PARNELL AND HIS TIMES

Marked by names such as W. B. Yeats, James Joyce, and Patrick Pearse, the decade 1910–20 was a period of revolutionary change in Ireland, in literature, politics, and public opinion. What fed the creative and reformist urge besides the circumstances of the moment and a vision of the future? The leading experts in Irish history, literature, and culture assembled in this volume argue that the shadow of the past was also a driving factor: the traumatic, undigested memory of the defeat and death of the charismatic national leader Charles Stewart Parnell (1846–91). The authors reassess Parnell's impact on the Ireland of his time, its cultural, religious, political, and intellectual life, in order to trace his posthumous influence into the early twentieth century in fields such as political activism, memory culture, history-writing, and literature.

JOEP LEERSSEN is Professor of European Studies at the University of Amsterdam. His books *Mere Irish and Fíor-Ghael* (1986) and *Remembrance and Imagination* (1996) helped establish the specialism of Irish Studies. His comparative work on national (self-) stereotyping and cultural nationalism earned him the Spinoza Prize in 2008 and the Madame de Staël Prize in 2020. He is also the editor of the *Encyclopedia of Romantic Nationalism in Europe* (2018).

Parnell memorial by Augustus Saint-Gaudens (1911; obelisk designed by Henry Bacon),
Parnell Square, Dublin.
Wikimedia Commons

PARNELL AND HIS TIMES

EDITED BY

JOEP LEERSSEN

University of Amsterdam

CAMBRIDGE
UNIVERSITY PRESS

CAMBRIDGE
UNIVERSITY PRESS

University Printing House, Cambridge CB2 8BS, United Kingdom

One Liberty Plaza, 20th Floor, New York, NY 10006, USA

477 Williamstown Road, Port Melbourne, VIC 3207, Australia

314–321, 3rd Floor, Plot 3, Splendor Forum, Jasola District Centre, New Delhi – 110025, India

79 Anson Road, #06–04/06, Singapore 079906

Cambridge University Press is part of the University of Cambridge.

It furthers the University's mission by disseminating knowledge in the pursuit of education, learning, and research at the highest international levels of excellence.

www.cambridge.org
Information on this title: www.cambridge.org/9781108495264
DOI: 10.1017/9781108861786

© Joep Leerssen 2021

First published 2021

Printed in the United Kingdom by TJ Books Limited, Padstow Cornwall

A catalogue record for this publication is available from the British Library.

Library of Congress Cataloging-in-Publication Data
NAMES: Leerssen, Joseph Th. (Joseph Theodoor), 1955- editor.
TITLE: Parnell and his times / edited by Joep Leerssen, University of Amsterdam.
DESCRIPTION: New York : Cambridge University Press, 2021. | Includes bibliographical references and index.
IDENTIFIERS: LCCN 2020018096 (print) | LCCN 2020018097 (ebook) | ISBN 9781108495264 (hardback) | ISBN 9781108817905 (paperback) | ISBN 9781108861786 (ebook)
SUBJECTS: LCSH: Parnell, Charles Stewart, 1846-1891–Influence. | Ireland–History–1837-1901. | Ireland–Politics and government–19th century. | Ireland–Politics and government–20th century. | Ireland–Historiography. | Politics and literature–Ireland–History–19th century. | Politics and literature–Ireland–History–20th century.
CLASSIFICATION: LCC DA958.P2 P425 2020 (print) | LCC DA958.P2 (ebook) | DDC 941.5081092 [B]–dc23
LC record available at https://lccn.loc.gov/2020018096
LC ebook record available at https://lccn.loc.gov/2020018097

ISBN 978-1-108-49526-4 Hardback

To Eamon Duffy

Contents

Illustrations

Note: Copyright clearance has been obtained from copyright owners for all images not in the public domain.

Contributors

THOMAS BARTLETT is Emeritus Professor at the University of Aberdeen. He is general editor of the *Cambridge History of Ireland* (4 vols., Cambridge University Press, 2018).

PAUL BEW was appointed Professor of Irish Politics in 1991 at Queen's University Belfast. The author of numerous books on Irish history (including *Charles Stewart Parnell*; *Enigma: A New Life of Charles Stewart Parnell*; *Ideology and the Irish Question*; and *Ireland: The Politics of Enmity 1789–2006*), he sits in the House of Lords as an independent cross-bench peer, where he chaired the Committee on Standards in Public Life from 2013 to 2018.

ANGELA BOURKE is Professor Emerita of Irish-Language Studies at University College Dublin. Joint editor of *The Field Day Anthology* IV and V: *Irish Women's Writing and Traditions*, her own books include *The Burning of Bridget Cleary: A True Story* and *Maeve Brennan: Homesick at the New Yorker*.

TERENCE BROWN is Professor Emeritus at Trinity College Dublin. Among his books are *Louis MacNeice: Sceptical Vision*; *Ireland: A Social and Cultural History*; *The Life of W. B. Yeats: A Critical Biography*; *The Literature of Ireland: Culture and Criticism*; and *The Irish Times: 150 Years of Influence*.

NICHOLAS CANNY is Professor Emeritus of History at the National University of Ireland, Galway, and was President of the Royal Irish Academy, 2008–11. His major monograph is *Making Ireland British, 1580–1650* and his forthcoming book *Imagining Ireland's Pasts* will be published in 2021.

CLAIRE CONNOLLY is Professor of Modern English at University College Cork. She has edited works by Maria Edgeworth and Lady Morgan and has published widely on eighteenth- and nineteenth-century culture, including *A Cultural History of the Irish Novel, 1790–1829*. With Marjorie Howes, she is General Editor of *Irish Literature in Transition, 1700–2020*.

DENIS DONOGHUE holds the Henry James Chair of English and American Letters at New York University. A leading Irish critic, he has published widely in the field of English and Irish literature, including *We Irish: Essays on Irish Literature & Society* and *Warrenpoint*, a volume of memoirs.

DAVID FITZPATRICK † was Professor of Modern History at Trinity College Dublin. His books include *Politics and Irish Society* and *Oceans of Consolation*.

R. F. FOSTER is Emeritus Professor of Irish History at the University of Oxford and Professor of Irish History and Literature at Queen Mary University of London. His books include *Modern Ireland 1600–1972*, the authorized two-volume biography of W. B. Yeats, *The Apprentice Mage* and *The Arch-Poet*, and, most recently, *Vivid Faces: The Revolutionary Generation in Ireland 1890–1923*.

RAYMOND GILLESPIE is a Professor of History at Maynooth University. He has written extensively on economic, social, and cultural change in early modern Ireland, particularly on religion and the role of print.

DECLAN KIBERD is Keough Professor of Irish Studies at University of Notre Dame. His recent book *After Ireland: Writing the Nation from Beckett to the Present* (2018) completes a trilogy begun with *Inventing Ireland* and continued with *Irish Classics*.

JOEP LEERSSEN is Professor of European Studies at the University of Amsterdam; author of *Mere Irish and Fíor-Ghael*; *Remembrance and Imagination*; and *National Thought in Europe*; and editor of the *Encyclopedia of Romantic Nationalism in Europe*.

EDNA LONGLEY is a Professor Emerita at Queen's University Belfast. She is the author of *Yeats and Modern Poetry* (2013) and *Under the Same Moon: Edward Thomas and the English Lyric* (2017).

OLIVER MACDONAGH † held professorships at Flinders University, University College Cork, and the Australian National University. His *States

of Mind: A Study of Anglo-Irish Conflict, 1780–1980 (1983) and his
biography of Daniel O'Connell (1988–89) remain benchmark studies.

FRANK MCGUINNESS, playwright, poet, and novelist, is Professor of
Creative Writing in the School of English, Film and Drama at University College Dublin.

HELEN VENDLER is Porter University Professor Emerita of English at
Harvard University, and the author of *Our Secret Discipline: Yeats and
Lyric Form*, as well as *The Art of Shakespeare's Sonnets* and books on
George Herbert, John Keats, Wallace Stevens, and Seamus Heaney.

CLAIR WILLS is King Edward VII Professor of English Literature at
Cambridge. Her books include *Reading Paul Muldoon*; *That Neutral
Island: A History of Ireland during the Second World War*; *Dublin 1916:
The Siege of the GPO*; *The Best Are Leaving: Emigration and Post-War
Irish Culture*; and *Lovers and Strangers: An Immigrant History of Post-
War Britain*.

Acknowledgement

The authors assembled in this volume share not only a general interest in modern Ireland but also the good fortune of having been able to pursue that interest, at one time or another, as visiting fellows at Magdalene College Cambridge. A gathering of the 'Parnell Fellows' held in 2017, when the centennial commemorations of the Revolutionary Decade 1913–23 were unrolling, sparked the idea to join forces and to reassess the many different aspects of Ireland's transition towards, and into, the twentieth century under the aspect of the looming presence (and absence) of Charles Stewart Parnell.

The authors mourn the passing, during the preparation of this volume, of their friend and colleague David Fitzpatrick. They gratefully acknowledge the kindness of the Master and Fellows of Magdalene College and dedicate this volume to their friend and colleague Eamon Duffy, who over many years has been the driving force behind the Parnell Fellowship at Magdalene College Cambridge.

Introduction
Charisma and Aftermath

Joep Leerssen

Ireland, though not a state in in own right until 1922, had its succession of statesmen: feudal leaders like the various O'Neills of the sixteenth and seventeenth centuries, civic and parliamentarian leaders from Flood and Grattan onwards, and revolutionaries from Tone to Pearse. In that tradition, Charles Stewart Parnell (1846–91) stands as the last great parliamentary statesman, successor to Grattan and O'Connell, more powerful yet ultimately less successful than either of his great predecessors. After Parnell, the Home Rule agenda, though ably continued by Redmond, had the wind taken out of its sails both by the Ulster Unionist Edward Carson (who wielded Parnellish power in his northern bailiwick) and by various extra-parliamentary forms of nationalism (cultural, separatist).

It is universally agreed that the downfall and death of Parnell marked a true crisis and a caesura in Irish politics and history. Born during the Great Famine into the landowning Protestant elite, Parnell had taken command of the process by which Ireland in the post-Famine decades embarked on a course towards modernization and self-empowerment. Between Land League and Fenians, Parnell pursued a two-pronged policy of dismantling both the landlord system and the parliamentary union with Great Britain, setting the agenda for both struggles. Parnell wielded great power and influence; at its zenith, he fell. He fell from a great height, as Westminster powerbroker and undisputed chief and champion of Irish national politics; he fell steeply and opprobriously, as the result of a divorce scandal right at the peak period of Victorian moralism and prudery; and he fell deep, losing his sway over his followers, attacked and injured, and dead by the age of forty-five. Parnell, in his downfall and death, affected Irish public opinion as profoundly as he had during his glory years; and Parnell's absence throughout the next decades left Ireland with a Parnell-shaped hole in the middle, filled only partially by a Parnell myth. The sudden void left in the wake of Parnell's passing was something the next generations had to come to terms with, consciously (as with Yeats and Joyce) or in

I

semi-articulate or deflected apprehensions at the turbulence and steerless-
ness of Irish modernity, at the disjointed incohesion of Irish society
between Dublin, Belfast, and the West.

Irish society after 1891 seems to exhibit the sudden withdrawal symp-
toms from a political elixir that between O'Connell, the Derrynane squire,
and Parnell, the Wicklow landlord, had become increasingly potent in
Irish public life: charisma. Ireland, though not a state, had got used to
having statesmen who could wield the informal but strong power of
charismatic leadership. Noticeable in its sudden absence, charisma seems
an important key to understanding the appeal of Parnell and the fact that
this appeal continued even after his passing and in the void he left behind.
That Parnell was a charismatic leader is almost a commonplace; but the
deeper meaning of that term is worth reflecting on.

* * *

Between the German defeat of 1918 and the Spanish Flu epidemic, which
would claim his life in 1920, Max Weber undertook a systematization of
various types of leadership; it was part – a small part – of the magnum opus
that was published, posthumously and in half-finished condition, as
Wirtschaft und Gesellschaft. In the chapter on leadership and authority
('Herrschaft'), Weber defined, alongside the established forms of 'dynastic'
and 'institutional' authority, a third type, which he dubbed 'charismatic'.
He took the term from theological usage, where 'charisma' denotes the fact
that the worship of God is not just a matter of dutiful obedience but also a
matter of joy (Fig. 1). Charismatic leaders, so Weber argued, derive their
authority neither from their lineage nor from their office, but by force of
personality inspire an almost religious fervour and devotion in their
followers, to the point of being credited with superhuman powers.

Weber's comments are brief, and although the term has become
famous, the concept of charisma remains unelaborated. It has been noted
how uncannily the thumbnail sketch of the charismatic leader foreshadows
the later cult of Hitler; but that only raises the question of who else,
historically rather than prophetically, Weber can have had in mind as a
prototype. Probably his implicit frame of reference included, generically,
the Hegelian hero-figures that Thomas Carlyle had made the subject of his
massively influential *On Heroes and Hero-Worship*.[1] Possibly also Weber

---

[1] The notion of hero-worship, *Heldenverehrung*, is explicitly mentioned: 'Über die Geltung des
Charisma entscheidet die durch Bewährung – ursprünglich stets: durch Wunder – gesicherte freie,

Fig. 1   Miss Tipperary embracing Parnell. Supplement to *Weekly Freeman*, 17 Jan. 1885

had noted, around the Paris Peace conference which embittered him so deeply, authority figures representing minority nations (Poland's Ignacy Paderewski, Czechoslovakia's Tomas Masaryk, or Norway's Fridtjof Nansen), who had gained their public stature and their authority as a pianist, writer, and polar explorer, respectively. Maybe he recalled the fervently acclaimed Boer leaders of South Africa, Kruger and De Wet; maybe even

aus Hingabe an Offenbarung, Heldenverehrung, Vertrauen zum Führer geborene, Anerkennung durch die Beherrschten' ('It is recognition on the part of those subject to authority which is decisive for the validity of charisma. This is freely given and . . . consists in devotion to the corresponding revelation, hero worship, or absolute trust in the leader'). Max Weber, 'Merkmale der charismatischen Herrschaft', par. 10 of chapter 3 of the first section of *Wirtschaft und Gesellschaft* (1922). English translation by A. M. Henderson and Talcott Parsons, *The Theory of Social and Economic Organization* (New York, 1947). Cf. also Joep Leerssen, 'Sacral States: The Politics of Worship, Religious and Secular', in *Great Immortality: Studies on European Cultural Sainthood*, ed. Marijan Dović and Jón Karl Helgason (Leiden, 2019), 15–27.

Marx. We do not know – Weber does not say. But few pre-1918 statesmen can be seen as more perfectly approximating the type of charismatic leadership than Charles Stewart Parnell.

Parnell was a charismatic leader in the full Weberian sense of the term. He embodies the Hegelian idea of the 'world-historical hero' which, directly or by way of Carlyle, underlies Weber's concept: someone who at crisis moments has a transcendent intuitive grasp of the direction that history is taking. Parnell was, in the eyes of his followers, one of those 'great historical men'

> whose own particular aims involve those large issues which are the will of the World-Spirit. They may be called Heroes, inasmuch as they have derived their purposes and their vocation, not from the calm, regular course of things, sanctioned by the existing order; but from ... that inner Spirit, still hidden beneath the surface, which, impinging on the outer world as on a shell, bursts it in pieces, because it is another kernel than that which belonged to the shell in question.... Such individuals ... were practical, political men. But at the same time they were thinking men, who had an insight into the requirements of the time – what was ripe for development. This was the very Truth ... which was already formed in the womb of time. It was theirs to know this nascent principle; the necessary, directly sequent step in progress, which their world was to take; to make this their aim, and to expend their energy in promoting it.[2]

We hear Yeats's 'long-legged fly' in these lines, and the anguished regrets of the bereft Parnellites in Joyce. Parnell, authoritarian and arrogant as he was, derived charisma in the Weberian sense from 'an extraordinary force of personality which caused him to be credited with, if not superhuman, then at least extraordinary powers of leadership'.[3]

Uniquely and almost uncannily suited to the Weberian notion of charismatic leadership, Parnell stands out among the great political champions of modern Ireland. O'Connell comes close, but his popular appeal was at least in part fed by a lingering Jacobite messianism which, as Breandán Ó Buachalla has shown,[4] had in the previous generation also

---

[2] Hegel, *Lectures on the Philosophy of History* (trans. Sibree, 1857), introduction. The 1837 German edition (by Gans) did not include Hegel's introduction; Sibree follows the 1840 edition (by Karl Hegel).

[3] Paraphrased from Weber, 'Merkmale der charismatischen Herrschaft'. In the original: 'Charisma soll eine als außeralltäglich (ursprünglich ... als magisch bedingt) geltende Qualität einer Persönlichkeit heißen, um derentwillen sie als mit übernatürlichen oder übermenschlichen oder mindestens spezifisch außeralltäglichen, nicht jedem andern zugänglichen Kräften oder Eigenschaften oder als gottgesandt oder als vorbildlich und deshalb als «Führer» gewertet wird.'

[4] Breandán Ó Buachalla, *Aisling Ghéar* (Dublin, 1997).

been projected onto Bonnie Prince Charlie and Napoleon; he was a saviour-figure rather than a hero-figure. And while the official post-1920 Irish cult of the Men of 1916 tried to turn the martyr-figure of Pearse into a sacral icon, that leader was singularly lacking in personal charisma, Parnell-style. Ditto for De Valera. If any of the 1916 generation would come close to charismatic leadership, it would have been Michael Collins. And that also means that Collins, had he survived and lived to lead the country, might plausibly have drifted into that military-style strongman authoritarianism that had also attracted other charismatic leaders such as the Polish condottiere József Piłsudski – to name no others.

Parnell's extraordinary hold over the hopes and imaginations of his followers is demonstrated in the anguish that he left behind: no one could fill his footsteps; Redmond, Pearse, and De Valera look puny in comparison. His downfall and death were more than a catastrophe: they were a trauma – which is a catastrophe that refuses to be laid to rest, which is obsessively, neurotically relived and renewed over and over again, much as in the post-Parnell poems of Yeats and, again, in the evocations and hauntings of Joyce. Parnell cannot be laid to rest the way O'Connell and Pearse were laid to rest. Tellingly, it is following the death of Parnell that the notion of resurrection begins to dominate Irish politics and the Irish imagination.

* * *

To be sure, nationalism in many cases will dream of a reconstitution of lost greatness and of the reversal of a historical decline. Thomas Davis wanted to see Ireland, long a province, be a nation once again. Germany throughout the nineteenth century was suffused by the *Reichsidee*: that the abolition of the Holy Roman Empire in 1806 had led merely to an interregnum, and the empire was merely in abeyance, not gone forever. But such notions usually hinged around the idea of restoration. What was new in the cultural nationalism of Romantic vintage was the idea of a rising, revivification, or reawakening from a death-sleep; or a rebirth or renaissance. Such terms are found in the Catalan Renaixença, the Galician Rexurdimento, the Albanian Relindja, the Bulgarian Văzrazdanie. Ireland applied no less than three such terms to itself in the post-Parnell decades: a Renaissance or Revival (in literature) and a Rising (at Easter 1916). And in the background of these reawakenings is the refusal of Parnell to be laid to rest – not so much like a Christ rising from the dead (as devout Pearse would like to see things) but as a Barbarossa, or King Arthur, or Holger

Fig. 2   John Tenniel, 'The Irish Vampire', *Punch*, 24 Oct. 1885

Danske, a Once and Future Leader waiting for the moment of his return from the underworld; or like a Dracula rising from the grave (Fig. 2). It was, after all, in the discussion of world-historical figures that Hegel had said that they always appear twice.

'The first time as tragedy, the second time as farce': that was Marx's sarcastic addition to Hegel. I do not want to go that way (De Valera as the farcical encore to tragic Parnell): Hegel's point is, rather, that the end of the great hero-leader is never the last word.

Another comment by Marx, made almost in the same breath, is more apposite: he points out that the great Hegelian hero-figures leave in their wake an oppressive absence, a dead weight stifling fresh departures. These words have often been applied to the condition of post-Parnell Ireland:

> The tradition of all dead generations weighs like a nightmare on the brains of the living. And just as they seem to be occupied with revolutionizing themselves and things, creating something that did not exist before,

precisely in such epochs of revolutionary crisis they anxiously conjure up the spirits of the past to their service, borrowing from them names, battle slogans, and costumes in order to present this new scene in world history in time-honoured disguise and borrowed language.[5]

Parnell gone made it impossible to get over Parnell. The most strenuous attempts to be post-Parnellite only emphasized this by the mere fact of trying so very hard. The stupor and death-sleep that Yeats and Pearse wanted to Revive or Rise from, to be Reborn from, was not just (as they foregrounded) the long centuries of subjection and self-alienation under English rule, but the one induced by the fall and death of Parnell. Tellingly, that project of Revival, Renaissance, and Rising was accompanied by the creaking coffin-hinges of Bram Stoker's book, published in 1895, and by the despairing paralysis of Joyce's Dubliners.

Stoker's Dracula and Joyce's Dubliners exist almost in tandem. One is the undead arrogant gentleman, refusing to be dead and gone, sucking the life-blood from the living, sapping their vital energies until they wither and decline. The characters in early Joyce are like his victims, limply struggling to escape from a nightmare which is not even history, but rather time marking time, time turned viscous, appointments missed and opportunities spoiled, a future indefinitely deferred. Parnell after dead turned into an undead presence, a Shade. Yeats summoned that shade to his side in his 1913 poem, mainly as a projecting screen for his own disenchantment with the deadness of Romantic Ireland:

> If you have revisited the town, thin Shade,
> Whether to look upon your monument
> (I wonder if the builder has been paid)
> Or happier-thoughted when the day is spent
> To drink of that salt breath out of the sea
> When grey gulls flit about instead of men,
> And the gaunt houses put on majesty:
> Let these content you and be gone again;
> For they are at their old tricks yet.

---

[5] Karl Marx, *The Eighteenth Brumaire of Louis Napoleon*, chapter 1, trans. Saul K. Padover, online at www.marxists.org/archive/marx/works/1852/18th-brumaire/cho1.htm. Among the first to apply this sentiment to late nineteenth-century Ireland was W. J. MacCormack, *From Burke to Beckett: Ascendancy, Tradition and Betrayal in Irish Literary History* (Cork, 1994). McCormack has also rightly drawn attention to the extent to which Parnell's charisma was described by Yeats (whose vocabulary was Golden Dawnish rather than Weberian) in 'demonic' terms: 'Yeats and Gothic Politics', in McCormack, *Dissolute Characters: Irish Literary History through Balzac, Sheridan LeFanu, Yeats and Bowen* (Manchester, 1993), 193–206.

. . .

Go, unquiet wanderer,

And gather the Glasnevin coverlet
About your head till the dust stops your ear,
The time for you to taste of that salt breath
And listen at the corners has not come;
You had enough of sorrow before death –
Away, away! You are safer in the tomb.[6]

Parnell's political downfall and death were more than the end of a career: they
were a sudden vacuum destabilizing the political order of things; an abrupt,
implosive disappearance, a disruptive vanishing, an annihilation. The annihilation of Parnell from Irish public life is almost like a Big Bang in reverse: it
brings into being a welter of turbulence, absences, and hollow spaces. These
fan out in three directions that seem unrelated and disparate unless we realize
that they originate from a common vanishing point. One of these is well-
known as the turn to culture – something presented as such by Yeats, but
slightly flatteringly so, in order to present himself as a revolutionary fresh
departure in Irish life. What distinguishes the self-proclaimed turn to culture
of Yeats and the Irish Literary Revival from its pre-Parnell run-up is, precisely,
the turn from an earlier mode of restoring justice (Repealing the Union, a
nation once again, Home Rule) towards a new mode of a national reboot: be
this phrased as de-Anglicization (involving revival of the Irish language), a
literary revival/renaissance, or a political rising. The other is an intensified
sense of Ireland as stagnation: as per the naturalism of Moore's Irish novels,
early Joyce, midlife Yeats, and indeed the Irish Gothic à la Stoker. The third
lies in a disparate array of small utopianisms, the scattered fallout of the great
Parnellite Home Rule movement which as a political force has fissioned into a
Redmondite successor party and Fenian, Irish-Ireland separatism.

* * *

The small utopian reform movements are perhaps the most intriguing, and
the most easily overlooked. At the European level,[7] they form part of a
wide reformist trend inspired by William Morris and with a figurehead in
Leo Tolstoy; they involve the Fellowship of the New Life, artists' colonies,

---

[6] 'To a Shade' (1913), in W. B. Yeats, *Collected Poems*, 2nd ed. (London, 1950), 123.
[7] The following comments on comparative aspects of European national-reformist movements have
   been collated taken from the *Encyclopedia of Romantic Nationalism in Europe*, ed. J. Leerssen, 2 vols.
   (Amsterdam University Press, 2018), online at ernie.uva.nl.

sexual libertarianism à la Edith Lees and Havelock Ellis, cooperative and agricultural credit initiatives, vegetarians, teetotallers, adepts of Dr Jaeger's sanitary woollen reform clothing, Thomas Allinson's wholemeal bread, sunbathing, and open-air excursions on foot or by bicycle; nudists, pacifists, Esperantists. The initiatives were rarely part of an overarching political doctrine and in many aspects shaded over into speculative occultism or hermetic societies (spiritism, Steiner's anthroposophy, and the weirder fringes of German *Lebensreform*). For that reason, they are nowadays often (not altogether fairly) dismissed as quirky, naïve, or quixotic; yet allotment gardening, the Garden Cities movement, the Fabians, and the suffragettes also formed part of this utopian-reformist spectrum. Within Ireland, reformist utopianism blended into the background of other movements. AE (George Russell) is now almost exclusively remembered as a star-gazing esotericist and speculative occultist; but he was also an activist on behalf of the Cooperative Movement. The fact that Shaw invariably wore Jaeger's *Normalkleidung* was not just his personal eccentricity. The Yeats sisters were not just helpmeets of W.B.'s preening aestheticism but adepts of Morrisite arts-and-crafts printing and reform clothing, and involved in the feminist networks around the Slade School of Arts (where they, like the Gore-Booths, had studied). Yeats's theatrical ventures interacted with grassroots amateur theatricals of a decidedly progressive-reformist, Ibsenite slant; indeed, the rift of 1903 saw the departure, precisely, of the more Ibsenite-reformist members (the Fays, Máire Nic Shiubhlaigh, and indeed Maud Gonne) away from Yeats's more elitist and exclusive Abbey Theatre venture. What is more, many of the revivalist activities of the Gaelic League are part of a wider, international folkloric turn that aimed to invigorate working-class and middle-class leisure culture with the wholesome energy of folk tradition. Irish dancing was revived in Ireland much as Morris dancing was in England, or folk dancing in Norway and Sweden; the introduction of an Irish kilt was part of a general European urban-bourgeois adoption of traditional rustic dress; artists everywhere in Europe, not just Jack B. Yeats in Ireland, were turning to a faux-naïf invocation of popular culture in the fin de siècle revival of the woodcut. And amateur theatre companies were active everywhere, not just in Dublin, following the Norwegian example.

In recent years, critics and historians have rightly drawn attention to the extent to which the pre-1916 generation of Irish national activists were part of a Europe-wide reformist movement.[8] This reformism spanned class

[8] Declan Kiberd, ed., *Handbook of the Irish Revival 1891–1922* (Dublin: Abbey Theatre Press, 2015); Roy Foster, *Vivid Faces: The Revolutionary Generation in Ireland, 1890–1923* (London, 2015).

divisions, involving both elite groups and aspiring lower middle classes. To the extent that their activities played into the political ambitions of non-dominant nationalities, they can best be identified in the term defined by Miroslav Hroch[9] as 'protagonists' (*Vorkämpfer*) of the national movements in Europe's imperial peripheries (Iceland, Norway, Finland, the Baltic, the Balkans, Bohemia, Hungary, Catalonia) – or, rather, in Europe's subimperial, subsidiary capitals: Reykjavík, Christiania/Oslo, Helsinki, Riga, Zagreb, Prague, Budapest, Barcelona. Here, a middle-class city culture, rooted in the increasing leisure interests of white-collar workers and expressing itself in café-chantants, theatrical, athletic, and choral societies and a burgeoning press, could draw on the rustic-regenerative nostalgia of its characteristic 'unspoilt' hinterlands to oppose an identity to the hegemonic metropolitan centres. Tellingly, choral and theatrical performances were often given in 'traditional' peasant garb, retrieved from grandparents' wardrobes or copied from plein-air genre paintings of 1870s–80s vintage. As that dress style was disappearing from the countryside, it was now adopted as 'national' by (sub-)urban actors, often for performative purposes (amateur theatre, choral concerts). This cultivation of rustic cultural specificity could be no more than a form of subsidiary regionalism in the Europe's pre-1914 empires: thus, in Andalusia and Galicia, Brittany, Bavaria, or Scotland (although in those regions and countries, too, autonomist sentiments would develop in some circles after 1914). But in many other cases, the new subimperial exceptionalism slotted into the discourse of nationalism and proclaimed the locality's character as being radically incommensurable with its imperial subordination, vindicating its separate standing amid an international palette, across Europe, of progressive civic communities asserting their separateness. Typically, the invocation of the peasant hinterland as a marker of traditional rootedness and separateness went hand in hand with a shared participation in a pan-European artistic modernity: art nouveau (Jugendstil, Catalan *modernisme*), Symbolism, and post-Ibsenite social realism or naturalism. Typically, also, the cultural and political activists in such cities (subimperial or provincial capitals aspiring to become national capitals) would show the contradictory impulses of conservative nativism (drawing inspiration from traditional peasant culture in the hinterland), and progressive cosmopolitanism (drawing inspiration from other European city and minority cultures). Macronationalisms like Pan-Slavism, Pan-Celticism, and Pan-Latinism were the

[9] Miroslav Hroch, *Die Vorkämpfer der nationalen Bewegung bei den kleinen Völkern Europas: Eine vergleichende Analyse zur gesellschaftlichen Schichtung der patriotischen Gruppen* (Prague, 1968).

natural development of such a mixed stance, combining ethnic nativism with a transnational outreach.

All this fits fin-de-siècle Dublin like a glove.[10] Miss Ivors, in Joyce's 'The Dead', is a good, albeit fictional, encapsulation of a European generational cohort and cultural-activist type; and readers will require little effort to fill in the Irish analogies for this European profile, from Yeats's theatre to Pearse's educationalism. Obviously, then, the specifically Irish dimension of the post-Parnell vacuum does not explain everything that happened in his wake.

* * *

Art-nouveau nationalism provided a robust cultural launching pad for most post-1918 states on the European continent – until they were engulfed, that is, by the totalitarian derailments of the 1920s and 1930s.[11] Ireland, despite its devastating civil war and corporatist sympathies, remained at least a constitutional multiparty democracy with an independent judiciary. But its nationalism by 1914 had abandoned almost all European sense of connectedness and turned wholly inward, driving its cosmopolitan modernists into exile: Joyce, O'Casey, Beckett, and for much of the time Yeats, a part-time Irishman at best.[12] Dublin-the-Irish-capital in the 1920s was less cosmopolitan than Dublin-the-imperial-subcapital in the 1910s.

It is here, in this strange death of cosmopolitan Ireland, that the influence of the Parnell vacuum can perhaps best be registered. Three important interrelated factors drove Irish nationalism away from its

[10] Cf. also my 'Cúchulain in the Post Office: Gaelic Revival, Irish Rising', *Journal of the British Academy*, 4 (2016): 137–68.

[11] Almost all of newly independent states (except Czechoslovakia and Finland) lurched into authoritarian or dictatorial systems even before they were engulfed by the fascist/communist juggernauts. Dictatorial or authoritarian rule was established in Hungary in 1920; in Italy in 1922; in Bulgaria in 1923; in Albania in 1925; in Poland, Portugal, and Lithuania in 1926; in Yugoslavia in 1929; in Austria and in Germany in 1933; in Estonia and in Latvia in 1934; in Greece in 1936; in Romania in 1938; and in Spain in 1939. Contemporary Europe would do well to heed that dismal track record, now obscured from our political rear-view mirror by the intervening Hitler/Stalin catastrophes.

[12] The aesthetic heritage of art-nouveau nationalism survived at best in the technicolour Book of Kells–inspired design of Bulmer Hobson's *Saorstát Éireann Official Handbook*, with which the country presented itself at the Chicago World Fair of 1933. The designer, Art O'Murnaghan (born as Arthur Murnaghan in Southampton in 1872), had designed badges for the Gaelic League and would go on to produce a sumptuous neo–Book of Kells dedicated to the Men of 1916, the *Leabhar na hAiséirghe*, or *Book of Resurrection*. It remained unfinished and has been retrieved from neglect only in the 2016 commemorations. Peter Figgis, 'Remembering Art O'Murnaghan', *Irish Arts Review* 2.4 (1985): 41–44.

European-modernist side. One was the continuing grip of confessionalism on the political spectrum. The other was the scant presence and lopsided distribution of actual modernity (industrial modernity rather than art nouveau aesthetics) in the country. The third was, paradoxically, the overriding, continuing preoccupation with nationality as the main defining issue of Irish political life.

Confessionalism affected most European politics post-1800. Papal ultra-montanism made itself felt as a powerful force in traditionally Protestant states (Prussia, the Netherlands, Britain) or secular states (France, Belgium); Orthodox countries such as Romania and the Ukrainian lands had important Uniate churches in communion with Rome. Accordingly, many national movements proclaimed shared nationhood as a transcendence of religious divisions: Muslim-Christian (Albania and Crete), Catholic-Orthodox (Illyrian/Yugoslavian), Catholic-Protestant (Czech/Slovak), Catholic-secularist (Catalonia, France, Slovenia).

In post-famine Ireland, any lingering Young Ireland ideal of uniting the Orange and the Green under a shared sense of nationhood proved quixotic. Gladstone's Home Rule drive had provoked the establishment of Loyalist or Unionist associations since the mid-1880s; following the 1885 election and Parnell's alignment with Gladstone's First Home Rule Bill, the natural result was that opposition Tories would align with Unionism in Ireland. Irish Unionism as a result abandoned whatever its earlier Liberal connections had been and, in the process, shifted its power base away from South Dublin towards Ulster's Presbyterian population and its Orange Lodges. The process was, ironically, triggered by Parnell's very success, and it is hard to see how he could have strategically prevented a nascent Presbyterian No Popery counterforce to Home Rule, as manifested in the career of Carson. Contrariwise, the decline of anything like a Protestant Home Rule and the antagonism of Ulster Unionism strengthened the link between Catholicism and nationalism. George Moore already poked bitter fun at the increasing dominance of Cork-based priests on the board (Coiste Gnótha) of the Gaelic League. The abdication of Douglas Hyde as the League's president in the face of the rise of Patrick Pearse reflects not just a political radicalization of the Gaelic League but also a confessional-religious shift of gravity. Between 1880 and 1905, the Protestant 'Anglo-Irish' landowning class (which was beginning to call itself the 'Ascendancy' precisely in these decades) saw themselves as the designated elite leading an Irish national movement: we see that paternalistic attitude in Standish O'Grady, Yeats, Moore, Hyde, even the Gore-Booths, and indeed it may have been derived from Parnell himself.

The fact that a more demotic, Fenian-rooted tradition of separatism moved away from their control proved the failure of that ambition, and it was a failure that was registered as much in religious terms as in class terms. Irish politics signally failed to de-confessionalize; or rather: Parnell, charismatic though he was, signally failed to prevent a split in Irish national politics along confessional, even sectarian lines.

The bitterness of the regret over Parnell's downfall was, obviously, strongest amongst his support base (not excluding the Catholic working and middle classes who had put their faith in his Home Rule, but not including Ulster Protestants, and with the rural peasantry perhaps fairly indifferent). Parnell's fall was caused by a loss of charisma. Being publicly branded an adulterer is bad enough, but what made it worse, truly tawdry and fatal to any sense of political probity, was the fact that Parnell had gone to great lengths to support, in the Galway by-election of 1885, the very man he had cuckolded, the oafish Captain O'Shea, against better, alternative candidates from within the ranks of his own party. Parnell's fall was, then, prepared by his own hubris; and part of the political disarray that followed had been prepared by his own strategy. But the execution – the party split, the church condemnation, Timothy Healy's denunciations, the quicklime, the undignified squabbles and riots: that was delivered by the rank and file of his former supporters.[13] For once, Ireland could not blame foreign foes for its plight: the fools and the knaves in the Parnell downfall were Irish one and all.

* * *

Ireland entered into the twentieth century with a new, unaccustomed sensation: that of self-reproach. It was a hard one to get used to and prevented Redmond, whatever his qualities as a parliamentarian, from ever achieving broad grassroots popularity.[14] Instead, Pearse's self-sacrificial mission may in part have been driven by a need to get Irish nationalist politics back on the track of a more edifying, old-school master narrative: asserting, in every generation, the unalienated rights of the Irish people, and if necessary asserting it in arms. Pearse's notion of the Irish people was extra-parliamentary, much more demotically rooted, less paternalistic,

---

[13] The details are in Frank Callanan, *The Parnell Split, 1890–91* (Syracuse, NY, 1992).

[14] Pace Michael Murphy, whose *The Parnell Myth in Irish Politics 1890–1956* (New York, 1986) celebrates an apostolic succession O'Connell–Parnell–De Valera. Accordingly, Murphy sees the post-Parnell trauma only in terms of Parnell's greatness rather than his ultimate, devastating loss of charisma and the disenchantment of his erstwhile followers.

and included, emphatically, both women and men, joined together by a common culture if not by class. It relied, crucially, and much more than in the case of Parnellite Home Rule, on a sense of kinship and solidarity with the native peasantry and its Gaelic-rooted culture.

Pearse's sense of nationhood relied for its mainstay on Irish folk culture. But neither Pearse nor the popular tradition, for all that they maintained vivid messianistic memories of O'Connell, shows many traces of charismatic Parnellism – so pronounced as a presence in the downwardly mobile middle classes of Joyce's *Dubliners* and in the disappointed elitism of Yeats and Moore.[15] Although the Land League and the Land War had been the original launching pad for Parnell's career (he had won street credibility by opposing the half-hearted Land Act of 1881 and being imprisoned in Kilmainham jail for it), the main concerns of the peasantry – land and religion – had been left behind by Parnellite Home Rule politics by the mid-1880s. Yeats put his finger on it in the wry 'Parnell' poem of 1938: 'Ireland shall get her freedom and you shall still break stone'. In agricultural politics, William O'Brien became the nationalist peasant leader that Parnell ceased to be. Root-and-branch agricultural reform – the dismantling of the landlord system – was the most important domestic policy galvanizing Ireland's rural society, with actual transformations effected by the Land Acts of 1903 and 1909, and land reform remaining high on the agenda for the Free State in the 1920s.

Seen in this light, Parnell's career and aftermath illustrate the failure of squaring a circle for Irish nationalism: how to embrace both Ireland's Protestant population, mainly in the North, and the native peasantry. Parnell managed to galvanize the nationally minded middle classes from both denominations, including, crucially, the freshly empowered Catholic lower middle classes. His support base could not include both the Presbyterian workers or lower-middle classes and the Catholic peasantry. The 'cultural turn' after his death was in fact a decision to embrace that latter constituency in the nationalist agenda, Fenian-style. No common ground was sought by the culturalists with the Ulster workers and lower-middle

---

[15] Breandán Ó Buachalla points out that the trope of the 'Once and Future Hero', whose return from a rumoured death is messianistically awaited, was only activated in the bourgeois theatrical culture of Dublin: Lennox Robinson's *The Lost Leader* (1918). Breandán Ó Buachalla, *History as Myth: The Return of the Hero* (the Parnell Lecture, 1998–99: Cambridge: Magdalene College 1999 [Magdalene College Occasional Paper, 20]), note 34. On the heroic afterlife of Parnell in non-peasant Ireland, see Alvin Jackson and Roy Foster, 'Men for All Seasons? Carson, Parnell, and the Limits of Heroism in Modern Ireland', *European History Quarterly* 39.3 (2009, special issue on 'Hero Cults and the Politics of the Past: Comparative European Perspectives', ed. Robert Gerwarth): 414–38.

classes (Hyde dismissed Ulster as an inconsequential 'Anglo-Saxon corner in the north-east', in his De-Anglicization lecture). Nor was there a Labour tradition strong enough to cross the denominational divide (as happened in Scotland).

The failure to avoid a re-confessionalization not only precluded any possible identification with an Irish nation among Ulster Protestants; it also meant that Irish nationalism missed out on an industrial, working-class power base. Most heavy industry was, after all, located in Protestant Belfast. True, there was a modern industrial hub around the Dublin port, and the lockout of 1913 is now universally celebrated as the starting point of what is called the Irish revolutionary decade. Much has been made of the participation of Connolly's Irish Citizen's Army in the Easter Rising; but Seán O'Casey's *The Plough and the Stars* should alert us that relations between Irish socialism and Irish nationalism may in fact have been more fraught than the habitual posthumous twinning of Pearse and Connolly might suggest. Irish nationalism, with only a slim basis in urban, industrial modernity, turned increasingly into a more conservative-nostalgic direction, ultimately leading to De Valera's vision of an Ireland of comely maidens dancing at the crossroads.[16] From Parnell to De Valera the mainstream tradition of Irish nationalism defined the country mainly in agrarian-cum-bourgeois terms. This emphasis rendered Irish nationalism different from that of more industrialized regions like the Basque Country, Catalonia, Poland, and the Czech lands. In those areas, nationalism was merged into the palette of emerging party politics and social democracy, becoming part of a general drive towards constitutional and economic reform. Nationalism there was a progressive reform movement against traditionalist empires; nationalism in Ireland would on the whole gravitate to a traditionalist stance opposing a modernizing empire.

This may be, then, a third element where Irish politics was caught in a post-Parnellite rictus. In most countries, nationalism was already being folded into party politics, and becoming, by this time, a meta-ideology, what is now known as a 'thin-centred' ideology: something that does not in itself constitute a complete political doctrine or societal agenda (like, for instance, Liberalism, Conservatism, or Social Democracy) but which is a general, almost moral-affective stance inflecting other ideologies;

---

[16] That is the habitual shorthand way to summarize De Valera's Rádio Éireann speech of 17 March 1943, 'On Language and the Irish Nation', celebrating St. Patrick's Day and the jubilee of the Gaelic League. Maurice Moynihan, ed., *Speeches and Statements by Eamon De Valera: 1917–73* (Dublin, 1980), 466. Online at ernie.uva.nl/viewer.p/21/54/object/351-227036.

nationalism as a 'flavouring' element in national liberalism, national conservatism, and so on.[17] Until 1848, 'love of the fatherland' had been a
powerful political mobilizer in its own right, against inherited privilege and
self-perpetuating elites. By the end of the century, it had become 'unpo-
litical', a general human virtue, diffused across the political spectrum and
equally shared among all right-minded people, including political conservatives. Douglas Hyde had sensed this when he presented his programme
for De-Anglicizing Ireland as something 'non-political' (which may raise
eyebrows among contemporary readers). Wherever nationalism became a
politically mobilizing agenda, it was as part of a progressive opposition
against reactionary imperial centralism, as in the peripheries of Spain and
the Habsburg and Russian Empires. Not so, however, in Ireland: following
the death of Parnell, the question of Home Rule and independence was,
and remained, a core issue in its own right, and parties divided mainly on
the best approach towards that ideal. Hence, ultimately, the divide of the
Civil War and the distribution of party politics in post–Civil War Ireland,
which cut squarely across the left-right spectrums of other countries.

Nationalism after Parnell remained frozen in the mode of the political
wedge issue. This precluded the development of anything like one-nation
Toryism (as in England) or the regionalism of Victorian and Edwardian
Scotland and Wales. Ireland was doomed by Parnell's failure never to
become normal, unremarkable, or just a given. Irish identity never sub-
sided into a mere status quo; it remained a challenge.

* * *

The various contributions in this volume chart the challenges (never the
comfort zone) of Irish identity during and after Parnell's heyday and fall.
They address how Irish artists and intellectuals responded to it in high and
popular politics, in their literary craft, in history-writing, in religious
affiliation, and cultural memory (literate, urban-popular, and oral-
traditional). The dark background radiation of Parnell, diffuse but never
absent, and constantly on the border between latency and salience, forms
the continuum between the various disciplines and specialisms
united here.

One reason to assemble various essays around the Parnell-shaped hole in
Irish politics and history was to recalibrate the relationship between the
man, his charisma, and his myth. On the one hand we have a number of

---

[17] Michael Freeden, 'Is Nationalism a Distinct Ideology?', *Political Studies* 46.4 (1998): 648–765.

fine biographical studies of Parnell (notably by F. S. L. Lyons and Paul Bew), on the other hand Seamus Deane's challenge still stands: that 'Parnell is a product of Parnellism'.[18] Arguably, the status of Parnell in twentieth-century Ireland is a function of cultural memory rather than professional history-writing, and the impact and influence of Parnell have been formulaically codified by the literary treatments of, notably, Joyce and Yeats – even more so than by his reminiscences, posthumously published in 1914. 'Afterlives' take on a life of their own; the myth overshadows the man, and how the past is recollected becomes more influential than the actual events and deeds of bygone times.

One reason to collect these various chapters was to map more long-term force lines in Irish history than the recent commemorative preoccupation with the incidents of the 'Revolutionary decade' might suggest. For better or for worse, Irish history is habitually periodized by those crisis moments, when the country 'changed utterly'. To be sure, that mode of viewing the past is legitimate; but it might obscure from our view the slower, tidal changes in Irish history that flowed on underneath those breakers in the surf. In addition, the case should be made that the entire Revolutionary decade (which in any case might need to be expanded to include the Ulster Covenant of 1912 as a starting date) formed part of the turbulence in the wake of Parnell's downfall and death.

The decision to bring that period in focus in terms of the ambient post-Parnellite depression of Irish modernity was anything but haphazard or contrived: the contributors are all of them 'Parnellites', and their collaboration in this volume was suggested and inspired by the shared experience of having held the Parnell Fellowship at Magdalene College Cambridge. It was there that we 'filled up all those glasses, and passed the bottle round', as Yeats exhorted his Parnellites to do. Over the past decades, Magdalene has been a congenial, hospitable, and inspiring setting for all of our musings on Parnell and his Ireland. To no one could this volume be more fittingly dedicated, therefore, than to the inspiring curator and convivial host of the Parnell Fellowship, our friend Eamon Duffy.

---

[18] Seamus Deane, 'Parnell: The Lost Leader', in *Parnell: The Politics of Power*, ed. Donal MacCartney (Dublin, 1991), 183–91. More generally, the literary record is covered in John Kelly, 'Parnell in Irish Literature', in *Parnell in Perspective*, ed. D. G. Boyce and A. O'Day (London, 1991), 242–83.

'Charles Stuart Parnell, President of the Irish Land League, Addressing a Meeting'.
Lithograph. New York: Currier and Ives, 1881. Library of Congress

PART I

Parnell's Ireland and Its Different Temporalities

CHAPTER I

O'Connell and Parnell

Oliver MacDonagh

Once upon a time people used to set crude examination questions which began, 'Compare and contrast ...'; and when someone suggested the title 'O'Connell and Parnell' to me, old habits stirred, and I could not help putting just such a schoolboy question to myself, apropos the two titans of nineteenth-century Ireland.*

I am well aware of the limitations of this form of comparative history. Time itself is a great distortionist: one cannot enter the same stream twice. Even a place's air and landscape are not immutable, let alone the generations on whom they act:

> O, how shall summer's honey breath hold out
> Against the wreckful siege of battering days,
> When rocks impregnable are not so strong
> ... but Time decays.

There is, perhaps, one special sense in which one can speak of a continuity between O'Connell, born in 1775, and Parnell, who died in 1891. O'Connell had still seven months to live at the time of Parnell's birth in 1846. Together, they spanned almost 120 years. But what a dozen decades of transformation! The very word 'revolution' seems to cling to them like a burr; and in no part of Europe were the changes more striking or profound than Ireland. During the years 1775–1891, its population, first, more than doubled, and was then almost halved; its native language, and the accompanying culture, fell from governing a considerable majority of the people to virtual disuse; its social structure altered and re-altered at its very base, under the impact of the great famine and its aftermath; and it witnessed no fewer than four of the six insurrections invoked as the sacred succession in

---

* This text was delivered by Oliver MacDonagh (1924–2002) as the second Parnell lecture at Magdalene College, Cambridge, in November 1993. It appeared at the time as a Magdalene College Occasional Paper (nr. 11).

the Proclamation of the Easter Rising in 1916. Thus, in comparing one of the lifetimes with the other, I shoot at targets in rapid motion.

There is, moreover, a peculiar disproportion in the spans of these lifetimes. If O'Connell had died as early as Parnell, he would have vanished from the Irish scene in 1820. Would he then have been much more than an interesting curiosity for the specialist? He would receive, I suppose, a mere 250 or 300 words, as a minor entry in the *Dictionary of Irish Biography*. Such an entry might recall that he was perhaps the most brilliant and successful junior ever to practise at the dazzling Munster Bar. It would certainly describe the duel of 1815 in which he killed D'Esterre, the spokesman of Dublin Corporation, for that was really a tournament between the reluctant champions of the Orange and Catholic factions of the day. It would probably recount his skilful capture and partial democratization of the Irish Catholic movement after 1808. But from 1815 on, the entry would be meagre. Apparently fruitless and often single-handed political drudgery, and failed agitations, are not generally recorded. As his son John wrote later of the years to 1820, 'By no kind of means, by no manner of exertion, and he *did* look about for means, and *did* use a thousand exertions, could he arouse the Catholics to action, or even to a defensive position.'

Had O'Connell died in 1820, he might possibly have been remembered for his support of the current causes of Queen Caroline and Simón Bolívar; but his grand undertaking to that date, Roman Catholic relief, was practically at a standstill. As Sheil recalled the state of things in 1820, 'we sat down like galley-slaves in a calm ... the country was palsied to the heart'. Actually, 1815–20 were the years of O'Connell's true apprenticeship as a popular leader. The craft that he was soon to practise with such astonishing virtuosity was learnt in the painful school of post-war failure. But without the later triumph, it would have blushed unseen.

It is not easy to project a political life for Parnell, had he lived to O'Connell's age and died in 1929 – and this not merely because projection is far more difficult than truncation when it comes to historical speculation. For one thing, the artistic quality of the actual Parnell story is beguiling. There is something so rounded, so finished, a *dénouement* – in the engineer being hoist with his own petard or, perhaps, conjoint petards, the O'Shea entanglement and the liberal alliance – that further chapters seem almost unimaginable. There is even a sense in which Parnell's political career might be said to have reached its conclusion in 1886. From then on, he fights, in general, to maintain a fixed position. Even his 'new departures' of 1890–91 were more apparent than real. They might, in fact, be better described as 'old returns' for, in essence, they repeat the tactics used by him in the later 1870s, in his first climb to personal dominion.

And then, how to conjure up convincing imaginary sequences for a Parnell of 1891–1929, even on the assumption that a Home Rule Parliament had been established? There is no difficulty in visualizing Parnell as a ruthless and domineering premier in a Dublin assembly. But would he have bestridden, for decades, a one-party state? Can we envisage the Ulster Unionists ever knuckling under to a Stormont-in-reverse, in which they were a perpetual opposition? How would Parnell's *idée fixe*, Protection, have fared early in the present century, when British politics were riven by this very issue, in terms of Empire? Above all, what of the possible return in force of the creeds of cultural division and separation and of revolutionary Republicanism, which the fall of Parnell did so much to release, but which he himself would surely have opposed implacably? Such trains of thought soon end in hopeless tangles.

***

The contrasts between the characters and social conditioning of the two men are quite as striking as those between the actual and the imaginary contracted and extended lives. I shall try to select some of the more significant.

Both O'Connell and Parnell were born into gentry families, but O'Connell's was much the lesser, for two main reasons. First, although the O'Connells had (through the quirks of the inheritance laws and the connivance of Protestant relations) retained some hereditary land, their substance derived principally from trade – the Continental traffic, smuggling, and even (in the case of O'Connell's own father) retailing goods. Second, as Catholics, they lived something of a dangerous and furtive life, even in O'Connell's boyhood. As late as the 1750s, the head of the clan, known universally as Hunting Cap, begged an antiquarian inquirer to spare him publicity in his book on Kerry: 'if you make mention of me and mine ... we too [may] be driven out upon the world without house or home'. All his life, O'Connell burned with resentment at what he saw as his lost or degraded status. At the Clare election of 1828, he burst out against the sneerers of the squireens, 'Of what use is my success [in life] to me? I have [often] wept over my lot in private ... [over] the cruel fate which places the Gores and other Protestants above me in my native land.'

Parnell, on the other hand, not only was socially secure in the long-settled ranks of the middling Ascendancy, but also his naturally commanding outlook on the world was reinforced by his distinguished ancestry, American as well as Irish, and by a forceful mother, who combined elitist American Republicanism (of the Daughters of the American Revolution variety) with easy entry into Dublin Castle sets and the presentation of her daughters to Queen Victoria. By right of birth and situation, as well as inherent disposition, Parnell assumed leadership like a glove. O'Connell had to fight his way *up* against an exclusive Catholic aristocracy and senior professionals of his own rank; and then to fight his way *in* to circles that had been closed to his co-religionists since the 1690s; and even this was only the beginning.

Apparently, the intellectual development of the two men was very different. We know much about O'Connell's but comparatively little about Parnell's, whose ideas have largely to be inferred from public actions and performances, which had specific audiences and aims in view. The only inclinations of interest to be discerned when he first stood for parliament as a Home Ruler were support for the secret ballot and some sympathy for Fenianism, this last being rare among his own class but quite commonplace among even moderate Catholics at the time. He was later spoken of as never opening a book, although he was most adept at borrowing others' knowledge. This cannot have been altogether so; and however derived, his judgements on the immediate Irish past were often extraordinarily penetrating.

Parnell's formal education was, of course, mainly English; but O'Connell's embraced a Kerry hedge-school, a tiny post-penal Jesuit academy, the great Continental recusant Colleges of Douai and St Omer, and the Inns of Court in London. Although he acquired, from each, some piece of his forensic equipment – and especially important was his grounding in Ciceronian rhetoric and concepts of public life at St Omer – he was essentially an autodidact. Strangely, for one later famed for troops of friends, he studied alone and secretly for the role, as he himself put it, of 'my country's Washington' and 'to appear with great eclat in the grand theatre of the world'. Whatever of Parnell, O'Connell was an endless reader: philosophy, history, science, poetry, even (while chastising himself for the waste of time) novels. And there were, of course, his law books, which he loathed for their inhumanity and pedantry, but forced himself to master as if they were the language of the enemy. His long self-education left him with not only an amazing breadth of reference but also lifelong habits of remorseless application.

There was one phase at least in which Parnell was equally the Industrious Apprentice. He would appear to have known virtually nothing of parliamentary forms when he entered the House of Commons in 1875, and during his first session he spoke little and badly. But he quickly acquired a meticulous knowledge of procedure. He too was mastering the language of the enemy, and would soon turn it into a weapon of his own. This was, however, a characteristically limited and pragmatic exercise, whereas O'Connell's was general and continuous.

In fact, there is a great gulf – a ratio of roughly five to one, if one can quantify such things – between the comparative efforts of the two. During the quarter-century 1804–29, for instance, O'Connell, when in Dublin, rose regularly at 5 a.m., worked on his briefs till 8, and then in the Four Courts from 10 until 3 or 4. The afternoons and evenings were devoted to political organization and correspondence, with reading and writing in his study until well into the night. For most of his long life, O'Connell laboured at this intensity. Although Parnell too was capable of sustained concentration, from 1881, and still more from 1886 on, he worked only occasionally at white heat. It is true that once the divorce crisis was upon him, he responded with wild bursts of energy. The Miltonic image seems inescapable:

> What though the field be lost?
> All is not lost: the unconquerable Will,
> And study of revenge, immortal hate,
> And courage never to submit or yield.

A rival image might well be the Viking gone berserk. Still, this was a final blaze. Overall, the contrast in stamina and persistence of labour is very great and of obvious political importance. It may well have been rooted as much in health and yielding to distraction as in early habits. Parnell was not strong physically; he was also emotionally susceptible – not least to the mild joys of domesticity.

Meanwhile, in 1796, along the trail of his solitary study, O'Connell had chanced on the book that was to provide him with his overriding public philosophy: the radical William Godwin's *Political Justice*. From it, he deduced his three fundamental principles of active politics: first, that violent means were *always* to be rejected, both because of their intrinsic evil and because, whatever they achieved, it would not be the object originally sought; second, that public opinion, properly marshalled and controlled, would, sooner or later, however laboriously or distantly, achieve any reform in view; and, third, that civil rights were at once absolute and universal, irrespective of religion, race, colour, sex, or condition. For all his gross demagoguery and tactical twists and turns,

O'Connell adhered to his three tenets with remarkable fidelity. I do not know of a single serious deviation from them throughout his long career.

Such schematization and abstraction were altogether foreign to Parnell's temperament. He was an instinctive constitutional politician, springing, as it were, fully armed and skilled upon the scene. Of course, he had to learn the mechanics of parliament. But in essentials he was straightaway complete. From 1875 to 1879 (and he was still only thirty-three years old when that year ended), he used parliament, residual Fenianism at home and rival Fenian factions in the United States, the Home Rule League of Great Britain, and the Mayo and National Land Leagues to climb from nothing to at least halfway up the ladder of unrivalled power. Politically, he was a *lusus naturae*. It was not his way to reflect generally, after O'Connell's fashion, on his own purposes and ambitions, or politics as a general science. He simply did.

The penultimate of my contrasts is largely negative, so far as Parnell is concerned. He was neither professionally trained nor forced to undertake the design or manufacture of his own political instruments. O'Connell, on the contrary, practised almost daily as a barrister for thirty years, for the last twenty of which he also toiled everlastingly at the trade of political organizer. Assiduity apart, perhaps, Parnell had the right qualities of mind and character, I think, to make a successful advocate. This is, however, a far cry from attributing to him the ingrained habits and acquired disposition of a near lifelong practitioner; and these did much to shape O'Connell's style of politics. For instance, O'Connell was quite extraordinarily resilient as a politician. Unlike Parnell's, O'Connell's career was marked by innumerable setbacks, and the frequent abandonment – for the time being, at least – of lines or policies that he had been pursuing. He could most readily shrug these off, and set off immediately on other tacks. No adverse verdict was ever crippling, let alone fatal. There was always tomorrow's case. There would always be another day in court.

Again, O'Connell was remarkable for his emphasis on measurable results. He himself once summed up the art of advocacy: 'A fine speech is a fine thing, but the verdict is *the* thing'; and in day-to-day politics too, the verdict remained, for him, *the* thing. Yet again, O'Connell was as prone to make ambitious claims on the platform or in his numerous 'proclamations to the Irish people', as in preliminary proceedings or the opening address in court. His initial demands for change were usually unrealistic, large, and wild. But this habit was accompanied by great readiness – even eagerness – to settle, so to speak, out of court, once things had reached the stage of dealing. Most important of all, perhaps, for

O'Connell's politics was his obsession with working to the limits of – but never crossing the border into – illegality. This is the key to understanding the structure of his associations and his management of the Repeal movement, both during and after 1843. There is no real counterpart in Parnell's career. Although Parnell was twice charged and once imprisoned, that was largely of his own choice. Governmental repression was not nearly so all-embracing, malignant, or severe in his day as in almost all the leading phases of O'Connell's agitation.

Parnell's own spell as agitator was comparatively short and restrained. Except for his broken campaigns of 1879–80 and 1890–91, he was an agitator in form rather than demagogic substance; and even in demagoguery he rarely lost his air of patrician superiority. O'Connell's case was very different. Down to 1829, during 1830–31 and 1840–41, and especially in his *annus mirabilis*, 1843, he was immersed in agitation, not merely in the sense of mass oratory and perfervid demonstrations but also in the very groundwork of its organization and detailed management.

Generally speaking, it was Parnell's fortune to take over going political concerns: the obstructionist faction in the House of Commons, the British Home Rule association, or the Land League. He secured their leadership by sheer force of personality or enigmatic lure, and went on to master rather than be used by them. Of course, he later shaped the parliamentary and national bodies, in part directly, in part through his lieutenants, to fit his particular personal and public purposes. Nonetheless, he was working with pre-existing units, and political machinery that ordinarily ran itself.

O'Connell was, on the contrary, the first cartographer of a then unknown continent: that of peaceful, mass, democratic politics. He was – he had to be – an unwearying political inventor and gadgeteer, with many failed experiments, as well as ultimate success, in creating, maintaining, or controlling popular pressure. Except for the final stage of the Catholic campaign, 1824–28, when R. L. Sheil and Thomas Wyse were effective colleagues, he lacked official subordinates of even moderate ability throughout his entire political life. Even as late as 1841, he himself chaired and set the agenda for not only the central council but also every subcommittee of the Repeal Association.

But the essence of agitation was the fieldwork; and this created a lasting dilemma for O'Connell. His power derived ultimately from the Irish masses, but ultimately, he had to deploy it in the House of Commons. This was then an assemblage of self-styled gentlemen, governed by esoteric codes of conduct; and O'Connell was the first of his class to be thrust into their ranks. Let me illustrate the difficulty by just one of his countless popular harangues. He was protesting, in 1831, against a proclamation suppressing Irish associations, which happened to have been signed by the Irish Chief Secretary, Sir Henry Hardinge, in the absence of the Lord Lieutenant. O'Connell began by assailing the hapless Hardinge as a 'paltry, contemptible, little English soldier ... [a] wretched English scribe, a chance child of fortune and of war'. Now the real purpose of O'Connell's speech was to induce peaceful submission to the proclamation. The cascade of scurrility was mere camouflage, intended to divert attention from a humiliating retreat. But one could not expect Hardinge to read it as just a rabble-calmer's line of business; and when O'Connell refused the consequent challenge to a duel – one of many such vain demands for satisfaction after he ceased duelling as a pacifist in 1815 – he was held to be totally unfit for the society of gentlemen. Nothing could have been more harmful to O'Connell in high London politics. All through the 1830s, he dragged behind him the chain of being a 'blackguard' or 'scoundrel': these were the conventional antitheses to 'gentleman'. Visiting London in 1840, Guizot was amazed to discover that O'Connell was not to be met with in the houses of even those Whigs with whom he had been in close political collaboration for many years.

Parnell lived in other, duel-free times; spoke to much more sophisticated popular audiences; and generally disdained vulgarity from the platform. Most of his public gibes, such as his celebrated dismissal of Gladstone in 1881 as 'a masquerading knight-errant', were well within the bounds of parliamentary abuse. More important still, it was part of Parnell's political stock-in-trade to be a 'gentleman', just as it was part of O'Connell's to be *vox populi*. It is a commonplace that Parnell's dominance over his followers, and nationalist Ireland as a whole, owed much to his Ascendancy accents, origins, and bearing: not quite, perhaps, an eye like Mars to threaten and command, but certainly an easy, unspoken assumption of the right to rule. Correspondingly, this class difference worked to his advantage in the House of Commons. Socially, he was an insider, accepted by the caste, one who knew instinctively the laws of personal behaviour, and spoke the same language in every sense. This helps to explain why his liberal alliance was much more easily attained, and sustained, than O'Connell's. But there were drawbacks too. He was demoted by Harcourt and others to the rank of 'blackguard' when in November 1890 he disclosed confidential conversations he had held with Gladstone. And when, for example, he asserted that he would emerge from the divorce proceedings without a stain on his reputation, his Irish public would take this to mean a great deal more than that he had comported himself honourably, according to the code. The final tragedy was to flow – to some small extent, at least – from such cross-purposes.

My last contrast is that of personality or, more exactly, public personality. O'Connell grew up in the shadow of both a tyrannical guardian, Hunting Cap, and institutionalized inferiority as a Papist; and, perhaps in consequence, deviousness and finesse were among his lifelong traits and what the harsh Hunting Cap condemned as 'the facility and softness of your disposition' – counterbalanced, be it said, by moral courage in the world at large. Growing up, Parnell was tyrant rather than tyrannized within his own family; his deviousness and finesse were chiefly reserved for party manoeuvring, and 'the facility and softness of his disposition' for his lover; and his courage of all sorts was manifested as aristocratic disdain, rather than tumultuous indignation.

Again, O'Connell was once innocently described by an Austrian horse boy as 'the man who invented Ireland'; and so, in a sense, he was. He had to mould the public opinion that was to be his sword out of an inert mass. For years, he had to struggle, as he himself said, against the inbred Catholic cringe, the Catholic crouch. For years, Byron's couplet:

> Hereditary bondsman! Know ye not
> Who would be free themselves must strike the blow

was his unceasing refrain from platforms. Such a protean endeavour demanded, or at least succeeded by, remorseless persuasion, dramatic exaggeration, theatricality of effects, flattery, effusion, and emotional appeal. Parnell took the other road of reticence, enigma, and repose. He committed himself as late as possible to as little as possible. He spoke only when he must, and then to some specific end, even in (or rather especially in) his numerous ambiguities. His form of leadership was opposite to O'Connell's. O'Connell, who was fifty years of age before he perfected and fully mastered his mass support, assumed the part of father of his people. As such, he chided and cajoled them, demanded their trust in his judgement and their obedience to his commands. He worked on their inmost drives as if they were his own. He was the very type of Gaelic clan chieftain, translated into nineteenth-century circumstances, and magnified ten-thousand-fold in scale. Parnell's rule was more in the Dalai Lama mode. His leadership was based on distance, and the instillation of a sense of awe in his crowd following; he even managed to hedge himself with some divinity. The king as popular apotheosis was O'Connell's form; but Parnell's, the king as removed and mysterious hero.

***

And now for the reverse side of the coin. Despite all the generational changes, differences in lifespans, and contrasts in character and bearing, O'Connell and Parnell were remarkably similar in political cast of mind and strategy. I wrote some years ago that Parnell's great parliamentary decade, the 1880s, was in many ways the evening performance of O'Connell's fifty years before. I would still hold to this firmly as a nutshell judgement. Of course (to maintain the theatrical metaphor), there were major differences in the available stagecraft and audience response, to say nothing of the actors' emphases. But so too there were between, say, Garrick and Kean, or Irving and Olivier, playing the same role.

We must not be misled by the extraordinary contrast in political styles. Each man's final objective was the utmost degree of constitutional independence that could be won by a combination of Irish popular pressure and disciplined voting in the House of Commons. Each man used shibboleths, 'The Repeal of the Union' and 'Home Rule', which constituted apparently precise demands, but which were in reality (in the language of contract law) 'an invitation to treat' rather than 'a firm offer'. Each man deployed the same symbolism (1782, the Volunteers, Grattan's Parliament, College Green, and all the rest), well aware that such references were utterly anachronistic but also aware that they possessed the priceless dualism of quasi-revolutionary and separatist connotations for one audience, and conservative and restorative connotations for another. The very incantation, 'The King, Lords and Commons of Ireland', could be turned this way or that.

The essential similarity of O'Connell's operation to Parnell's is apparent in this extraordinary passage towards the end of O'Connell's great Mansion House speech of 1843 on the desirability of Repeal:

> a Parliament inferior to the English parliament I would accept as an instalment if I found the people ready to go with me, and if it were offered to me ... It must first be offered to me – mark that ... I will never ask for or look for any other save an independent legislature, but if others offer me a subordinate parliament, I will close with any such offer and accept that offer.

Despite the initial hedges of 'an instalment' and 'the people ready', O'Connell was showing considerably more of his hand than Parnell would ever do. Still, they worked within the same ambience. Each sought to force out what we might call a counter-offer. Each sought to force out a declaration, and make none himself. Parnell's devices were silence and an ambiguous and amorphous name, Home Rule; O'Connell's garrulity, inconsistency, and a merely ostensible objective, a return to the status quo ante 1801. But these were only differences in technique. Parnell and O'Connell were at one in being 'comparative separatists', who recognized that the *degree* of separation would be determined ultimately by Great Britain, and who committed themselves to no abstraction or ideal form of state.

Pari passu, they reached their launching fields in a substantially similar fashion. The land legislation of 1881–82 was, for Parnell, the equivalent of the 1829 Catholic Relief Act for O'Connell. From 1800 onwards, O'Connell had steadily proclaimed that the religious issue was secondary to, though an indispensable preliminary for, the Repeal of the Act of Union. Correspondingly, even at the fiery height of the land agitation in 1880, Parnell declared to the Irish world in general that he would never 'have taken off his coat' to fight the land war if he did not think that it would lead on to Irish independence. This general resemblance in the opening phases contains many lesser fragments of a common pattern. For instance, if Parnell depended heavily on Fenian and ex-Fenian organization in his early associations, O'Connell's Catholic movement of the 1820s owed much – and this is not generally appreciated – to the support of ex–United Irishmen and veterans of 1798. Again, if Parnell retained control of the mass of the tenant farmers by his formula of 'Test the Act' (that is, the 1881 Land Act) in the courts, O'Connell maintained control of the rural masses in the late summer of 1828 (with particular difficulty in the flashpoint area of Tipperary) by his equivalent formula of 'Test the Cabinet' – meaning, do not dissipate all the pressures built up by the Clare election, but await the government's *enforced* response.

When it came to the ultimate objectives, both men knew well, from the beginning, that success depended on reaching a constructive understanding with one of the major, office-holding British parties; and that meant, realistically, the Whigs or Liberals. This by no means ruled out common action with the Tories, even if only on the basis of some temporary or tactical coincidence of interest. At no stage could O'Connell hope to reach an accommodation with the Conservative Party per se. All else apart, Peel's personal enmity towards him was, and remained, unremitting. But between 1831 and 1834 he repeatedly sought a rapprochement with the Irish Tories, as a means of turning the Whig-Liberal flank. Of course, from 8 June 1885 (when Parnell combined with the Conservatives to bring down Gladstone's government) to 10 November of the same year (when he directed the enfranchised Irish in Great Britain to vote against the Liberals in the coming General Election), *he* was pursuing essentially the same end – though with much more success.

The most difficult phase in each case was when a Liberal government was in office without any Liberal alliance in the offing. This situation called for three lines of conduct which, in the short run, at least, exacerbated Irish-Liberal relations. O'Connell and Parnell had, first, to maintain menacing organization and agitation at home; second, to repudiate most of the government's Irish measures as inadequate or injurious; and, third, to use a more or less disciplined Irish party to provide both a running fire and selective procedural disruption in the House of Commons. On all counts, but particularly the last, Parnell was in a stronger position than O'Connell.

By use of a Repeal test in the general election of 1832, O'Connell secured forty nominal supporters and about twenty-five on whom he could fairly generally rely; and we can, more or less, reverse these figures to some twenty-five original and forty ultimate, as the outcome of the 1880 general election for Parnell. These were significant blocs of votes, especially in the more disciplined 1880s. Yet even O'Connell's much looser party conducted a protracted, and partially successful, campaign of parliamentary obstruction against the Whig Irish Coercion Bill of 1833, a campaign which constantly bears comparison with (and indeed foreshadows in many details) the much more celebrated Parnellite scenes of January–February 1881.

During 1830–32 and 1880–82, respectively, O'Connell and Parnell, on the one hand, and the Whig and Liberal governments of Grey and Gladstone, on the other, were exploring unknown terrain, with very similar eventual results. From the start, Parnell was heading an agrarian campaign; while O'Connell almost immediately set up successive Repeal organizations to force out concessions by the threat of popular excitement (he also greeted the European revolutions of the summer of 1830 with a national call to 'agitate – agitate – agitate'). The official response to the two thrusts was identical: a combination of repressive and conciliatory legislation, and the arrest of the contumacious leaders – O'Connell, in January 1831, and Parnell, first in November 1880, and again in October 1881, when he ended in Kilmainham prison.

The next stage, after unabated Irish disturbance, was the *modus vivendi*. In O'Connell's so-called treaty with the government, in March 1831, he agreed to disband the current Repeal movements in return for the quashing, in effect, of his own conviction, and some ameliorative Irish measures. The Kilmainham Treaty of May 1882, between Gladstone and Parnell, was essentially the same sort of agreement writ large. Part of the larger writing was, of course, Parnell's own release from imprisonment.

We should note, particularly, that apart from marking the end of full belligerence and a stage on the road to thorough compacts, the 'treaties' signalled major advances on the parts of both O'Connell and Parnell. First, each had quite clearly established himself as national leader, with a *demonstrated* capacity to deliver and substantial, if not total, control over the forces of Irish disaffection. And, second, each was enabled to free himself from an agitation that had become a political encumbrance. In O'Connell's case, his first Repeal campaign could only have ended in parliamentary humiliation in 1831; and, in Parnell's, the land agitation was, by 1882, hindering rather than hastening the formation of a moderate, broad-based, and Church-blessed Irish movement.

These were necessary preliminaries on the way to full-scale, if unwritten, Liberal alliances. In each case, they took four more years, and various intervening game-plays, to achieve. They were very different in form. O'Connell's Lichfield House Compact of 1835 was designed to maintain a Liberal government in office, and had for its condition-precedent the shelving of Repeal. Parnell's was designed to support the Liberals in opposition, and had for its condition-precedent that party's undertaking to commit itself wholeheartedly to Home Rule. Yet the differences were not really so very large, at least in terms of ultimate achievement. After all, O'Connell *did* secure much of his major political objective of the 1830s: a degree of power-sharing, executive favour, and Catholic parity in Ireland. So far as it went, this constituted an actualization of what the Emancipation Act of 1829 had theoretically implied. Moreover, however meagre and mutilated the legislative fruits of his Compact turned out to be, the Irish Grand Jury, Tithe, Poor Law, and Municipal Reform Acts did weaken Protestant and Tory Ascendancy, and *pro tanto* brought civil equality a little closer, and Irish self-government with it. Parnell's alliance achieved much the same sort of result by other means. Through forcing the Conservative party on to the track of positive Unionism ('killing Home Rule by kindness'), it ultimately wrung out measures of land purchase, denominationalism in education, democratic local government, and state investment in the infrastructure, all fundamental objects of conventional Irish nationalism, as it had gradually developed since the 1820s.

***

In all this, I do not at all mean to measure one man against another, in terms of political ability. It is enough to say that both belonged, as it seems to me, to the very first rank of nineteenth-century politicians. If we allow for the much smaller scale and shorter span of action, Parnell can, I believe, be compared without absurdity to Bismarck or Cavour, so sure was his assessment of the forces of the day, so unerring his sense of timing. Correspondingly, given his perpetual banishment from governmental power, O'Connell can, I believe, be compared, without absurdity, to Andrew Jackson or even Lincoln, as supreme artist in popular politics.

And when I draw out the high degree to which Parnell's strategy, tactics, and devices followed those of O'Connell (*mutatis mutandis*, of course), I am not at all implying that Parnell owed anything to his predecessor, other than the fact that his advances were made from the more forward bridgehead that O'Connell had done so much to establish. O'Connellism (by that name at least) was in deep eclipse throughout Parnell's political performance; and he would probably have found its tone and *modus operandi*, had he ever studied them, altogether antipathetic to his own. Instead, the common contours of the two careers derive, in my estimation, from two different factors: first, the interior logic of Anglo-Irish conflict in the nineteenth century meant that a mainly Catholic nationalism had to mobilize, weld, and concentrate its weight of numbers and aggregation of grievances, if it were to produce fundamental change in Ireland; and, second, both its great orators, O'Connell and Parnell, were fully committed to, and expert in, the parliamentary and constitutional form of politics. It is these factors in combination which, I believe, explain why the same role was replayed in different generations.

As parliamentarians, O'Connell and Parnell excelled. One experienced American observer wrote of the years 1834–37, 'O'Connell is, I think, the finest orator [of the age]. I have heard him at least fifty times, and in every variety of question; and every new display gave me a higher opinion of his varied, astonishing and exquisite powers ... next to him, I would rank Lord Stanley; then Sir Robert Peel.' Morley judged that Parnell's speech in the Home Rule debate of 1886, which, he said, made 'even able disputants on either side look like amateurs', was only one of his masterly performances. More to the point, perhaps, than their individual supremacy, both men – despite occasional misleading signals to the contrary – adhered absolutely to the parliamentary mode. To apply the acid test, their respective threats to withdraw their followers from the House of Commons were never carried through, not even, in Parnell's case, in the coercion crisis of 1881, when it seemed to be the last card left for him to play. A withdrawal was out of the question, although in Gladstone's view, a 'withdrawal *en bloc*' would have been 'by far the worst thing' that could have happened, from the standpoint of any British government. On the contrary, what were the battlefields, and what the trophies fought for, in Parnell's last desperate campaign, but by-elections and seats in parliament?

O'Connell repudiated violence specifically in a way that Parnell avoided; but even he was capable of a Parnellite sleight-of-hand in his popular speeches. In lacerating Sir Henry Hardinge (to return to our earlier example), he declared that 'Irish conditions were not *yet* ripe for the use of physical force', before going on to say that he, himself, would not support it in any circumstances. All this was merely what Conor Cruise O'Brien has called, in his book *Parnell and His Party,* 'the capework of the pseudo-revolutionary gesture', a rhetoric of militancy designed to flatter and inspirit Irish listeners as well as concentrate the minds of British cabinets. After all, what did the whole gamut of Parnell's dark ambiguities between 1877 and 1882 represent but a sort of haka? The essence of the matter seems to me to be that both men entered politics in the aftermath of armed revolutions, and worked through periods when jacqueries and incalculable bloodshed seemed real threats. It was their business to divert, and channel into constitutional campaigns, the powerful forces of violence, past and potential.

Soon after the rebellion of 1798, O'Connell, who might well have been a victim or even a reluctant participant himself, wrote in his private journal, 'Good God! What a brute man becomes when ignorant and oppressed! Oh, Liberty, what horrors are perpetuated in thy name! May every virtuous revolutionist remember the horrors of Wexford.' Such language and sentimentalism would, doubtless, have jarred upon Parnell. But he was certainly at one with O'Connell in distrusting the course and fearing the consequences of any, let alone violent, mass action from below. And again, at one monster meeting of 1843, with almost half a century of adherence to rely upon, O'Connell told his vast audience: 'The principle of my political life has been that all improvements in political institutions can be obtained ... by peaceful means, and cannot be obtained by forcible means, or if they could be got by forcible means, such means create more evils than they cure.'

Parnell was, characteristically, silent on such a theme. But the whole course of his political career – even its demonic close – bears tacit witness to the same conviction.

In the very end, it seems to me that, for all their power-hunger, equivocation, and deceit, O'Connell and Parnell nonetheless stand out, in the long, sad sweep of modern Irish history, as great carriers of reconciliation – even if the world was too much for them in their own, or perhaps any other day.

CHAPTER 2

The Paradoxes of Parnell

Paul Bew

> Parnell was amenable to liberal considerations but utterly immune from liberal sympathies.
>
> —Francis Hackett[1]

Everything about Parnell is contested. 'Was Parnell good hearted?' T. P. O'Connor asked.[2] The young George Bernard Shaw, working unhappily as a clerk in a Dublin land agency from 1871 to 1877, found Parnell a 'deucedly disagreeable person'. But was this only because, as Francis Hackett surmised, he had no 'gift of the gab'.[3] T. P. O'Connor gave an answer to his own question:

> It would have appeared to many people a ridiculous question, so plain seems the answer of Parnell's expression and manner and speech. I remember hearing quite a distinguished Englishman once speak of Parnell as a fish-blooded man. Justin McCarthy, who was not only a good but a benignant judge of human character, often said that he never knew Parnell to say a kind word of his colleagues, that there was always underneath an inner sneer.[4]

T. P. O'Connor felt it necessary then to give evidence 'to the contrary', indicating Parnell's occasional generosity of spirit. William O'Brien directly contradicted Justin McCarthy: there was no 'scornful masterfulness in dealing with his own lieutenants ... to his appreciation and admiration there were no bounds'.[5] Michael Morris, the Irish Lord Chief Justice, noted, however, that Parnell's respect for his colleagues was limited

---

[1] Francis Hackett, *A Shady Nationalism* (New York, 1918), 330.
[2] T. P. O'Connor, *Memoirs of an Old Parliamentarian* (London, 1929), 1:345.
[3] Michael Holroyd, *Bernard Shaw: The Search for Love* (London, 1988), 52–53; St John Ervine, *Bernard Shaw* (London, 1956), 45; Ralph Ellison, 'Shaw and Wells', *The Atlantic Monthly* 187 (1951): 71.
[4] O'Connor, Memoirs of an Old Parliamentarian, 1:346.
[5] William O'Brien, *Evening Memoirs* (London, 1920), 62.

to the 'hard men' amongst them;[6] even William O'Brien was inclined to accept that such men were in some sense privileged.

When did he first take account of Fenianism, the popular Irish movement which launched a poorly organized insurrection in March 1867? 'I have heard Parnell say that the first (and I suspect last) time he ever found himself singing was when he followed the heady chorus of Michael Scanlon's "Out and make way for the Fenian men!" as it was roared by the bronzed soldiers of the Civil War in his mother's drawing room.'[7] Or was it, later in the year, as he claimed, when at Magdalene College, Cambridge, he was affected by the execution of the Manchester martyrs – three Fenians hanged for killing a policeman during an attempted rescue of comrades – in November 1867?

Most profoundly of all, the historical debate is now focused on the apparently conflicting strains in Parnell's political activity: Was he a republican revolutionary or a Tory landlord? The reasons for seeing Parnell as a revolutionary are clear enough. He asked Charles Fay, the Monaghan MP, to commend him to the republican movement. His first major public act was to give money to the parliamentary campaign of John Mitchel, a true revolutionary who believed that the British parliament would never carry out a pro-Irish reform and was motivated instead by genocidal intentions as proven by the famine. He led the Land League (1879–82), a peasant-based Catholic nationalist movement of 600,000 mostly Catholic tenants, against 10,000 mostly Protestant beleaguered landlords. He worked closely at the apex of this movement with men who were revolutionaries, many of them having been involved in the failed Fenian attempt at insurrection in 1867. These men believed that a British parliament would never act decisively against the garrison 'landlord class' in Ireland and that, therefore, an aggressive campaign against them would lead to a withdrawal from the Westminster parliament in favour of a Dublin one or, even better, an insurrection backed this time by angry peasants in contrast to the rural apathy which had marked the revolt of 1867.[8] This movement included leaders who believed that to achieve maximum mobilization it might be necessary to appeal to the class interests of small farmers against strong ones: strong farmers, although mostly Catholic and nationalist, were strongly suspected of lacking the necessary spirit of daring and self-sacrifice for the national cause. Moderate home rulers – well aware of

---

[6] W. H. Hurlbert, *Ireland under Coercion* (Edinburgh, 1889), 55.
[7] O'Brien, *Memoirs of an Old Parliamentarian*, 59.
[8] Paul Bew, *Land and the National Question in Ireland* (Dublin, 1978), chapter 3.

Parnell's visible respect for the 'hard' men – looked on aghast as Parnell placed himself at the centre of this drama. They expected an almighty crash as Britain moved it to quell this movement as easily as it had put down the 1867 revolt. But the very presence of Parnellite parliamentary respectability made it more difficult for the British authorities: they hit on a course which combined major reform – the 1881 Land Act – with major repression and mass internment of Parnell and hundreds of his supporters.

All this revolutionary activity by Parnell has led some scholars to an unavoidable conclusion. Professor Liam Kennedy has written:

> There is no doubt that Parnell envisaged a role for the Anglo-Irish in his home rule Ireland. The key question is the extent of this role, particularly after the confrontations of 1879–81. Given the consistency as well as the ferocity of his attacks on landlordism, and, on occasion, on individual landlords, one suspects that Parnell, the political realist, can hardly have entertained serious notions of a leading role for the remnants of the *ancien regime* in a self-governing Ireland. Even if he did, the strategies he pursued during the 1880s suggest that he accorded the prospect a low priority.[9]

At first sight, Professor Kennedy's conclusion cannot be challenged. It fits many of the facts and much of the actual impact of Parnell's career. But it does not quite catch the allusive references to cross-class conciliation in Parnell's platform speeches, even in the most revolutionary times from 1879 to 1882. The sense was that he was, even in revolutionary times, held back by 'a strain of sympathy', as Harold Spender put it for the landlords.[10] Winston Churchill in his book *Great Contemporaries* wrote that Parnell was

> himself a man of Conservative instincts, especially where property was concerned. Indeed, the paradoxes of his earnest and sincere life were astonishing: a Protestant leading Catholics; a landlord inspiring a 'No Rent' campaign; a man of law and order exciting revolt; a humanitarian and anti-terrorist controlling and yet arousing the hopes of Invincibles and Terrorists.[11]

But was Parnell really a man of conservative instincts on the property issue? Actually, he told Andrew Kettle during the 1880 election: 'Do you know, Kettle, what I have been thinking about for the last few minutes? Well,

[9] Liam Kennedy, 'The Economic Thought of the Nation's Lost Leader', in *Parnell in Perspective*, ed. D. G. Boyce and Alan O'Day (London, 1982), 171–200.
[10] Harold Spender, 'John Redmond: An Impression', *Contemporary Review* 113 (April 1918): 375–76.
[11] Winston Churchill, *Great Contemporaries* (London, 1938), 268.

I give it up so you may as well tell us! Why the land does not belong to the landlords at all? I answered, Is it only now that you found that out?'[12]

Parnell's private ruminations need, however, to be treated with care. He told Kettle once that the Catholic religion was the only religion which connected this world to the next – but, at other times, became angry with colleagues who suggested he would die a Catholic and even seemed to some (like Tom Healy) to be attracted to extreme Protestantism. All this is different from political calculation, albeit unrealistic calculation. Despite Parnell's remark on land ownership, Andrew Kettle believed that Parnell believed (as did Kettle) that in the circumstances of the 1880s, Parnell felt that home rule as a project needed greater social cachet to be acceptable to a UK parliament.[13] A land reform based on purchase was the way to create a more variegated political leadership.

Parnell once said to William O'Brien, 'The only good thing the Irish landlords have to show for themselves are their homes and perhaps in Roscommon County, their horses.' But that was not the end of the matter. Parnell also told Andrew Kettle that 'he was always very hopeless about the older landlords ever throwing in their lot with the people of Ireland, but he expected that the young man would, if the land question was settled by purchase'.[14] It is worth noting that Kettle did not regard this aspiration as conflicting in any way with Parnell's assertion that the landlords did not really own the land.

In the spring of 1882, Parnell sent increasingly conservative and reassuring signals to Gladstone. On his release from jail in early May 1882, he appears to have asked P. J. Sheridan – a key figure in the perpetration of acts of terrorism – to calm things down in the west of Ireland and, in exchange, offered a secret oath of allegiance to republican ideals. Parnell's intention is clear: he sent messages to Gladstone mentioning Sheridan in precisely this context. Almost immediately, the Phoenix Park murder of Lord Frederick Cavendish, the incoming Irish Chief Secretary, and of Thomas Burke, the Catholic head of the civil service, took place. As late as June, Sheridan's close friend P. J. Gordon – a man well known to Parnell – was responsible for the murder of Col. Walter Bourke in Mayo. These were seriously embarrassing developments. The Irish Chief

---

[12] L. J. Kettle, ed., *The Material for Victory: Being the Memoirs of Andrew J. Kettle* (Dublin, 1958), 31.
[13] F. S. L. Lyons, 'The Land War', *Irish Times* (12 May 1979).
[14] Kettle, *The Material for Victory*, 34.

Secretary was well aware of the connections between 'Parnellism' and the Bourke murder.[15]

It is clear that Parnell inhabited a different mental universe from that of his revolutionary colleagues: the public hints of this can be seen in the many assertions during the land war of the necessity of a reformist course of action. But what decisively tips the balance is his meeting with Mrs O'Shea, the wife of a parliamentary colleague in mid-1880. Their intense love affair intensified the conservative elements in Parnell's political make-up: Katharine was the niece of a former Lord Chancellor and intensely political. Within weeks of his meeting with her, Parnell's correspondence reveals a man happy to see the collapse of the agitation. His refusal to move the popular movement at a key meeting in Paris in early 1881 along a revolutionary path was attributed to influence of his mistress by his colleagues. The bloody Phoenix Park murder placed Parnell in a most difficult position. English public opinion turned against him. Redmond has given one of the best descriptions of the moment:

> A blind unreasoning fury took possession of the public, and there was but one thought in every English mind, Parnell was the man responsible. Parnell was the man who ought to suffer. Imagine yourselves in the House of Commons at its first meeting forty-eight hours after the murder. All London surged down towards Westminster. The police with difficulty cleared a passage for Members to enter the building through the crowds in the street outside. Such one or two of the Irish Members as were recognised were greeted with howls of execration. Inside the House there was the stillness of the tomb. By a strange and mysterious instinct every Member had come down dressed in black as to a funeral. Mr Parnell, however, did not falter. In a few simple words, expressed without any outward sign of the influence of the scene upon him, he expressed his horror at the crime and sat down the most hated, distrusted, and feared man in England.[16]

Parnell also issued a public statement which appeared to urge the Irish people to inform on the assassins. It was to please British public opinion. But it also infuriated Ireland's revolutionary subculture:

> On the eve of what seemed a bright future for our country, that evil destiny which has apparently pursued us for centuries, has struck at our hopes

---

[15] Patrick Maume, 'Parnell and the IRB Oath', *Irish Historical Studies* 39.115 (May 1995): 363–70; Shane Kenna, *War in the Shadows: The Irish American Fenians Who Bombed Victorian Britain* (Dublin, 2014). Kenna states to have in his possession an oath for the Invincibles written in P. J. Sheridan's handwriting (343 n. 60).

[16] John Redmond, *Home Rule* (London, 1910), 82.

another blow which can not be exaggerated in its disastrous consequences. In this hour of sorrowful gloom we venture to give expression to our profoundest sympathy with the people of Ireland in this calamity which has befallen our cause through this horrible deed, and with those who were determined at the last hour, that a policy of conciliation should supplant that of terrorism and national distrust. We earnestly hope that the attitude and action of the Irish people will show to the world that this assassination which has befallen us has led almost to the abandonment of hope in our country's future, is deeply and religiously abhorrent to their every feeling and instinct. We appeal to you, to show by every manner of expression, that amid the universal horror which the assassination has excited, no people feel so deep a sympathy with those hearts which must be seared by it, as the nation upon whose prosperity and reviving hopes it may entail consequences, more ruinous than those that have fallen to the lot of unhappy Ireland during the present generation. We feel that no act that has ever been perpetrated in our country during the exciting struggles of the last fifty years has so stained Ireland as this cowardly and unprovoked assassination of a friendly stranger, and that until the murderers of Cavendish and Burke are brought to justice that stain will sully our country's name.[17]

Parnell was fortunate in that after the Phoenix Park murders those land leaguers who had the closest connections with the funding of violence fled to the United States: the treasurer, Patrick Egan, who became eventually in 1897 after Parnell's death a US ambassador in Chile; Thomas Brennan, a businessman; Patrick Sheridan, a rancher in Colorado; M. M. O'Sullivan, a priest; and so on. The departure of such men – Mitchel supporters to a man – made Parnell's switch to moderation much easier. In December 1882, Parnell respectfully but decisively dismissed Mitchel's strategy of withdrawal from Westminster.[18] Even before that, however, Parnell was working to move his movement away from the Egan–Brennan nexus. Two reports of Parnell's conversation, prepared by Labouchere for Chamberlain, are of particular interest. On 22 May, Labouchere wrote to Chamberlain after a further interview with Parnell:

He says that he is most anxious for a *modus vivendi*, and believes that if the present opportunity for establishing one be let pass, it is not likely to recur. He and his friends, he says, are incurring the serious risk of assassination in their efforts to bring it about, and he thinks that his suggestions ought to be judged on their merits.

[17] Paul Bew, *Enigma: A New Life of Charles Stewart Parnell* (Dublin, 2012), 98–99.
[18] *Irish Times*, 18 Dec. 1882.

On 9 June the same writer reported:

> Egan and his section of the League are furious at the idea of the League
> being converted into a moderate tenant right association with its headquar-
> ters in Dublin. This he desires. Parnell indicated that he would rather
> withdraw from politics than allow Egan's line to win – but added that once
> he withdrew, his 'own life will not be worth a day's purchase' and that 'the
> Fenians will be masters of the situation'.[19]

Of course, this policy had deep implications. Revealingly, in 1883, when
Parnell was rewarded a cheque of £37,000 in Dublin – to help him out of
some pressing financial difficulties – the money came not from those poor
western counties which had provided the impetus for the Land League but
from the richer, more politically cautious counties like Meath. Meath, not
much involved in the Land League, gave £1,454; Mayo, the very heart of
the movement, gave £174 4s 3d. Serjeant Sullivan noted how Parnell had
become 'by a dispensation hard to understand ... the hero of the
bourgeoisie'.[20]

   Now all circumstances favoured Parnell. The franchise reform of
1884 guaranteed him and his party eighty-five seats at the heart of the
Westminster system: Gladstone, who by 1882 had privately accepted
home rule in principle, contemplated a Dublin parliament. The political
personality of Parnell was, of course, central to Gladstone's thinking. As
Churchill put it:

> Without Parnell, Gladstone would never have attempted Home Rule. The
> conviction was borne upon the Grand Old Man in his heyday that here was
> a leader who would govern Ireland, and no one else could do it. Here was a
> man who could inaugurate the new system in a manner which would not be
> insupportable to the old.[21]

But then Parnell, to the surprise of many, sought out the Tories in the
spring and summer of 1885 and tried to make a deal with them. Winston
Churchill explained the *Realpolitik* behind the move: 'His own Conservative instincts, his sense of realism, the anger excited against Liberal coercion, led him a long way towards the Tories. After all, they could deliver
the goods. Perhaps they alone could do so, for the House of Lords in those
days was a barrier which none but Tories could pass.'[22]

---

[19] Bew, *Land and the National Question*, 104.   [20] A. M. Sullivan, *Old Ireland* (London, 1927), 47.
[21] Churchill, *Great Contemporaries*, 270.
[22] *Ibid.*, 272; Paul Bew, *Churchill and Ireland* (Oxford, 2016), 21–24.

Parnell had another reason for his Tory dalliance. He believed the Tories would be more likely to concede protection of Irish industry than the Liberals. In this he was quite correct – as his conversations with senior figures on both sides of British politics agreed. Parnell's protectionism was probably one of his inheritances from the social ideology of Fenianism. In this ideology, post-famine Ireland was set along a path of structured underdevelopment and subservience to England: a mere cattle farm to feed English cities. To break with this, Ireland needed to establish self-government, smash the existing land system, and protect native Irish industries. As one Republican writer, P. J. P. Tynan, puts it: 'Establish ... manufacturing industries all over the island, first creating a native market by shutting out all foreign goods, as soon as Irishmen can make them at home.'[23]

Parnell had echoed this sentiment in his February 1880 speech in Cincinnati: 'You have been much criticised because you insist upon protecting your manufacturers against the worthless products of many English looms.... I can not help seeing that by this protection policy you have protected your manufacturers and escaped many of the worst ends of British civilisation in the great towns.'[24] The question of Parnell's protectionist views has received not quite the attention it deserves. It may be that subsequent scholars have been overly influenced by Conor Cruise O'Brien's work in this respect. In his superb *Parnell and His Party 1880–1890*, published in 1957,[25] he offered a rebuttal of the work – 'stimulating' and 'original' as O'Brien thought it was – of the Marxist historian E. Strauss, whose *Irish Nationalism and British Democracy* (1931) had laid great stress on Irish protectionism. But even O'Brien, while convincing in his analysis of the weakness of support for protection more generally in the Irish party, substantively accepts that it was Parnell's personal conviction.

At Arklow, in late August 1885, Parnell said that 'without a freely elected National Assembly with power to control all the affairs of Ireland, and with power to protect her struggling industries ... it is impossible for us to revive our native industries'.[26] The speech surprised his friends.

---

[23] P. J. P. Tynan, *The Irish National Invincibles and Their Times* (London, 1894), 14.
[24] *Special Commission Act*, 1888. Report of the shorthand notes of the speeches, proceedings and evidence taken before the Commissioner appointed under the Above Named Act, 12 Feb. 1880, 5:155.
[25] Conor Cruise O'Brien, *Parnell and His Party 1880–1890* (Oxford, 1957), 109–14.
[26] *Freeman's Journal*, 21 Aug. 1885.

Everyone knew that it would annoy Liberals, who were increasingly seen as friends of Ireland. What was he up to?

The Liberal unionist *Spectator* noted Parnell's personal strategic selfish motive: 'In the Arklow speech, Parnell explained how he had persuaded the Dublin Corporation not to buy in the cheapest market their stone for the paving of Dublin streets, but to encourage native industry by buying from his own quarries stone dearer than the Welsh quarry-owners professed themselves willing to apply.' The editorial went on to note, sourly: 'It is his good fortune to find the profession of patriotism, thoroughly genuine we are sincerely convinced, very profitable to him.' The *Spectator* denounced the whole project: 'First sent asunder by Home Rule, and then hermetically sealed from all by a policy of Protection, Ireland would, indeed, rue the blighting influence of Mr Parnell's ascendancy.'[27] Whatever the *Spectator* thought about the matter, Parnell was perfectly sincere. In the last months of his life, he told his loyal friend Dr Kenny MP, 'Well, the first thing I do, would be to put a protective duty on imports of British manufacturers.'[28]

Shortly after giving the Arklow speech, Parnell met one of his lieutenants, Andrew Kettle. Kettle was a keen observer of Parnell. He questioned him closely on the matter:

> You were at Arklow yesterday, I said, opening the quarry and selling the stones to the [Dublin] Corporation, but what was the meaning of your strange speech on protection and Irish industries? Are you going to break with the Free Traders? 'Yes', he said, 'we have a rather big project on hand.' He then explained the meeting with Lord Carnarvon and the project of Aristocratic Home Rule, with the colonial right to protect our industries against English manufacture. I seemed to be knocked dumb as I really was, by the unexpected news, and he went out to explain that it was not from a motive of justice or generosity that the Conservative party was making the proposals. Inspired chiefly by Lord Randolph Churchill, the classes in Britain were afraid that if the Irish democratic propaganda were to continue, in conjunction with the English radicals, class rule might be overturned altogether. So to save themselves, they are going to set up a class conservative government in Ireland, with the aid and consent of the Irish democracy, having no connection with England but the link of the Crown and an Imperial Contribution to be regulated by circumstances.

---

[27] 'Home Rule and Free Trade', *Spectator*, 29 Aug. 1885.
[28] *Irish Weekly Independent*, 4 Oct. 1941, 4.

Kettle's response was striking:

> The world will be surprised and astounded when this becomes known, but
> you know what I always thought on this subject? England could not afford
> to delegate the governing powers of England into the hands of any class
> other than that ruling England at the time. Here was I thinking that we
> would have to wait for home rule until the English radicals and the Irish
> democrats would become powerful enough to rule the Empire, and now it
> is coming from the top instead of the bottom. It is simply astounding but
> I fear it will not come to pass. You will not be able to get the Tories in a
> majority to do this. The Irish in Britain will not vote for them, and besides
> I fear that the Irish landlords, owing to their crimes in the past, are not
> destined to be placed so easily at the heads of the people's affairs in Ireland.
> But all the same, I am intensely interested, and I shall do the little I can to
> help you with the experiment. [29]

What is revealed here is that though we can defend the Conservative-
Parnellite alliance of 1885 purely in terms of calculations concerning the
balance of power at Westminster, it had a very much deeper significance
for Parnell. It was his old dream of a 'class conservative government' in
Ireland which inspired him: a government dominated by forces of respectability and an ethos of Conservatism. In the end, the Conservative rank
and file vetoed the potential Parnell alliance; had they not done so, the
Irish nationalist rank and file would have done the same.

In general terms, the Parnellites fought the election on an aggressive but
perfectly legitimate constitutionalist programme. Home Rule meant a
parliament in Dublin, though it did not mean a complete separation from
Britain or a separate army, navy, and foreign service; but that was all that
was known, except that the Irish would try to obtain for their parliament as
many powers as possible, including, as far as Parnell was concerned, trade
protection.

In Ireland the expected electoral triumph was achieved. Parnell won
every seat outside eastern Ulster and the University of Dublin. He now
had eighty-six MPs at his back 'pledged' to 'sit, act and vote' with the party
and to resign if a majority of the party felt that obligations had not been
fulfilled. In terms of actual votes cast, for Home Rule and against, the
result was perhaps less stunning. Nevertheless, the electoral map of Ireland
now seemed to show an almost complete Parnellite dominance except for
the north-east, where Unionism remained strong. For the first time the
majority of the Irish electors had clearly declared for Home Rule. Parnell

[29] Kettle, *The Material for Victory*, 63–64.

was in an exceptionally strong moral position. But what was the reaction of the leadership of the two main British parties? To put it briefly, the Conservatives turned against the Irish, while the Liberals moved towards them.

The overall result of the election could hardly have suited the Irish purpose better. Outside Ireland the Liberals won eighty-six seats more than the Conservatives, but since eighty-six was also the number of Parnellite MPs, the Nationalists now appeared to hold the balance of power. The consequences were soon apparent. The Conservatives realized that Parnell's delivery of the Irish vote in England – which Chamberlain estimated as giving them twenty-five seats – had not given them a majority. They were quick to end the flirtation with Parnell. Lord Salisbury's government announced to the new parliament in January 1886 that a return to coercion in Ireland was in prospect. Combining with the Liberals, Parnell immediately threw them out of office.

Parnell turned back to Gladstone but, even then, he did not forget the interests of the landlords. Using Mrs O'Shea as an intermediary, he passed a message to Gladstone:

> A communication, the substance of which I append, has been forwarded to me by the representatives of one of the chief landlord political associations in Ireland. It is thought that if this arrangement were carried out there would remain no large body of opinion amongst the landowning class against the concession of a large measure of autonomy for Ireland, as the Protestants, other than the owners of land, are not really opposed to such a concession.[30]

This document clearly reveals that Parnell was in contact with Irish landlord leaders. It reveals also, of course, a rather foolish reduction of the problem of the Protestant minority to that of the problem of the landlord minority. But the main thing to note is Parnell's determination to reach some workable compromise with the Irish landowners. He wanted to get them out of their difficulties on the best possible terms.

There seems to be little doubt that Gladstone shared Parnell's vision of the new Ireland. He was certainly well acquainted with Parnell's hope that landlords 'as individuals' and people in Ireland were about to enter an era of conciliation. As the premier expressed it: 'Yes, I believe it may be possible that even the Irish Nationalists may perceive that those marked out by leisure, wealth and station, for attention to public duties, and for

---

[30] Parnell to K. O'Shea, 6 Jan. 1886, Gladstone papers, B.L. Add. MS 44628.

the exercise of influence, may become, in no small degree, the natural and effective and safe leaders of the people.'[31] Gladstone even assumed that Irish public opinion more generally was conservative. 'He [Gladstone] believed it was a mistake to suppose that Irishmen were imbued with real democratic tendencies. Instead, he should not be surprised if, when they governed themselves, they would not cut a somewhat Tory figure in the Imperial Parliament.'[32]

The Gladstone/Parnell alliance to achieve Home Rule in 1886 failed because Gladstone's own party split on the issue – Parnell's belief in protection having played a not insignificant part. Having come so close to success, Parnell became the object of much political hatred and intrigue. Michael Davitt wryly commented:

> In fact had the classes of Ireland and Great Britain really known Parnell, in his inward political convictions and strong bias against the very methods of agitation he had been constrained to adopt as a means to attain his ends for the good of Ireland, they would have hailed him as absolutely safe for their interests, and as a conservative ruler of the country in 1886, instead of approving a conspiracy to destroy him in 1887.[33]

On 18 April 1887, the London *Times*, at the end of a series of articles on the theme of Parnell's links with crime, published a letter purporting to have been written by Parnell, seeking to excuse his public condemnation of the Phoenix Park murders by pleading necessity. The amazing document, dated 15 May 1882, ran as follows:

> Dear Sir: I am surprised at your friend's anger but he and you should know that to denounce the murders was the only course open to us. To do that promptly was plainly our best policy. But you can tell him and all others concerned that though I regret the accident of Lord F. Cavendish's death, I cannot refuse to admit that Burke got no more than his deserts. You are at liberty to show him this and others whom you can trust also, but let not my address be known. He can write to House of Commons.
>
> Yours very truly,
> Charles S. Parnell.

Parnell knew that he had never written such a letter. Before long, he had a pretty shrewd idea who the forger (a hapless journalist and pornographer, Richard Pigott) was. However, when a commission of three judges was set

---

[31] T. J. Dunne, 'The Political Ideology of Home Rule' (MA thesis, University College, Dublin, 1972), 209–10.

[32] D. W. R. Bahlman, ed., *The Diary of Sir Edward Walter Hamilton* (Hull, 1993), 110.

[33] Michael Davitt, *The Fall of Feudalism in Ireland* (London, 1904), 637.

up to enquire about these allegations, he had another more serious concern. The *Times* attempted to offer a cash incentive to P. J. Sheridan, now in Colorado, to return to London to testify. Had Sheridan testified, as he was privately claiming, that he had sworn Parnell into a republican oath-bound conspiracy on the eve of the Phoenix Park murders, it would have been explosive. P. J. Sheridan appears to draw up the oath for the 'Invincibles'.[34] Although Parnell no doubt wished to use him as a force against violence in the west, it was Sheridan's closest friend, P. J. Gordon, who was believed by the authorities to have murdered Col. Walter Bourke in June. It was Sheridan's wife, along with Gordon's wife, who had created the original 'Land for the People' banner at the first Irishtown meeting of the Land League; Gordon's wife was also at the heart of the miracle cures of Knock in the same period – which boosted her husband's business. Mercifully for Parnell, Sheridan rejected the *Times* approach.

With the collapse of the forger, Parnell became the golden hero of progressive politics in both Britain and Ireland. On Christmas Eve, 1889, Captain O'Shea filed a petition of divorce from his wife, citing the National leader as co-respondent. Nationalists chose to believe that this was another knavish plot which would soon evaporate. The party gave Parnell a forty-fourth birthday party at the dismal Westminster Palace Hotel – where many Irish members normally stayed. Parnell spoke optimistically: 'We all of us must see that the time can not be long distant when the sands of the present government are nearly run out ... I do not see the slightest hope for them.'[35]

But it was Parnell himself who was soon to run out of time. It did not help that he had not visited Ireland between 1886 and 1890, and despite the fame of his name could walk around Dublin unrecognized as he returned to defend his position. The party split as the allegations in the O'Shea divorce case became known. Parnell was seen as a destroyer of a Catholic marriage. He fought to retain his influence at first in good heart. But now, in his last struggle, he created the Parnell legend. Michael MacDonagh left us with the following picture of Parnell, as the last struggle began. It is a rare moment of relaxation at Avondale.

> As it was a sunny day, and rather warm, we sat on our rugs in the Vale of Avoca for the lunch of sandwiches, hard-boiled eggs and a bottle of sherry which Ker produced from the well of his side-car.
> During the meal Parnell gave us an odd glimpse of his superstitious nature. As he was breaking the shell of an egg, Kerr held towards him a

[34] Kenna, *War in the Shadows*, 60.   [35] *Spectator*, 5 July 1890.

twisted slip of paper containing salt. 'No, no,' he cried. 'Don't you know it is very unlucky to serve anyone with salt?'

I was disposed to smile, but when I saw Parnell's face I realised that he was not joking. His look seemed to express what a narrow escape we had or that he alone had, of arousing the enmity of unseen agencies of evil by – and this is my comment, of course the friendly and innocent act of passing the salt at meals. None of us made any remark. He had also – as we are soon to see – a sense of awe in Nature and showed that he was not so devoid of poetic feeling as was often assumed.

Where we lunched is celebrated by Moore, in one of the most endearing of his Irish melodies, 'The Meeting of the Waters' – the junction of two streams, the Avonmore and the Avonbeg as they meet on the Avondale estate.

An enchanted spot! On our left, the Avonmore flowed from Glendalough between wooded heights, behind us the Avonbeg came down the hill from Glenmalure. The Avonmore, as it approached us, was at first extraordinarily placid. Not an undulation wrinkled the mirror-like smoothness or disturbed the deep silence of its flow, as if it were wrapped in day dreams. But reaching where we sat, a rough bottom broke it into a lulling ripple and this the Avonbeg, encountering rocks up stream a short distance from us, appeared to answer. To my fancy the meeting of the waters was like the meeting of two lovers. The Avonmore (meeting the big Avon) suddenly bursts into a love call on catching sight of the Avonbeg (meaning the little Avon) and she, joyously answering to his hail, rushes down, bubbling and sparkling, to his embrace. Thus mingled the streams relapse into tranquillity and smoothness and dropping their original names flow on at the Avoca river.

It was, indeed, a place for sweet thoughts and quiet breathings. Parnell was visibly affected. As we were sitting close to 'Tom Moore's Tree' where, according to tradition, the poet composed the song in the summer of 1807, Parnell asked whether its words were known to any of us. I said I knew them, and began to recite the opening lines:

> *There is not in this wide world a valley so sweet,*
> *As the vale in whose bosom the bright waters meet.*

Parnell interrupted me, calling out 'Ah, sing it man; sing it' in a tone that made us laugh – as if he did not think much of my reciting and expected less from my singing. However, as I sang for him he listened attentively. In the third verse the poet declares it was not the soft magic of streamlet or rill that he'd remember for ever –

> *'t Was that friends, the belov'd of my bosom were near.*
> *Who made every dear scene of enchantment more dear,*
> *And who felt how the best charms of Nature improve.*
> *When we see them reflected from looks that we love.*

As I repeated the two last lines on a higher note Parnell said in a dreamy voice, 'True, true.' Then I gave out the last verse where the poet speaks of how calmly he could rest in that 'bosom of shade' with the friends he loved best:

Where the storms that we feel in this cold world should cease,
And our hearts like thy waters be mingled in peace.

'No, no,' said Parnell decisively, in a swift change of mood. Death even in the tender and sentimental associations of the song, appeared at the moment to be repellent to him. Rather than lie at rest in that 'bosom of shade' he preferred to live to retrieve the disaster which had come to his cause. The poet might think all was vanity, but not he. The recovery of his position was but a matter of time, and he was determined to live long enough to achieve it.[36]

The passage gives some indication of Parnell's ability to entrance and become a force in the imagination. There are other elements of interest in the last year. F. S. L. Lyons. Parnell's greatest biographer, declared in an interview with Terence de Vere White that 'the north' was Parnell's blind spot.[37] But he did in this last crisis, as the majority of his colleagues turned on him, try to make amends: in Belfast in May 1891, a sickly[38] Parnell told a decidedly uneasy audience of Belfast Nationalists, 'It is undoubtedly true that until the prejudices of the [Protestant and unionist] minority are conciliated ... Ireland can never enjoy perfect freedom, Ireland can never be united.'[39] Also, as Frank Callanan noted, he maintained a different tone on the land issues as against his more radical colleagues.[40]

Parnell combined this increased moderation with a last parliamentary appeal on behalf of Irishmen convicted of terrorism. In his last words in parliament, he declared: 'Those conspiracies in America have been abandoned for many years, and nobody now wants to blow up the British Empire with dynamite.... These events terrible as no doubt they were have passed away, and could not a powerful Government of a powerful nation consider the case for clemency and mercy?'[41] His successor John Redmond was to reproduce these tropes, insisting on the need for class and

---

[36] *Irish Weekly Independent*, 4 Oct. 1941.   [37] *Irish Times*, May 1977.
[38] *Northern Whig*, 23 May 1891.
[39] See 'Old Fogey' E. G. Robinson's later account. Belfast Newspaper Library, Cutting collection 17:8.
[40] Frank Callanan, 'Charles Stewart Parnell', in *Dictionary of Irish Biography* (Cambridge, 2009).
[41] Michael MacDonagh, *Parliament: Its Romance, Its Comedy, Its Pathos* (London, 1902), 388.

sectarian unity amongst the Irish while displaying sympathy for the dynamitards.[42] This was Parnellism without Parnell.

> What has been the real stumbling block on the way of the English people granting us home rule? It has been the fact that Ireland herself has been divided upon the question of home rule in two camps, and that many thousands and tens of thousands of Irish people have held aloof from the national movement or a movement in favour of an Irish nation, which, I desire to see, and when if it once came into existence, would mean the obtaining of home rule within six months – in a movement in which all creeds and classes could unite.[43]

Was Parnell at heart an Irish rebel? He certainly walked on 'the verge of treason/felony' in the years from 1876 to 1882 – he gave good reasons for the fears of moderate home rulers, let alone unionists. But even in these years of political enthusiasm Parnell's differences with the revolutionary agenda are clear enough. As the Irish American extremist 'Transatlantic' of the *Irish World* (1 June 1881) commented on Parnell's view that the younger landlords would throw their lot in with the home rule cause if the land question was settled by purchase: 'Individual landlords are well fitted to take their place as leaders of the Irish nation. Who are these landlords, Mr Parnell? Except yourself, I see not one in the crowd.' In later years the double effect of the Phoenix Park trauma and the O'Shea relationship undoubtedly reinforced the conservative side of his nature.

Unionists complained about Parnell's betrayal of his own class. 'Mr Parnell', wrote W. Hart Westcombe in 1886 in his *The Irish Question: A Monograph in the Form of a Letter to the Prime Minister*, was 'compelled to join the Crusade against the class to which he himself belonged. I don't know and I don't care whether Mr Parnell was sincere in his landlord *hetze.*' In 1895, W. O'Connor Morris discussed Parnell's conciliatory course in the later 1880s towards Irish unionist opinion as merely a trick to lure Gladstone deeper into the home rule trap: 'His success in Ireland with the classes he sought to conciliate was hopeless because they knew him well; but Mr Gladstone and those who acted with him were deceived.' Three years later he revised the judgement – acknowledging that he never knew Parnell and may have done 'less justice' to his 'motives' than he deserved.[44] But

---

[42] Dermot Meleady, ed., *John Redmond: Selected Letters and Memoranda 1880–1918* (Dublin, 2018), 49 (Memorandum of meeting with John Morley MP, 17 Oct. 1892). Redmond liked to say that nationalists should behave with 'moderation' and 'sobriety'. 'Morley: Have you any suggestion as to securing a peaceful winter? Redmond: Amnesty – Amnesty – Amnesty!'

[43] *Spectator*, 18 June 1897; *Freeman's Journal*, 11 Nov. 1898.

[44] W. O'Connor Morris, *Ireland, 1798–1898* (London, 1898), vii.

nationalist opinion increasingly portrayed Parnell as a patriot but also a Tory and a landlord.

With even greater insight, Francis Hackett wrote that Parnell was 'amenable to liberal considerations but utterly immune from liberal sympathies'. This catches the political temper of 'The Chief' exactly: the Irish *ancien regime*, he felt, could not survive the combination of the economic crisis of the late 1870s plus the democratization of the mid-1880s without drastic change. He saw it as his role to bring about that change on the most conservative basis which was available. As his radical friend Henry Labouchere put it, 'home rule apart, he was himself a Tory'.

Parnell is a particular hero of John Hume. There is a notable similarity between the two careers. Parnell was the dominating politician of the home rule crisis. Hume has been the dominating politician of the 'troubles'. It is no surprise that Hume was a key figure in the successful 1980s campaign to place the Parnell bust – by the Breton fascist sculptor Yann Goulet – in the House of Commons.[45] Hume has identified himself with the Parnellite theme of the need to lower the barrier between different sections of the Irish people. In 1988, in the course of the published public debate with Sinn Fein, the Social Democratic and Labour Party (SDLP) made much use of Parnell's Belfast speech of May 1891. But it is perhaps worth noting one of the lessons of Parnell's political life: entanglements with the physical force tradition are a risky business, and if the constitutional politicians' luck does not hold, they can be career threatening.

---

[45] Patrick Maume, 'Goulet, Yann', in *Dictionary of Irish Biography* (Cambridge, 2009). Goulet was one of an interesting group of wartime Nazi collaborators who reconstructed their careers in Ireland.

CHAPTER 3

Parnell to Pearse

R. F. Foster

When considering the shattering effect of Parnell's fall from the vantage of the revolution that eventually followed, the old Home Ruler (and Governor-General of the newly-minted Irish Free State) Tim Healy remarked: 'If we [the anti-Parnellites] had the voters, Parnell had their sons.'[1] One implication of Healy's remark is that the more extreme and uncompromising nationalist politics that characterized the pre-revolutionary period was an inheritance from Parnell; another implication is that there was a generational shift in politics in this era, bringing about a repudiation of accepted values.[2] These are the themes of this essay. But the title 'Parnell to Pearse' also suggests another, more famous quotation: W. B. Yeats's assertion that the fall of Parnell heralded the inception – even the conception – of the Irish revolution, mediated through cultural transformation rather than politics (as suggested by Joep Leerssen in the Introduction to this volume). 'The modern literature of Ireland, and indeed all that stir of thought which prepared for the Anglo-Irish War, began when Parnell fell from power in 1891. A disillusioned and embittered Ireland turned from parliamentary politics; an event was conceived; and the race began, as I think, to be troubled by that event's long gestation.'[3] Subsequent historians have tried to complicate this picture, but it still has resonance.[4] This reading of a quarter-century of Irish history raises questions that recur in any consideration of that 'long gestation' – the title chosen by Patrick Maume for his ground-breaking study of the

---

[1] T. M. Healy, *Letters and Leaders of My Day* (London, 1929), 1:355.
[2] See my *Vivid Faces: The Revolutionary Generation in Ireland, 1890–1923* (London, 2014), chapter 1.
[3] 'The Irish Dramatic Movement', reprinted in W. B. Yeats, *Autobiographies* (London, 1955), 559.
[4] See my essay 'Thinking from Hand to Mouth: Anglo-Irish Literature, Gaelic Nationalism and Irish Politics in the 1890s', in *Paddy and Mr Punch: Connections in Irish and English History* (London, 1993), 262–80.

period between Parnell's fall and the revolution symbolized by Pearse, which subtly queries the determinist version suggested by Yeats.[5]

This raises the question of whether Parnell, and the phenomenon of Parnell-lism, represents the end of something or the beginning. The cult of the leader, in a Parnellite sense, would later be invoked by both Eamon de Valera and Charles James Haughey, but the line back to Parnell might seem somewhat tendentious, as Paul Bew suggests. (Nonetheless, it might be pointed out that Parnell, like Haughey, may not have been a stranger to the old Irish tradition of the brown envelope.) More nobly, we might invoke Yeats, this time referring to his key political poem of 1934, 'Parnell's Funeral'. Here Parnell is seen in a tradition of nationalist martyrs (all Protestant) – but differing from his predecessors in being dispatched by the Irish themselves, not by the Saxon oppressor.

> An age is the reversal of an age:
> When strangers murdered Emmet, Fitzgerald, Tone,
> We lived like men that watch a painted stage.
> What matter for the scene, the scene once gone:
> It had not touched our lives. But popular rage,
> *Hysterica passio* dragged this quarry down.
> None shared our guilt; nor did we play a part
> Upon a painted stage when we devoured his heart.
>
> Come, fix upon me that accusing eye.
> I thirst for accusation. All that was sung,
> All that was said in Ireland is a lie
> Bred out of the contagion of the throng,
> Saving the rhyme rats hear before they die.
> Leave nothing but the nothings that belong
> To this bare soul, let all men judge that can
> Whether it be an animal or a man.

At the end of the poem, Parnell is decisively relegated to an Anglo-Irish tradition now part of the past:

> The rest I pass, one sentence I unsay.
> Had de Valera eaten Parnell's heart
> No loose-lipped demagogue had won the day,
> No civil rancour torn the land apart.
>
> Had Cosgrave eaten Parnell's heart, the land's
> Imagination had been satisfied,
> Or lacking that, government in such hands,
> O'Higgins its sole statesman had not died.

[5] Patrick Maume, *The Long Gestation: Irish Nationalist Life, 1891–1918* (Dublin, 1999).

Had even O'Duffy – but I name no more –
Their school a crowd, his master solitude;
Through Jonathan Swift's dark grove he passed, and there
Plucked bitter wisdom that enriched his blood.

As Conor Cruise O'Brien put it, Parnell had 'deviated into literature' from politics; and, in O'Brien's view, the 'collective emotional explosion of 1890 helped to set free the imaginative forces which for a time in the early 1900s made Dublin – the Parnellite city – an important centre of world literature. One cannot prove it to be so, but one does feel in that literature the Parnellite shock.'[6]

This essay tries to counter this by considering how Parnell and Parnellism *stayed* political, the ways in which historians have dealt with him, and some of the shifts and processes that characterized the period between Parnell and Pearse. We might, for one thing, go back to that Healy quote and ask: If Parnell had the voters' sons, how about their daughters? The revolutionary generation that some of us discern in that period was remarkable not least for the leading part played by radical women, as historians have come belatedly to realize. Reasserting their importance, in the commemorations of the revolution, has been an important part of complicating the narrative. This was the clarion call issued by the research director of the National Archives, Dr Catriona Crowe, a long-standing advocate of the new emphasis on the history of Irish women, particularly in the revolutionary era. Following the pioneering work of Margaret Ward, Maria Luddy, and others from the 1970s on, there has been a plethora of studies of the lives of Irish women in the late nineteenth and early twentieth century – magisterially surveyed in Senia Pašeta's path-breaking *Irish Nationalist Women 1900–1918*.[7] Significantly, Pašeta's book is part of a larger enterprise and will shortly be followed by her volume on Irishwomen and politics in the same period. And 'politics' here does not necessarily mean 'nationalism'. As the work of Diane Urquhart has shown, Irishwomen in the early twentieth century were politically active in the cause of unionism too; and the suffrage issue mobilized and galvanized women from various political backgrounds in Ireland (though the Catholic Church's attitude towards the issue meant that Protestant Irishwomen played a disproportionate part in the leadership). [8]

---

[6] Conor Cruise O'Brien, *Parnell and His Party 1880–90* (Oxford, 1964), 356.
[7] Senia Pašeta, *Irish Nationalist Women 1900–1918* (Cambridge, 2013).
[8] Diane Urquhart, *Women in Ulster Politics 1890–1940* (Dublin, 2000).

Moreover, during the revolutionary period 1890–1923, from the Parnell Split to the end of the Civil War, women's lives and opinions were radicalized in various directions; and this was more evident in Ireland than has sometimes been realized. But the important precedent is a movement that was central to Parnell's career, though he broke it in the end. If we project the beginning of the revolutionary period a decade back to 1880, with the potentially revolutionary Land War, we find the Ladies' Land League mobilizing Irishwomen, keeping the agitation going when the male leaders were imprisoned – and taking a much more radical stance on the question of landlordism, rent strikes, and the politics of social protest than their male colleagues (who did not thank them for it). It was the leader of the Ladies' Land League, Parnell's sister Anna Parnell, who – after she left the front line of political agitation, in disillusionment – in fact forecast that change would come in Ireland through the activity of a dedicated revolutionary minority. In a memoir (written about 1907 but unpublished in its entirety till long after her death) she remarked that under the Irish Parliamentary Party (IPP) the hypocritical, collaborationist, and imperial tendency of the Home Rule movement had now become absolutely clear. All that could be hoped for was 'the infinitesimally small chance . . . of a minority being able to seize some exceptionally magnificent opportunity and by its aid turn the national rudder against the dead weight of the majority'; 'armed rebellion', she added, would 'be the next thing either tried or played at here'.[9] This was in 1907. Anna died in 1911, but the uncompromisingly revolutionary scenario which she forecast would be played out almost exactly five years later. It seems apposite that Parnell's feminist and socialist sister should have anticipated the handover – so to speak – to Patrick Pearse.

Other kinds of revolutionary thought were in the air too. It should not surprise us that in the age of Rosa Luxemburg in Germany, Virginia Woolf in England, Katharine Mansfield in New Zealand, and Margaret Sanger in the United States, there were many women in Ireland who wanted to break the accepted mould of female existence and embark on various kinds of liberation – which could be social and sexual as well as political. The reason why this has not been widely recognized, perhaps, is because women's existences were so rapidly reassigned to the hearth and home in

---

[9] Quoted in my *Charles Stewart Parnell: The Man and His Family* (Hassocks, 1976), 282. The reflection is from Anna's then-unpublished account of the Ladies' Land League and the Land War, *The Tale of a Great Sham*, later edited and published by Dana Hearne for Arlen House (1986).

the post-revolutionary dispensation, as was bitterly noted by the revolutionary generation of women activists who lived to see this retrograde development.[10] When Parnell's widow Katharine published her extraordinary and unabashed account of their life together, in 1914, one of the most insightful and distinctly modern-sounding reviews was published in the suffragist journal the *Irish Citizen,* most probably by Hanna Sheehy-Skeffington. This concluded that Parnell's fate was 'the Nemesis of the antifeminist ... to fall victim to a woman of the highly sexed unintellectual type, developed by the restriction of women's activities to the sphere euphemistically styled "the Home"'.[11]

Hanna Sheehy-Skeffington, though from an old Home Rule dynasty, reflected and expressed the changes coming in Irish life from the 1890s. The desire to break out of accepted modes of life, and to challenge conventional expectations, was closely linked to the advances in Irish women's education in Ireland in the late nineteenth and early twentieth century – especially at the third level. In the late nineteenth century, the old Royal University, essentially an examining body linked to third-level institutions, was a route to higher education for many women. And in terms of ancient teaching universities, Trinity had a better record than Oxford or Cambridge in admitting women on more equal terms, in 1903. A few years later the foundation of the new National University created a vital forum where women of the revolutionary generation could meet, interact, and hear new ideas. Geraldine Plunkett, sister of the 1916 signatory Joseph Mary Plunkett, and like all her siblings a radical Republican, came from a rich and privileged background, her wealthy parents living off a large rent-roll from Dublin property and moving between large houses in and around the city. She went to the elite convent school Mount Annville, which she despised for its conventional and snobbish values, and subsequently found her métier as a medical student; joining student societies, she realized that they often had an agenda 'to nationalize the students and subsequently the professions ... It was only in the students' hour late at night, walking home through the deserted streets, that we learned what was happening and the correct revolutionary point of view.'[12] This suggests a different political culture from that of Parnell's ascendancy. Though he had been seen as a revolutionary in his day too, and was surrounded by strong-minded and politically active women in his family, his ideas about

[10] See my *Vivid Faces,* 313–19.   [11] *Irish Citizen,* 6 June 1914.
[12] Typescript autobiographical draft, 'The Battle Is Over', in Military Archives of Ireland, Bureau of Military History Contemporary Documents, 5-6/1, pp. 69, 71.

social and gender issues stayed resolutely conventional. Irish historians of
the period have been more interested in the fault lines of conflict that run
through Irish rural society and erupt at critical moments such as the Land
War of 1879–82; these have been suggestively connected to later outbreaks
of violence. But in terms of the change in Irish political culture between
Parnell and Pearse we might also take note of less spectacular events, such
as the 1898 reforms in Irish local government, which not only democra-
tized (and nationalized) local government but enfranchised about 100,000
women and made them eligible to stand in elections. (It is one of the
issues, as with gay rights in our own day, where Irish legislation, after
lagging behind British advances, suddenly leap-frogs them.) In the Introduction to this volume, Joep Leerssen draws attention to Miroslav Hroch's
concept of 'protagonists', and it is helpful to see the Irish nationalist
revolution in terms of the radical mindset and input of students, women,
intellectuals, journalists, and émigrés – who succeeded the Parnellite
dispensation. And the pre-revolutionary generation might be reconsidered
in terms of secondary and university education, the absorption of
new ideas about society in general, and the expectation of a future that
never happened.

The Ladies' Land League supplies one of the moments when the later
shift to radicalism is anticipated; as a movement run by women, they saw
themselves as trying to counter what they saw as the conservative and even
hypocritical stance taken by the Land League leaders, in terms of stabiliz-
ing the land agitation in the interests of the 'strong farmers' (and the IPP),
while the cottier classes were left to the tender mercies of poverty and
emigration.[13] The women of the Ladies' Land League wanted to push
things to the logical extremes of rent strikes, rather than paying rent 'at the
point of a bayonet'; this was in marked contrast to Parnell's belief that, as
the effects and implications of Gladstone's 1881 Act worked through, the
movement was 'breaking fast' and could now be wound down. His belief
that the desirable future was a land of peasant proprietors (and perhaps a
reformed landlord class, as suggested long ago by Paul Bew[14]) was
very far from the radical vision of his sister – or his colleague Michael
Davitt's belief in land nationalization, dismissed by Parnell as 'a chaotic
socialist experiment'.

---

[13] As reflected in Angela Bourke's contribution, Chapter 6 in this book.
[14] See his short but suggestive biography *Charles Stewart Parnell* (Dublin, 1980), later extended and
republished as *Enigma: A New Life of Charles Stewart Parnell* (Dublin, 2011).

It is significant that recent historiography of the period has turned to these countering themes, rather than the mainstream or high-political aspects of Parnellism (as Bew himself points out in Chapter 2 in this book). The themes which seem of most interest currently are the more challenging and radical aspects of the Parnellite era, such as the Ladies' Land League, the violent or conflictual aspects of land agitation, and the persistence and influence of Fenian and neo-Fenian activity. The latter theme has been explored by Matthew Kelly and Owen Magee, while Patrick Maume has unearthed the possibility (indeed, probability) that Parnell himself took the Fenian oath (in Trinity College Library of all places).[15] Eugenio Biagini has explored the effects of the Home Rule movement on larger questions of British radical culture.[16] Carla King has produced a large-scale study of Davitt's life after the Land War, which brings to the fore his profile as a labour politician and internationalist, and his consistent advocacy of land nationalization, right up to his death in 1906.[17] Ged Martin has recently explored further the question of Parnell's finances, showing them to be even more straitened than I found them to be forty years ago.[18]

By contrast, the classic historiography of the Home Rule era which Paul Bew and I grew up with – so to speak – was dominated by high politics, with classic studies by David Thornley, Conor Cruise O'Brien, and Leland Lyons.[19] Professor Bew's first book, *Land and the National Question in Ireland*, helped break the mould, as did work on the Land War by Samuel Clark, James Donnelly, William Vaughan, Donald Jordan, Philip Bull, and Laurence Geary; while in retirement Theo Moody, who had taught and influenced so many of us, finally produced his great book *Davitt and*

---

[15] Matthew Kelly, *The Fenian Ideal and Irish Nationalism 1882–1916* (Woodbridge, 2006); Owen McGee, *The IRB: The Irish Republican Brotherhood from the Land War to Sinn Féin* (Dublin, 2007); Patrick Maume, 'Parnell and the I.R.B. Oath', *Irish Historical Studies* 29.115 (May 1995): 363–370.

[16] *British Democracy and Irish Nationalism 1876–1906* (Cambridge, 2007).

[17] Carla King, *Michael Davitt: After the Land League 1881–1906* (Dublin, 2016).

[18] See 'Charles Stewart Parnell: Economics and Politics of a Building Trade Entrepreneur', online at www.gedmartin.net/martinalia-mainmenu-3/263-charles-stewart-parnell-economics-and-politics-of-a-building-trade-entrepreneur. A fragmentary 1891 diary kept by Parnell's mother shows a deep preoccupation with the prospect of her son's estate making a claim on the £190,000 left by Katharine [O'Shea] Parnell's aunt, and disputed by her relatives. (It also shows an implacable belief that the Pope was behind her son's fall, reminding us of the fundamentalist Protestantism shared by several members of his family.)

[19] David Thornley, *Isaac Butt and Home Rule* (London, 1964); O'Brien, *Parnell and His Party*; F. S. L. Lyons, *The Irish Parliamentary Party 1890–1910* (London, 1951), *The Fall of Parnell 1890–1891* (London, 1960), *John Dillon: A Biography* (London, 1968), *Charles Stewart Parnell* (London, 1977).

Irish Revolution.[20] It is significant that the 'revolution' in Moody's title was the revolution in landownership, initiated by the Land War and then implemented by the British government's policy of underwriting land purchase by the occupying tenantry, and compensating the landlords.

There was another kind of revolution – an armed rising against British rule – which Davitt had devoutly supported in his youth but repudiated later on, though Matthew Kelly has drawn attention to his continued readiness to play to a hillsider audience and the continued interest that police observers took in him. But this was of less interest to Parnellite historians, at least back then. The glamour and enigma of 'The Chief' tended to monopolize attention, rather than the contrasting figure of Davitt – different in so many ways. A fascinating 1919 study by a journalist, Michael O'Hara, referred to them as 'Chief and Tribune', which is a good distinction.[21] Their backgrounds could not have been more different: Davitt's youth of poverty, eviction, disablement through a factory accident; Parnell's of landowning privilege and aristocratic connections. (When the realities of Davitt's early life were recounted during the Special Commission hearings, Parnell was visibly moved – a rare sight.) These contrasting backgrounds may also explain a different kind of contrast: Davitt's hunger for education, his intellectual sophistication, his wide reading, compared with Parnell's philistinism, lack of interest in intellectual culture, and limited acquaintance with books. (Apart from a taste for *Alice in Wonderland*, Parnell's reading was apparently restricted to journals about mining and Youatt's compendium *The Horse*). It was Davitt, after all, who defined the phenomenon of Parnellism, when the National League emerged out of the ashes of the Land League in October 1882. 'The outcome', Davitt wrote, was

> the complete eclipse, by a purely parliamentary substitute, of what had been a semi-revolutionary organization. It was in a sense the overthrow of a movement and the enthronement of a man: the replacement of nationalism by Parnellism; the investment of the fortune and guidance of the agitation, both for national self-government and land reform, in a leader's nominal dictatorship.[22]

[20] Paul Bew, *Land and the National Question in Ireland 1858–1882* (Dublin, 1979); Samuel Clark, *Social Origins of the Irish Land War* (Princeton, 1979); James S. Donnelly Jr, *The Land and the People of Nineteenth-Century Cork: The Rural Economy and the Land Question* (London, 1975); W. E. Vaughan, *Landlords and Tenants in Mid-Victorian Ireland* (Oxford, 1994); Donald Jordan, *Land and Popular Politics in Ireland: County Mayo from the Plantation to the Land War* (Cambridge, 1994); Philip Bull, *Land, Politics and Nationalism: A Study of the Irish Land Question* (Dublin, 1996); Laurence Geary, *The Plan of Campaign 1886–1891* (Cork, 1996); T. W. Moody, *Davitt and Irish Revolution 1846–1882* (Oxford, 1982).

[21] M. M. O'Hara, *Chief and Tribune: Parnell and Davitt* (Dublin, 1919).

[22] Quoted in King, *Michael Davitt*, 52–53.

But if Davitt and what he represented used to be of less interest to historians than Parnell and Parnellism, that is no longer the case. We might note that one trait which they seem to have shared was an antipathy to British imperial claims – in marked contrast to Parnell's predecessor Isaac Butt, and his successor John Redmond, both of whom endorsed the Empire and wanted Ireland to have a share in it. Here, perhaps, the fact that Parnell was half-American should be taken into account – as it too rarely is. And the question of Ireland's complex relation to the British Empire in this period is another area of historiography where the narrative has been creatively complicated in recent work. The imperial strain in Home Rule has been brilliantly explored by Alvin Jackson, Colin Reid, and others, while anti-imperial themes in other varieties of Irish nationalism have been explored by Matthew Kelly and Niall Whelehan.[23] The decade of centenary commemorations which began around 2012 has seen the publication of many works relating to the revolutionary generation (from Parnell to Pearse), but we still await a substantial analysis of the ideas and ideology of early Sinn Féin, on the lines of Michael Laffan's exemplary and still unrivalled study of the movement from 1917.[24] One of the important aspects of such a subject must concern a new, or at least remastered, analysis of imperialism – as was happening contemporaneously in other parts of the Western world (see Hobson, see Lenin). This was a distinctive part of Sinn Féin's contribution, forged initially in Griffith's opposition to the Boer War. The complex and sometimes contradictory approach of the Home Rulers to imperial questions has received more attention but still needs explication; this is an area where the shift in political culture between Parnell and Pearse might appear most marked.

And if there is such a shift, where do we place Parnell's legacy to the political world that came after him? Paul Bew has bracingly explored the essentially conservative strains in Parnell's thought and policies. But as always with a political cult, people took what they wanted from it.[25] Given

---

[23] Alvin Jackson, 'Ireland, the Union, and the British Empire, 1800–1960', in Kevin Kenny, ed., *Ireland and the British Empire* (Oxford, 2004), 123–53, and 'Irish Unionists and Empire', in *An Irish Empire?*, ed. K. Jeffery (Manchester, 1996), 123–49; Colin Reid, 'An Experiment in Constructive Unionism: Isaac Butt, Home Rule and Federalist Political Thought during the 1870s', *English Historical Review* 129.537 (2014): 332–61; Matthew Kelly, 'Irish Nationalist Opinion and the British Empire in the 1850s and 1860s', *Past and Present*, 204.1 (2009), 127–54; Niall Whelehan, *The Dynamiters: Irish Nationalism and Political Violence in the Wider World 1867–1900* (Cambridge, 2012).

[24] Michael Laffan, *The Resurrection of Ireland: The Sinn Fein Party 1916–1923* (Cambridge, 1999).

[25] See Roy Foster and Alvin Jackson, 'Men for All Seasons? Carson, Parnell and the Limits of Heroism in Modern Ireland', *European History Quarterly* 39.3 (July 2009): 414–38.

that radicalization of political culture, what the revolutionary generation took from Parnell was the profile he presented in his last campaign, where – despite his subtle understanding of party politics, highlighted by Paul Bew – he repudiated the very idea of doing business with the Liberal Party to deliver Home Rule, or indeed any question of ever trusting the British. (Here at least the resolutely Anglophobic C. J. Haughey walked in his footsteps.) The revolutionary generation projected this aspect of Parnell's legacy further, to the point of never trusting or doing business with the IPP. Even though that party had been reunited under a Parnellite leader, John Redmond, it was the values of the anti-Parnellites that seemed to be dominating, at least in the eyes of young radicals. The party, they felt, was subservient to the hierarchy; it was too closely linked to the Ancient Order of Hibernians (sworn enemies of Sinn Féin); it was far too favourable towards the British Empire and far too antagonistic to female suffrage. But the image of Parnell himself could be worshipped, as different from this: a kind of anti-self to Redmond. For the cultural revolutionary James Joyce, Parnell had been betrayed by Irish political venality and sexual puritanism; for him as for several members of the revolutionary generation, Parnell's sexual transgression added to his lustre.

For Patrick Pearse the political revolutionary, Parnell represented (if only symbolically) the necessity of violent resistance to British rule. Pearse grew up in a Home Rule household and remained an adherent of that cause till surprisingly late. After 1912 he remained preoccupied with Parnell but now had to recruit him for Fenianism, in line with the Fenianization of his own politics. In *Ghosts*, written in 1915, Pearse postulated that

> the conception of an Irish nation has been developed in modern times chiefly by four great minds ... Theobald Wolfe Tone, Thomas Davis, James Fintan Lalor, and John Mitchel. It is a question here of political teachers, not of mere political leaders. O'Connell was a more effective political leader than either Lalor or Mitchel, but no one gives O'Connell a place in the history of political thought. He did not propound, he did not even attempt to propound, any body of political truths. He was a political strategist of extraordinary ability, a rhetorician of almost superhuman power. But we owe no political doctrine to O'Connell except the obviously untrue doctrine that liberty is too dearly purchased at the price of a single drop of blood.

Parnell, however, was in Pearse's view different:

> If one had to add a fifth to the four I have named, the fifth would inevitably be Parnell. Now Parnell was less a political thinker than an embodied

conviction; a flame that seared, a sword that stabbed. He deliberately disclaimed political theories, deliberately confined himself to political action. He did the thing that lay nearest to his hand, struck at the English with such weapons as were available. His instinct was a Separatist instinct; and, far from being prepared to accept Home Rule as a 'final settlement between the two nations', he was always careful to make it clear that, whether Home Rule came or did not come, the way must be left open for the achievement of the greater thing.

Pearse inevitably buttressed this by Parnell's 1885 speech where 'The Chief' had said:

> It is given to none of us to forecast the future, and just as it is impossible for us to say in what way or by what means the national question may be settled – in what way full justice may be done to Ireland – so it is impossible for us to say to what extent that justice should be done. We cannot ask for less than the restitution of Grattan's Parliament, with its important privileges and wide and far-reaching constitution. We cannot, under the British constitution, ask for more than the restitution of Grattan's Parliament, but no man has a right to fix the boundary of the march of a nation. No man has a right to say 'Thus far shalt thou go, and no further'; and we have never attempted to fix the ne plus ultra to the progress of Ireland's nationhood, and we never shall. But, gentlemen, while we leave these things to time, circumstances, and the future, we must each one of us resolve in our own hearts that we shall at all times do everything that within us lies to obtain for Ireland the fullest measure of her rights. In this way we shall avoid difficulties and contentions amongst each other. In this way we shall not give up anything which the future may put in favour of our country; and while we struggle to-day for that which may seem possible for us without combination, we must struggle for it with the proud consciousness that we shall not do anything to hinder or prevent better men who may come after us from gaining better things than those for which we now contend.

And again, in the same year:

> Ireland a nation! Ireland has been a nation: she is a nation; and she shall be a nation.... England will respect you in proportion as you and we respect ourselves. They will not give anything to Ireland out of justice or righteousness. They will concede you your liberties and your rights when they must and no sooner.... We can none of us do more than strive for that which may seem attainable to-day; but we ought at the same time to recollect that we should not impede or hamper the march of our nation; and although our programme may be limited and small, it should be such a one as shall not prevent hereafter the fullest realisation of the hopes of Ireland; and we shall, at least if we keep this principle in mind, have this consolation that, while we may have done something to enable Ireland in

some measure to retain her position as a nation, to strengthen her position as a nation, we shall have done nothing to hinder others who may come after us from taking up the work with perhaps greater strength, ability, power, and advantages than we possess, and from pushing to that glorious and happy conclusion which is embodied in the words of the toast which I now ask you to drink – 'Ireland a nation!'

According to Pearse's selective reading,

If words mean anything, these mean that to Parnell the final and inevitable and infinitely desirable goal of Ireland was Separation; and that those who thought it prudent and feasible, as he did, to proceed to Separation by Home Rule must above all things do nothing that might impair the Separatist position or render the future task of the Separatists more difficult. Of Parnell it may be said with absolute truth that he never surrendered the national position. His successors have surrendered it. They have written on his monument in Dublin those noble words of his, that no man has a right to fix the boundary of the march of a nation; and then they have accepted the Home Rule Act as a 'final settlement' between Ireland and England. It is as if a man were to write on a monument 'I believe in God and in Life Everlasting' and then to sell his chance of Heaven to the Evil One for a purse, not of gold, but of I.O.U.'s.[26]

For IRB hardliners, this compromise approach was part and parcel of the radical-nationalist repudiation, not only of the IPP but also of Arthur Griffith, seen from about 1910 as falling back on an unacceptable dual-monarchy tradition, and therefore nearly as bad as Redmond.[27] But principally *Ghosts* was written and published as part of the drama of the Easter Rising, and it is notable that one of its chief choreographers should have summoned up Parnell as an apostle of separatism by violence. Parnellism features less in the agendas of Tom Clarke and Sean MacDiarmada, and not much in Connolly's – unsurprisingly, given Par-nell's views on socialism, trade unions, and his chilly jest to Davitt that in a Home Rule Ireland, his first action would be to lock his troublesome colleague up. Connolly did instance Parnell's late and rather desperate call to the Irish working classes, but only as a stick with which to beat his successors in the IPP.[28]

---

[26] All the above quotations come from 'Ghosts' as printed in *Collected Works of Padraic H. Pearse: Political Writings and Speeches* (Dublin, 1922), 219–50.

[27] For this dip in Griffith's reputation, see my *Vivid Faces*, 212–13, 261.

[28] A point made by F. S. L. Lyons in 'The Parnell Theme in Literature', in *Place, Personality and the Irish Writer*, ed. A. Carpenter (Gerrard's Cross, 1977), 83.

Paul Bew has, in Chapter 2 of this book, instanced Henri Le Caron's private report about Parnell's knowledge of the extremist side of Irish nationalism, and the Special Commission certainly managed to assert a certain amount of guilt by association – though this was obscured by the drama of Pigott's unmasking and suicide. Nonetheless it should be pointed out that in collating Parnell's political pronouncements, you could find far more instances of accepting a continued connection with Britain than endorsements of what Pearse called the 'separatist idea'. His own campaigns, victories, and achievements were principally fought in Westminster – an arena dismissed by the revolutionary generation as 'John Bull's Circus' but the forum where Parnell was at home, and which he manipulated with genius. After 1883, indeed, he spent extraordinarily little time in Ireland; and his lack of contact with Irish opinion, as well as his tendency to eccentric solipsism, goes some way to explain his arrogant and self-destructive tactics (or lack of them) when the long-ticking bomb of the O'Shea connection finally blew up in his face.

So not the least important part of Parnell's legacy is what was wrongly assumed about him after his death – above all by the revolutionary generation who were determined to make a new Ireland and to repudiate the British Empire ('a thing of unspeakably evil import', as Pearse described it in 1913) along with England's 'tyranny' over Ireland.[29] Home Rule was tainted with that imperial connection, while 'Parnellism', officially laid to rest with the reunification of the IPP in 1900, mutated into something claimed by the various contending nationalist bodies as it suited them. And from 1916, Pearse's claim for Parnell as 'Separatist' notwithstanding, the martyrs of Easter would replace 'The Chief' as the symbolic figures of sacrifice for the sake of national probity.

In the pre-revolutionary era, what Pearse and his fellow-revolutionaries were most preoccupied by was the fear that Ireland would, by means of the materialist and collaborationist tactics of the IPP, be assimilated into a sort of sub-England. For all the rhetoric of 'tyranny', their real fear was that England was exerting its evil influence by means of seduction rather than rape. In the pre-war period, for all the rhetoric of oppression and victimhood, the Ireland being created by Edwardian repressive tolerance was a land of peasant proprietorship, Old Age Pensions, reformed local government, Catholic control of education, and the comfortable certitudes of clientelist IPP hegemony. The revolutionary generation's worries on this

---

[29] See Joost Augusteijn, 'Patrick Pearse and Ireland's Position in the Empire', in *The British Empire and Its Contested Pasts*, ed. Robert J. Blyth and Keith Jeffery (Dublin, 2009), 247.

score were drastically intensified by the Irish response to the war effort in 1914, which seemed to many young republicans to threaten even the ideal of Ireland's separate existence. The nationalist intellectual Desmond Fitz-Gerald put it unequivocally:

> The movement on which all our dreams had centred seemed merely to have canalized the martial spirit of the Irish people for the defence of England. Our dream castles toppled about us with a crash. It was brought home to us that the very fever that possessed us was due to a subconscious awareness that that the final end of the Irish nation was at hand. For centuries, England had held Ireland materially. But now it seemed she held her in a new and utterly complete way. Our national identity was obliterated not only politically, but also in our own minds. The Irish people had recognized themselves as part of England.[30]

The remedy was obvious, at least to the IRB, and we know the results.

* * *

In conclusion, I would like to look at the implications of those results. Before the revolution, Pearse spoke for many when he anticipated Ireland overcoming Anglicization by recreating a spiritual empire, when

> the bard and the *seanchaidh* and the teacher of the Gael will once more be held in honour. A better, purer and happier world will be listening to the grand old epics and time-honoured *sgealta* of our race. Men's gods will no longer be empire, ambition and gold: but the homage that is paid to those things today will be paid in that happy age, as it was in the days of yore, on the hills and in the valleys of Eire, to the mysterious potencies of nature, the beauty and virtue of woman, the heroic dignity of man, the awful and incomprehensible majesty of the Divinity.[31]

Of course, an essential part of this was an Irish-speaking Ireland: the Irish nation simply could not survive, Pearse said, while people spoke English. It was Pearse, too, who coined (in 1901) that phrase which Leland Lyons later used to resonant and bleak effect in *Ireland since the Famine* and *Culture and Anarchy in Ireland*: 'the battle of two civilizations'.

That battle became overt, for the radical minority at least, in 1916; and the country that emerged six traumatic years later was ostensibly a very different place, 'changed utterly' from the pre-war world of constitutional

[30] Quoted in John Horne and Edward Madigan, eds., *Towards Commemoration: Ireland in War and Revolution 1912–1923* (Dublin, 2013), 27.

[31] 'Three Lectures on Gaelic Topics' (1898), in *The Literary Writings of Patrick Pearse: Writings in English*, ed. S. Ó Buachalla (Cork, 1979), 235–36.

nationalism and anticipated Home Rule. But in conclusion, I would like to look at the questions with which I began, of legacy and inheritance. In his *Reflections on the Revolution in France* (1790), Edmund Burke remarked that after a revolution, people wished to reaffirm all they now possessed, in the new dispensation, as 'an inheritance from our forefathers'. Looking at the Ireland that emerged in the 1920s, on its way (as Michael Collins forecast) to achieving at least a measure of 'freedom', it is worth asking whose legacy it epitomized. It was certainly very far from that Gaelic Utopia envisioned by Pearse, for all the top-dressing of compulsory Irish; 'nominalism', as Joep Leerssen reminds us, went only so far.[32] Nor did the new state embody the radical reordering of property and politics dreamt of by Anna Parnell. A two-party democratic system, a bicameral parliament, a powerful and independent civil service, the (by now well-established) replacement of landed estates by independent small farms, the continued prevalence of the English language, and over all a conservative Catholic ethos, enabled by the partition of the island, all enabled Arthur Balfour, ex-Chief Secretary of Ireland in the 1880s as well as retired Conservative PM, to say in 1928, 'The Ireland of today is the Ireland we made.'[33]

If 'we' means the so-called constructive unionist policies of his heyday, this is claiming too much; but it does make one wonder who had 'made' the Ireland of the 1920s and 1930s. The old radical Hanna Sheehy-Skeffington described it contemptuously as 'a Catholic statelet under Rome's grip ... with a very narrow provincial outlook, plus a self-satisfied smugness', ruled by a 'professor-type'.[34] Others were disillusioned by the close links kept with Britain and the Commonwealth. There is a case for saying that this was the Ireland Arthur Griffith made; and the extraordinarily Houdini-like way in which Griffith wriggled out of his increasingly marginalized pre-war position, into negotiating the Treaty that split the revolutionary movement, is worth more attention than it usually gets. Before 1914 his adherence to his dual-monarchy idea had alienated the Young Turks of the IRB, and many of his old Sinn Féin contacts, whose private correspondence bristles with sulphurous comments about their old guru as a sell-out. Though the war, and his 'mosquito press' journalism, brought him back into radical circles, people such as Michael Collins remained suspicious of his '1782' ideas.[35] Griffith is generally seen as

---

[32] J. Leerssen, 'Cúchulain in the General Post Office: Gaelic Revival, Irish Rising', *Journal of the British Academy* 4 (2016): 137–68.
[33] See B. E. C. Dugdale, *Arthur James Balfour* (London, 1936), 2:392.
[34] See *Vivid Faces*, 315–16. [35] Ibid., 261.

accepting Lloyd George's blandishments over the Treaty out of a sense of duty and wishful thinking; it might make just as much sense to see him as intentionally and cleverly manoeuvring the negotiations, to revive exactly what he had been preaching before the revolution of 1912–22: a dual-monarchy status with increased autonomy for Ireland in terms of economic and social policy, but far from the republic dreamed of by irreconcilable revolutionaries. Yet by the late 1920s the 'Ireland of today' was not the Ireland Griffith made, either; for one thing, the political system of the new state was closer to the British model than the corporate-representative plan which he had from time to time floated, and neither did it embody the drastic national economic protectionism which he had advocated – since this was hardly feasible under Commonwealth membership (though they tried their best, and it would later be discovered *faute de mieux* by his rival Eamon de Valera).

In fact, it could be argued that the person who left his stamp most firmly on the way independent Ireland turned out had died thirty years before the Treaty was signed – on 6 October 1891. Paul Bew's book on Parnell reminds us of a conversation between Andrew Kettle and Parnell in 1885, where Parnell casually outlined to an astonished Kettle the deal he hoped for from the Tories regarding Home Rule: a 'small-c' conservative government in Ireland, backed by the Irish democracy and peasant proprietary, linked to the Empire by Crown and an imperial contribution, and with enough economic autonomy to protect and encourage Irish industries. The twists and turns of politics, Tory opportunism, and Gladstone's *démarche* in 1886, and the crash of 1890–91, projected events in another direction. But twenty-two years after that conversation between Kettle and Parnell, not only did the status of the Free State approximate (constitutionally speaking) to this kind of Dominion Home Rule; the new Dominion, and subsequently its further incarnations as Eire and the Republic, were characterized by the social results of the subsidized revolution in landownership which Parnell had brought into being; by the kind of Westminster-inspired political structures which he had mastered and dominated in his heyday; by the concordat between national politicians and the Catholic hierarchy which he had endorsed (notably over denominational education in 1884, but also – to his own eventual undoing – in political representation); by the clientelist structures of local politics which were pioneered by the IPP and faithfully practised by Cumann na nGaedheal, Fine Gael, and Fianna Fáil; and by the relegation of ambitious and independent women, who were excluded from public life every bit as ruthlessly as Parnell had suppressed his sister's Ladies' Land League. That last shortcoming, as well as much else, has been altered if not fully remedied in our own time. But despite the upheavals brought by Pearse and his companions a hundred years ago, much of the 'Ireland of today' observed by Balfour in 1928 could arguably be seen as the Ireland Parnellism made. Perhaps in some ways it still is.[36]

---

[36] This – if nothing else – makes the Parnell Fellowship, Magdalene College's imaginative celebration of a founder of modern Ireland, pioneered and sustained by Eamon Duffy, enduringly relevant; long may it continue.

CHAPTER 4

Race, Nation, State

Denis Donoghue

A few autobiographical sentences may not, I hope, be amiss. I was born in Tullow, one of the minor towns of County Carlow, itself a minor county of the Irish Free State, as it was then constituted. But my home – though I rarely felt at home there – was in Warrenpoint, a town only slightly larger than Tullow, in County Down, just across the Border in Northern Ireland. My father was the sergeant-in-charge of the local police force, then called the Royal Ulster Constabulary (RUC). We were a Catholic family, living in the 'married quarters' of the police barracks, not a comfortable situation in domestic, social, or political terms. My impulses were entirely nationalist, and I regarded the RUC as an alien instrument of occupation: its function was to enforce the status of Northern Ireland, a political entity I deplored. Whatever misgivings my father and mother felt on this issue, they did not discuss them in my presence. Religion and politics were beyond the pale of conversation.

Warrenpoint is a seaside resort on Carlingford Lough, but it is also distinctive for having the largest public square in Ireland. For that reason, when I was growing up, it was famous for political marches, Unionist flourishes, nationalist shows of resentment. Those occasions were equal in one respect, though not ecumenical in any: each party had two days in the year to itself. We had not yet learnt to call the summer months the marching season, but the lines of ideological possession were not in dispute. Nationalists started off the year on 17 March, St. Patrick's Day. Unionists took over the town on 12 July, the not-quite-accurately calcu-lated anniversary of the victory of King William III at the battle of the Boyne in 1690. There were two further occasions. Nationalists who were also Roman Catholics – as nearly all of them were – celebrated the Feast of the Assumption of the Blessed Virgin on 15 August. But they marched to a softer tread on that day than on St. Patrick's Day, since they could hardly claim that the Blessed Virgin was Irish. Finally, on the last Saturday of August, Unionists celebrated Royal Black Preceptory Day, a festival I did not understand. The success of an occasion was measured by the number of bands that joined the parade and the distances the celebrants had travelled by bus or train. Unionists included members of the Orange Order and the Apprentice Boys: they wore black suits and bowler hats, with orange sashes diagonally across their chests. The bands featured banner images of King William on his white horse casting King James to the ground.

Nationalists had no event to show as dramatic as that one, but their banners in green, white, and orange presented a communal figure of Ireland that supposedly included the mythical Kathleen Ní Houlihan as vividly as the historical Wolfe Tone, Robert Emmet, and Daniel O'Connell. The lettering on nationalist banners was Celtic, a notional mark of allegiance to Irish, a language we laboured to learn and on rare occasions to speak. The music on those marching days consisted of political songs and ballads that could be played to brass, pipe, and drum; on the Unionist side 'The Sash My Father Wore', on the nationalist side 'Who Fears to Speak of Ninety-Eight?' and 'A Nation Once Again'.

It seemed a harmless custom: there were grim faces, steadfast to some undefined purpose, but I did not feel obliged to take them too seriously. Political passions on display in Warrenpoint were not as fierce as in other towns and villages in the North – in Harryville, Dunloy, and Drumcree, for instance – as in recent years.

I will put an end to these reminiscences now, because my memory has been shown to be fallible. When I published a memoir called *Warrenpoint* some years ago, I relied on my powers of recall to an extent I soon had cause to regret. Errors of fact are there to embarrass me. So I will not claim that my relation to the marches was analytic or otherwise thoughtful. I did not wonder, for instance, as I have wondered since, when precisely Ireland had been a nation rather than a site of quarrelsome tribes, such that in Thomas Davis's poem of 1842 or thereabouts it must become a nation once again. It had certainly ceased to be a nation on 1 January 1801 when the wretched Act of Union came into force. Presumably that was what Davis had in mind:

> When boyhood's fire was in my blood
> I read of ancient freemen
> For Greece and Rome who bravely stood,
> Three hundred men and three men.
> And then I prayed I yet might see
> Our fetters rent in twain,
> And Ireland, long a province, be
> A nation once again.[1]

---

[1] *The Poems of Thomas Davis* (Dublin, 1853), 73.

Davis's reference to Greece and Rome recalls the three hundred who died
at Thermopylae – the hot gates – and the three Romans who kept the
Sublician Bridge. I did not know the references, or stop to learn them,
when I committed the song to memory or let it inhabit my mind. I should
have wondered why Ireland, to become a nation rather than a province,
must exhibit the bravery of Greece and Rome.

In the south of Ireland, so far as I recall, there were no parades of
Orange or Green, except for an Orange march every year in Bundoran,
County Donegal, for reasons I do not understand. The anthologies read in
schools south of the Border featured patriotic poems but not marching
songs. The most memorable poem in that context was Thomas D'Arcy
McGee's 'The Celts':

> Long, long ago, beyond the misty space
> Of twice a thousand years,
> In Erin old there dwelt a mighty race,
> Taller than Roman spears;
> Like oaks and towers they had a giant grace,
> Were fleet as deers,
> With wind and wave they made their biding place,
> These Western shepherd-seers.[2]

The Celts were thought to be mighty because epic tradition required them
to be.

It is customary to say that Ireland was a nation in the twelfth century,
but I do not understand how the conspiracies and struggles for power
among local kings fulfilled the concept of a nation. We read of Diarmait
MacMurchadha in conflict with Tighernan Ua Ruairc not only because
MacMurchadha abducted Ua Ruairc's wife Devorgilla but because the
province of Meath was to be won or lost. We hear of the High King Ruairí
Ua Conchobhar in league with Ua Ruairc; of MacMurchadha submitting
himself to King Henry II of England to gain his support in recovering his
territory; of the bishops giving Henry their allegiance in the expectation
that he would reform the Irish church, in the twelfth century a notoriously
corrupt institution. Davis's 'A Chronology of Ireland' gives the relevant
dates without comment, as if they spoke their own truth, as they would if
they were accurate. I give them so far as they have been corrected:

1156: Pope Hadrian V's bull *Laudabiliter* granting Henry II the right to
incorporate Ireland in his realm

---

[2] Thomas D'Arcy McGee, *Poems* (Boston, 1869), 176–77.

1169, May: First Landing of the Normans

1171, October 16: Henry II arrives in Ireland

1172: Synod of Cashel assembled under the authority of Henry II. A Council, called by some a Parliament, held by Henry II at Lismore.[3]

Davis does not mention the unforgivable Diarmait and Dervorgilla 'who brought the Norman in', as the Young Man on the run from the General Post Office in 1916 keeps reminding us in Yeats's *The Dreaming of the Bones*.[4] However, since 1172, according to Davis and the Young Ireland writers, Ireland has been merely a province.

In the middle of the nineteenth century, it was not universally agreed that Ireland had ever been a nation. Between December 1865 and May 1866, Matthew Arnold gave four lectures at Oxford on the study of Celtic literature, in which he asserted that the Celts, and specifically the Irish and the Welsh, had for centuries been a race but not a nation. He spoke of 'the shrunken and diminished remains of this great primitive race', but only to remark on their 'failure to reach any material civilization sound and satisfying, and not out at elbows, poor, slovenly, and half-barbarous'. Arnold claimed that the Celts had never achieved the degree of composition that would be embodied in a polity. The epigraph he chose for the lectures was a line from Macpherson's Poems of Ossian: 'They went forth to the war, but they always fell.' Taking his bearings from Renan's *Essay on the Poetry of the Celtic Races* and Henri Martin's *France before 1789*, Arnold spoke up for the Celts, but on the clear assumption that they had never become a nation or entered into history. They were a race, recognizable in their spirit or genius, but they had never exceeded that condition. The genius of the Celtic peoples counted for something 'in the inward world of thought and science', but for nothing 'in the outward and visible world of material life'. As late as 1887, Arnold said that the Irish could be regarded as 'a nation poetically only, not politically'.[5]

I use the words 'race' and 'nation' with the liberty of an amateur. I will assume, in default of an erudite sense of the matter, that a race, as distinct from a nation, is what sociologists call a 'social imaginary'. Its status is ideal or virtual rather than palpable. It is what people living in the same country – a certain small island in the Atlantic Ocean, say – think of themselves as being: their feeling is primordial rather than historical, social,

---

[3] Thomas Davis, *Essays*, ed. D. J. O'Donoghue (New York, 1974; reprint of 1914 ed.), 250.

[4] W. B. Yeats, *Plays*, Variorum edition, ed. Russell K. Alspach (London, 1966), 773.

[5] Matthew Arnold, 'From Easter to August', *The Nineteenth Century* 22 (September 1887): 321.

or economic. In that sense – Arnold's – the Irish race had left traces of itself
in poems, sagas, and artefacts, but it had not otherwise entered into the
history of peoples. It is what one imagines, on the evidence of archaeological and linguistic remains. But a nation is what one projects, on the
strength of that imagining. A race is a people-in-waiting, exemplifying
the condition of being possible, a long 'perhaps'. Or it marks what once
was: an immemorial folk that has left evidences of itself in legends and
landscapes but cannot otherwise be produced for inspection. We think of a
race as a tribe or breed, descended from putative common ancestors; but
we say that it has not – or not yet – taken to itself the relatively stable
character of a society. Or perhaps it has been ejected from historical or
territorial existence, like the Jews in Leopold Bloom's sense of them. In the
Cyclops chapter of *Ulysses* John Wyse Nolan asks Bloom: 'But do you
know what a nation means?' 'A nation is the same people living in the
same place,' Bloom answers. 'What is your nation if I may ask?' the Citizen
intervenes to say. 'Ireland', says Bloom, 'I was born here. Ireland.' After a
paragraph of Joyce's linguistic finery, Bloom adverts to another attribute of
his inherited life. 'And I belong to a race, too ... that is hated and
persecuted . ... At this very moment ... sold by auction in Morocco like
slaves or cattle.'[6] Bloom is not ready to expound the differences between
Jews as a race and Irish men and women as a nation, but his use of the
terms is acceptable so far as it goes.

   Arnold derived his typology of races from scholars of ethnology, lin-
guistics, and the historical study of the Celtic languages. He did not know
the languages, so he was indebted to O'Curry, Zeuss, O'Donovan, and
other scholars for his access, limited indeed, to Celtic literature. But he was
charmed by the little he knew, and gratified to think of the Celtic
languages as distinctive so long as he could take pleasure in their being
dead. He referred to 'the practical inconvenience of perpetuating the
speaking of Welsh' and maintained that

> the fusion of all the inhabitants of these islands into one homogeneous,
> English-speaking whole, the breaking down of barriers between us, the
> swallowing up of separate provincial nationalities, is a consummation to
> which the natural course of things irresistibly tends.

He did not hesitate, apparently, over the metaphor of 'swallowing up'. He
regarded the genius of the Celtic race as beautiful but fatally defective in its
inability to engage with the real conditions of life. For his main argument,

---

[6] James Joyce, *Ulysses*, ed. Hans Walter Gabler, 3 vols. (New York, 1984), 2:713–17.

he endorsed a claim of Henri Martin's: that the Celts were 'always ready to react against the despotism of fact'. They were imaginative, sentimental, vivid, in every respect Nature's children, but they were incapable of acting upon the real world; they lacked the power of composition and therefore the social and political capacity. It followed that the only reasonable thing for 'the Celtic members of this empire' to do in 1865 was to bring their nationalist desires to a quiet end and join with English people to create a better polity in Britain, 'a new type, more intelligent, more gracious, and more humane'.[7] Ireland had no future of its own, but it could help to improve an English society dismally Philistine when left to its proclivities. England, in turn, should do everything to attach Ireland to itself. On Ireland's part, there must be no thought of independence.

Arnold's advice got a poor reception. Within two years, the Fenian Rising – despite its being a botched enterprise in every practical respect – at least made it clear that the Act of Union of 1 January 1801 was still in dispute. Sixteen years after lecturing on the study of Celtic literature, Arnold reported with dismay in an essay called 'The Incompatibles' that England had 'completely failed to attach Ireland'. Worse still: 'we find ourselves the object of a glowing, fierce, unexplained hatred on the part of the Irish people'. But there must still be no thought of Home Rule or separation. In the spirit of Edmund Burke, Arnold urged that Ireland should be brought 'to acquiesce in the English connection by good and just treatment'. Specifically: Ireland would be appeased not by better Land Bills but by 'the equitable treatment of Catholicism' in regard to schools and universities and by the development of a society in England which Irish people would find worth joining.[8]

It may be said that Arnold is merely a particular manifestation of prejudice and vivacity, that he is not representative of the relation between England and Ireland. True, but he was not alone in maintaining that the Irish were a race, not a nation. George Moore, apparently an Irish writer, expressed much the same attitude, especially in *A Drama in Muslin* and *Parnell and His Island*. Ireland was 'a primitive country and barbarous people'. The western Celt, as Moore described him, was 'a creature quick to dream, and powerless to execute; in external aspects and in moral history the same tale is told – great things attempted, nothing done'.[9]

[7] Matthew Arnold, 'On the Study of Celtic Literature', in Arnold, *Lectures and Essays in Criticism*, ed. R. H. Super (Ann Arbor, MI, 1962), 291, 296–28, 344–45, 385, 395.

[8] Matthew Arnold, *English Literature and Irish Politics*, ed. R. H. Super (Ann Arbor, MI, 1973), 238–42, 269.

[9] George Moore, *Parnell and His Island* (London, Lowrey, 1887), 55, 233.

You could find Ireland interesting so long as you were not invited to take it seriously. In *Hail and Farewell* Moore made fun of Yeats for his rejection of the social class – the middle one – to which Yeats himself belonged on both sides of his family. In the *Autobiographies* Yeats paid Moore back for this affront and many other indelicacies. Moore's face, he reported, was carved out of a turnip, his body was 'insinuating, upflowing, circulative, curvicular, pop-eyed'. He was so ill-mannered that 'he wrote a long preface to prove that he had a mistress in Mayfair'.[10] In *Hail and Farewell* Moore, who knew no Irish, laughed at Douglas Hyde for speaking it ('a torrent of dark, muddied stuff flowed from him, much like the porter which used to come up from Carnacun to be drunk by the peasants on midsummer nights when a bonfire was lighted'[11]) and he gave a farcical account of a pilgrimage he himself made with George Russell (AE) to Slievegullion in honour of Cuchulain and Finn. Moore's sarcasm always preceded the need of it. But the main difference between Moore and Arnold on the question of the Irish as a race was that Arnold proposed to rescue them from their civic penury by attaching them to England; Moore tormented them for the fun of it. Arnold blamed successive British governments for keeping the Irish in their barbarous condition. Moore sneered at every institution in sight: Gladstone, Parnell, the Catholic Church, the Land League, Irish peasants, and the worthies of Dublin Castle. It was as if his rhetoric had only one figure of thought and he meant to keep it employed.

But Moore's insults did not inhibit the work of cultural nationalists, nor did Joyce's gibes at Yeats and the literary movement. I have in mind 'The Holy Office' (1904), 'Gas from a Burner' (1912), and the account of political life after Parnell, as Joyce gives it in 'Ivy Day in the Committee Room' – a story set in the Dublin of 6 October 1902. But these ironies are not definitive; they do not tell the whole story of Joyce's relation to nationalism or even to Yeats and his companions. Joyce was as deeply involved in the values of 'kinship, race, and inheritance' as he was committed to those of art and the Europe of Dante, Flaubert, and Ibsen.[12] There is no reason to think that he is being sarcastic at Stephen Dedalus's expense when he has him exclaim: 'I go to encounter for the millionth time the reality of experience and to forge in the smithy of my soul the uncreated conscience of my race.'[13] It is possible to read that declaration ironically, but the irony soon becomes ashamed of itself.

---

[10] W. B. Yeats, *Autobiographies* (London, 1966), 406, 422.

[11] George Moore, *Hail and Farewell*, 3 vols. (New York, 1925 reprint), 1:139.

[12] Emer Nolan, *James Joyce and Nationalism* (London, 1995), 42.

[13] James Joyce, *A Portrait of the Artist as a Young Man*, ed. Hans Walter Gabler (New York, 1993), 282.

In any event, none of Joyce's interventions, or Moore's, deflected Yeats from his purpose as a cultural nationalist to summon the Irish race into historical existence as a nation. I do not claim that he accomplished this with his own hands. The work of cultural nationalism began, according to one persuasive account, when the antiquarian Edward Bunting and his assistants transcribed and published the songs played at the great harpists' festival in Belfast in 1792.[14] Bunting's achievements are clear in his *A General Collection of the Ancient Irish Music* (1796 and 1809) and *The Ancient Music of Ireland* (1840).

The early phase of modern Irish nationalism also includes pre-eminently Samuel Ferguson, Isaac Butt, Michael Davitt, John O'Leary, and Parnell, and in other respects Hyde and the Gaelic League, Michael Cusack and the Gaelic Athletic Association, Lady Gregory and the Abbey Theatre, and many men and women whose purposes did not coincide with Yeats's. Nor was Yeats the first to prepare the ground; he had many precursors, none of them his equal: Davis, Gavan Duffy, Standish O'Grady, Mangan, Ferguson, and Allingham. In 1886 Yeats published his first essay, 'The Poetry of Sir Samuel Ferguson', in which he said that Ferguson's

> special claim to our attention is that he went back to the Irish cycle, finding it, in truth, a fountain that, in the passage of centuries, was overgrown with weeds and grass, so that the very way to it was forgotten of the poets; but now that his feet have worn the pathway, many others will follow, and bring thence living waters for the healing of our nation, helping us to live the larger life of the Spirit, and lifting our souls away from their selfish joys and sorrows to be the companions of those who lived greatly among the woods and hills when the world was young.[15]

This became Yeats's own ambition in his early poems, plays, and essays. But he did not express Ireland at every point of its feeling and desire, as reference to Maud Gonne, Countess Markiewicz, Pearse, Connolly, Griffith, and Collins is enough to indicate. But Parnell, Yeats, and Hyde are the major figures in the early years of modern Irish nationalism, at that time a sacred cause. Yeats's main achievement in his early work was to bring to composition and form a plethora of national desires that hardly knew themselves to be desires. He told many Irish men and women what they felt, what they wanted, and the more strenuous things they should

---

[14] Katie Trumpener, *Bardic Nationalism: The Romantic Novel and the British Empire* (Princeton, NJ, 1997), 10ff.
[15] W. B. Yeats, *Uncollected Prose 1: First Reviews and Articles 1886–1896*, ed. John P. Frayne (New York, 1970), 82.

now want. It was an achievement the more remarkable because he spoke from the experience of a social class in decline, the Protestant professional class of parsons and businessmen, and he thought to arouse from their sleep a people mainly Roman Catholic, a type he always disliked and in his later years feared.

The question of nationalism, its origin, and the conditions of its rise is contentious. I assume that national sentiment is a feeling of kinship with the other people in one's vicinity rather than with people as such or in general. It is a tendency to think of one's race on the analogy of one's family. This does not entail thinking well of them; it is enough that the analogy with one's family be retained even in disappointment. The national sentiment may also provoke a habit of regarding people outside the circle of kinship as different and probably hostile. Julia Kristeva has urged people – French, to begin with – to break this habit by reflecting on the 'unconscious' in Freud's description of it. By this reflection we find that we are strangers to ourselves. So we should find it possible to appreciate the strangeness of other people – the foreigners – 'instead of striving to bend them to the norms of our own repression'.[16] I suppose, too, that nationalism contains an aspiration to see one's kinship embodied in a nation, a territory, and ultimately a state. We are also being urged these days to think of nationalism in relation to the factors that enabled it – the printing press, modernization, Romanticism, and the rejection of Enlightenment values. Some scholars of nationalism present it as a discursive formation without any ground in one's experience. This is implausible. At least in Ireland, the nationalist conviction has not begun or ended in words; it has been provoked by issues of land, ownership, tenancy, trade, the Famine, and apparently continuous humiliation by those in power.

I am willing to be persuaded by Hans Kohn that the sentiment of nationalism reached its clearest formulation in Rousseau's *Social Contract* with his concept of the 'general will'. If nationalism is, as Kohn describes it, 'the state of mind in which the supreme loyalty of the individual is felt to be due to the nation-state', it seems reasonable to posit the general will as an essential condition of its thriving: it is not the sum of individual wills but the common will, released from every merely accidental desire and turned towards the fellowship of one's kind.[17] In that sense the United States is the first community of people who thought of themselves, at least

---

[16] Julia Kristeva, *Nations without Nationalism*, trans. Leon S. Roudiez (New York, 1993), 29.
[17] Hans Kohn, *Nationalism: Its Meaning and History*, rev. ed. (Princeton, NJ, 1965), 9.

on that occasion, as bringing a nation into existence. But it is necessary, with Irish nationalism in view, to add to Rousseau's 'general will' the post-Herderian concept of the *Volksgeist*, if only to take account of the emphasis – in Davis, Hyde, Daniel Corkery, and D. P. Moran, to name four otherwise disparate figures – on the Irish language and the valued differences between the cultures of Ireland and England. Herder devoted his work to the idea of a nation rather than the nation-state, but that, too, was a factor in some Irish nationalists. An uncle of mine, Seamus O'Neill, a rebel before 1916 and imprisoned in Ireland and England at various times thereafter, told me that the Irish people suffered far more by the loss of the Irish language than by their subjection in other respects to the British Empire.

As a cultural nationalist, Yeats set out to invigorate a sentiment closely resembling Rousseau's 'general will'. He hoped to do this by invoking a sense of the Irish people as they were expressed primordially in a legendary history, the sagas and lore of a people before the coming of Christianity, myths of Oisín wandering; Cuchulain killing his son and fighting the sea; Maeve and her children, Baile and Ailinn; Angus and his fellow-immortals:

> I would, if I could, add to that majestic heraldry of the poets, that great and complicated inheritance of images which written literature has substituted for the greater and more complex inheritance of spoken tradition, some new heraldic images, gathered from the lips of the common people. Christianity and the old nature faith have lain down side by side in the cottages, and I would proclaim that peace as loudly as I can among the kingdoms of poetry, where there is no peace that is not joyous, no battle that does not give life instead of death; I may even try to persuade others, in more sober prose, that there can be no language more worthy of poetry, and of the meditation of the soul than that which has been made, or can be made, out of a subtlety of desire, an emotion of sacrifice, a delight in order, that are perhaps Christian, and myths and images that mirror the energies of woods and streams, and of their wild creatures.[18]

If myth is, as Marcel D'Etienne has described it, 'an autonomous discourse extracting from reality the elements over which it maintains sovereignty',[19] it corresponds to a selected communal experience, as desire would have it, free from the despotism of fact. The three major cycles – the mythological cycle, the Red Branch cycle, and the cycle of the Fianna – gave Yeats enough motifs for any of his early purposes in poetry, fiction, and drama.

---

[18] Yeats, *Plays*, 1283, 1290.
[19] Marcel D'Etienne, *Dionysos Slain*, trans. L. Muellner and M. Muellner (Baltimore, MD, 1979), 15.

He could use those sagas to appeal to unity of race as a force prior to historical divisions. They allowed him to say, and to urge others to say: I am of Ireland, not of England. England had given itself over to industrialism, the printing press, and the counting house.

Several years after the little island was partitioned, Yeats maintained that 'Ireland, divided in religion and politics, is as much one race as any modern country.'[20] But he did not maintain a strict distinction between race and nation. The word 'race' occurred to him when he scanned the far horizon of myth and legend, and when he consulted the evidences drawn from Celtic anthropology, folklore, and archaeology. In 'J. M. Synge and the Ireland of His Time' he claimed that Synge 'sought for the race, not through the eyes or in history, or even in the future, but where the monks found God in the depths of the mind'.[21] The word 'nation' occurred to Yeats when he thought of a people being impelled towards self-expression and self-transformation. In the same essay he spoke of the nation as 'a dumb struggling thought seeking a mouth to utter it or hand to show it, a teeming delight that would re-create the world' (*Essays*, 317). The poet was its representative voice, the bard.

Yeats's first authority for these motifs was Standish O'Grady's *History of Ireland*, especially its first volume, *The Heroic Period* (1878). The second volume, *Cuculain and His Contemporaries* (1880), was more easily superseded in later years by the stories Lady Gregory assembled in her *Cuchulain of Muirthemne* and *Gods and Fighting Men*. Although Yeats protested that he wanted to see pagan Ireland and Christian Ireland reconciled in peace, it was crucial to him that he could divine the unity of the Irish race, to begin with, mainly in pagan terms. In the debate between Oisín and Patrick, Oisín should have the deeper experience and the better lines. Christianity must be made to appear a fine enough thing in its way, though Yeats did not emphasize the monastic and the missionary traditions as Joyce did, especially in his lectures in Trieste in 1907. Nor did he speculate on linguistic relations between Phoenicia, Crete, Greece, Egypt, and Ireland, as Joyce did when his mind was on *Ulysses* and *Finnegans Wake*. It was rhetorically compelling for Yeats to present early Irish Christianity as a much-reduced system of belief and practice, by comparison with the heroic values of the legendary, pagan Ireland it displaced.

When it came to a further choice, after the Reformation, Yeats settled for an undemanding Protestantism as providing a more agreeable form of

[20] W. B. Yeats, *Explorations* (London, 1962), 347n.; hereinafter cited as *Exp.*
[21] W. B. Yeats, *Essays and Introductions* (London, 1961), 341; hereinafter cited as *Essays.*

life than Catholicism. He was often bitter, as O'Grady was, when he pondered the declined social status of Protestants in nineteenth-century Ireland. In several essays and two or three poems Yeats maintained that a distinctively Irish form of nationalism had been promulgated by Molyneux, Swift, and especially by Berkeley; that it animated the otherwise diverse lives of Burke, Goldsmith, Grattan, Wolfe Tone, Lord Edward Fitzgerald, Robert Emmet, Davis, and Mitchel; and that it culminated in Parnell. It was a Protestant achievement, but Yeats liked to think of it as being at one with heroic, pagan, antinomian impulses. A primitive form of it was expressed in Gavan Duffy's and Davis's work for the Young Ireland movement, but Yeats knew that he must refine upon the spirit of the *Nation* by submitting its patriotic zeal to a much wider range of feelings and a more intense scrutiny. That was his justification for claiming, in 'To Ireland in the Coming Times', that his rhymes, more than those of Davis, Mangan, and Ferguson, told 'Of things discovered in the deep, / Where only body's laid asleep.'[22] He respected Davis, but he thought that the Young Ireland movement had encouraged Irish people to settle for facile sentiments and vulgar arguments:

> Young Ireland had taught a study of our history, with the glory of Ireland for event; and this, for lack ... of comparison with that of other countries, wrecked the historical instinct. The man who doubted, let us say, our fabulous ancient kings running up to Adam, or found but mythology in some old tale, was hated as if he had doubted the authority of Scripture. Above all, no man was so ignorant that he had not by rote familiar arguments and statistics to drive away amid familiar applause all those that had found strange truth in the world or in their minds, and all whose knowledge had passed out of memory and become an instinct of hand or eye. There was no literature, for literature is a child of experience always, of knowledge never. (*Essays*, 316–17)

In 'To Ireland in the Coming Times' Yeats included himself in the kinship of Protestant nationalists, and in other poems he took up in cultural terms the work that Parnell had tried to do in parliamentary terms. The sentiment he proclaimed was Parnell's, a Protestant impulse, different in kind from the Catholic drive of O'Connell, a man Yeats affected to despise as 'the great comedian'. O'Connell was a populist. Parnell was a tragic hero, lonely, subjective, antithetical; an ambiguous, equivocal force, maintaining his personality as a secret, his demon. He spoke in whatever voice he chose and on his own authority.

---

[22] W. B. Yeats, *Collected Poems* (New York, 1952), 50; hereinafter cited as *CP*.

Yeats's strategy was culturally emphatic. Parnell regularly invoked 'the Irish nation' and 'the Irish race' which he proposed to lead, but – as F. S. L. Lyons has noted – he seems never to have asked himself what he meant by those phrases, 'and the idea that Ireland might possibly contain two nations, not one, apparently never entered his head'.[23] Yeats proclaimed Unity of Race, at least to begin with: divisions would be admitted later and with regret. It is often maintained that he posited for the Irish people a fixed identity, as if such a quality were independent of circumstances. I do not think he did. His reflections on race, type, and national character seem to me not at all essentialist. He allows for mobility by making every postulate yield to the transforming power of one's imagination. He submits the ostensibly fixed concepts of nature, history, character, self, and origin to subjective transformation, such that they become one's particular forms of freedom, gesture, personality, and style. Irish identity is what he wants to create, by many acts of summoning and conjuring; it is not deemed to be already there in an immutable form. Yeats's motive was Nietzschean long before he had read Nietzsche. In 'The Use and Abuse of History' Nietzsche says that we seek a past from which we may spring rather than that past from which we appear to have derived.

This explains why Yeats's typical attention to a concept or a value displaces it and submits it to his own imagination. In 'A General Introduction for My Work' he says that a poet 'is never the bundle of accident and incoherence that sits down to breakfast; he has been reborn as an idea, something intended, complete'. Evidently, the particular idea is his own, a poet's, not a novelist's:

> A novelist might describe his accidence, his incoherence, he must not; he is more type than man, more passion than type. He is Lear, Romeo, Oedipus, Tiresias; he has stepped out of a play, and even the woman he loves is Rosalind, Cleopatra, never The Dark Lady. He is part of his own phantasmagoria and we adore him because nature has grown intelligible, and by so doing a part of our creative power. (*Essays*, 509)

Similarly, in his considerations of time and history, Yeats was not willing to see history as mere chronology, 'the cracked tune that Chronos sings' (*CP*, 7). In his diary of 1930 he wrote, 'History is necessity until it takes fire in someone's head and becomes freedom or virtue' (*Exp.*, 336). In 'The Celtic Element in Literature', as if he were ready to exchange life for art, he wrote:

---

[23] F. S. L. Lyons, *Charles Stewart Parnell* (New York, 1977), 623.

> Certainly a thirst for unbounded emotion and a wild melancholy are troublesome things in the world, and do not make its life more easy or orderly, but it may be the arts are founded on the life beyond the world, and that they must cry in the ears of our penury until the world has been consumed and become a vision. (*Essays*, 184)

The problem was not how to consume the world but how to make this apparently opaque thing appear to be transfigured, become transparent by virtue of one's imagination.

I bring these considerations forward to clarify the relation between Yeats's work as a cultural nationalist and his dealings with magic. We have only to note his emphasis on subconscious, collective experience, in the essay on Magic, to see how compatible they were:

> I believe in the practice and philosophy of what we have agreed to call magic, in what I must call the evocation of spirits, though I do not know what they are, in the power of creating magical illusions, in the visions of truth in the depths of the mind when the eyes are closed; and I believe in three doctrines, which have, as I think, been handed down from early times, and been the foundations of nearly all magical practices These doctrines are:
>
> 1. that the borders of our minds are ever shifting, and that many minds can flow into one another, as it were, and create or reveal a single mind, a single energy,
> 2. that the borders of our memories are as shifting, and that our memories are a part of one great memory, the memory of Nature herself, and
> 3. that this great mind and great memory can be evoked by symbols.
>
> (*Essays*, 28)

So everything begins to cohere: ancestral memories, magic, the spiritus mundi, the summoning of a race to become a nation, the practice of an antinomian politics as cultural nationalism, the politics of difference, the tragic theatre, the sacred book of the arts. In the 1892 version of 'To Ireland in the Coming Times', Yeats clarified the propinquity of magic and cultural nationalism by claiming for himself, by comparison with Davis, Mangan, and Ferguson, that

> My rhymes more than their rhyming tell
> Of the dim visions old and deep,
> That God gives unto man in sleep
> For round about my table go
> The magical powers to and fro.[24]

---

[24] W. B. Yeats, *Poems*, Variorum edition, ed. Peter Allt and R. K. Alspach (London, 1957), 138.

It follows that Yeats must assert that Ireland was a nation to the extent of its cultural difference from England. If England was, as Yeats thought, rotten with positivism and industrialism, Ireland – and especially the west of Ireland, Synge's mythical place – must be an antinomian culture, a place of islands, villages, and townlands, mindful of ancient lore and natural magic. He must find in the west sufficient reasons, aesthetic and spiritual, for rejecting the lure of modernism. In 'Literature and the Living Voice' he wrote

> Irish poetry and Irish stories were made to be spoken or sung, while English literature, alone of great literatures, because the newest of them all, has all but completely shaped itself in the printing-press. In Ireland to-day the old world that sang and listened is, it may be for the last time in Europe, face to face with the world that reads and writes, and their antagonism is always present under some name or other in Irish imagination and intellect. (*Exp.*, 206)

Those reflections justified Yeats's recourse to the theatre. 'Wherever the old imaginative life lingers', he said, 'it must be stirred to more life, or at the worst, kept alive, and in Ireland this is the work, it may be, of the Gaelic movement' (*Exp.*, 208–9). By the Gaelic movement I think he meant to include what he later called the Celtic Renaissance, with the Abbey Theatre its significant form.

But Yeats's boldest gesture was to join his work as a cultural nationalist with that of European Symbolism and the occult. By that designation I mean to include not only Mallarmé and the other poets and dramatists presented in Arthur Symons's *The Symbolist Movement in Literature* but the whole neo-Platonic tradition with Blake as its greatest adept. Symons wrote of Symbolism that it is 'a literature in which the visible world is no longer a reality, and the unseen world no longer a dream'.[25] It may seem a wild project to act upon that emphasis while conjuring a race to come forth as a nation and to take its place in history. But Yeats did not want Ireland to become a nation like any other. In 'The Celtic Element in Literature' he makes the antithetical nature of his desire quite clear. Taking up the theme where he thought Renan and Arnold had left it, he did not engage with Arnold's talk of race and nation, but he construed the strange qualities of early Irish stories as cognate with the transfiguring force of Symbolism:

---

[25] Arthur Symons, *The Symbolist Movement in Literature*, rev. ed. (London, 1908), 4.

> I will put this differently and say that literature dwindles to a mere chronicle of circumstance, or passionless fantasies and passionless meditations, unless it is constantly flooded with the passions and beliefs of ancient times, and that of all the fountains of the passions and beliefs of ancient times in Europe, the Slavonic, the Finnish, the Scandinavian, and the Celtic, the Celtic alone has been for centuries close to the main river of European literature. (*Essays*, 185)

I am not sure that Yeats knew those literatures well enough to pronounce upon them or to make an invidious comparison, but we may pass over that consideration. I should note, however, Yeats's insistence on the transforming, subjective power of imagination. History becomes freedom or virtue; the force of will is changed to the creative force of imagination; character as something given is changed to personality as something chosen; nature becomes fruitful power; time is changed to what Yeats calls 'the Moods'; image is transformed into symbol, mind into dream – 'the generative aspect of the mind', as Allen Grossman called it[26] – and at last knowledge is transfigured as wisdom. It follows that in Yeats's early work as cultural nationalist, the poet is the exemplar, the one in whom desire knows itself for what it is. He is the bard, reciting ancient lore for the benefit of the people for whom he sings. This motive animates his early work and persists, despite many inducements to disgust and rage, till the end of his life.

David Lloyd has argued in *Anomalous States* that Yeats's work as a cultural nationalist came to a crisis if not to an end in 1916. When Pearse and the other leaders of the Easter Rising took to arms, they appropriated Yeats's Ireland, seized his myths and symbols, and removed the sources of his authority. After Easter Week and the execution of the rebels, Yeats could appeal to no authority but his own: he could no longer be the national bard. In his poems of Easter 1916 he could only pay tribute to the heroic, transforming power of men who had chosen to go their own militant way – which was not his way – and to bring the people with them. The peremptory tone of Yeats's poems and plays after 1916 is partly explained by their being 'speech acts' in a particular mode: performatives, imperatives.

The evidence is not decisive. It could be argued that in the years from 1907 to 1913 – that is, from the disturbances at the first performances of Synge's *The Playboy of the Western World* to the controversy over Hugh

---

[26] Allen R. Grossman, *Poetic Knowledge in the Early Yeats: A Study of 'The Wind among the Reeds'* (Charlottesville, VA, 1969), 40.

Lane's paintings and the Dublin Lock-Out of 1913 – Yeats was no longer a cultural nationalist in the original sense; he was a poet at a distance from the people he summoned to come forth; he was a critic, a satirist, a polemicist; his note was contempt rather than exhortation. But leaving Yeats aside for the moment, it would be reasonable to argue that the work of cultural nationalism came to a crisis in 1915 when Hyde resigned from the presidency of the Gaelic League because the League had become a political rather than a cultural organization. In the same year Pearse dissociated himself, in his pamphlet *Ghosts*, from constitutional nationalists as men who had allowed themselves to be defeated by the fall and death of Parnell. It soon became clear that the conviction of identity which Yeats, Hyde, Lady Gregory, and their colleagues provoked in those who attended to them had issued in desires that those writers could not have anticipated, desires that could not be appeased by Home Rule in any of the forms in which it might be proposed.

Pearse was the crucial figure in bringing about this change and in forcing Ireland to the extremity of becoming a state after his execution, much bloodshed, and the Civil War. The word 'state' appears only once in the Proclamation of the Irish Republic – the text is the work of Pearse, James Connolly, and Thomas MacDonagh, but of Pearse mainly – but that once is resolute: 'we hereby proclaim the Irish Republic as a Sovereign Independent State'. There are four references to the Irish 'people', three to the 'nation', one to 'nationhood', three to the 'republic', and one to 'Poblacht na hÉireann'. It was as if the founding of a state were the culminating act in a series of acknowledgements testifying to a conviction of nationhood and identity. The sense of identity floats free of its mere history. Like Yeats, and like de Valera in the Constitution of 1937, Pearse appeals not to Irish history as the record of events in the order in which they have occurred but to the nation that has existed and continues to exist 'in the minds and loyalties of its people', as Liam de Paor has expressed it, 'independently, as it were, of its own history of some centuries past'.[27] Pearse implies that the true history of Ireland, as distinct from the specious history it has officially had, is not a record of the English presence in Ireland for more than 700 years but of the six attempts in the past 300 years to remove that presence (he means the acts of insurrection in 1641, 1689, 1798, 1803, 1848, and 1867). The only reference in the Proclamation to the refusal of Unionists in certain parts of Ulster to countenance any nationalist proceeding is in this sentence:

[27] Liam de Paor, *On the Easter Proclamation and Other Declarations* (Dublin, 1997), 36.

The Republic guarantees religious and civil liberty, equal rights and equal opportunities to all its citizens, and declares its resolve to pursue the happiness and prosperity of the whole nation and of all its parts, cherishing all the children of the nation equally, and oblivious of the differences carefully fostered by an alien government, which have divided a minority from the majority in the past.[28]

Pearse knew, as everyone should have known since 1886, that the minority he referred to would not acquiesce in a Republic of the entire island of Ireland, any more than it had acquiesced in Home Rule, but he hoped – as Hyde did, and de Valera at least for some years – that Unionists would come to acknowledge that they were Irish rather than British, and subside into an Irish republic, if such a thing were to be brought about. The Good Friday Agreement of 1998 has made it clear that no such yielding, on the part of Unionists, is to be contemplated.

Meanwhile the Proclamation of 1916 summoned the Irish race not only to believe in a transfigured history but to take part in an insurgent politics. Pearse did not have an elaborate political philosophy, but his thinking seems to have been compatible with a tendentious politics enunciated fifteen years later by Carl Schmitt. The state, according to Schmitt, is 'the political status of an organized people in an enclosed territorial unit'. In its literal sense and its historical appearance, 'the state is a specific entity of a people'. Jacques Derrida has phrased it differently: the state is 'the particular modality of the mode of existence of the people (*Volk*)'.[29]

The main point of Schmitt's theory is that 'the specific political distinction to which political actions and motives can be reduced is that between friend and enemy'.[30] It follows that the political does not exist without the figure of the enemy and the determined possibility of an actual war. The state is the teleological 'end' of the political, and it is necessarily characterized by the designation of friend and enemy. In this spirit, Pearse turned Yeats's cultural nationalism of difference – between Ireland and England – into a politics of friendship and hostility. We are friends with our Unionist brothers and sisters in the North, but England – at least for the moment – is our enemy.

It is still a dispute whether the Home Rule bill that passed in Westminster in September 1914 but was suspended for the duration of the war would have led, in the fullness of a few more years, to the complete

---

[28] Ibid., 10.
[29] Jacques Derrida, *Politics of Friendship*, trans. George Collins (London, 1997), 119.
[30] Carl Schmitt, *The Concept of the Political*, trans. George Schwab (New Brunswick, NJ, 1976), 19, 26.

independence of Ireland. I doubt it. I cannot regret that Pearse and his companions acted as they did and when they did, without anything resembling a mandate. Revolutions hardly ever have a mandate. What Pearse had – and justly claimed – was the authority of understanding Irish history and tradition as a long travail issuing in revolution by force of logic and desire. The fact that previous revolutions failed only made it more urgent that this latest one succeed. It is difficult to deny to Pearse the right to his own understanding, which was so much more convinced than anyone else's. Some students of Easter Week have wondered how the Rising would have turned out if it had been led by Connolly rather than by Pearse; would Ireland have turned towards European Socialism for its identity? I don't think it would. Socialism, indeed Marxism in any of its forms, needs, if it is to have a chance of thriving, an industrial society and the whole concatenation of factories and trade unions. Ireland has never had an Industrial Revolution, except for a brief period in Belfast and the Lagan Valley. Connolly understood this, and eventually committed himself – as Constance Markiewicz and other feminist leaders did – to the separatist movement under Pearse's leadership. But I feel some misgiving when I reflect that one of the main consequences of Pearse's being the leader of the Rising was the identification of nationalism and Catholicism, after more than a hundred years in which most of the leaders of nationalism were Protestants. The continuity of Pearse, Cosgrave, and de Valera meant that, in practice, Irish politics would be deduced – to the scandal of many Catholics, let me say – from Roman Catholic theology, a procedure from which the institutions of both church and state have inevitably suffered, as in the debacle of the Mother and Child Scheme of 1951.

Pearse could not have foreseen the consequences of the Easter Rising: the assembly of the first Dáil Éireann in January 1919, the British Government of Ireland Act of 1920 that established Northern Ireland and guaranteed its part in the United Kingdom, the Articles of Agreement between Britain and Ireland in 1921, the ratification of those articles by Dáil Éireann in 1922, the Constitution of the same year, the Civil War, the defeat of de Valera's republicans, the victory of his Fianna Fáil party in 1932, the new Constitution of 1937, and the declaration of the Irish Republic in 1948, an entity recognized by the United Kingdom in 1949. It is sometimes maintained by disaffected nationalists that this sequence of events has merely extended British colonial rule in Ireland under the guise of independence. Such critics point out that Ireland has adopted most of its administrative institutions from the United Kingdom and has not radically changed the disposition of power and wealth among the social classes. Yeats anticipated this expression of disappointment:

> Parnell came down the road, he said to a cheering man:
> 'Ireland shall get her freedom and you still break stone.'
>
> (*CP*, 309)

Ireland has taken over from the United Kingdom most of its arrangements for the conduct of law: a two-tier system of government, a similar police force, a system of class formations favourable to the middle and upper-middle classes, much the same arrangements in economics, banking, and investment. I am not convinced that this decision on the part of the Free State and later governments has been either an error or a crime.

Besides, it is a fact of inescapable significance that since 1922 Ireland – most of it, twenty-six of the thirty-two counties – has been governed by Irish men and women and is otherwise subject only to the institutions the Irish people have chosen to join, notably the European Union. That makes such a difference that I am content to put up with every defect in the government of Ireland, even beyond the third generation. Perusal of Gramsci's *Prison Notebooks*, Fanon's *The Wretched of the Earth*, and later work by Benedict Anderson, Edward Said, Partha Chatterjee, and Homi Bhabha has not weakened my resolve in that respect. I deplore the follies and corruptions of successive Irish governments: a misguided policy on the Irish language, a futile economic war between Ireland and England in the 1930s, meanness of spirit regarding the censorship of books and films, the confounding of politics and religion, the bad faith of governments on the question of Northern Ireland, the greed of Charles J. Haughey and other politicians. But I do not regret that de Valera's Ireland stayed neutral in the Second World War or that it has chosen – at least for the present – to stay out of NATO and to maintain its independent judgement, at least occasionally, in the European Union and the United Nations.

What I most deplore is the habit of Irish governments to suppress the republican tradition in practice while paying lip-service to it on the standard anniversaries. I understand that the Free State government had its hands full: it had to set up a working system of administration, entailing arrangements in matters of law, agriculture, education, economic development, transportation, and so forth. It had to deal with the aftermath of a civil war, continued violence, assassinations. But I cannot believe that the execution of republican prisoners, even for crimes of murder, was justified. What do you do with your gunmen when the revolution is over? Long-term imprisonment would have been a just response. I concede that in such circumstances the Free State government could not have been expected to bring patient and imaginative consideration to these questions: What should we do with the separatist passions we ourselves felt and acted upon a few years ago; and how are we to comport ourselves in relation to the United Kingdom and, more particularly, to those in Northern Ireland who would take up arms rather than make common cause with us?

De Valera had less excuse than Cosgrave for doing nothing. The institutions of the state were more settled, though not entirely to his satisfaction. By 1937, after five years in power, he was in a position to bring forward a new Constitution to replace the one enacted by the Free State with effect from 6 December 1922, and to have it pass. It is clear that he tried to respect the republican tradition by making a distinction between the nation, the matter of the first three Articles of the Constitution, and the state, the matter of Articles 4 to 11. The Preamble pays tribute to the Irish people and their 'unremitting struggle to regain the rightful independence of our Nation'. Article 2 declares that 'the national territory consists of the whole island of Ireland, its islands and the territorial seas'. Article 3 begins 'Pending the re-integration of the national territory', but then goes on to accept that the jurisdiction of the parliament and government extends only to the twenty-six counties established as subject to the laws of the Irish Free State. These provisions have weathered many disputes in law, including a dissenting judgment in *Russell* v. *Fanning* (1988) in which Justice Hederman said that the reunification of the national territory is

> by the provisions of the Preamble to the Constitution and of Article 3 of the Constitution a constitutional imperative and not one the pursuit or non-pursuit of which is within the discretion of the government or any organ of the state.[31]

This view was later endorsed by the Supreme Court in *McGimpsey* v. *Ireland* (1990) interpreting Hederman as saying that the reunification of the national territory is a constitutional imperative rather than a policy to be pursued or not according to the wishes of the government that happens to be in power. But the fact is that no government since 1937 has in any consistent degree obeyed the instruction. Gerry Adams is the only politician who has continued to speak of 'the constitutional imperative of pursuing Irish unity'.[32] The Good Friday Agreement has silenced him,

---

[31] J. M. Kelly, *The Irish Constitution*, ed. Gerard Hogan and Gerry Whyte, 3rd ed. (London, 1994), 6.
[32] Gerry Adams, 'We Have No Exit Strategy', *Ireland on Sunday*, 8 March 1998, 3.

too: he has settled, however sadly, for the permanent existence of Northern Ireland as a constituent of the United Kingdom. De Valera accepted, after 1932, that there was nothing he could do to get rid of Partition. He continued to bring the issue up in discussions with the British government in 1932, 1936, 1938, and later years. But the Anglo-Irish Agreement, in April 1938, promised the northern parliament, yet again, that it would never be separated from the United Kingdom. The part that Northern Ireland played – and suffered – in the Second World War was a further bond of loyalty to the United Kingdom, a fact embodied in the Ireland Act of 1949. De Valera gave up the ghost of Irish unity in 1938, though he continued to keep the aspiration notionally alive. He regarded it as the most acute tragedy of his life that he had failed to bring Partition to a peaceful end.[33]

One of the consequences of de Valera's dismal belief, as early as 1938, that he could do nothing to bring about Irish unity was the handing over of republican conviction, in effect, to the Irish Republican Army (IRA), especially in the years of the war, and the establishing of a new republican party, Sean MacBride's Clann na Poblachta, in time to contest the general election in January 1948. In 1957, when de Valera took up his last administration, the Northern Ireland parliament and the single-mindedness of Unionist zeal for the union of the United Kingdom and Northern Ireland seemed to be scripted in stone. Governments in Dublin could yearn and make diminished noise on the appropriate public occasions, but they soon gave up even imagining a united Ireland. Until the Northern Ireland Civil Rights Association started protesting in the North in 1968, with violent consequences for several years, every Irish government regarded the question of Northern Ireland as beyond its reach: it was, in practice, Britain's business. As a result, no government seriously tried to imagine how republican sentiments and desires, either in the North or the South, might be acknowledged. This situation was not changed by the Sunningdale Agreement of December 1973, the Anglo-Irish Agreement of 15 November 1985, the Downing Street Declaration, the Framework Document, and the Good Friday Agreement. None of these has even committed itself to saying what 'a majority of the people of Northern Ireland' means. Does it mean 51 per cent? Not at all. These documents are repugnant to a few Unionists; they should also be repugnant to nationalists, because they give Unionists a veto on every proposal that might lead, in however distant a future, to a united Ireland. As a further consequence

---

[33] Cf. John Bowman, *De Valera and the Ulster Question 1917–1973* (Oxford, 1982).

of this neglect, over a period of forty years, the leaders of Sinn Féin are in a position to claim – with some justification – that they, rather than the government in Dublin, are the authentic guardians of the republican, separatist tradition.

As for my own sentiments, I remain a nationalist, but I think it most unlikely that Unionists in the North will ever be persuaded to make common cause with the South. Ian Paisley, David Trimble, Peter Robinson, and their ancestors have been in the North for 370 years; they still think of themselves as British rather than as Irish. Perhaps de Valera and his associates could have done more to persuade them to sink their differences with us in a united Ireland. A few political commentators have argued that unity, according to some definition of it, is logically inescapable. I hope so. In the meantime, I do not condone a single act of bloodshed, nor do I think that the social conditions in Northern Ireland, wounding to Catholics as they have been, have ever justified the taking up of arms. At the same time, the desires embodied in the republican tradition cannot be merely suppressed, any more justly or effectively than loyalist desires which have a strong historical right to persist.

I have referred to bad faith on the part of Irish governments and especially of de Valera's administrations. But I do not share the common view, represented accurately enough by Neil Jordan's film *Michael Collins*, that de Valera was a sinister figure, a murderous angel. He was a devout Catholic, something of a scholar, a teacher, a leader, ardent in the cause of the Irish language and the unity of Ireland. But he was also spiritually constricted, such that he determined to express his love of Ireland even if it entailed repressing its citizens. It was hard to feel alive and at ease in the country he governed. Not surprisingly, many Irish writers deplored the narrowness of de Valera's Ireland, its joylessness. I have in mind particularly Sean O'Faolain, Frank O'Connor, Austin Clarke, Flann O'Brien, Elizabeth Bowen, and Kate O'Brien. But a state is always disappointing, especially one that has issued from a high rhetoric of race and nation. It is bound to incur the sardonic note of disillusion. Think of the state of Israel, the grand hopes of its setting forth in the years before and after 1948, the heartbreak of its racial history, and now the degree to which Netanyahu's Israel has become a state like any other. Ireland, too: the discrepancy between the race divined through its myths, the nation it was summoned and supposed to become, and the state it became is hard to be patient with, subject to the consideration that at least it is independent in part and a feasible place, on the whole, in which to live. It does not own any nuclear or hydrogen bombs or germ weapons. That's something worth making a note of. But it could have been a better country. In 'Parnell's Funeral' (1933), Yeats wrote:

> The rest I pass, one sentence I unsay
> Had de Valera eaten Parnell's heart
> No loose-lipped demagogue had won the day.
>
> (*CP*, 276)

I don't think of de Valera as a loose-lipped demagogue – he was tight-lipped to a fault. But I respond to Yeats's motif in later lines, according to which one eats the heart of a dead man to acquire his qualities.[34] No Irish leader has eaten Parnell's heart or imagined what form a politics would take that honoured Swift and Parnell.

But 'Parnell's Funeral' was not Yeats's last word on politics, race, nation, and state. I will end with a reference to two literary episodes in 1938. In that year Samuel Beckett published his first novel, *Murphy*. The fourth chapter is set, briefly, in the General Post Office in Dublin, Pearse's chosen place for the Rising and, outside, for the Proclamation of the Republic. Neary is contemplating from behind the statue of Cuchulain, Oliver Shepherd's work:

> Neary had bared his head, as though the holy ground meant something to him. Suddenly he flung aside his hat, sprang forward, seized the dying hero by the thighs and began to dash his head against his buttocks, such as they are.

A policeman approaches, but one Wylie, a former pupil of Neary's, leads Neary off to the exit. When the policeman shouts to them, Wylie says: 'John o' God's. Hundred per cent harmless ... Stillorgan ... Not Dundrum.'[35] That is: a nursing home for mentally ill patients, not an asylum for the criminally insane.

Beckett wrote *Murphy* between August 1936 and June 1938. I have no evidence that Yeats read the novel then or later. We are dealing with a coincidence. In April 1938 he wrote one of his last poems, 'The Statues', which is based on a conviction he arrived at by reading Adolf Furtwangler and other historians of art:

> There are moments when I am certain that art must once again accept those Greek proportions which carry into plastic art the Pythagorean numbers,

---

[34] Peter Ure has traced this motif to Sordello da Goito's lament on the death of Sir Blancatz, a poem translated in free verse by Ezra Pound in *The Spirit of Romance*; cf. Ure, *Yeats and Anglo-Irish Literature*, ed. C. J. Rawson (Liverpool, 1974), 130–32.

[35] Samuel Beckett, *Murphy* (London, 1969; reprint of 1938 ed.), 33.

those faces which are divine because all there is empty and measured.
Europe was not born when Greek galleys defeated the Persian hordes at
Salamis, but when the Doric studios sent out those broad-backed marble
statues against the multiform, vague, expressive Asiatic sea, they gave to the
sexual instinct of Europe its goal, its fixed type. (*Exp.*, 451)

Yeats asks, in the last stanza of 'The Statues':

> When Pearse summoned Cuchulain to his side,
> What stalked through the Post Office?
> What intellect,
> What calculation, number, measurement, replied?
>
> > (*CP*, 323)

Pearse revered the name and legendary bearing of Cuchulain only less
devoutly than the more ascertainable memory of Columcille, one of the
three patron saints of Ireland. Summoning is what Yeats is doing, too, in
this poem as in 'Parnell's Funeral'; it is the most typical act of his later
poems. 'Sect' is his word now for the earlier 'race' as he bodies forth Pearse
the representative Irish figure and opposes him to the filthy modern tide of
democracy, and opposes Greek sculptural form – as in Phidias – to Asiatic
formlessness. In several of these later poems Yeats deduces a politics from
an aesthetic, more particularly from the history of sculpture. The Pythag-
orean theory of numbers is supposed to have made possible not only
Phidias but Michelangelo and a corresponding praxis of great men. Yeats's
pamphlet *On the Boiler* gives some theory in favour of the politics and is
chiefly to be read as indicating not what the poems mean but how close
Yeats was, in 1938, to the end of his tether. His talk of 'rule of kindred' is
noxious. In the poems it hardly matters, because there it is merely part of
an elaborate mixture of allusions and invocations: it is to be valued mainly
for its enabling the poet to achieve his distinctive, desperately driven tone,
his personal sense of the world rather than the world as it might appear to
other people. I construe the violence of the last poems as a sign of rage and
desperation. He hoped against hope that the Irish people would resist the
claims of democracy and climb to 'our proper dark', the same darkness of
subjectivity and transformation in which he found Swift and Parnell.

Yeats knew that Ireland would have nothing to do with it, and would
not take pains to understand what he was saying. Modern Irish politics is a
politics of the same, not a politics of difference. Many Irish people have
grown tired of being told that they are interesting beyond their numbers,
or that the trajectory from race through nation to state has made them
distinguished among their European associates. They want to be the same

as everyone else, the same as England to begin with and as the United States later on. It is their right. But only with misgiving: there are other values, which we advert to when we murmur name upon name – Davis, Parnell, Yeats, Hyde, Synge.[36]

[36] Originally delivered as the 1997–98 Parnell Lecture, this essay appeared in *Yeats and the Nineties* (ed. Warwick Gould; *Yeats Annual* 16 [2001]) and in revised form in Donoghue's *Irish Essays* (Cambridge, 2011).

CHAPTER 5

Parnell's Other Ireland
Irish Religion in 1891

Raymond Gillespie

Charles Stewart Parnell died in Brighton on 6 October 1891. His political legacy was to be a deeply contested one resulting in the fragmentation of the Parliamentary Party and a schism between the Catholic Church and some nationalist politicians that shaped Irish political life up to the eve of the First World War. The world that Parnell left, and which he had in part created, was recorded and atomized some six months before his death when, on the night of 5 April 1891, census enumerators recorded the names and social and cultural characteristics of the 4.7 million people on the island of Ireland.[1] The practice of taking a census of the Irish population was by then well established. The methodology, created by Sir William Wilde for the 1841 census, was, by 1891, well tried and many of the initial difficulties had been resolved. The main census return (form A) differed little from earlier census forms asking the head of each household to list the names of the inhabitants of the house, their relationship to the head of the family, religious profession, education (as measured by their ability to read and write), age, sex, occupation, marital status, birthplace, ability to speak the Irish language, and whether they had any infirmities and, if so, what they were. Should the householder be illiterate or unable to understand the form the enumerator was there to assist.[2]

Unfortunately, the original returns have not survived so it is not possible to retrieve Parnell's census form with the details of his household; but there is no reason to think that completing the form would have posed any

---

[1] *Census of Ireland, 1891, Part i: Area, Houses and Population; Also the Ages, Civil or Conjugal Condition, Occupations, Birthplaces, Religion and Education of the People for Each County*, vol. i, *Province of Leinster* [C6515], H.C. 1890–1, xcv; vol. ii *Province of Munster* [C6567], H.C. 1892, xci; vol. iii, *Province of Ulster* [C 6626], H.C. 1892, xcii; vol. iv, *Province of Connacht* [C6685], H.C. 1892, xciii. All 1891 data for this essay are taken from this source unless otherwise stated.

[2] A sample form is reproduced in *Census of Ireland, 1891, Part ii: General Report with Illustrative Maps and Diagrams, Tables and Appendix* [C6780], H.C. 1892, xc, p. 549. The method of taking the census is described on pp. 1–2 of this report.

96

difficulties for him. Only one question might have raised eyebrows: that of religion. Such a question had been included in the Irish, and indeed the English, census since 1861 but had not provoked any antagonism.[3] Indeed, of the 4.7 million people who returned the 1891 census form, only 871 refused to answer the question on religion, the bulk of those coming from Ulster with a mere thirty in Connacht refusing to answer. However, unlike literacy, marital status, or occupation, which are readily measurable, religion is a complex idea embracing beliefs about the super-natural, acting as a marker of identity, and determining local institutional affiliations with their associated sociability. This complexity is reflected on the census form in the long note at the head of the column for religious profession asking for precision in description, preferably the use of a denominational label. Parnell's case, however, was an example of the problems that this could create. There is little reason to doubt that he would have entered 'Church of Ireland' in this column.[4] He was, after all, a baptized member of that church. He served on the parish vestry and presumably attended services occasionally when he was in Rathdrum. However, those who knew him painted a rather different picture of Parnell's relationship with religion. Timothy Healy, probably his closest political ally, confided that Parnell's 'religious views tended towards those of an uncle who was a "Plymouth Brother". Ignorant as I was of the tenets of that creed, I asked him to enlighten me, but he could not do so. He said Paley's *Evidences of Christianity* upset his faith.'[5] Parnell's mistress, Katharine O'Shea, who encountered another aspect of him, described Parnell as having

> no religious conviction of creed or dogma ... he personally believed in a vast or universal law of 'attraction' of which the elemental forces of Nature were part and the whole of which tended towards some unknown and unknowable end, in the immense distant periods of time ... of deist 'cause' and predestined end he was convinced though he believed their attributes to be unknown and unknowable.[6]

In some ways Parnell's complex belief system is a reflection of his family background. As his comments to Healy suggest, while a nominal Anglican and perhaps also a deist he was also deeply influenced by his family

---

[3] For the question, see Malcolm Macourt, *Counting the People of God? The Census of Population and the Church of Ireland* (Dublin, 2008), 13–17, 22.
[4] For Parnell's views on religion, see Pauric Travers, 'Parnell and Religion', in *Parnell Reconsidered*, ed Pauric Travers and Donal McCartney (Dublin, 2010), 61–75.
[5] T. M. Healy, *Letters and Leaders of My Day* (London, [1929]), 367.
[6] Katharine O'Shea, *The Uncrowned King of Ireland* (reprint, Dublin, 2005), 274.

background and the ideas of John Nelson Darby and his Plymouth Brethren movement. This group had originated in the evangelical circle surrounding Lady Powerscourt in Wicklow in the 1830s and dabbled in apocalyptic ideas of the second coming, drawing on evangelical fears of Daniel O'Connell's growing political support.[7] By the end of the nineteenth century they had grown considerably in size, with more than 2,000 Irish adherents in 1891. They were a significant presence, and the standard work on religious groups in the late nineteenth century described them as a 'rather widely spread and growing sect' in which 'there is much attraction for the leisurely class of what may be called semi-professional society which is found in towns inhabited by retired officers etc. . . . and the sect is largely recruited from this class of persons'.[8] Parnell's religious ideas were clearly more complex than any entry on a census form might suggest.

This disjuncture between confessional allegiance and belief in the case of Parnell was not unusual in modern Ireland and in some cases could be dramatic. Consider, for example, the case of Kathleen Goligher. Kathleen, one of four daughters and a son, had been born in Londonderry in June 1898, the daughter of a Donegal shirt cutter and a Tyrone woman. By 1901 the family had moved to Balfour Avenue in Belfast and by 1911 they were living in Artana Street in the Cromac ward of the city. The family, according to the census, was solidly Presbyterian. However, when William J. Crawford, a lecturer in mechanical engineering in the Belfast Technical Institute, met Kathleen in 1914 it was as a spiritualist medium. Indeed, according to Crawford all the members of the family were mediums, well versed in trance speaking, automatic writing, and table movements, skills that they had inherited from their mother. There was no doubt in Crawford's mind that 'the whole family look upon Spiritualism as their religion. They attend no church other than the Spiritualistic but they are devoted in their attention to that.'[9] It seems clear that confessional allegiance to Presbyterianism, for census purposes at least, did not align with the beliefs held by the Goligher family. We should not regard the Goligher case as unusual. Spiritualism barely featured as a religious

[7] For a portrait of that world, see D. H. Akenson, *Discovering the End of Time: Irish Evangelicals in the Age of Daniel O'Connell* (Montreal, 2016), and for other apocalyptic figures, see Myrtle Hill, *The Time of the End: Millenarian Beliefs in Ulster* (Belfast, 2001), esp. 33–47.

[8] John Henry Blunt, *Dictionary of Sects, Heresies, Ecclesiastical Parties and Schools of Religious Thought* (London, 1874), 433.

[9] W. J. Crawford, *The Reality of Psychic Phenomena: Raps, Levitations Etc.* (London, 1919), esp. 1–4; National Archives of Ireland, 1911 census, Belfast, Cromac Ward, Artana Street. Crawford's papers on Goligher are among the papers of the Society for Psychical Research, now in Cambridge University Library.

category in the Ulster part of the 1901 and 1911 censuses but that did not prevent more than 100 members of the Belfast Christian Spiritualist Association turning up at a funeral service in Belfast City Cemetery in July 1926, some with cameras trying to take photographs of 'the spirits of the departed friends of those around the grave'.[10] Again in Dublin some of the more esoteric elements of spiritualism were well established by the late nineteenth century. The Dublin Heremetic Society was founded in 1885, and the Dublin lodge of the Theosophical Society was established the following year by Charles Johnston, a former candidate for the Church of Ireland ministry.[11] Whatever beliefs that those who adhered to those bodies held, like the Golighers, they had difficulties in describing themselves outside the normal confessional framework. Despite the institutional framework, the 1891 census recorded only two spiritualists and two Theosophists in all of Leinster (including Dublin).

Such problems of aligning confessional allegiance with belief may seem to be insoluble or at times marginal and insignificant, but for some they were real. Esoteric beliefs might lurk under the most conventional of disguises. Some of Parnell's own circle came closer to that unorthodox supernatural world than they may have liked. In July 1898 Rose Downey, an Irish-American emigrant, visited the St Louis coroner's office to report that her daughter-in-law, Mary Downey, who had arrived in America three years previously, accused her of bewitching her grandson to death. She claimed to be the sister of William O'Brien, the Parnellite MP at whose wedding Parnell had been the best man.[12] Again the old Fenian and Parnellite supporter, John O'Leary, was so shocked by the dabbling of his acolyte, W. B. Yeats, in the world of the supernatural that he wrote him a strongly worded letter, provoking an equally trenchant reply from Yeats about the importance of magic in his life.[13] However, it is not necessary to examine such dramatic examples of active involvement with the supernatural to detect the difficulties in interpreting the religious returns from the census. Esoteric ideas such as those of the British Israelites or Freemasonry happily survived within a more formal confessional context. Indeed, in 1891 one of the council members of the British Israel Association in London was Denis Hanna, Church of Ireland rector of Tipperary, and

[10] *Belfast Newsletter*, 19 Aug. 1926; *Irish Independent*, 28 July 1926.
[11] R. F. Foster, *W. B. Yeats: A Life*, vol. 1: *The Apprentice Mage, 1865–1914* (Oxford, 1997), 45–48, 51.
[12] Owen Davies, *America Bewitched: The Story of Witchcraft after Salem* (Oxford, 2013), 77.
[13] Foster, *W. B. Yeats*, 120–21.

the leading authority within Ireland on ghost stories and demonology was St John D. Seymour, archdeacon of Cashel.[14]

We can begin to understand the way that people in Parnell's Ireland thought about themselves and their religion through two sometimes competing ideas: believing and belonging. For some religious affiliation was more an expression of belonging, a cultural or political affiliation, rather than belief. Equations between political positions and confessions in Parnell's Ireland were one indication of that. It was assumed that Catholics were automatically nationalists, and Protestants of various hues could not be regarded as such.[15] There were other indications that some regarded churches as cultural and social bodies at least as much as they were religious ones. In the case of the Church of Ireland, comparison of the returns of church membership from the census forms for Dublin with the entries for congregational size in the preacher's books of parishes show significant differences between those who simply regarded themselves as part of that Church and those who actively participated in religious worship on a Sunday. In middle-class Dublin in the 1860s, perhaps about 60 per cent of the Church of Ireland population attended church on a Sunday, while in more working-class areas that figure fell to about 35 per cent. These figures were rather higher than in larger English industrial cities and have been at least partially explained by the defensive mindset of a minority of Church of Ireland population in a largely Catholic city.[16] Outside Dublin the situation may have been rather similar. In Arklow, near Parnell's own Wicklow home, some 727 individuals returned themselves as Church of Ireland on the 1891 census form, yet average weekly worshipers came to only 423 across that year and communicants only thirty-one in the low-church Church of Ireland community. There were some grounds for optimism since these attendance figures were significantly higher than those for the census years of 1871 and 1881.[17] For at least some of these non-attenders at worship on Sunday, a confessional statement on a census form was not a statement of belief but a way of describing who one was. In slightly differing ways some of those who filled in census forms made statements about belonging. In the Leinster census return, twenty-six people described themselves as being

---

[14] On the British Israelites in Ireland, see Mairéad Carew, *Tara and the Ark of the Covenant* (Dublin, 2003).

[15] For such attitudes for a slightly later period, see Heather K. Crawford, *Outside the Glow: Protestants and Irishness in Independent Ireland* (Dublin, 2010).

[16] John Crawford, *The Church of Ireland in Victorian Dublin* (Dublin, 2005), 74, 80.

[17] Jim Rees, *The Fishery of Arklow, 1800–1952* (Dublin, 2008), 33.

'Christians – Merrion Hall'. These few souls defined themselves not by confession but by the congregation to which they belonged. Merrion Hall in Dublin was opened in 1863 as an evangelical outreach centre but in 1886 was acquired by some Dublin Brethren who had been meeting there almost since it had been established.[18] It seems highly likely that those who returned themselves as adherents of Merrion Hall might also be classified as Brethren, but their sense of belonging to one congregation or local group led them to record it as the place to which they belonged rather than indicating a bare denomination.

Against this sense of belonging to a local group, either confessionally or congregationally, the 1891 returns recorded that many individuals' religious sense was underpinned by a strong, though sometimes poorly articulated, set of beliefs. Individuals grappling with the census form often struggled to articulate a set of beliefs that they felt were not expressed in any denominational creed. Thus, in Ulster, form fillers declared that they were a 'Saint in Christ Jesus meeting with others of like profession' (unfortunately, only one person of this persuasion was returned, making a meeting difficult), a 'Christian in separation from the denomination', or that 'we belong to the Lord and worship him with Christian brethren' or 'Church of the First Born whose names are written in Heaven'. Indeed, across the 1891 census return there was a significant minority who wished to stress their nondenominational status, relying for a spiritual side to their nature on their beliefs rather than an organizational badge of belonging. Such statements are evidence that religious ideas, though sometimes not articulated in a philosophically discussable system, were important to those who held them. Ten years after the 1891 census, William James would wrestle with these ideas in his Gifford Lectures that became his *The Varieties of Religious Experience* (1902). For James, religion came in two varieties. The first was the religion of the 'ordinary religious believer' whose 'religion has been made for him by others, communicated by tradition, determined to fixed forms by imitation and retained by habit', in short, religion as badge of belonging to a group. For James as a psychologist this held little interest. He wanted to penetrate behind this to the 'original experiences' which were 'an acute fever' causing people to live on the margins of social acceptability. At times they 'presented all sorts of peculiarities which are ordinarily classed as pathological' that 'have helped to give them their religious authority and influence', in short,

[18] Steven C. Smyrl, *Dictionary of Dublin Dissent: Dublin's Protestant Dissenting Meeting Houses, 1660–1920* (Dublin, 2009), 258–59.

people driven by their vision and belief.[19] In individuals there were shifts in the balance between the importance of custom and religious experience over time. The success of the 1859 revival, for instance, validated the importance of experience over custom and institutions and often provided the confidence that allowed lay people to question religious structures and institutions such as clergy. The disputes between the Methodist maternal grandmother and the father of the Ulster poet John Hewitt and the clergy over doctrine and other matters led to one generation of the family not being baptized.[20] The motives of those who completed the religion question on census night in April 1891 do not fall into two neat categories of custom and experience. Both ideas could motivate one individual and sometimes in different combinations. It is possible to see something of this at work in the comments of Robert Harbinson growing up in Belfast in the 1930s and Max Wright's memoir of his relations with the Brethren movement in Ulster in the early twentieth century.[21] Given the Brethren's lack of centralized organization and the absence of a professional ministry, the church was defined by a sense of an exclusivity of belief and a set of rituals of inclusion and exclusion, thus defining who might belong to the group. Central to the experience of belief was the conversion experience, the testimony, the baptism, and the continual awareness of the end of time and the second coming of Christ. This articulation of vivid religious experience was controlled by a series of rituals that had been built up over time. Ways of preaching, listening, and singing were all central to the Brethren, and it is no accident that long after he had left the movement Max Wright would wonder, '[W]hy so many years later do so many of these mindless ditties [Brethren hymns] complete with their tunes still rattle about my head?' Singing combined believing and belonging and acted as a ritual of inclusion for the group (and by doing so created boundaries with a wider world) as well as expressing experienced faith.

This broad framework of a balancing of belief and belonging allows us to use the returns of religious affiliation from the 1891 census, within the limits of confessional definitions, to sketch the main outlines of religion in Parnell's Ireland. Statistically, the dominant religious group was Roman Catholicism, which, according to the 1891 census, claimed the allegiance

---

[19] William James, *The Varieties of Religious Experience* (Edinburgh, 1902), 6.

[20] On Hewitt's grandmother, see Barry Sloan, *Writers and Protestantism in the North of Ireland* (Dublin, 2000), 346 n. 20, and for his father, see W. J. McCormack, *Northman: John Hewitt, 1907–98* (Oxford, 2015), 15–16.

[21] Max Wright, *Told in Gath* (Belfast, 1990). The allusion is to 2 Samuel 1:20; Robert Harbinson, *No Surrender: An Ulster Childhood* (Belfast, 1960; reprint, 1987), 54–57, 61, 65–67, 73–74.

of 75.4 per cent of the Irish population with its greatest concentrations in the west and south-east of the country.[22] Clearly, within this area there were significant variations in how this devotion manifested itself. Fifty years earlier, for example, there was a dramatic disparity between the frequency of Mass attendance in south-east Ireland and attendance in north and west Ireland.[23] While religious practice may have converged somewhat by the time of the 1891 census, mainly due to the efforts of Cardinal Paul Cullen's Romanization and standardization of the Irish Catholic Church, dramatic variations in devotional practices still remained. A massive church building programme in the late nineteenth century demonstrated both the tenacity with which the poor supported this cause and the organizational sophistication that underpinned it. This was a world that Parnell understood. At the elite level he knew the organization of Catholicism and its main managers, and at a popular level his tenants provided a model that informed him of the popular understanding of belief.[24]

The second largest religious grouping from the 1891 census were the 12.7 per cent (or just over 600,000) who described themselves as members of the Church of Ireland. While members of the Church of Ireland could be found across the island, their numbers were lowest in Connacht and the west and strongest in Ulster and Leinster (especially Parnell's Wicklow) and to a lesser extent in the main cities of Dublin and Cork. Some may have feared their position under threat, and the disestablishment of the Church in 1871 suggested that. However, there were more positive signs. Significant church-building campaigns, not least in the dramatic rebuilding of the cathedrals of Christ Church in Dublin, St Finbarr's in Cork, and St Brigid's in Kildare, point to a church prepared to invest in its future. Parish life in Dublin and elsewhere was lively, and in some places parishes were enlivened by the passage of control to the laity after disestablishment. In places such as Arklow and in some Dublin parishes, the Church of Ireland population was growing at parish level.[25] At national level the story was less sanguine. Nationally, in 1891 the Church of Ireland population was down 5 per cent on what it had been a decade earlier. This masks

---

[22] See the maps in Ian Gregory et al., *Troubled Geographies: A Spatial History of Religion and Society in Ireland* (Bloomington, 2013), 76.

[23] David Miller, 'Mass Attendance in Ireland in 1834', in *Piety and Power in Ireland, 1760–1960: Essays in Honour of Emmet Larkin*, ed. Stewart Brown and David Miller (Belfast, 2000), 172–73.

[24] C. J. Woods, 'Parnell and the Catholic Church', in *Parnell in Perspective*, ed. D. G. Boyce and Alan O'Day (London, 1991), 9–37.

[25] Rees, *The Fishery of Arklow*, 33.

significant variations across the country. In the late nineteenth century, only Belfast and Dublin saw significant growth in the Church of Ireland population, while across the Irish midlands and Connacht emigration was taking its toll with falls of over 40 per cent in the Church of Ireland population over the period 1861–1911.[26] However, disestablishment had changed religious relations in a subtle way. Ideas of dissent and nonconformity had now been removed from Ireland's religious vocabulary, and within the Church of Ireland the laity were given a much enhanced influence in the church, especially in the control of parish life. It would take some time before these changes could be properly assimilated.

Close on the heels of the recently disestablished Church of Ireland was almost 10 per cent of the population that described itself as Presbyterian. These were concentrated almost exclusively in the nine counties of Ulster, Louth, and Dublin, with a small Presbyterian population in Cork. While in the 1850s the Presbyterians, free from the establishment connections of the Church of Ireland, had supported liberal reform, particularly the reform of tenant rights, they recoiled before Parnellite nationalism, fearing that any sort of Home Rule arrangement would result in a new establishment – that of Catholicism – that would impose a set of beliefs that many felt to be heretical and even anti-Christian. As one anti–Home Rule tract of 1887 addressed to the Presbyterian tenant farmers of north Antrim feared, 'his [Parnell's] reign of terror [might] trouble for a season our unhappy country'.[27] Moreover, since they were concentrated in the industrialized north-east, they also feared that economic policy in an independent Ireland would be dominated by agricultural interests and protectionist policies. [28]

These three large denominations together comprised almost 97 per cent of the Protestant population of Ireland, leaving the remainder to be split between some 55,500 Methodists and a roughly equal number of 'others'. These two groups had much in common. Neither had been established churches, like the Church of Ireland, nor aspired to be, like the Presbyterians. They were genuine dissenters. Equally significant was the fact that they managed to increase their numbers over the numbers recorded in the 1881 census, Methodists by a remarkable 13.6 per cent and the 'other' religious groups by a more modest 3.8 per cent. While in 1861 Methodists

---

[26] Gregory et al., *Troubled Geographies*, 79.
[27] J. B. McMinn, ed., *Against the Tide: A Calendar of the Papers of Rev. J. B. Armour, Irish Presbyterian Minister and Home Ruler* (Belfast, 1985), 201.
[28] For an examination of this across all the Protestant positions, see David Hempton and Myrtle Hill, *Evangelical Protestantism in Ulster Society, 1740–1890* (London, 1992), 161–87.

had comprised only 0.79 per cent of the population, that had grown to 1.18 per cent by 1891, and the 'other religious groups' had increased their share of the national population from 0.54 per cent to 1.21 per cent. In this they outperformed all other denominations. Methodist numbers had always proved to be volatile largely because of Methodism's evangelical nature, with sudden surges in numbers following revival campaigns and an equally sudden fall-off in adherents as enthusiasm waned. Like Presbyterianism it was not a religious body that Parnell or his supporters would have known or had much sympathy with. It had, for instance, strong connections with the Orange Order, which certainly would not have been welcome in the nationalist circles in which Parnell moved.[29]

In some ways the most interesting religious groups are not the mainstream religious denominations of Parnell's Ireland but rather those groups who made up the 'other Ireland' of Parnell. The lists included in the 1891 census return of these groups were bewildering. Almost 300 groups to which those completing the census returns said they belonged were listed in the 'other' category. There was a significant scattering of atheists, Free Thinkers, secularists, and sceptics who amounted to just over a hundred, of whom almost 90 per cent were located in Ulster with its strong tradition of religious independence in which belief dominated belonging. Indeed, Ulster was the heartland of these 'other' groups, with seven of the nine census districts in which the 'other' group constituted more than 1 per cent of the population being located there. Not surprisingly, the large cities of Belfast and Dublin, where one might escape too much curiosity about one's beliefs, were prominent in this list. Leaving aside nonbelievers, most of the vast majority who declared a belief in God were Christians, though not all were. Inward migration, sometimes temporary and occasionally permanent, into larger cities had brought a diverse group of beliefs to Ireland. For instance, sailors whose ships docked in Ireland on census night were recorded in the census, and this probably explains the references in the Leinster returns to the Norwegian and Swedish churches as having adherents there. The largest and best-documented case of such immigration is the Jewish settlement in Dublin, comprising 1,135 out of a total Jewish population in Ireland of 1,779 in 1891, but they were not alone.[30] The census as a whole produced two

---

[29] David Fitzpatrick, 'Methodism and the Orange Order', in his *Descendancy: Irish Protestant Histories since 1795* (Cambridge, 2014), 78–104.

[30] Eugenio Biagini, 'Minorities', in *The Cambridge Social History of Modern Ireland*, ed. Eugenio Biagini and Mary Daly (Cambridge, 2017), 442–50.

Buddhists, three Hindus (two of whom were Brahmins), a Zoroastrian and three Muslims. Migration also brought various and exotic forms of Christianity to the country. Both Greek and Russian Orthodox were present, as were a range of European denominations. Particularly prominent were various forms of Swiss Protestants, nearly all of whom were women. As the general report on the census pointed out, more than half of the Swiss in Dublin were governesses, ladies' maids, or domestic servants, which would certainly explain the gender distribution of adherents to Swiss Protestantism in Dublin. The vast bulk of this 'other' group in the returns was made up of smaller but still substantial non-Catholic denominations such as Quakers, Unitarians, Congregationalists, Baptists, Brethren, Salvation Army, and various forms of Presbyterianism who had seceded from the main denomination such as the Covenanters and nonsubscribers. Congregationalists and Unitarians accounted for some 8,000 members each, reducing to 1,000 in the Salvation Army before moving down sharply into groups whose membership could be measured in tens. Of the 295 smaller denominations, only thirty-four could boast above twenty members; the remaining 261 could claim only a handful of adherents. It is sometimes difficult to know what to make of these very small groups, often comprising one or two members, who simply describe themselves as 'Christian', 'Saved', 'Christian follower', or 'Disciple of Christ'. For some, such bland descriptions may well have been attempts to adhere to the Christian consensus of nineteenth-century Ireland while having no active religious or denominational life. For others, as suggested above, such descriptions were attempts to make some sort of meaning out of the welter of religious experience that they encountered in many circumstances, such as evangelical street preaching, which could, and did, morph into religiously inspired political violence.[31]

Many of these smaller religious groupings had their origins outside Ireland. Some, such as the Quakers or Baptists, had been long established in Ireland as a result of migration in the seventeenth century and later. Others, who came from a denomination that was formally organized, had recently arrived in the country as part of a planned mission, supported and organized by the institution to which they belonged. In March 1834, for instance, the dedicated fieldworker of the Ordnance Survey John O'Donovan witnessed in the square at Moira, County Down, 'a venerable

---

[31] For examples, see Janice Holmes, 'The Role of Open Air Preaching in the Belfast Riots of 1857', *Proceedings of the Royal Irish Academy* 102 (2002): 47–66; Rees, *The Fishery of Arklow*, 33–34.

old man with a beard hanging down to the middle button of his waistcoat, repeating aloud one of the psalms of David'. At first O'Donovan thought that he was a Jew but he 'soon learned that he had abandoned the old cause of his tribe, and is now going about preaching the morality and doctrine of Jesus of Nazareth'.[32] In fact what O'Donovan had witnessed was a preaching tour by one of the prophets of John Wroe, a farmer and wool comber from near Leeds who had become a follower of a prophetess from an earlier generation, Joanna Southcott, who prophesied the birth of a new messiah. Wroe created the new sect of Christian Israelites that attempted to blend Christianity and Judaism with clear rules of dress and a requirement of circumcision. Internal disputes and scandals in the 1830s severely weakened the sect, but it survived to the present in Australia.[33] However, in June 1834 Wroe himself appeared in Belfast and set out on a preaching tour in north Down, and in Belfast the police had to be called out to protect him. There was probably a second preaching tour shortly afterwards, and during this preaching tour he issued a prophecy at Dromore. A Christian Israelite community appears to have been formed near Dromore, and a number of people wrote regularly to Wroe in the following years asking for interpretations of particularly difficult passages of Scripture and advice on the Second Coming.[34] By the time of the 1861 census, the preaching campaigns of thirty years earlier had borne fruit, for there were fifty-five Christian Israelites reported in the census in Ulster, nineteen of whom were in County Armagh. A further ten could be found in Belfast, eight in County Down, and a scattering in Monaghan and Tyrone. By 1891 the Ulster numbers had fallen to thirty-three, but the influence of the sect had spread, with four adherents in Leinster, probably in Dublin, and sixteen in Munster.

The Christian Israelites were not the only group from elsewhere who actively proselytized in Ireland. The Salvation Army, formed in England in the 1860s, had established some seventeen corps in Ireland by 1883 and returned 1,052 adherents in the 1891 census.[35] By 1891 the Mormons had

---

[32] Michael Herity, ed., *Ordnance Survey Letters: Down* (Dublin, 2001), 14.

[33] For Wroe, see Edward Green, *Prophet John Wroe: Virgins, Scandals and Visions* (Stroud, 2005), and J. F. C. Harrison, *Second Coming: Popular Millenarianism, 1740–1850* (London, 1979), esp. 138–52.

[34] Wroe's Irish venture and his Irish correspondents can be traced in *The Life and Journal of John Wroe with the Divine Communications Revealed by Him*, 5th ed., 3 vols. (Gravesend, 1861), most of the Irish material being in vol. 2.

[35] Glenn K. Horridge, *The Salvation Army: Origins and Early Days, 1865–1900* (Goldming, 1993), 38.

also established a small, but active, presence in the country.[36] The census reported forty-four Mormons in Ireland, although Mormon sources claimed fifty-four members in that year. However, to judge this in isolation would be a mistake. Mormon missionary activity in Ireland was well organized, and by 1891 the third Mormon mission to Ireland was well under way, having begun in 1884. The first, an overspill from the English mission, had lasted from 1840 to 1850 and the second from 1850 to 1867. The first mission, mainly concentrated in Ulster, peaked in 1842 with a relatively modest seventy-one members. With five missioners in the field at one point, there were considerable possibilities for making converts. However, attitudes to Mormonism in the middle of the nineteenth century were hostile and conversions consequently difficult. Of the handful of Irish converts whose backgrounds can be established, roughly half were artisans or working-class, while the others were middle-class. The established church proved a poor source of recruits, with Methodism and Presbyterianism being more fruitful hunting grounds.[37] Much of the work of this mission was undone by the migration of converts to the Mormon American settlement in Salt Lake City. The second mission branched out into Dublin from the Ulster base, with eight missionaries active in the peak year of 1857. That had generated 210 members in 1856. However, the third mission was the most successful, with some twenty-six missionaries active at its peak just before the First World War. By 1914 the Mormon church claimed 353 Irish members. Thus the 1891 membership figure, while apparently low, was only the beginning of an upswing in the denomination's fortunes. Even more impressive was the fact that baptisms outstripped deaths in every year, pointing to a community growing from within as well as by conversions. This was clearly a well-organized mission with committed elders who became involved in a number of aspects of Irish society. Samuel Kerr, for instance, first came to Ireland in 1854 as an elder on the Irish Mormon mission working in Down and Armagh. Sometime later he moved to Belfast where he met Frank Roney, the Presbyterian radical and Fenian. Roney was then working with Kerr in a foundry and he recruited him to the Fenian movement in which he became 'an active organizer' and attempted to convert other Protestants to Fenianism. Not content with this, Kerr became involved, with Roney,

---

[36] For what follows I have drawn on Brent A. Barlow, 'History of the Church of Jesus Christ of Latter-Day Saints in Ireland since 1840' (MA thesis, Brigham Young University, 1968). Most of the Mormons' own calculation of membership figures is in appendix 1 of that thesis.

[37] Malcolm R. Thorp, 'The Religious Backgrounds of Mormon Converts in Britain, 1837–52', *Journal of Mormon History* 4 (1977): 66.

in the early trade Union movement in Belfast through the moulders union.[38] The Mormon elders were clearly figures of determination backed by evangelical resources such as the Mormon Tract Society, established to produce printed material for the Irish mission; they clearly had an impact on late nineteenth-century Ireland.

Even where denominations were much less clearly structured than the Christian Israelites or the Mormons, the movement of key figures and groups could open up new missionary territory. The Brethren, one of the largest of the minor sects in Ireland with their origins in Parnell's Wicklow, were in an expansionary mode and as a result were most feared by other Protestant churches as competitors. As William Alexander, Church of Ireland bishop of Derry (and later archbishop of Armagh), observed in 1892, presumably having read the religious returns of the 1891 census, 'the hill up which our own little host must march is steep, and the hail beats on our faces. We hear the steady tramp of the serried ranks of Rome around us; the shout of the marauders of Plymouth [Brethren] rises as they . . . cut off a few stragglers'.[39] The Brethren movement was characterized by John Henry Blunt's 1874 *Dictionary of Sects, Heresies, Ecclesiastical Parties and Schools of Religious Thought* as having 'little organic unity, being broken up into many sections by differences of opinion arising from their "many men" ministry'. They had no ordained clergy, 'every "brother" and "sister" having a full right to "prophesy" or preach whenever he is moved to do so'. There was no centralized leadership.[40] Yet, despite this, Brethren assemblies were very effective in establishing new fields of endeavour and in generating converts, and in this the lack of a centralized structure may have helped by allowing flexibility of response to opportunity. The mechanism by which this happened is clear from the example of Belfast, recorded in the memoir of William Gilmore about the progress of the Brethren in the city.[41] According to Gilmore, in the middle of the 1880s there were three Brethren assemblies in Belfast, which had been preceded by tent preaching at Donegall Pass. Each of these meetings divided and spawned new meetings as some of the Brethren in one meeting simply decided to work in another area. Thus the origins of one of these early meetings, that based in Sandy Row, was the result of the efforts of R. M. Henry, a Church of

---

[38] Frank Roney, *An Autobiography*, ed. Ira B. Cross (Berkeley, 1931), 75, 151.
[39] William Alexander, *Verbum Crucis: Being Ten Sermons on the Mystery and the Words of the Cross* (London, 1892), 161.
[40] Blunt, *Dictionary*, 433.
[41] William Gilmore, *These Seventy Years, 1883–1953: Memoirs of Christian Life and Activity in Belfast* (Kilmarnock, [1954]).

Ireland clergyman and father of the artist Paul Henry, who left that church, became a Baptist pastor, and seceded there, also taking some of the congregation with him. He held meetings in Sandy Row Orange Hall and from that founded the Apsley Street Hall. From Apsley Street, which had open-air meetings on the Ormeau Road in south Belfast, 'some brethren thought they should go to the Ormeau Road and so they went and quite a number followed them', building a small wooden hall there. Again in East Belfast, Gilmore records there was a street of six houses called Campbell's Row, and 'some local brethren started a gospel work in one of the houses and a few people were converted'. They began to meet in Mountpottinger Orange Hall and from that developed Mourne Street Hall, which later grew into Albertbridge Road Hall. These were prompted not by theological splits or even formal missions, such as those organized by the Mormons, but simply by a natural process of creating new bodies, helped by the Brethren's lack of formal structure which allowed such natural evolution without secession from a formal organization.

Some of these smaller religious groupings arrived in Ireland not as a result of formal mission or even the movement of people with religious motivations but rather as the result of immigration for other reasons. The most prominent example of this was the Jewish population in Dublin.[42] In 1871, the census noted there were 285 Jews in Ireland; by 1891, Ireland's Jewish population had exploded to 1,779, with 1,135 in Dublin; by 1911 there were 5,148 in Ireland. Most of the newcomers were Litvaks from Russian Lithuania. The collective memory of the migration emphasizes the outbreaks of persecution and discriminatory legislation by the Russians; but Lithuania was almost pogrom-free, suggesting that the impact of these forces was more indirect than might appear. Most of the Irish settlers came from a relatively small cluster of villages and towns in Lithuania. It appears that they were unsettled by a fear of pogroms rather than actual persecution and an 'emigration mania' that set up a network of chain migration that brought the first settlers to England and then to Dublin. Once established there, the first settlers recruited friends, relatives, and former neighbours. What formed was a geographically cohesive community in the smaller streets around South Circular Road, an area that became known as 'Little Jerusalem'. This community remained remarkably stable for a long period before finally fragmenting

---

[42] For most of what follows, see Cormac Ó Gráda, *Jewish Ireland in the Age of Joyce: A Socioeconomic History* (Princeton, 2006).

under the pressures of suburbanization from the mid-twentieth century.[43] By 1892 the community had built a shul at Adelaide Road at the centre of this new world. School records suggest that in the 1890s this community was largely dominated by shoemakers, butchers, furniture dealers, and, above all, pedlars or drapers. In the following two decades it would diversify, with tailors, dealers, carpenters, and cabinet makers all appearing in the community, mostly self-employed.

The experience of being part of a small religious denomination is difficult to define and is perhaps best caught in memoirs such as Max Wright's *Told in Gath* and in fiction; but the 1891 census also captured some of the features of belonging to one of the smaller religious groups. Literacy figures, for example, point to them being highly literate. Only some 5 per cent of the 'other' groups could not read or write in 1891, about the same as the Presbyterians but lower than those of the Church of Ireland and very considerably lower than the 22 per cent reported as illiterate within Catholicism. Perhaps significantly, the lowest proportion of literates among the 'other' group was in Ulster at 86.7 per cent, while the highest was in Connacht at 92.8 per cent. If literacy rates were high, lunacy rates were not. Only twenty-one lunatics (about half in Ulster) were uncovered by the 1891 census among the 'other' denomination group despite the fears of 'religious melancholia' or 'religious enthusiasm' that some writers, such as William James, entertained of such people. Their numbers were no higher than those of Methodists in lunatic asylums. Although the 'other' denominations were 1.2 per cent of the total population, they comprised only 0.09 per cent of the total lunatic population, suggesting underrepresentation among the mad.

Literacy and sanity were useful attributes that allowed those from the 'other' religious denominations to make a living. They chose almost every occupation imaginable in a pattern similar to that followed by Methodists. The largest occupational group for men was farming with some 2,300 employed, while the linen trade came a close second with some 2,000 employed. However, men from the 'other' denominations could be found as civil servants, soldiers, physicians, merchants, commercial travellers, carpenters, shopkeepers, sailors, and labourers. Women from 'other' denominations equally went to work as schoolmistresses, grocers, shirt makers, dressmakers, and in the linen trades. If anything, those from 'other' denominations tended to gravitate towards towns and urban

---

[43] Stanley Waterman, 'Changing Residential Patterns of the Dublin Jewish Community', *Irish Geography* 14 (1981): 41–50.

employment rather more than the population at large, but that was not a marked trend. In general, there were few areas of human existence that those who adhered to smaller religious groups, or indeed any formal denomination, did not penetrate.

Parnell's Ireland was a more diverse and complex place than it might appear at first glance. The statistical dominance of a few confessional groups in the 1891 census conceals the presence of other diverse worlds of religious ideas and practice. It is true that many of these were small groups exercising little or no wider political influence or having no apparent national significance. However, such groups served as markers of belonging and provided a framework of beliefs that guided their adherents through a difficult and sometimes dangerous world. Just because these bodies were small does not mean that they were unimportant. As Parnell's brother, John Howard Parnell, recalled of Charles's obsession with superstitions, such as his fear of the colour green, 'although these superstitions may seem trivial, and even ridiculous, they certainly had a great influence on Charley's actions and sometimes even decided him at a critical turning point in his affairs'.[44] Historians in search of the ways that people in the past understood their worlds and tried to find their own salvation cannot afford to confuse the small with the unimportant.

[44] John Howard Parnell, *Charles Stewart Parnell: A Memoir* (London, [1914]), 267.

CHAPTER 6

Inside History
Storyteller Éamon a Búrc and the 'Little Famine' of 1879–1880

Angela Bourke

Born when Charles Stewart Parnell was a twenty-year-old student at Magdalene College, Cambridge, the Irish-language storyteller Éamon a Búrc (otherwise De Búrc, Burke, Bourke; 1866–1942), spent his childhood in Carna, on the Atlantic seaboard of County Galway, one of the remotest parts of the west of Ireland. He died five miles from there, aged seventy-six, in November 1942 while Europe was at war, never having learned to read or write.[1]

Búrc was seventy when Walter Benjamin made his statement that 'the storyteller in his living immediacy is by no means a present force'.[2] Poor, rural, and unlettered, in a world increasingly urban and literate, he seems at first to have lived, in Eavan Boland's term, outside history. His life was more eventful, however, and has left a larger mark, than his birth and death suggest. For his own community he was very much a present force, his living immediacy considerable, as people gathered to listen to him. We know this because an early cultural project of the Irish Free State has preserved a substantial intellectual and artistic legacy in his name. His stories, collected and catalogued by the Irish Folklore Commission (IFC) and preserved in the National Folklore Collection (NFC), are celebrated for their verbal artistry and vivid, vigorous narrative style.[3] I shall argue here that they can also be read 'aslant' for what they reveal about Búrc's life

---

[1] Peadar Ó Ceannabháin, ed., *Éamon a Búrc: Scéalta* (Baile Átha Cliath [Dublin], 1983), 11–22. National schools brought literacy in English to most parts of Ireland from 1831, but John MacHale, Archbishop of Tuam (1834–81), excluded them from his archdiocese, which covered almost all of County Galway. See Miriam Moffitt, *Soupers and Jumpers: The Protestant Missions in Connemara 1848–1937* (Dublin, 2008), 9, 137.

[2] Walter Benjamin, 'The Storyteller', in his *Illuminations*, ed. Hannah Arendt (London, 1992 [1973]), 83.

[3] The Folklore of Ireland Society and its journal *Béaloideas*, both founded in 1927, preceded the IFC, set up in 1935. The National Folklore Collection is now at University College Dublin. Búrc's longest story has been published with facing English translation as *Eochair, mac rí in Éirinn/Eochair, A King's Son in Ireland*, ed. and trans. Kevin O'Nolan (Dublin, 1982). For Irish-language story-texts with introduction and notes, see Ó Ceannabháin, *Éamon a Búrc*.

and attitudes and those of his community. In combination with other sources, they offer vivid detail about living conditions at the time of the Land War and the 'Little Famine' of 1879–80, together with insight into *mentalité* and memory in the west of Ireland.[4]

Eavan Boland died suddenly in Dublin on 27 April 2020. In her land-mark poem of thirty years earlier the stars stand forever 'outside history':

> They keep their distance. Under them remains
> a place where you found
> you were human, and
> a landscape in which you know you are mortal.
> And a time to choose between them.[5]

Boland's contemporary essay, also called 'Outside History', recalls the first poem of the sequence, 'The Achill Woman'. As a student in the 1960s, she spent a few days alone in a borrowed stone cottage near Keel, Achill Island, County Mayo, revising for university exams. The woman who carried a bucket of water to that house each evening was the first person ever to speak to her about famine.[6] She made it personal, pointing out local landmarks, like the 'blond strand' nearby where people had converged 'to eat the seaweed'; she almost certainly spoke Irish as well as English. Like the Breton women painted by Roderic O'Conor in the 1890s, Boland's Achill woman, so evocatively and precisely described, remains nameless. Clearly, however, she had a voice and a mind. She carried the memories of earlier generations and shared them with the young poet, to international effect. Similarly, the celebrated Manchester-born painter Hughie O'Donoghue, whose mother was born near Achill in Erris, County Mayo, and emigrated young, works with her recounted memories and with his own experience of that landscape and the stories through which it is known. People appear in his work as shadowy faces emerging from a painted surface that speaks to the topography and history of north Mayo.[7]

In Dublin, the NFC includes meticulous transcriptions of some 200 tales, legends, and items of *seanchas* – local and family history – which

---

[4] See also Angela Bourke, 'The Baby and the Bathwater: Cultural Loss in Nineteenth-Century Ireland,' in *Ideology and Ireland in the nineteenth century*, ed. Tadhg Foley and Seán Ryder (Dublin, 1998), 79–92; 'Economic Necessity and Escapist Fantasy in Éamon a Búrc's Sea-Stories,' in *Islanders and Water-Dwellers*, ed. Patricia Lysaght, Séamas Ó Catháin, and Dáithí Ó hOgáin (Dublin: DBA, 1999), 19–35; and 'Legless in London: Pádraic Ó Conaire and Éamon a Búrc', *Éire-Ireland* 38.3–4 (Fall–Winter 2003): 54–67.

[5] Eavan Boland, *Outside History: Selected Poems, 1980–1990* (New York, 1991).

[6] Eavan Boland, 'Outside History', *American Poetry Review* 19.2 (March/April 1990): 32–38.

[7] Some of this material is discussed, with images, in my *Voices Underfoot: Memory, Forgetting, and Oral Verbal Art* (Hamden, CT, 2016).

Éamon a Búrc told for Liam Mac Coisdeala of the IFC in the last sixteen years of his life.[8] They bring us a vital step closer to this superb verbal artist, to the memories he curated and the consciousness he shares with Boland and O'Donoghue, of mortality and of inhabiting a haunted landscape. We have no sound recordings, but his voice lives on in the cadences of his spoken language. The hero tales and local legends he told bear vivid, if sometimes oblique, witness to his experience of famine, emigration, and the unrest that gave rise to the Land War. Material he divulged to the collector months before his death tells a more personal story, borne out by written testimony.

When Mac Coisdeala first met him in 1929, Éamon Liam, as he was known, was a tailor, small farmer, and fisherman living high on a hill above the sea in Aill na Brón, Cill Chiaráin, a place renowned for storytelling but not reached by roads until his lifetime. Mac Coisdeala, twenty-two and a member of the Folklore of Ireland Society, had come to the area to teach evening classes, helping native speakers in Irish to become literate in their own language; his students told him that Búrc was the best storyteller around. He found Éamon Liam sitting on a stool outside his house, a knife in his hand and a pile of hazel rods in front of him. He had finished making one lobster pot and was starting on a second.[9]

Búrc's parents, Liam and Bríd, both aged forty in 1880, had survived the Great Famine of 1845–52. Liam was active in the Land War in Carna and is thought to have been involved in the 1880 burning of a boat owned by the local 'big man', Martin Lydon (Máirtín Ó Loideáin), who owned islands and cattle as well as boats: a smuggler and a grazier. A local oral poet, Seán 'Bacach' [lame] Ó Guairim, immortalized that event in the song 'Bád dóite Loideáin' ('Lydon's burnt boat'), whose circumlocutions bear witness to the deference demanded by such 'big men' and the danger of identifying perpetrators.[10] Liam and Bríd emigrated to Minnesota with their five children soon after.[11]

---

[8] Liam Mac Coisdeal(bh)a, 'In Memoriam Éamonn (Liam) a Búrc (Aill na Brón, Cárna, Co. na Gaillimhe', *Béaloideas* 12 (1942): 210–14, and 'Im' bhailitheoir béaloideasa', *Béaloideas* 16 (1946): 141–71.

[9] Mac Coisdeala, 'Im' bhailitheoir', 149.

[10] Transcribed by Seamus Ennis from Seosamh Ó hÉanaí, NFC 1280: 365–66. See also Ríonach Ní Fhlathartaigh, *Clár amhrán Bhaile na hInse* (Baile Átha Cliath, 1976), 194–95; Tim Robinson, *A Little Gaelic Kingdom* (Dublin, 2011), 174–75 and passim; and *Graceville: The 'Connemaras' in Minnesota* (DVD), researched and narrated by Seosamh Ó Cuaig, written by Bob Quinn (Cinegael, 1997).

[11] Massachusetts Archives, passenger manifest, SS Austrian www.sec.state.ma.us/ArchivesSearch/PassengerDetail.aspx?ID=8386537, accessed 1 April 2017.

On 11 June 1880, the SS *Austrian* embarked from the port of Galway with 390 emigrants bound for Boston, en route to a new Catholic colony in Minnesota, where the coadjutor bishop of St Paul, John Ireland, had taken options five years earlier on 75,000 acres of railway land.[12] Éamon, the second son, was fourteen; he had three younger sisters.

When he died on 5 November 1942, Búrc had been ill for a year, but had rallied for a while during the summer. Mac Coisdeala visited him in July, and spent some weeks transcribing local legends and history, including precise and harrowing memories of the Great Famine from his parents' generation, which the storyteller recounted with some reluctance.[13] Búrc also told him about people he had seen as a child in the 1870s, living in shelters thrown up against rocks and in sod huts on wet cut-away bog, on the north side of the road that runs west into Carna village. They worked for Martin Lydon, he said: most likely cutting turf (peat) for fuel, drying it by frequent turning, and hauling it to Lydon's boats for transport to the Aran Islands. Carefully dissociating his own family from those squalid conditions, he pointed out that they lived south of the road, where the land was better. He spoke about Bishop Ireland's free emigration scheme, saying that almost all the people living on the poorer side of that road put their names down for free passage, houses, and land in Minnesota.[14] He did not mention that his family was among those the Catholic Colonization Bureau of St Paul sponsored to travel there.

When their train halted in Chicago on its way west from Boston, the local St Patrick's Society met the travellers at the rail depot with a hot meal and fresh clothing. Prominent Chicago citizen William J. Onahan, the Society's secretary, was shocked when he saw them: 'The famine was visible in their pinched and emaciated faces, and in the shriveled limbs – they could scarcely be called legs and arms – of the children. Their features were quaint, and the entire company was squalid and wretched. It was a painful revelation to all who witnessed it.'[15] The storyteller and his siblings were among those children. In talking to Mac Coisdeala, Búrc often referred to the hardship he had experienced when young, and a newspaper report from the Catholic colony of Graceville records that in the unusually harsh Minnesota winter of 1880, he had no shoes.[16] The colonization was

---

[12] James P. Shannon, *Catholic Colonization on the Western Frontier* (New Haven, CT, 1957), 46. Cf. Bridget Connelly, *Forgetting Ireland: Uncovering a Family's Secret History* (St. Paul, MN, 2003); and *Graceville*.
[13] Cormac Ó Gráda, *Black '47 and Beyond: The Great Irish Famine* (Princeton, NJ, 1999), 212.
[14] NFC 850: 290–306.   [15] Quoted in Shannon, *Catholic Colonization*, 157–58.
[16] Connelly, *Forgetting Ireland*, 136.

badly planned and managed; only a few families managed to break the prairie and farm the unfamiliar land, and a year later Bishop Ireland removed the others, including the Búrc family, to St Paul, where they settled near the rail yards.

Éamon Liam was seventeen when he lost a leg in a railway accident in St Paul. The family returned to Carna, settling in An Aird Mhóir, where Liam's father, also called Éamon, was a tailor. The young man learned that craft, managed his disability, and made a frugal living, negotiating the rocky local terrain and vaulting dry-stone walls with a crutch tied under his arm; for a while, he kept a small shop. Alert to all around him, articulate and animated, he became much sought after as a storyteller, his time in America reflected only occasionally in his speech and preoccupations. He was an accomplished fisherman and sailor, and took a keen interest in boxing and in current affairs. When Mac Coisdeala visited him in the 1930s to record stories as fascism spread in Europe, Búrc's first question was always about the news: Had he seen a newspaper? Forty years after his death Seán Ó Súilleabháin of the IFC described Búrc as 'possibly the most accomplished narrator of folktales who has lived into our own time'.[17]

Folktales are long, formulaic stories of the kind that in English begin 'Once upon a time'. Irish listeners specially appreciated those about heroes and giants, *scéalta gaisce*, and Búrc told many for Mac Coisdeala, including one tour de force that ran to 30,000 words.[18] Another hero-tale, 'Céachlann, mac rí in Éirinn agus Rí an Deachma' ('Céachlann, the King in Ireland's son, and the Tithe King'), which he told over two evenings in September 1936, reminds us that almost every household in Connemara owned a cow or two and that earlier generations had watched their animals starve.[19] Búrc was in his twenties, long back from America, when the Reverend T. A. Finlay, Jesuit priest, university economist, and social activist, came to Carna in 1898. The essay the priest published after his visit is famous:

> For the most part the cattle are gaunt and hungry-looking quadrupeds, with skins tightly stretched on their bones, heads that seem much too large for the bodies to which they are attached, and horns out of all proportion with the rest of the skeleton. Thirty shillings is not an unusual price for one of these beasts, full grown; it may be doubted whether a Roscommon or Meath grazier would accept a present of a drove.[20]

[17] Sean O'Sullivan, ed. and trans., *Folktales of Ireland* (London, 1966), 262.   [18] See note 3 above.
[19] Ó Ceannabháin, *Éamon a Búrc*, 89–107.
[20] T. A. Finlay, 'The Economics of Carna', *New Ireland Review* 9 (1898): 65–77.

Búrc's 'Céachlann' clearly conveys memories of similar sights, as the young
hero leaves home and enters the service of the impoverished 'Tithe King'
whose lands a giant has usurped. This king requires each of his champions
to spend a month herding his bull and cow, but their condition horrifies
the young hero:

> thiomáin sé an bhó agus an tarbh roimhe agus ní raibh ann ach go raibh
> siad in ann siúl. Ní raibh orthu ach an cnáimh [*sic*] agus an craiceann, agus
> mac rí in Éirinn ag déanamh an-iontas díobh, go raibh siad in ann siúl chor
> ar bith. Agus is í an áit ar ordaigh an rí dó iad a chur ansin . . . isteach i dtoir
> chlocha in áit nach raibh seamaide féir dár chruthaigh Dia riamh ag fás
> ann . . . Agus bhí páirceannaí féir ar gach aon taobh de, chomh hard leis an
> sconsa agus leis an gclaí ins gach uile áit, agus gan aon ghair ag na beithigh
> bhochta breathnú air. (93)

> He drove the cow and the bull before him, but they could barely walk.
> They had nothing on them but skin and bone, and the King in Ireland's
> son was amazed that they could walk at all. And the place the [Tithe
> K]ing . . . ordered him to drive them was into a stony wasteland, where
> not a blade of all the grass God ever created was growing . . . . And in fields
> on every side grass was growing as high as the ditch and the wall, but the
> poor beasts couldn't even look at it.

After showing the young man his duties, the king leaves him:

> Ghabh Rí an Deachma abhaile agus d'fhága sé mac rí in Éirinn agus an bhó
> agus an tarbh ansin. Bhí scrúd agána chroí do na beithígh – an bealach a bhí
> leo agus gan aon bhlas acu ach ag cuimilt a dteanga de na clocha, gan ní dár
> chruthaigh Dia le n-ithe ná le n-ól acu (93).

> The Tithe King went home and left the King in Ireland's son there, with
> the cow and the bull. His heart was broken for the animals – the condition
> they were in, and that they were so hungry they were licking the stones, and
> that among all God ever created there was nothing for them to eat or drink.

The usurping giant here is a 'big man' of the Martin Lydon type, or
perhaps a landlord, backed up by forces reminiscent of the Royal Irish
Constabulary. Búrc explicitly contrasts his lush pastures, protected behind
stone walls, with the miserable grazing left to their former owner. The hero
breaks down the giant's gate and allows the animals to graze in grass up to
their horns till evening. He drives them home, proud of their sleek
appearance, and the cow gives twice as much milk that evening as ever
before. Next morning, when the giant comes to kill him, the hero beheads
him, the animals graze as before, and that night the cow's milk fills every

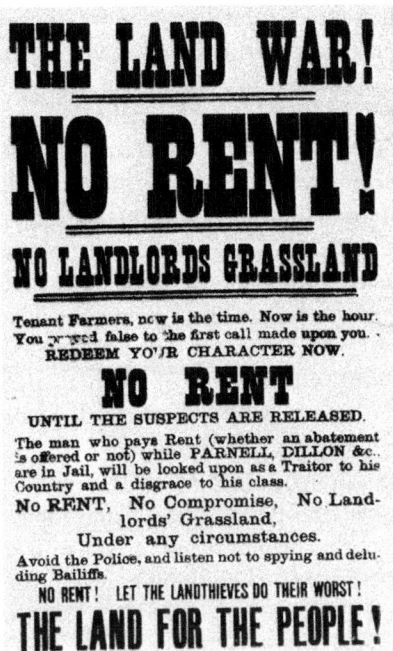

Fig. 3   Irish Land League poster, 1881.
Alamy

vessel in the house. On the third day, he breaks another gate and drives the cow and bull into a new field, where another giant, with three heads, threatens to kill him. He cuts off all three heads, and when he drives the animals home that evening, the cow gives even more milk; he repeats this feat on the fourth day, when he slays a four-headed giant.

Land League posters around 1880 insisted 'No RENT, No Compromise, No Landlords' Grassland, Under any circumstances' (see Fig. 3). Listeners who had seen cattle go hungry must have found solace in the storyteller's fantasy of resistance and redress, with its echo of the campaign against graziers, as the king's lands are restored and the hero marries his daughter, to live happy and well fed ever after.

Búrc also excelled in telling belief-legends about the 'good people', or fairies. His versions weigh conflicting obligations carefully and are much longer and more complex than most. If disasters like the Great Famine cause the disarticulation of cultural systems, as economic historian Cormac

Ó Gráda suggests, then these storytelling performances demand to be read as creative exercises in repair, re-membering, and rearticulation.[21]

Fairy legends are about people and about strange events that befall them. Storytellers achieve authority and credibility through detailed realism in their telling, but gain a reputation as artists by fitting their ideas and images into a shared framework of supernatural reference.[22] Their legends map the grey areas of human thought and interaction, including the moral dilemmas that arise especially in crises and catastrophes. Calling someone a fairy puts them outside humanity. It justifies the savage treatment of changelings in legends, and may have helped real people to live with unbearable choices. As access to food diminished after the potatoes first failed in 1845, numerous accounts tell of a brutal triage that could mean feeding the child who had a chance of survival, but not the emaciated, shrivelled infant who probably would not make it.

Humans encounter 'the good people' on boundaries – of time, space, and social status – or in the Foucauldian heterotopia that is the 'fort' – often a circular earthwork – where they are said to live. Usually wild and overgrown, a fort is a place where anything may happen. In vernacular oral tradition, it marks the limits of accountability and the site of legends – fictions that can take over where reality ceases to cope, the most sensitive spot in a haunted landscape.

In September 1938 Éamon a Búrc told a story evidently set in the bleak upland of stone and bog behind his own house, about a young man who inadvertently damages the roof of an underground dwelling while cutting heather for bedding. Later, the fairies take their revenge when his sister loses her way on the mountain. Blundering into a fort as darkness falls, she finds a crowded room brightly lit, and a table covered with food. A woman warns her not to eat for fear of remaining there for ever, and she barely escapes with her life.[23]

As the young man works on the hillside a voice suddenly speaks beneath his feet:

> Lá, ghabh duine de na fir óga amach chun cnoic ag baint ualach fraoigh agus nuair a ghabh sé i mbun an fhraoigh dá bhaint bhí aill ann agus bhí fraoch an-bhreá air, agus suas leis i mullach na haille ag baint an fhraoch [sic]. Agus dúirt an rud insan aill: 'Céard tá tú a dhéanamh ansin?' (267)

---

[21] Cormac Ó Gráda, 'Famine, Trauma and Memory', *Béaloideas* 69 (2001): 121–43 (141).

[22] See Angela Bourke, 'The Virtual Reality of Irish Fairy Legend,' *Éire-Ireland* 31.1–2 (Spring–Summer 1996): 7–25.

[23] Ó Ceannabháin, *Éamon a Búrc*, 268–71. Further references in the text.

One day, one of the young men went out to the hill to cut a load of heather, and as he began to cut, he spotted a big rock with fine heather growing on top. Up he went, and started to cut it. Then something inside the rock said, 'What are you doing there?'

He explains what he is about, but the voice warns him to stop, and as he turns for home with what he has cut, he hears a woman's voice behind him: 'You're not done yet . . . We're not finished with you yet by any means. You've let the rain in on top of us and left us in a terrible state!'

The coast around Carna and Cill Chiaráin saw new settlers arrive throughout the nineteenth century, following evictions inland, with results that were visible in the bodies of the 1880 migrants. Twenty years later, Dr Charles Browne told the Royal Irish Academy that the poorest kind of house in the area was

> dug out of the sandhills and lined with walls of dry stone; the roof is low with scarcely any pitch, and the walls rise above it to the height of two or three feet to prevent the strong gales of autumn and winter from blowing the thatch away. There is no window, a space a foot or so in height being left at the top of the door to admit light . . . These houses are of small size, about 10 feet by 8 feet, and consist of only one room.[24]

A house in a sand dune must have been slightly more habitable than one dug out of a bog, and would have done duty for longer, but it is clear that Búrc's legend describes the kind of temporary dwelling so often described in reports of the Great Famine, which he saw a generation later as a child in Carna during the 'Little Famine' of 1879–80. Destitute or seriously ill newcomers arriving in an area whose people were barely subsisting put enormous pressure on a moral economy of cooperation and mutual aid, forcing impossible choices. Thousands of the kind of oral belief-legends Búrc told concern strangers who lurk on the edges of a community's life and make demands, exacting revenge when refused, or rewarding those who help them. Storytellers identify the strangers obliquely, in terms that mark them as not of the human community, and leave the emotional conflict of hard choices implicit.

Unlike folktales, where things happen in threes, and the protagonists are the children of either kings or poor widows, legends are realistic. Stitched closely into local landscape and practice, they name people and places, and claim to be true. Medieval Irish literature offers episodes like those in

---

[24] Charles R. Browne, 'The Ethnography of Carna and Mweenish, in the Parish of Moyruss, Connemara', *Proceedings of the Royal Irish Academy* 6 (1900–1902): 503–34 (524).

modern Irish fairy legends, as do other oral traditions across northern Europe. It is impossible to estimate their currency in Ireland before the nineteenth century, but they occurred in huge numbers then, in English as well as Irish, continued strong throughout the twentieth century, and can still be heard in the twenty-first.

People versed in oral fairy legend had access to a paradigm outside reality with which to think or speak about horrific memories. The magical realism that emerges in art and literature during violent social upheaval has something in common with the strategy of defensive disassociation in children who are abused. Both accommodate the overwhelmingly incomprehensible alongside the mundane and necessary in a single narrative, yet somehow keep them separate. Fairy legends allowed traumatized people to express nightmare horrors alongside fantasies of plenty. And stories about babies taken away and replaced with changelings evidently carry memories of real children whose appearance changed as they starved, making them look 'quaint,' like the children observed in Chicago, fleeing from the 'Little Famine', or like those observed thirty years earlier, during the Great Famine, 'wrinkled with care, so that they appeared like aged persons'.[25]

Walter Benjamin reminds us that an orientation towards practical interests is a common characteristic of born storytellers and that the story, openly or covertly, contains something useful. His essay dwells on the artisanal quality of storytelling – the coordination of soul, eye, and hand, through which a practitioner brings his whole life experience to bear on what he is producing. Éamon a Búrc, thoughtful storyteller, tailor, and maker of lobster pots, exemplifies that quality, while the contrast Benjamin drew eighty years ago between story and information is exponentially more pertinent today:

> The value of information does not survive the moment in which it was new. It lives only in that moment; it has to surrender to it completely and explain itself to it without losing any time. A story is different. It does not expend itself. It preserves and concentrates its strength and is capable of releasing it even after a long time. (89–90)

Like the light from the stars in Boland's poem, reaching us only after they have died, the memories, endurance, resistance, and consolation encoded in Búrc's stories are only now becoming visible. We have yet to discern the full meaning and weight of the thousands of oral narratives whose transcriptions the NFC preserves.

---

[25] *Illustrated London News*, 29 December 1849.

CHAPTER 7

Digesting the Past
Anthologies and Bicultural Memory in Ireland

Joep Leerssen

Nous marchons vers l'avenir à reculons.

—Paul Valéry

Reading and Writing Ireland around Parnell

The fall and death of Parnell are traditionally seen as incisive moments in Irish literary history. They are usually linked to the beginning of the 'Irish Literary Revival', marked as that movement was by the establishment of an Irish Literary Society, twinned across London and in Dublin, and by the establishment of the Gaelic League, following Douglas Hyde's lecture on 'The Necessity for De-Anglicising Ireland'. The wreckage of political and parliamentary Home Rule ambitions, so the argument goes, triggered a shift in Irish nationalism towards the field of culture. And in its cultural sanctuary – so the traditional view continues – the ideal of Irish independence was kept alive and transfigured, to return to politics again with the establishment of the Irish Volunteers and the Easter Rising.

To be sure, the overly facile cause and effect chain in this reductive master narrative has been challenged by historians and literary historians alike. Roy Foster, for instance, has usefully pointed out that the literary figures and concerns that dominated the 1890s had started their career well ahead of Parnell's downfall, and did not need it to set them going. And although the sequential concatenation is by no means wrong, it is only one strand in a much more complex skein of traditions, influences, and inspirations. I will explore some of these tangled traditions in what follows.

By way of a preliminary, I plead for a realignment of what is habitually understood when we speak of Irish literary history. By that term, we usually refer to a succession of memorable texts with aesthetic merit arranged by date of production – so that the nineteenth century opens with Edgeworth, Moore, and Lady Morgan, followed by the fiction of Griffin and the Banims, then the poetry of Mangan and Young Ireland,

and then an in-between period. The decades 1845–90 are marked at best by a novelistic tradition moving from comic tales (Carleton, Lover, and Lever) towards realism and naturalism (Kickham, and later Somerville and Ross and George Moore), with, in the background, a sustained Gothic tradition (from Maturin by way of LeFanu to Stoker). Post-famine poetry is dominated by Allingham and Ferguson, drama by Dion Boucicault. These authors are increasingly caught up with a mainstream-British tradition – something that also holds for George Moore, Shaw, and Wilde – but it is in the drama of Yeats and his fellow-Revivalists that a national renewal takes hold.

That chronological template has, indeed, a Parnell-shaped hole in it: the fallow years of the 1880s – the Parnell Decade. Anyway, who could argue with chronology?

Three elements make this template, for all that it is factually true to the chronology of literary production, insufficient. The first is the focus on 'Anglo-Irish' texts and authors; the second is its restriction to the genres of prose fiction, poetry, and drama; the third its reliance on a one-dimensional chronology of literary production.

The Other Language

The marginality of a Gaelic-language participation in this tradition stands out. Even authors who came from a Catholic background, who had a personal familiarity with the native tradition, wrote in English and marketed Gaelic Ireland to an English-language audience for historicist or local colour. Then again, this absence is not just the result of some blind spot but reflects the actual lack of participation of the Gaelic tradition in Ireland's literary productivity. That state of affairs is part and parcel of the subaltern, disenfranchised position of the Catholic, Gaelic-speaking portion of the Irish population, which also brought about greater poverty and greater exposure to calamities such as famines. The communicative and culture-productive opportunities of modernity became available to them much later than they did to the Protestant, English-speaking portion, which developed playhouses, printing presses, periodicals, and literary associations from the early eighteenth century on. In contrast, the Gaelic tradition failed to reach the printing press to any meaningful extent; there are no Gaelic-language playhouses, reviews, novels, or even broadsheets or almanacs, even in the early to mid-nineteenth century, even after Catholic Emancipation. This is egregious, and stands in contrast even to the other marginalized minority languages in Europe. Breton, Bulgarian,

Estonian, Finnish, Galician, Latvian, Lithuanian, Maltese, Slovak, Ukrainian/Ruthenian, Yiddish, and Hebrew (not to mention Czech, Flemish, Catalan, and Basque, with their urban, middle-class demographic base) developed a print culture, minor and demotic though it was in many cases, which formed the basis of a literary audience for the revival movements of the 1860s and later. Gaelic is both tardy and tenuous in comparison, comparable rather to the revivalist chronology of Albanian, Belarusian, and Macedonian.[1]

Gaelic-language literary production subsisted, orally and in manuscript, in the 1820s and 1830s but died out, to all intents and purposes, with the Famine. The names that have come down to us (and they have done so thanks to a posthumous retrieval effort by Anglo-Irish folklorists and philologists – Mícheál Óg Ó Longáin, Antoine Ó Raifteirí, and Amhlaoibh Ó Súilleabháin) represent a literary tradition on the brink of disappearance. That fact must be taken for what it is, even though it might gall the sympathies of patriotically minded critics, reluctant to see the native tradition in terms of victimhood or subjection.[2] But historical injustice cannot be undone or argued away by celebratory pep-talks stoutly maintaining the vibrancy, vitality, and robustness of the native tradition. While the language may have been widespread and culturally productive orally in the first half of the century, the only traces of it in print culture are by scholars or Protestant proselytizers; and Gaelic was not so robustly entrenched or vibrantly resilient that the Famine's survivors should cling to it in the century's second half. By the 1870s, Gaelic was being dropped like a hot potato by its cradle speakers, rejected as a socially stigmatizing

---

[1] A comparative survey of cultural revival movements in the nineteenth century is given in the *Encyclopedia of Romantic Nationalism in Europe*, ed. J. Leerssen, 2 vols. (Amsterdam, 2018), accessible online at http://ernie.uva.nl.

[2] Critics have taken issue with this view as stated by me on previous occasions, and with my contention that the Gaelic-language literary and communicative activities of the period did not amount to the ambience of a nationwide Habermassian 'public sphere', bereft as they were of the large-volume, deep-penetration, long-distance medium of commercially distributed print (i.e., the infrastructural modernity of what Benedict Anderson calls 'print capitalism'). For my part I stand by this contention. The oppression of the Catholic majority in pre-Emancipation Ireland was marked by that majority's exclusion from the elite's public sphere as much as its institutions. Asserting the existence of a parallel Gaelic-language public sphere scrapes the barrel of documented evidence, magnifies sporadic exceptions into representative typicalities, and stretches the terms of the definition; the case that is made thus must rest on the (undisputed) vibrancy of what was essentially an oral/manuscript culture with texts and manuscripts spreading translocally and taking note of current affairs elsewhere, and on the argument that, even though writers could not make use of the printing press, modern print capitalism reached Gaelic Ireland by virtue of the fact that Gaelic readers had access to non-Gaelic printed material. This argument confuses a shared culture with a public sphere, and the visible proximity of modernity with active civic participation in it.

handicap, linked to the trauma of the Great Hunger. It is only when we acknowledge this fact, uncomfortable though it is, that we can appreciate what a truly extraordinary process took place in the later century, when the language became an object of revivalist interest among English speakers; its literature was retrieved from oral praxis and manuscript documentation to be printed by those revivalists; and its cultural memories were adopted as national ones by an altogether differently rooted mnemonic community.[3]

The process, not of cultural memory but of cultural anamnesis, retrieving cultural traditions from their oblivion, makes the Irish case stand out among all European national movements. The Irish Literary Renaissance would be a plain-vanilla phenomenon if it were just that: a renaissance, like all the other *renaixenças, rexurdimentos, risorgimentos, văzrazdanies,* and *relindjas*; if it were based on the mere reactivation and activist empowerment of an existing demotic-cultural base. But it was more than that: it amounted, almost, to a Resuscitation, a rising from near-death oblivion.

The Other Genres

To do justice to Ireland's unusually complex cultural retrieval and resuscitation in the post-Parnell decades, we must look to more than the productivity of the established canon of Anglo-Irish poets, novelists, and dramatists. Besides widening the cultural field beyond the English-language ambit, we must also widen our notion of what went on in literary history, both in genre terms and in the relationship between literary production and cultural memory.

Literary history-writing has traditionally focused on the poetically creative genres: lyrical poetry, drama, and prose fiction. Along with this focus on creative literature as an art form went a privileged foregrounding of originality and innovation as the *primum movens* in literary history: literary history did not just develop, nay, it *progressed*, with younger authors boldly striking out beyond the limitations of the previous generation. Hence, literary histories are invariably records of innovatory production in the creative genres. It goes without saying that this is a very partial view. It marginalizes all literary traditions that were less progress-oriented, that is to say, all of world literature pre-1500 and all non–West European literature (as well as Gaelic literature) pre-1800. And it marginalizes literary genres

---

[3] Cf. my 'Cúchulain in the Post Office: Gaelic Revival, Irish Rising', *Journal of the British Academy* 4 (2016): 113–36. I take the notion of a mnemonic community from Eviatar Zerubavel, *Time Maps: Collective Memory and the Social Shape of the Past* (Chicago, 2003).

other than poetry (lyrical or satirical), drama, or fiction. A more inclusive view of the literary record should include nonfictional fields such as literary criticism, history-writing, (auto-)biography, travel writing, and what Walter Benjamin called the 'panoramatic' genres so typical of late nineteenth-century urban modernity.[4] It is in genres such as these that the position of writers vis-à-vis their society and culture is most explicitly articulated. Scholars of the Irish eighteenth century know this full well: antiquarian writings and other forms of disquisition are at the core of their corpus; but this wider definition of the corpus is less obvious for literary historians of the Parnell decades. However, if we want to find out not just what the authors of the Parnell generation did but what they thought they were doing, we must turn to sources like the autobiographical writings of Moore and Yeats, or Yeats's occasional criticism and cultural journalism. It is in his occasional pieces that Yeats reflects most interestingly on his own position in Irish, and in literary, history. And what drives him is not just the crisis of Parnell but a general sense of a literary climacteric.

The sense of a Europe-wide decadence, an imminent senectitude or historical belatedness, makes his Irishness both European and exceptional. European, in that his Celtic-inspired symbolism chimes with what is happening at the time (1897) 'in Germany in Wagner, in England in the Pre-Raphaelites, in France in Villiers de l'Isle-Adam and Mallarmé, and in Belgium in Maeterlinck'.[5] These all share, however, a sense of historical belatedness. Yeats sees this in stadial terms: any literature, so he argues, develops from a golden to a silver to a bronze age by progressing through the genres of epic, drama, and lyric poetry, which relate to each other like the root/trunk, branches, and twigs/foliage of a tree. Greek literature went from Homer to the Attic tragedians to the disembodied mixed emotions of the Anthology; English from Beowulf and Malory to Shakespeare to Shelley. Where does that leave the latter-day post-Shelley poets? 'Are we not, perhaps, merely a little eddy cast up by the advancing tide of English literature and are we not doomed, perhaps, to its old age and coming decline?' On the contrary, Yeats affirms. He chooses not to see himself as

---

[4] Thus Walter Benjamin, in his 'Paris, Capital of the Nineteenth Century' (1935): 'Contemporary with the panoramas is a panoramatic literature. *Le livre des Cent-et-Un, Les Français peints par eux-mêmes, Le diable à Paris, La grande ville* belong to this. These books prepare the bellettristic collaboration for which Girardin, in the 1830s, will create a home in the *feuilleton*. They consist of individual sketches, whose anecdotal form corresponds to the panoramas' plastically arranged foreground, and whose informational base corresponds to their painted background.' Walter Benjamin, *The Arcades Project*, ed. and trans. Howard Eiland and Kevin McLaughlin (Cambridge, MA, 2002), 20–21.

[5] W. B. Yeats, *Essays and Introductions* (Basingstoke, 1961), 187.

part of the English post-Shelley stage, but as an Irish author in a literary tradition which has not yet moved from the mythic/epic to the tragic/ dramatic stage. He is, in other words, not old but young, not decadent but emergent. His Twilight is that of the morning as well as the evening. 'On the contrary, I affirm that we are a young nation with unexhausted material lying within us in our still unexpressed national character, about us in our scenery, and in the clearly marked outlines of our life, and behind us in the multitude of our legends.'[6]

Here, perhaps, lies the most important reaction to the Parnell crisis and to the sense of political stagnation that had taken hold in political life. The turn to literature is a return to cultural memory, an escape from senile decline, with literature as a way of revitalizing the past and bringing dormant traditions into new life. It closely resembles Romantic-Historicist responses to the political crises of the Napoleonic period: Von der Hagen's edition of the *Nibelungenlied* in 1807, Tegnér's *Svea* of 1811, Helmers's *De Hollandsche Natie* of 1812. In that light, we can also understand the fact that it is in these years that Douglas Hyde should write his *Literary History of Ireland* (1899), with its tell-tale dedication to the Members of the Gaelic League, 'the only body in Ireland which appears to realise the fact that Ireland has a past, has a history, has a literature, and the only body in Ireland which seeks to render the present a rational continuation of the past'.

Literature as cultural memory:[7] the phrase is well known by now, but hides a multitude of complexities largely unexplored. In what follows I want to look at Irish literature not as a process of production but as an ongoing process of retrieval.

Literary Production, Literary Retrieval, Literary Reflection

It is a truth universally acknowledged, but not always put into practice, that the history of literature is not just that of literary production but also

---

[6] W. B. Yeats, 'Nationality and Literature' (1893), in *Uncollected Prose*, vol. 1, ed. John P. Frayne (Basingstoke, 1970), 359–64.

[7] On cultural memory: Ann Rigney, 'The Dynamics of Remembrance: Texts between Monumentality and Morphing', in *Cultural Memory Studies: An International and Interdisciplinary Handbook*, ed. Astrid Erll and Ansgar Nünning (Berlin, 2008). Cf. also Zerubavel's notion of 'collective memory' in *Time Maps*. Oona Frawley's *Memory Ireland*, 4 vols. (Ithaca, NY, 2010–14) is a benchmark application to Ireland.

of literary circulation, reception, and recycling. The importance of Keats as a poet is almost wholly posthumous, and the great vernacular epics of German, English, and French literature slumbered unnoticed and unread on unvisited library shelves for centuries until they hit the literary system in the Romantic period: the *Nibelungenlied* in 1807, *Beowulf* in 1814, and the *Chanson de Roland* in 1836. Oblivion and Anamnesis are as much part of literary history as Convention and Innovation.

If, then, we want to thematize the role of literature as cultural memory, we need to factor in a broader sense of literature than merely the production of new verbal artworks, and to factor in two important dimensions: one, that literature, as Hyde would put it, has a history. It is not just a static accumulation of texts on a shelf but an evolving praxis over time, leaving long contrails and paper traces behind it on its trajectory across the years. The other, that literature as a sentient cultural praxis does not only *do* things but also *thinks about how it does things*. Metaliterary self-reflection is the constant accompanying shadow of whatever literary activity we encounter; and in any of these we can thematize the element of cultural memory.

Schematically we could organize these thoughts as follows. Literary production leaves behind a legacy of texts that is received and reproduced (like post-1821 editions of Keats's poetry). This legacy is engaged with by later generations in a dynamic that we can call (like the pre-Raphaelites engaging with Keats) 'recycling'. And it is commented and reflected on by literary critics and literary historians.

Each of these has its own historicity over the years. This historical dimension could be tabulated as follows:

literary production	history of literary production
literary legacy (reception)	history of literary reception
literary recycling	history of literary recycling
literary criticism and history-writing	history of literary criticism and history-writing

The element of cultural memory or anamnesis would then manifest itself as follows:

literary production	cultural memory in literary production
literary legacy (reception)	cultural memory in literary reception
literary recycling	cultural memory in literary recycling
literary criticism and history-writing	cultural memory in literary history-writing

Of these four classes, the first and fourth are unproblematically self-explanatory: Lady Morgan's National Tales, the verse and journalism of Thomas Davis, and Hyde's *Literary History of Ireland* are obvious examples. It is, however, the second and third classes that can shed fresh light on the relationship between literature and history in Parnell's Ireland, when literary production was (as we have noted) at a low ebb. How did the presence, ongoing reception, and recycling of a literary legacy in Ireland affect the cultural memory that the generation of Yeats and Hyde wanted to reactivate? What were the Irish equivalents of the *Nibelungenlied*?

In order to address this question, I turn to the omnipresent but often-overlooked genre of the anthology.

* * *

How did pre-1800 Gaelic texts reach the decades of Parnell and Yeats? Given the dearth of a native print culture, the main carrier medium was centuries of manuscript transmission flanked (in the case of verse) by oral transmission, with all the attendant philological pitfalls this entails: substantial textual variants and substantial uncertainties as to authorship. Yet it is precisely this corpus – hard to pin down in terms of authorship, date of origin, or textual variant, and understandable to the vast majority of modern readers only in translation, from *Táin Bó Cuailnge* to the Jacobite *aisling* – which is usually seen as the most authentic embodiment of true, native Irishness in Irish literature, unarguably Irish and nothing but, with none of the categorical cross-over problems that we encounter in the case of known and datable authors like Eriugena, Luke Wadding, or Jonathan Swift.

But it was not as manuscripts or in oral performance that the Táin or the Jacobite aisling reached Yeats. The corpus had been remediated (like much of Europe's vernacular epics and pre-Gutenberg literature) by a *via philologica*. That reception history is nothing if not complex, with ever-renewed efforts at translation and adaptation, none of these apparently being definitively satisfactory. All Táin translators from Lady Gregory to Ciaran Carson by way of Thomas Kinsella vie with each other. Again, certain perennial 'classics' of the Irish tradition such as the 'woman's complaint' entitled *Dónall Óg* have no known author, no fixed date of origin, and even in their textual substance are variable: the order of the stanzas, the stanzas' appurtenance to this or that version or parallel poem: all that differs considerably from manuscript to manuscript. Much like the situation of performed art (jazz, folktales), we can at best extrapolate an ideal-type textual template from a shifting praxis of diverging performances.[8]

In recycling the native corpus for a print-culture audience, intractable difficulties had to be faced. This was a literature that often has no identifiable authors and no precise datability of its texts, and no living successors or continuators except in the field of popular verse, between literature and folklore. James Joyce's symbol of the 'cracked looking-glass of a servant' is often applied to the bifurcation and discontinuity of Ireland's literary past: Gaelic and English halves, Ó Rathaile and Swift, that share a frame but somehow do not match up, presenting the onlooker with only a fractured and riven self-image.

However, cracked though the mirror may have been, it was held together by a frame; and that frame was provided by cultural memory and literary recycling. It is here that the anthology played a crucial role.

Anthologies

Reflections on the genre (or medium) of the anthology are only occasionally encountered in Irish literary history. An honourable exception should be made for Margaret Kelleher, especially her contribution to the *Oxford History of the Irish Book*, 'The Anthology and the Duanaire'.[9] Kelleher's study is richly documented and traces the interaction between traditional Gaelic poem-books and modern print-culture anthologies admirably; but while it has an eye for the anthology as a medium for literary transmission and canonicity, her analysis is primarily book-historical in orientation rather than concerned (as I am here) with the anthology as a vehicle for cultural memory transmission and an agency in the history of literary recycling.

The anthology as a book form antedates by many centuries the rise of print culture and the rise of the author.[10] The genre receives its name from

---

[8] Cf. my 'For a Post-Foucauldian Literary History: A Test Case from the Gaelic Tradition', *Configurations* 7 (1999): 227–45.

[9] Margeret Kelleher, 'The Anthology and the *Duanaire*', in *The Oxford History of the Irish Book, vol. 4: The Irish Book in English, 1800–1891*, ed. James H. Murphy, (Oxford, 2003), 448–59. Cf. also her 'The Cabinet of Irish Literature: A Historical Perspective on Irish Anthologies', *Éire-Ireland* 38.3–4 (2003): 68–89.

[10] The notion of authorship has, of course, its own historical dynamics which I mention only in passing. Originally, the word 'author' was tantamount to 'authority' and referred to the texts invoked to bolster an argument. Later on, it came to stand specifically for the individual who had written those texts. The 'authors' known as individuals were originally philosophers and Church Fathers; they were also the earliest 'authors' to be given opera omnia editions of their works as somehow forming a coherent corpus held together by the informing personality of their individual

the great prototype, the Greek Anthology, that collection of Greek epigrams and poems made by Meleager in the first century AD, and continuously added to until well into Byzantine times. The Bible itself may be seen as an anthology containing a collection of texts belonging to many different genres. Any medieval codex can be seen as an anthology of sorts, a collection of texts, almost never organized by author but by the preference of the scribe, the needs of the readership, or the availability of material. And the anthology is perhaps the pre-print genre that has most successfully survived the Gutenberg revolution. Anthologies are still being published in great numbers, from school collections to the *Field Day Anthology of Irish Writing* (which will serve as my terminus ad quem here).

Anthologizing has remained an important part of literary practice. To begin with, it has a long-standing and intimate relationship with the notion of literary canonicity. From the Bible onwards (those Bible books were 'canonical' which were included in the collection) to the Greek Anthology, being included in an anthology was tantamount to an induction into a Textual Hall of Fame. Indeed, scholars are now realizing that canonicity is not merely a function of being critically celebrated but also a function of being recirculated and remediated; prestigious books that remain on the shelf unread get lost in a mummified state of inert canonicity (*The Pilgrim's Progress* or Matthew Arnold's *Empedocles on Etna* might count as examples). Canonicity is always posterior to textual production: texts are not born canonical but become so after having left their author's hands; and canonicity is therefore not a mode of textual production but a mode of textual circulation, specifically, an enduringly successful mode of textual circulation. The process is illustrated schematically in Appendix A.

It is in the difference between textual production and textual circulation that interesting things happen in literary history, and particularly in Irish literary history.

In particular, in the field of poetry we may surmise that the canonicity of certain poems owes more to their being anthologized than to reprintings under the poet's own authorship,[11] celebrity and recognizability counting

---

mind. The earliest secular and nonphilosophical writers to become personally known as authors were the poets of the twelfth and following centuries. It was in the context of print culture that the individual author became the premier marker of a text's identity; the first secular poet to be given an opera omnia edition being Giovanni Pontano. The centuries between Dante and Pontano present the period of the 'rise of the author'. Cf. generally also Seán Burke, ed., *Authorship from Plato to the Postmodern: A Reader* (Edinburgh, 1995).

[11] A point also made by Leah Price in the introduction to her *The Anthology and the Rise of the Novel: From Richardson to George Eliot* (Cambridge, 2000).

for more than actual sales figures. In the canon of English verse, the influence of set anthologies used in school and university courses (Oxford Anthology, Norton Anthology, etc.) is one obvious, institutional factor; but even outside educational settings, in the wider literary marketplace, collections such as *Palgrave's Golden Treasury of English Verse* and the *Oxford Book of English Verse* have been formative in shaping tastes and preferences, as well as registering the shifting poetical outlooks, of succeeding generations of readers. Palgrave brought out his original *Golden Treasury* in four volumes in 1861, followed by a second series in 1897 and a supplement in 1921. Laurence Binyon added a volume in 1931; C. D. Lewis one in 1954; Christopher Ricks produced a Penguin version in 1994; and a new *Golden Treasury* was published in six volumes by Oxford University Press in 1994. That same Oxford University Press had throughout the twentieth century been running the competing *Oxford Book of English Verse*, originally edited by Arthur Quiller-Couch in 1900 and re-edited in 1939, with new editions coming out in 1972 (Helen Vendler), 1990 (John Wain), and 1999 (again Christopher Ricks). Both the frequency and the august editorial roll call indicate the undemonstrative importance of poetic anthologizing.

A similar role of 'canonization by reselection and recycling' was played by certain anthologies in Irish literature over the last two centuries. The anthology *Éigse: Duanaire na hArdteistiméarachta* (ed. Breandán Ó Conaire, 1974) was the set anthology for Irish literature courses in secondary school and presented school pupils with the canon of Gaelic literature; a similar use was intended for the three-volume *Nua-Dhuanaire* (ed. Pádraig De Brún, Breandán Ó Buachalla, and Tomás Ó Concheanainn, 1975 and following years). For the wider English-reading market, there were formative and influential collections such as those by Kathleen Hoagland (1947), Donagh Mac Donagh and Lennox Robinson (1948, given a new profile by Kinsella in 1986), Frank O'Connor (1959), Derek Mahon (1972), Seán Lucy (1973), John Montague (1974), Brendan Kenelly (1981), Paul Muldoon (1986), and Michael Longley (2002) (Appendix B, at the end of this chapter, contains a chronological checklist).

Again, the frequency is striking, as is the high-prestige nature of the writers involved; any poet of note seems to have been approached by some publisher or other to lend his name to an Irish anthology over the last half-century. Some of these may even have been commercially driven pot-boilers, aimed at the literary tourist market when 'Anglo-Irish literature' was one of the country's main export products (roughly 1960–2000). One gets the impression that editing an anthology was an even more efficient marker of canonicity than being merely included in one. W. B. Yeats himself, with his epoch-making edition of the *Oxford Book of Modern Verse* (1936), may have acted as a role model. In fact, many succeeding generational shifts in Irish literature and Irish poetry have been signalled not only by the emergence of new authors, journals, and periodicals but also by way of the anthology as self-presentation. Poets who individually were relatively powerless newcomers in the literary marketplace could make a more forceful entrance on the scene by collectively showing their colours. That practice reaches from the days of the Irish Literary Revival to the feminist assertions of women poets: from anthologies edited by W. B. Yeats (1895) to Ailbhe Smyth (1989), Éilís Ní Dhuibhne (1995), and Katie Donovan, Norman Jeffares, and Brendan Kennelly (1995), and of course volumes 4 and 5 of the *Field Day Anthology* (2002). Similarly, in the 1970s, the Northern Irish troubles and their literary repercussions gave rise to important anthologies of 'Ulster poetry', for example, those edited by Pádraic Fiacc (1974) and Frank Ormsby (1979). Thus, anthologies in their own right can document not only the recycling of past literature but also the emergence of new currents.

None of these patterns is specifically Irish; they merely serve to highlight the important, albeit under-recognized role played by anthologies in the dynamics of literary history. There are, then, important parallels between Irish and English anthologizing and, indeed, crossovers, from Yeats's *Oxford Book of Modern Verse* to Seamus Heaney's and Ted Hughes's *The Rattle Bag* (2005). But in addition, anthologies in Ireland also have a specific function, and a longer and richer history, which I propose to highlight now.

Irish Anthologies: Cultural Transfer, Cultural Memory

Much of nineteenth-century Irish culture was deeply engrossed in acts of translation: in the root sense of the word, the relocating of something from one place to another; in this case: the salvage of Gaelic literature and Gaelic culture from the wreck of the Gaelic language and giving it a new lease on life in an English-speaking social setting. It amounts, almost, to a brain transplant: an entire personality, character, and life story is lifted from one body and fitted into a new one. Even so, the Irish writers at the latter end of that process (who, for all that they are native speakers of the language of Shakespeare, have de-Anglicized their sense of affiliation to the extent that they acknowledge Gaelic-language forerunners such as Aogán Ó Rathaile as 'us' while they disavow Milton or Wordsworth as 'them') are uncomfortably aware of the discontinuity within the Irish tradition, the crack in the servant's looking-glass.[12] Thus, Thomas Kinsella, in his essay 'The Irish Writer', encounters a 'great cultural blur' when he looks for 'the past in [him]self': 'I must exchange one language for another, my native English for eighteenth-century Irish.' Kinsella sees this bifurcation in his cultural memory as if he comes, 'so to speak, from a broken and uprooted family, [in] being drawn to those who share my origins and finding that we cannot share our lives'.[13] John Montague plays on linguistic discontinuity as trauma in 'A Severed Head' (part of the celebrated cycle *The Rough Field*, 1972): 'To grow a second tongue: as harsh a humiliation as twice to be born'; and Brian Friel's *Translations* remains, despite its wilfully counterfactual distortion of cultural change in nineteenth-century Ireland, widely accepted as a valid 'poetic' representation and interpretation of real-world events: linguistic alienation as a deliberate instrument of colonial hegemony.[14]

However, this view of radical disruption and irretrievable loss is contradicted by the remarkable intensity, even in this colonial context, of cultural transfers. Keating's *Foras feasa ar Éirinn* was translated into English as early as 1723. A historiographical tradition based on native sources emerged in the eighteenth century: Abbé James MacGeoghegan's *History of Ireland* (Paris, 1758–62) or Sylvester O'Halloran's *General History of Ireland* (1778), which in turn informed nationalist historians like A. M. Sullivan and John Mitchel in the nineteenth.[15] Intellectuals versed in the antiquities and philology of the native tradition did much to communicate its riches to metropolitan scholars and academics, a process starting in the eighteenth century and leading from Aodh MacCruitín, Charles O'Conor, and Theophilus O'Flanagan to the great nineteenth-century figures of Eugene O'Curry and John O'Donovan.

---

[12] Cf. Michael Cronin, 'The Cracked Looking Glass of Servants: Translation and Minority Languages in a Global Age', *The Translator* 4.2 (1998): 145–62, and various essays in Maria Tymoczko and Colin A. Ireland, eds., *Language and Tradition in Ireland: Continuities and Displacements* (Boston, 2003).

[13] Thomas Kinsella, 'The Irish Writer', in *Davis, Mangan, Ferguson? Tradition and the Irish Writer* (Dublin, 1970), 57–70.

[14] On the role of the Ordnance Survey in Irish cultural history, see Gillian M. Doherty, *The Irish Ordnance Survey: History, Culture and Memory* (Dublin, 2004); P. S. McWilliams, 'The Ordnance Survey Memoir of Ireland: Origins, Progress and Decline' (PhD thesis, Queen's University Belfast, 2004); Stiofán Ó Cadhla, ed., *Civilizing Ireland. Ordnance Survey 1824 1842. Ethnography, Cartography, Translation* (Dublin, 2007).

[15] Generally, Clare O'Halloran, *Golden Ages and Barbarous Nations: Antiquarian Debate on the Celtic Past in Ireland, c. 1750–1800* (Cork, 2004).

It is against this background of a general process of cultural transfers that the Irish anthology gains its full importance. Recuperation and appropriation of Gaelic literature in an urban, English-speaking setting takes on added resonance. Anthologies are a prominent platform for the translation of Gaelic literary heritage into the language of the modern print-based readership; it is striking, but not surprising, how many anthologies have been discussed in Robert Welch's studies of translations.[16] While the written production of Irish literature languished and stalled, in a slow decline that would lead from Aogán Ó Rathaile (†1728) by way of Mícheál Óg Ó Longáin (†1837) into the Famine, the Irish anthology became an increasingly potent vehicle for literary salvage. Charlotte Brooke's *Reliques of Irish Poetry: Consisting of Heroic Poems, Odes, Elegies, and Songs, Translated into English Verse* (1789) is recognized as a 'classic' in Irish cultural history, but usually for other reasons than for what it fundamentally is. It is seen as a manifestation of Grattanite-Patriot appreciation of Gaelic antiquity; as part of the Irish vindication against Macpherson-style Ossianism; as an Irish counterpart to Bishop Percy's *Reliques of Ancient Poetry* and, as such, as part of the climate of Irish antiquarianism; as a first benchmark in the history of translations from the Irish; and, indeed, it is all those things. But first and foremost it is one of the first, and greatest, Irish *anthologies.* Brooke's *Reliques* is the prototype of the great showcases retrieving and re-presenting the riches of the native tradition, such as Charles Read's *Cabinet of Irish Literature* (4 vols., 1880) and Seamus Deane's *Field Day Anthology of Irish Writing* (3 + 2 vols., 1991/2002).[17]

Even more importantly, perhaps, her collection, in deliberately straddling the Gaelic-English linguistic divide, is the mainspring of similar anthologies which, since then, have formed crucially important stepping-stones in the development of Irish literature as a bilingual system, for example, Hardiman (1831), O'Daly and Walsh (1844), O'Daly (1849 and 1860), Ferguson (1864), Brooke and Rolleston (1900), Greene and O'Connor (1967), Ó Tuama and Kinsella (1981), Bolger (1986), and Kiberd and Fitzmaurice (1991). All of these present texts from one

---

[16] Robert Welch, *A History of Verse Translation from the Irish, 1789–1897* (Gerrards Cross, 1988). For the idea of 'cultural transfer', see the seminal collection by Michel Espagne and Michael Werner, *Transferts: Les relations interculturelles dans l'espace franco-allemand (XVIIIᵉ et IXᵉ siècle)* (Paris, 1988).

[17] On Read's Cabinet, and on anthologies in general: Kelleher, 'The Cabinet of Irish Literature'. In 'The Anthology and the *Duanaire*', Kelleher mentions some Reliques collections in the wake of Brooke (which was itself reprinted several times), such as Daly/Walsh 1844 and Thaddeus Connellan 1825. She highlights as 'significant' two small Irish-language collections by Connellan, both from 1829. On these: Donal O'Sulllivan, 'Thaddeus Connellan and His Books of Irish Poetry', *Éigse* 3.4 (1941–42): 278–304.

language for readers in another, often giving original and English translation side by side on facing pages – a procedure first devised by Brooke, in
an obvious denunciation of Macpherson's reluctance to produce the
originals for his Ossianic 'translations', and still followed by Kinsella and
Ó Tuama in their highly influential *An Duanaire: Poems of the Dispossessed*
of 1981. These anthologies thus in themselves bring two languages
together, that of the text and that of the reader, often indeed in their very
textual substance and page layout, and thus form an almost Hegelian
Aufhebung of the opposition between Gaelic and English: their polarity
is both enshrined and transcended.

And that, too, was their function, certainly in the nineteenth-century
process of rediscovering Ireland's Gaelic past. The work of Hardiman,
O'Daly, Ferguson, and Sigerson is generally recognized as being of cardinal
importance in this process, yet hardly thematized as forming part of a
concerted praxis and tradition; yet without their anthologizing, the poetic
rise of Mangan or the boom of patriotic verse by the poets of *The Nation*
(themselves largely disseminated by canonical and oft-reprinted anthologies like *The Spirit of the Nation* (1843) and its spin-offs) would have been
unthinkable. The process is known as 'productive reception': the fresh
production of Irish texts in the English language taking themes, topics,
inspirations, and settings from the Gaelic cultural inheritance – in short,
an entire Gaelic *cultural memory* – retrieved and appropriated in a reception process.

Anthology, Philology, Manuscript Tradition

That reception and retrieval process was carried by philologists and
anthologists jointly, throughout the nineteenth century. The source-
referencing notes to Thomas Moore's *Irish Melodies* – an early instance
of productive reception – feature antiquaries like O'Halloran and anthologists like Brooke; Thomas Davis's mid-century verse and critical essays
are replete with similar references to antiquarian, historical, and anthologized literary sources; and philological text editions like those of Standish
O'Grady as well as anthologies like Douglas Hyde's *Love Songs of Connacht*
and *Religious Songs of Connacht* (1893 and 1906) provide the repertoire for
the drama and verse of the Irish Literary Revival.

In order to place the activities of anthologists in their proper and
congenial context, from Charlotte Brooke to Charles Read, we should
consider them not just as outriders in the production history of creative
literature but as partners in the rise of the philological text edition, in the

field of knowledge production. Text editions, too, are a form of retrieval and recycling; they, too, often bridge the gap between the language of the text and the language of the reading audience; they, too, had the dual role of bringing a receding, no-longer-active cultural tradition back from oblivion and reintegrating it into the literary imagination of a different (urban, modern, English-speaking) society. And they rose almost conjointly with the Irish anthology. Indeed, with her *Reliques*, Charlotte Brooke stands godmother over the philological-editorial tradition as much as over that of the anthology. The first great editorial works were undertaken around the mid-nineteenth century under the aegis of the Royal Irish Academy and its spin-off, the Irish Archaeological Society (later merged with O'Daly's Ossianic Society),[18] the high points being undoubtedly John O'Donovan's edition of the Annals of the Fours Masters,[19] and the edition of the Brehon laws by W. N. Hancock and others, made on the basis of preparatory work by O'Curry and O'Donovan. From these beginnings rose the discipline of the Celtic philology; and in many cases its early achievements (certainly when nonauthored verse or imaginative-fictional texts like legends or myths were assembled thematically, edited, and translated) were almost indistinguishable from the anthologizing tradition highlighted here – for example, the seminal Hardiman (1832), Montgomery (1846), O'Grady (1892), Sigerson (1897), Meyer (1901), and Hull (1912). After independence, T. F. O'Rahilly (1925–26), Osborn Bergin (1970), and Seán Ó Tuama (1981) have continued this editing/anthologizing outreach from the academic into the wider literary field.

Strikingly, the Irish materials edited by Celtic philologists rarely fit the default form of a given author's *opera omnia*. Granted, text editions of individual authors do exist: the works of Aogán Ó Rathaille as edited by Dinneen and O'Donoghue, of Dáibhí Ó Bruadair as edited by MacErlean, and of Tadhg Dall Ó hUiginn as edited by Elanor Knott (all of these in the publication series of the Irish Texts Society, in 1909, 1910–17, and 1920, respectively). Post-1945, the Dublin Institute of Advanced Studies has continued to bring out author-based work editions. But these collections had to be assembled, and arranged, around an individual author, from a disparate manuscript tradition; and as an editorial-philological endeavour they are heavily overshadowed by editions that are in themselves

---

[18] Damien Murray, *Romanticism, Nationalism and Irish Antiquarian Societies, 1840–80* (Maynooth, 2000).

[19] Bernadette Cunningham, 'The Nineteenth-Century Legacy: Publishing the Annals of the Four Masters', in *Writing Irish History: The Four Masters and Their World*, ed. E. Bhreathnach and B. Cunningham (Dublin, 2007), 68–73.

selections – indeed, philological anthologies. Seen in this light, the editions of poetic materials by Lambert McKenna (also the compiler of the standard English-Irish dictionary *Foclóir Béarla agus Gaedhilge* of 1935) stand out as being of immense value and importance. His collections of 1938, 1939, 1947, and 1951 mark him as one of the unsung giants of the Irish literary tradition.

Often the anthologizing nature of such editions is not just the result of editorial selection from amid diverse manuscript sources but a reflection of the anthological nature of the edited manuscript itself. McKenna's edition of the 'Contention of the Bards', *Iomarbhágh na bhFileadh* (1917), is a case in point: a corpus always transcribed and transmitted as multiparty controversy between altercating poets. In other cases, what is edited is in fact itself a *duanaire* or poem-book, with texts by different poets organized around the addressee: the patron or family to whom such poems were addressed and dedicated, and by whom the collection was kept. Ó Donnchadha (1931), Carney (1945 and 1950), and McKenna (1947 and 1951) (poem-books for the Clannaboy O'Neills, Butlers, O'Reillys, Magaurans, and O'Haras, respectively) are examples in point.

Two patterns emerge from this. One is that early-independence Ireland, for all that it is often perceived as stagnated and unproductive, in fact achieved an immense amount in making literary material from pre-1600 Gaelic literature available for circulation and recirculation in twentieth-century print culture. The other is that this modern anthologizing tradition in Ireland reconnected with a pattern of nonauthorial text organization which was in fact a long-standing feature of Gaelic literature itself.

The Gaelic term *duanaire* – signifying 'aggregate of poems' – may already alert us to this.[20] The manuscript transmission of Gaelic literature rarely proceeded authorially; the usual organization of any manuscript being in itself a type of scribal anthology. The most important Gaelic codices from the eleventh to the sixteenth century (Leabhar na hUidre, and the Books of Glendalough, Leinster, Ballymote, Lecan, and Fermoy, listed at the head of Appendix B and all of them printed between 1875 and 1937) were, as hinted earlier on, anthologies themselves. After the catastrophic defeat of the Ulster Earls, an anthology-in-exile was produced on the continent around 1630, *Duanaire Finn* – and this collection may stand as a 'missing link' between a retrieval and recycling effort from within the

---

[20] Cf. Kelleher, 'The Anthology and the *Duanaire*'; Kelleher registers the occasional use of the word in titles and sets off the decline of Gaelic anthologizing against the rise of the English anthology, but does not address the pre-1800 specimens or their post-1870 recyclings.

stricken Gaelic tradition itself and the later retrievals heralded by Charlotte Brooke and by the 1795 collection entitled, again with a native phrase, *Bolg an tSolair* ('The Provider's Bag', connoting a cornucopia of miscellaneous 'goodies').

In all these respects, the anthology transcends divisions. It remains a constant in textual (re-)production from the Gaelic scribal tradition to the modern academic and commercial press; it reaches across different literary fields from academic philology to patriotic propaganda verse; and, most importantly, it rivets together the two different and competing literary languages of Ireland. In the last two centuries Irish anthologies have truly created, and embodied within their pages, the unity of Irish literature that they often strove to achieve or facilitate. That the lack of such a unity and continuity could at the same time be deplored in other quarters only shows how undervalued and unnoticed the anthologizing tradition has been. If there is, at the beginning of the present century, a sense that despite historical discontinuities and linguistic differences there is such a thing as an 'Irish Literature', then the credit is in no small part due to Ireland's anthologizing tradition.

A Flowchart Model of Textual (Re-)production and Literary Canonicity

The vastly simplified flowchart shown in Fig. 4 visualizes how canonicity is not a static condition but a dynamic function of reception processes involving constant reactivation ('endurance' or 'rediscovery'). It also suggests at which points this reactivation and retrieval process can cross language borders and cross over between different literary systems; in other words, that 'cultural transfers' are made possible by literary recycling.

Reading the chart from top to bottom, we can trace its processes as follows: *New writing* adds continually to the available reservoir of *reading supply*. Owing to complex mechanisms (e.g., taste, marketing and critical response, prestige of the author or endorsing critic) here subsumed under the notion *appeal*, some of this reading material meets with *failure* and drops into a disregarded, largely unread category here called *non-canon*. There it remains as long as it fails to obtain *appeal*, and is relegated to *oblivion*.

Other portions of *reading supply*, however, meet with a positive response (*success*) and as a result enter a category here called *canon* – which is, in fact, a diverse array of different 'canons' current in different parts of the reading market at large, with all sorts of crossovers, overlaps, and transfers between them. A text's position in that category is, however, subject to constant reappraisal. As long as it continues to obtain *appeal*, its *endurance* in the canon is ensured; once that fails, however, it falls, by way of *obsolescence*, into the category of *non-canon*ical texts.

With the exception of a few works of perennially enduring canonicity (the Bible, Homer, Dante, Shakespeare), a gravitational downward pull seems to draw most texts towards the limbo of non-canonical (unread or unappreciated) texts. The speed and trajectory of that process is complex and unpredictable, depending as it does on recurring and complex 'appeal' moments.

There is, however, an escape from *non-canon*icity: texts may, after longer or shorter periods of obsolescence or oblivion, gain fresh appeal

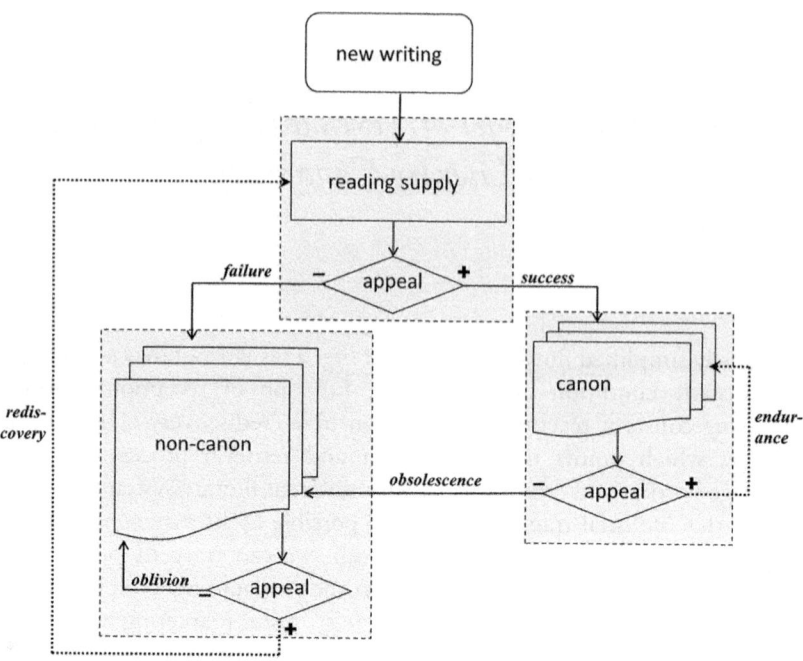

Fig. 4   Flowchart model of the dynamics of canonization, decanonization, and
recanonizaton

and re-enter the reservoir of available *reading supply* by means of *redis-covery*. From that moment onwards, the cycle begins afresh: the *rediscovery* may be more or less lasting or successful, depending, once again, on the complexities of what constitutes, among different readers and in different generations, literary appeal.

We can infer four things from this schematization.

1. *Endurance* of canonicity and *rediscovery* (dotted arrows) work in the opposite direction (upward in this chart) from the processes of *success, failure,* or *obsolescence* (downward in this chart). They illustrate the renewed availability of old material, rather than the downward vector, which illustrates the attrition of newly available material. Between them, these opposing vectors define the essence of what we call 'recycling'.

2. The 'downward' processes of *success, failure,* and *obsolescence* are the ones usually foregrounded in production-oriented literary histories; conversely, *endurance* and *rediscovery* come to the fore in the history of literary reception.

3. It is in these recycling processes of *endurance* and *rediscovery* that anthologies play their specific role.

4. The three 'appeal' moments in the flowchart, gathered in grey rectangles, are each in principle monolingual and occur within a reading public united by a shared language. The process of *success* may cross a linguistic frontier (translations), as well as the processes of *obsolescence* and *failure* (unread works being unread in any language, and obsolescence possibly occurring as a result of language death). Crucially, the process of *rediscovery* can cross linguistic borders and ensure texts' passage from one language to a different-language audience. (The same holds for the *endurance* process: canonicity can spread or radiate from one language to another, as the cases of Flann O'Brien and Nuala Ní Dhomhnaill show.) This seems particularly suggestive for multilanguage literary systems like Ireland.

A Thousand Years of Irish Anthologies: A Checklist of Some Representative Titles

Pre-1600

Leabhar na hUidhre, XId, RIA 1844, transcript facs 1870, Best/Bergin ed. 1929

Book of Glendalough, XIIb, BL, facs. ed. Kuno Meyer 1909

Book of Leinster, XII, Killiney/TCD, transcript facs ed. 1880

Book of Ballymote, XIVd, RIA 1875

Book of Lecan, XIVd-XVa, TCD>RIA, facs. ed. Kathleen Mulchrone 1937

Yellow Book of Lecan, XIVd-XVd, TCD, facs ed. 1896

Leabhar Breac, XVa, RIA 1789–1844, transcript facs. ed. 1872–76

Book of Fermoy, XIVd-XVI, incl Roche duanaire, RIA/BL XIXb

1600–1800

Book of the O'Conor Don, XVIIb, private

Duanaire Finn, XVIIb, MacNeill/Murphy ed. 1907–53

1789   Charlotte Brooke, *Reliques of Ancient Irish Poetry*

1795   *Bolg an tSolair*

1800–1920

1831   James Hardiman, *Irish Minstrelsy, or Bardic Remains of Ireland*

1839   Thomas Crofton Croker, *Popular Songs of Ireland*

1843   *The Spirit of the Nation*

1844   John O'Daly and Edward Walsh, *Reliques of Jacobite Poetry*

1845   M. J. Barry, *The Songs of Ireland*

1845   Charles Gavan Duffy, *The Ballad Poetry of Ireland*

1846   H. R. Montgomery, *Specimens of the Early Native Poetry of Ireland*

1846   Denis Florence MacCarthy, *The Book of Irish Ballads*

1847   Edward Walsh, *Irish Popular Songs*

1849 John O'Daly, *The Poets and Poetry of Munster* (with Mangan versions)

1852 William Hamilton Drummond, *Ancient Irish Minstrelsy*

1860 John O'Daly, *The Poets and Poetry of Munster*, 2nd ser. (with Sigerson versions)

1864 Samuel Ferguson, *Lays of the Western Gael*

1880 Charles Read, *The Cabinet of Irish Literature* (4 vols.)

1892 Standish Hayes O'Grady, *Silva gadelica*

1892 D. O. Crowley, *Irish Poets and Novelists*

1893 Douglas Hyde, *Love Songs of Connacht*

1894 Martin MacDermott, *The New Spirit of the Nation*

1894 *Poetry and Legendary Ballads of the South of Ireland*

1895 W. B. Yeats, *A Book of Irish Verse*

1897 George Sigerson, *Bards of the Gael and Gall*

1900 Justin McCarthy et al., *Irish Literature* (10 vols.)

1900 Stopford Brooke and T. W. Rolleston, *A Treasury of Irish Poetry in the English Tongue*

1901 Kuno Meyer, *Selections from Ancient Irish Poetry*

1906 Douglas Hyde, *Religious Songs of Connacht*

1909 John Cook, *The Dublin Book of Irish Verse*

1912 Eleanor Hull, *Poem-Book of the Gael*

1912 Mary J. Brown, *Historical Ballad Poetry of Ireland*

Post-1920

1921 L. D'O. Walters, *Irish Poets of To-day: An Anthology*

1922 Lambert McKenna, *Dán Dé*

1925 Lennox Robinson, *A Golden Treasury of Irish Verse*

1926 T. F. O'Rahilly, *Dánta Grádha*

1927 T. F. O'Rahilly, *Measgra Dánta*

1931 Tadhg Ó Donnchadha, *Leabhar Cloinne Aodha Buidhe*

1938 Lambert McKenna, *Dioghluim Dána*

1939 Lambert McKenna, *Aithdioghluim Dána*

1939 Colm Ó Lochlainn, *Irish Street Ballads*

1945 James Carney, *Poems on the Butlers, 1400–1650*

1947 Kathleen Hoagland, *1000 Years of Irish Poetry*

1947 Lambert McKenna, *Leabhar Meig Shamhradháin*

1948 Donagh MacDonagh and Lennox Robinson, *The Oxford Book of Irish Verse*

1950 James Carney, *Poems on the O'Reillys*

1951	Lambert McKenna, *Leabhar Í Eadhra*
1952	Colm Ó Lochlainn, *More Irish Street Ballads*
1958	Pádraig Ó Canainn, *Filíocht na nGael*
1959	Frank O'Connor, *Kings, Lords, & Commons: An Anthology from the Irish*
1967	David Greene and Frank O'Connor, *A Golden Treasury of Irish Poetry*
1967	Seán Lucy, *Love Poems of the Irish*
1967	Georges-Denis Zimmermann, *Songs of Irish Rebellion*
1969	Frank O'Brien, *Duanaire Nuafhilíochta*
1970	Osborn Bergin, *Irish Bardic Poetry*
1972	Derek Mahon, *Sphere Book of Modern Irish Poetry*
1973	Seán Lucy, *Irish Poets in English*
1974	Breandán O Conaire, *Éigse: Duanaire nua na hArdteistiméarachta*
1974	Párdaic Fiacc, *The Wearing of the Black*
1974	John Montague, *The Faber Book of Irish Verse*
1976–81	De Brún, Ó Buachalla, and O Concheanainn, *Nua-Dhuanaire* (3 vols.)
1979	Frank Ormsby, *Poets from the North of Ireland*
1979	Maurice Harmon, *Irish Poetry after Yeats: Seven Poets*
1981	Seán Ó Tuama and Thomas Kinsella, *An Duanaire: Poems of the Dispossessed*
1981	Brendan Kennelly, *Penguin Book of Irish Verse*
1985	Seán Dunne, *The Poets of Munster*
1986	Thomas Kinsella, *New Oxford Book of Irish Verse*
1986	Dermot Bolger, *The Bright Wave: An tonn gheal*
1986	Paul Muldoon, *The Faber Book of Contemporary Irish Poetry*
1988	A. A. Kelly, *Pillars of the House: An Anthology of Verse by Irish Women*
1989	John Montague, *Bitter Harvest*
1989	Ailbhe Smyth, *Wildish Things: An Anthology of New Irish Women's Writing*
1990	Derek Mahon and Peter Fallon, *Penguin Book of Contemporary Irish Poetry*
1991	Declan Kiberd and Gabriel Fitzmaurice, *Crann faoi bláth/The Flowering Tree*
1991/ 2002	*Field Day Anthology of Irish Writing* (3 + 2 vols.)
1995	Eilís Ní Dhuibhne, *Voices on the Wind: Women Poets of the Celtic Twilight*

1995	Patrick Crotty, *Modern Irish Poetry*
1995	K. Donovan, A. N. Jeffares, and B. Kennelly, *Ireland's Women*
1996	Theo Dorgan, *Irish Poetry since Kavanagh*
1997	Seán Dunne, *The Ireland Anthology*
1998	Andrew Carpenter, *Verse in English from Eighteenth-Century Ireland*
1999	Theo Dorgan and Noel Duffy, *Watching the River Flow*
1999	Seán McMahon, *1000 Years of Poetry: A Millennial Anthology*
2000	Gréagóir Ó Dúill, *Fearann Pinn: Filíocht 1900–1999*
2000	Colm Tóibín, *The Irish Times Book of Favourite Irish Poems*
2000	W. J. McCormack, *Ferocious Humanism*
2002	Michael Longley, *20th-Century Irish Poems*
2003	Andrew Carpenter, *Verse in English from Tudor and Stuart Ireland*
2004	Stephen Regan, *Irish Writing: An Anthology of Irish Literature in English 1789–1939*

CHAPTER 8

The Writing of County Histories in Parnell's Ireland

Nicholas Canny

In the course of my Parnell lecture for 2005 I reminded the audience that insufficient recognition has been given to the weight of historical material that was published both before and during the years associated with the Irish Literary Renaissance.[*] Then histories of all kinds were being written on Irish subjects, and editors were also busy compiling historical documents that were intended to authenticate the arguments being expounded in the historical tomes. My principal purpose in 2005 was to make the case that the contours of what today we describe as the early modern period of Irish history were then delineated as historians of opposing political views contested the merits of what everybody accepted were the two transformative achievements of the sixteenth and seventeenth centuries: the government's designation of Protestantism as the official religion of the state, and its securing most of Ireland's wealth for the British and Protestant interest, principally through the process of plantation.

The histories to which I then made reference took several forms; some authors wrote biographies of those they identified as either villains or heroes of the past; others traced the course of events in particular dioceses or individual parishes; some wrote the histories of particular cities or towns; and yet others tracked the fate of particular lordships down the centuries. Some of the histories published were single-volume works, while others extended to several volumes, and some, such as Maurice Lenihan, *Limerick: Its History and Antiquities* (1866) (a city rather than a county history), were serialized in newspapers before they were finally put between covers. Historians also brought their subject to the people (or at least to the increasing proportion of the population who were literate in English) by defending their findings or challenging the contentions and evidence of rival interpreters in the pages of newspapers. Also many of the conclusions proposed by those who had

---

[*] I am grateful for Dr Ciaran Ó Murchadha for the valuable advice he offered me on an earlier draft of this chapter.

invested time in archival research on special topics reached a wider public when they were repeated in the general narratives on Ireland's history that sought either to justify or to condemn the discontinuity with Ireland's more ancient past that all authors dated to the early modern centuries.

This summary of what I presented in 2005 will explain why in Parnell's Ireland, past history, and particularly the history of the early modern centuries, became present politics. Indeed as I researched my subject I found that almost all Irish-based historical scholars of the time had been drawn to their subject because it provided them with a platform from which to pronounce on particular political or denominational positions that were important to them.

More recently, I have come to realize that I would have discovered some historians in Parnell's Ireland who were more concerned to understand what had happened in the past and to reduce political and religious animosities had I looked to those who were then involved with the writing of Irish county histories. Now that I have consulted several county histories written at that time, I find that the authors of county histories could be more even-tempered than most other historians of the time and for a variety of reasons. To begin with, the Irish county had been an English creation that dated back either to medieval times or to the sixteenth and early seventeenth centuries. Since the county was a unit associated with the extension of English law and administration throughout the country, those attracted to writing county histories tended to be those who admired this endeavour because either they themselves or their patrons had been involved with county administration.

County histories, whether written by Protestant or Catholic authors, tended therefore to be patriarchal in tone. Most authors assumed the existence of a county community whose prosperity and well-being relied upon the benevolent oversight of the principal landed proprietors who, regardless of political or religious differences, best understood the needs and the problems of their respective counties. Authors also usually considered that the county gentry were best placed to seek remedies for any deficiencies in the affairs of the counties in which they held their property, because they, or their ancestors, had customarily provided for its defence and because two of their number had usually served as county representatives in parliament, initially in Dublin and later at Westminster.

Insofar as would-be Irish authors of county histories in the late nineteenth century had models to follow, they may have consulted earlier Irish county histories such as those on Cork and Waterford written by Charles Smith, a client of the Boyle family, or *The History, Topography*

and Antiquities of the County and City of Limerick, published in
1826 by the Reverend P. Fitzgerald, a vicar of the Church of Ireland.
However, it is likely that the county histories of England that were being
published intermittently over the course of the nineteenth century, and
that were to become institutionalized in 1903 as the Victoria County
Histories of England, were also a potent influence on such authors.
Certainly, when F. Elrington Ball brought a multivolume *History of the
County of Dublin* to completion in 1902 he explained that he had taken the
parish as the most logical 'geographic unit' around which to organize his
succeeding chapters, 'because in England it has been found the most
convenient division for local history'.[1]

It is likely that English models would have been in the minds of W. G.
Wood-Martin, who devoted several years to compiling data for his *History of
Sligo: County and Town*, which was published sequentially in three volumes
in 1882, 1889, and 1892.[2] The author, who came from a Church of Ireland
minor gentry family (whose descendants still reside in the county), was
associated with the Sligo Artillery, and we can see that as his volumes were
appearing in print he had been moving up the ranks from being major to
becoming lieutenant colonel and finally colonel. His military service indicated his political allegiance, as did his previous historical work on the
contribution made by Sligo recruits to the Inniskilling Fusiliers. While some
of the prejudices that one would expect from a person of his position and
denomination feature in his writing, he did not pursue any political or
religious agenda in strident fashion. Rather, his objective, as he put it in his
first volume, was to offer 'a thoroughly faithful and vivid picture of the
whole life of the county of Sligo from its cradle upwards . . . to historic and
comparatively modern days'. By the time he came to his third volume,
which had 1892 as its terminal date, he expressed the hope that his
endeavour might have aroused in his readers 'a feeling and more lively
interest and more earnest love for the County and Town of Sligo'.[3]

Wood-Martin set about his task, as did most historians of Irish counties,
by discoursing on the topography, etymology, and legendary lore of the
county, and in so doing he also drew upon the records of the Ordnance
Survey. Then as he coursed through the medieval centuries, he paused
only to record the imprint made by more forceful rulers on the county as,

---

[1] F. Elrington Ball, *A History of the County of Dublin: The People, Parishes and Antiquities from the Earliest Times to the Close of the Eighteenth Century*, 3 vols. (Dublin, 1902), preface.
[2] W. G. Wood-Martin, *History of Sligo: County and Town*, 3 vols. (Dublin, 1882, 1889, 1892).
[3] Ibid., preface to vol. 1, and preface to vol. 3. Further references are cited in the text.

for example, Richard de Burgo, the Red Earl, 'the most powerful subject in Ireland' who had 'made war, raising and deposing at his pleasure the native chiefs of Connacht and Ulster, but also founded numerous monasteries and castles in various parts of Ireland' including 'the castles of Ballymote, Corran and Sligo, in the present County Sligo' (1:213). While he took due account of the cultural achievements of Ireland's ancient past, and particularly of the contribution to this legacy made by institutions and people with Sligo associations, he concluded, rather condescendingly, that the totality marked 'no remarkable advance in civilization or education ... except in the case of those who were destined for the priesthood'. Then, on the political front, Wood-Martin asserted that the history of the county in earlier centuries had been modulated by 'feuds among petty rival chiefs', occasioned principally by 'the absence of a fixed law of succession' (1:ix–xi). This, he contended, had been exacerbated when Spain became embroiled in the affairs of the county in 1588 when some of the ships of the defeated Spanish Armada were wrecked off the coastline of Sligo, at which point 'every one's hand [was] uplifted against his neighbour'. The only positive development of the sixteenth century that Wood-Martin could discern was the Composition of Connacht of 1585 when, as he understood it, 'O'Connor Sligo voluntarily renounced his Irish style and title, agreed to abolish Irish gavelkind and tanistry, and to hold his land by English tenure'. An even more positive outcome, according to Wood-Martin's interpretation of events, was that this placed all other 'chiefs in Sligo under his authority' when they 'agreed to follow his example'. 'Thus', Wood-Martin proclaimed, 'Sligo theoretically was brought to the status of an ordinary English county' (1:300, 312, 317).

This conspectus of what had transpired in Sligo down to its establishment as a county prepared the way for his second volume that dealt with developments in Sligo 'from the accession of King James 1 to the Revolution of 1688', a period during which 'Sligo, in common with many other parts of Ireland ... frequently – we might say almost continuously – felt the cruel scourge of war' (2:4). His investigation of the ownership of land in Sligo during the earlier part of the seventeenth century left him satisfied that the amount of land 'forfeited to the crown, and given or sold to Protestant settlers' was 'surprisingly small', and he believed that stability and harmony would have persisted were it not for the intervention of Lord Deputy Wentworth, who, treating 'Saxon and Celt alike' with his 'iron rule', set himself a task that was 'nothing less than the establishment of British settlers in the entire western province', including in Sligo.[4] It was

---

[4] Vol. 2, chapter 11, treats of the Wentworth episode.

this external interference, he believed, that provoked the 'popular uprising' of 1641, which he likened to the eruption of a volcano, and which he was able to describe graphically by drawing upon the so-called 1641 depositions for that county. He, like most credible authors before and since, believed that the disturbance in Sligo was precipitated by 'the lords of the Irish,' whose 'original intentions' he could not fathom, but who, after they had broken the mould, became powerless 'to restrain their subordinates' once their 'passions had been aroused', this being 'but the natural result of stimulating the passions of an ignorant people' (2:59).

The long-term consequence of the popular outburst and assault upon the Protestant population of Sligo was, according to Wood-Martin, the confis-cation of much of the land of the county held by Catholics, the enlargement of the estates held by Protestants already present in the County, and the addition of new proprietors to the Protestant ranks. This redistribution, as Wood-Martin saw it, gave rise to 'internecine strife' between the Protestant and Catholic landed interests in Sligo that spilled over into military conflict from 1688 to 1691. Wood-Martin explained that the consequence of this war for Catholic proprietors was a further loss of land once William and Mary were secure on the British throne. While he expressed sympathy for the plight of those who lost their estates, he insisted also that 'at the close of the struggle many Protestants found themselves ruined', and he expressed particular concern for the poorer elements of the county's population – 'the unfortunate inhabitants who had joined neither of the rival parties under arms' – who had been impoverished by the conflict (3:1–2). The tragedy, as he saw it, was that the outcome had been a foregone conclusion because the Protestant landowners had formed themselves into 'local military organiza-tions' long before 1688. These, he claimed, were 'in great part' descendants of those who had upheld the Protestant interest in the county in the decades following the insurrection of 1641, including 'members of Colonel Richard Coote's regiment of horse, [and of] Colonel Charles Coote's regiment of horse and his regiment of foot' (3:4). His positive invocation of parts played by members of the Coote family in the history of the county would not have endeared him to Catholic readers given the negative portrayal of the Cootes in popular memory because of the forceful part they had played in suppres-sing the cause of the Catholic Confederacy. However, Wood-Martin seems to have considered it worth taking the risk of offending Catholic sensibilities in the interest of emphasizing how many of the Protestant landed families in Sligo of his own day pre-dated the Cromwellian conquest of Ireland. He made this same point graphically in his second volume when, in the course of discussing how Mr Parke had been 'shut up' in Newtown Castle by the insurgents of 1641, he published, on the facing page, a nineteenth-century drawing of Newtown Castle on Lough Gill, 'the property of Major Roger Parke, 3rd dragoon guards' (2:60).

Having thus explained how the Protestant gentry of Sligo had come into being, Wood-Martin detailed how, through the eighteenth and into the nineteenth centuries, they had lived up to their responsibility of defending and contributing to the well-being and good governance of the county. He mentioned also that some had served the British crown in foreign assignments. When it came to local service and representation he gave credit to the Gore, Wingfield, Morgan, Coote, Ormsby, Wynne, O'Hara, and Cooper families, while in the matter of international distinction he made special mention of Richard Coote, son of the first Baron Collooney, who had supported King William III, was rewarded with the title of earl of Bellamont, served as Treasurer and Receiver General to Queen Mary, and was then appointed in 1690 as Governor of New England and New York and 'Admiral of those seas'. Wood-Martin also explained how after 1776, when Ireland was exposed to the possibility of French invasion during the course of the American Revolutionary War, the Sligo gentry, commanded by Mr Wynne, had contributed generously to the Volunteers – 'a body of 100,000 men, self clothed, self disciplined and without pay', who, as he put it, performed commendably in discharging 'the duties of the army' until 'unfortunately they afterwards turned their attention to politics upon which rocks they made shipwreck' (3:4–5, 8).

Wood-Martin believed that 'prior to the year 1790, Protestants and Roman Catholics lived on very good terms' in Sligo and that this harmony had prevailed until 1794 when the 'Defenders' began to commit 'outrages' and to take 'unlawful oaths'. Even then, he remained confident that 'the peasantry would not have risen' without the French invasion at Killala (3:11, 17). Thus, as in 1641 and in 1688, he considered that external interference rather than any failure of local leadership had precipitated disturbances in Sligo in 1798. These disturbances, he stated, led to the flight of the Protestant clergy from the county, the destruction of their churches, the plundering of the houses of the gentry, and again the impoverishment of the ordinary people, who were the invariable sufferers in all such uprisings. Nonetheless, he remained satisfied that order was quickly restored to the county and that Sligo fighting men – Catholic as well as Protestant – contributed significantly to the British war effort both at the battle of Vinegar Hill in Wexford and in the continuing conflict in France right down to 1814 (3:25–34).

Sligo's normal communal harmony continued, according to Wood-Martin, until 1822 when 'the titular bishop of Killala' intervened to impose a 'religious effect' upon the elections of that year in Sligo with the result that 'religious feeling was greatly excited' in the county. Tension became even more acute when Daniel O'Connell visited the county in 1828 with a view to 'hunting' a sitting Member of Parliament to make way for a nominee of his choosing. Wood-Martin cited with disapproval 'a specimen of O'Connell's style or oratory' designed to mock and belittle the rival candidate named Martin (possibly an ancestor of Wood-Martin himself) and 'to inflame passions'. The consequence was that in 1829 'the mob broke the windows of almost every Protestant household in Sligo'. Worse was to follow, according to Wood-Martin, until 'in short liberty had degenerated into licence [and] votes were almost openly sold' (3:39–40, 51, 53, 62).

At this point Wood-Martin's narrative of political events tapered off even though his terminal date was 1892. It is likely that he took this decision because he found nineteenth-century politics distasteful given that the political role of the cohort of Sligo's population that he represented had been brought to an end by the rise of O'Connell and what he believed to be clerical involvement in politics. This elision meant that the name of Parnell was never once mentioned by him and his only oblique reference to Parnell's achievements was his complaint that the 'popular element' in the courts of the Land Commission had been 'too strong and the legal element too weak' with the result that rents had been 'worked down' because 'a too willing ear' had been 'given to the extravagant claims made by the tenants for alleged improvements'. While not disputing that 'rack-renting' had been practiced in the county, his vindication of landowners was that rack-renting was not 'general, nor as a rule, common' and was, to some degree, offset by land improvements implemented by some landlords at their personal expense (3:293–94, 296–97).

While Wood-Martin seemed reconciled to landowners (and particularly Protestant landowners) becoming eclipsed as political leaders of their county, his continuing narrative made it clear that the Protestant community had played a continuing role in improvement. What they had already done before the 1820s included the creation of 'plantings' at Markree, Annaghmore, Hazlewood, and Templehouse; the 1756 investment by Lord Shelburne in promoting Ballymote as a linen town; experiments in the hatching of salmon fry and the production of kelp; and the establishment of Sligo town in 1750 as a provisioning port for British fleets and later again as a steam shipping port to Liverpool (3:241, 248, 259, 284). Wood-Martin also gave attention to the role the gentry had played in reducing, and even staving off, the sufferings of the 'population' in times of pestilence and also whenever the potato or flax crops fell short of expectations or failed outright. He dated such calamities to 1765, 1802, 1812, 1816, 1817, 1821, 1832, and 1845–48. This sequence persisted, he insisted, even to 1879 when 'the potato crop was again almost an entire failure'. He reported ruefully that the efforts of landowners, combined with those of the government and philanthropic bodies, had not been sufficient to prevent the calamity of the Great Famine, but he suggested they were not the only ones whose endeavours had fallen short when he mentioned that 'even so late as the year 1861' it still rankled in the minds of the merchants' how the food intended to relieve hunger in Sligo had been disposed of (3:83).

While he acknowledged that the landed elite had been incapable of averting the Great Famine, he credited them with lessening the effect of a catastrophe that he considered inescapable because of the excessive 'dependence' of the population upon the potato crop. They had done so, he claimed, by promoting emigration schemes from as early as 1832. He also chronicled the general positive record of landowners in combating disease. This led Wood-Martin to a detailed consideration of the major contribution made by the gentry, and by the Victorian state, to the spectacular improvement of the county and town of Sligo through the construction of roads, bridges, canals, ports, workhouses, artisan dwellings, a gaol, a fever hospital, a lunatic asylum, police barracks, a waterworks, cemeteries, and eventually the railroad. As he described the physical improvement to Sligo town that had been achieved by official bodies in a relatively short time, Wood-Martin detailed also the vital contribution made by businesses, philanthropic bodies, and churches of all denominations to the construction of banks, churches, a Catholic cathedral, schools, and accommodation for clubs and voluntary societies. Several of these developments, such as the consecration of the Catholic cathedral in 1874 'in the presence of Cardinal Cullen and most of the Roman Catholic bishops of Ireland, and also some from England and America' must have reminded Wood-Martin how the once dominant Protestant community, who were now more numerous and diverse, had been eclipsed politically by Catholics. However, while he voiced concern over occasional popular attacks upon the property of Protestants he attributed these to incendiary priests or illegal societies, and he remained satisfied that the Catholic population at large had remained well disposed to their Protestant neighbours. Thus, he exuded confidence that, in this changed political environment, the Protestant community of the town and county of Sligo would continue to play an important role in the improvement of a community to which all belonged. In his optimism he clearly parted ways with the authors of typical Unionist grand narratives of Ireland's past who invariably cited the demonstrable failure of Irish Catholics to govern themselves rationally in the past as proof that they would be equally incapable of doing so in the future.

When James Frost[5] set himself the task of writing a history of County Clare, which was duly published in 1893, he is likely to have been guided considerably by the example of Wood-Martin, whose first two volumes had already appeared in 1882 and 1889 and whose third volume was published in 1892 as Frost would have been about to go to press. The late appearance of Wood-Martin's third volume would not have troubled Frost since his history spanned only from the earliest times to the beginning of the eighteenth century.[6] He began, as had Wood-Martin with Sligo, with a topography of the Gaelic lordship of Thomond 'before the English settlement of the county', and, as with Wood-Martin, this drew heavily on the description of the county and its antiquities composed by the authors of the Ordnance Survey (1). Again, like Wood-Martin with Sligo, Frost believed that 'before the territory of Thomond was formed into a county by the English it [had been] divided into distinct districts by the native inhabitants' and that the baronies into which the English segmented the county correspond roughly with these districts. Each such area, according to Frost, had been 'owned by its separate clan and presided over by its particular chieftain' all of whom had Brian Boroimhe and his successors, kings of Thomond, as their 'lord paramount' (4). Frost indicated at one point in his narrative that the political conditions were then idyllic with 'the natives, being masters of the land of their birth' and with each sept, and each individual of the sept, having the opportunity to enjoy his 'property absolutely free from any control of a man calling himself his landlord' (235). However, he later retracted this appraisal (without seeming to realize he was contradicting himself) when he pronounced (and here again he was agreeing with Wood-Martin) that

> of all the political institutions ever devised by human ingenuity the system of clanship, as it had prevailed in Ireland, was the best contrived for retarding the progress of civilization and preventing the material prosperity of a people. (256)

This was so, he averred, because the system encouraged each lord to transgress upon the territory of his neighbours, and Frost, like Wood-Martin in the case of Sligo, looked favourably on the incorporation in 1580 of the various segments of Thomond into the single county of Clare. This confidence was not disturbed by his belief that the establishment of

[5] Cian O'Carroll, 'A Thomond Scholar: James Frost, MRIA, 1827–1907', *The Other Clare* 2 (1979): 28. I am grateful to Dr Ciaran Ó Murchadha for this reference.

[6] James Frost, *The History and Topography of the County of Clare: From the Earliest Times to the Beginning of the Eighteenth Century* (Dublin, 1893). Further references are cited in the text.

the rule of England and the 'endeavour to subdue the people and bring them under the British system of land tenure' had been proceeded with in 1542 only when the government brought over the ruling O'Brien 'to their intentions' by the offer to him of 'enormous bribes'. This bribery, he contended, extended to granting the ruling O'Brien the entire lordship of Thomond 'in fee simple' together with a grant to him of the abbey lands within the lordship (235).

Thus, while Frost, like Wood-Martin, provided a substantial account of developments in the Irish lordship during the medieval centuries, he too believed that his story really began only with the formation of Thomond into an English County in 1580 (226). The commonality of the approaches of the two authors and the favourable response of each to the introduction of English rule into their respective counties may be attributed to the fact that Frost, like Wood-Martin, came from minor gentry background and, therefore, would have been a strict upholder of the law, as it was administered in the nineteenth century, and suspicious of any subversive threat to the existing social order.

If we can take it that the social position of our two authors accounts for the cautious conservatism of each, Frost experienced difficulty in always seeming to support official policy for Ireland because, while he was a landowner he was also a Catholic and would have been keenly aware of the disabilities under which Catholic landowners, like his ancestors, had operated because of their continued loyalty to their faith. Moreover, he would have known many of the details concerning the religious persecution that Catholics in Ireland and in Clare had suffered in past centuries, because these were deeply imbedded in popular memory and were regularly recounted by Catholic priests in their sermons. The author's religious attachment would explain why, when detailing the positive attributes of Gaelic society in Thomond before it was fashioned into a county, he made special mention of how 'the church of the people ... had [had] its rights clearly defined, and enjoyed the lands bestowed upon it by the munificence of pious benefactors' (235).

For Frost, therefore, the negative aspect of the extension of English rule into the former lordship was its religious dimension when 'the monasteries of Clare were suppressed ... [and] the brethren were expelled'. He instanced the experience of Quin Abbey, which had been endowed and supported by the Mc Namara sept, only to be 'converted into a barrack by the English garrison'. Then, after Quin Abbey had been recovered and restored by the Mc Namaras, Frost explained that it had been again destroyed by the forces of Cromwell and that Rory Mc Namara, a friar, was then taken and shot by Cromwell's officers near Clare Castle in 1651. This served as a preliminary to his listing others in Clare who had died for their faith in Cromwellian times, when the inhabitants of the county 'for the greater part' 'were either slain or driven into exile; its priests proscribed and forced to flee into the mountains and woods for the performance of the divine offices; its pastures were denuded of cattle; and poverty and sorrow reigned throughout the land' (52–53, 527).

The ultimate 'policy of the English party' at this time was, he contended, 'to extirpate the Catholic clergy' rather than to convert the population to Protestantism as could be proven by the fact that 'the Puritans under Cromwell and Ireton ... thought three Protestant ministers sufficient for the want of the whole county' (551–53). This, for him, contrasted poorly with the experience of previous decades when 'it was part of the plan devised for the subjugation of Ireland, that the Protestant religion should supersede the old faith of the inhabitants'. To sustain his point that the authorities had then been sincere about conversion, Frost cited from the report of the Commission of 1622 that identified the Protestant clergy, most of them from England, who had been listed by the bishops of Killaloe and Kilfenora as holding appointments in the various parishes of County Clare (550–51).

For Frost, the period of most intense persecution of Catholic clergy had been the Cromwellian era when Catholicism had survived only because the people successfully hid some priests from the authorities. Then, as he traced the narration of religious developments in the county from the Restoration of 1660 to the accession of William and Mary, Frost found but occasional breaks in 'English persecution' of the Catholic clergy in Clare. Despite such persecution he celebrated the endurance of many Catholic priests in the county when he identified those who had been 'listed' by the state authorities in 1704 as the authorized Catholic clergy for the county (552).

Frost also provided a political narrative of the 'sanguinary struggle between the rival races that did not come to an end till the time of Cromwell and William III'. This, he believed, had been provoked by the efforts of the authorities to establish 'the rule of England' and 'to subdue the people, and bring them under the British system of land tenure'. We already noted his belief that the cooperation of the O'Brien dynasty with the wishes of the state in this matter had been for the better, even if it had involved bribery. Therefore, he lacked sympathy for the effort of Red Hugh O'Donnell to reverse this achievement by invading the county in 1599 during the course of the Nine Years' War (256–57). His principal criticism of the state during those years concerned the efforts of successive rulers to raise excessive rents from the property owners of the county. It was discontent over these levies, he believed, that had persuaded the Catholic landowners of Clare to join the 'rising of the Catholics that was general throughout the country'. The more dramatic actions in Clare that Frost mentioned concerned attacks made by Catholics upon the Protestants who had settled in the County, principally as tenants on the O'Brien estates. The detail he provided for such attacks came from the depositions collected from those Protestants who had survived them, including the account given by Maurice Cuffe, a merchant of Ennis, who had defended himself, and many other Protestant settlers, in the siege of Ballyalla Castle.

This rising and the effort of the Protestants in Clare to retain their positions led to what Frost described as 'the disastrous period of the Civil War of 1641' after which the Catholic people of Clare, 'like all other Catholic Irishmen of the time', took an 'active interest' in the proceedings of the Confederation of Kilkenny (338). As he skimmed over what happened in 'these disastrous times', he thought it was 'to be lamented that the heads of the great family of O'Brien lent their support to the cause of the English invader' (388). In this respect he made particular mention of Morrogh O'Brien, baron, and later earl, of Inchiquin, who 'at one moment was a Confederate Catholic, at another a Protestant and Parliamentarian. After changing his political and religious creed no less than four times, he at last died a Catholic.' However, while he expressed doubts about the character of Inchiquin – popularly remembered by Catholics in Clare as *Murchadh na dTóiteán*, Morrogh of the Burnings – Frost refrained from dwelling on 'his exploits', on the grounds that these belonged 'to the general history of the country' and were relevant to the history of the county only insofar that 'it may be assumed that, amongst his followers and soldiers, were many of his kinsmen and tenants from Clare'. And while Frost considered that the 'conduct' of Inchiquin during the Civil War in Ireland proved him to be 'an unscrupulous politician', he pronounced that it also marked him out as 'an able general' (371, 388).[7]

This led Frost to a consideration of the Cromwellian settlement in Clare where existing Catholic proprietors were dispossessed to make way both for Protestant grantees and for 'innocent Papists' from within the county and from other counties of Ireland who were assigned land in Clare as part of the transplantation of Catholics to Connacht and Clare. One is left to assume that Frost's own ancestors were among these grantees, which would explain the attention he devoted to the usually futile efforts of dispossessed Irish Catholic proprietors to secure a return of their property

---

[7] For a biographical sketch of Inchiquin, see that by John A. Murphy, in *Dictionary of Irish Biography* (Dublin, 2009), 7:67–69.

under the Act of Settlement that was operated in the 1670s by the government of King Charles II. As he did so he mentioned the success of Donogh O'Brien, son of Conor O'Brien of Lemenagh and Dromoland, who 'had been slain in the king's service', and of his wife Máire Rua Mc Mahon, in securing a recovery as 'an innocent Protestant' of the estates of which the family had been deprived by the 'usurped powers'. While mentioning that the children of Donogh O'Brien and Máire Rua had been brought up as Protestants, Frost did not explain the methods used by Máire Rua to recover the family estates for her son despite the fact that her role in the matter was deemed notorious in the historical memory of Catholics in Clare (394).

Frost's account of further forfeitures and distributions in subsequent decades was in effect a chronicle of the decline of Catholic proprietorship in County Clare as 'the inhabitants continued to be driven out to make way for the new settlers'. He also explained how those who escaped confiscation were impoverished by the poll tax imposed by 'Ireton's Lieutenants' that continued to be levied under the guise of subsidies during the reign of Charles II (527, 531–32). This, as he saw it, explained why those Catholics who continued to hold land in the county mobilized under the command of Viscount Clare to support King James II when William of Orange challenged that king's authority. The members of 'Clare's dragoons' who supported James were, according to Frost, but 'raw recruits' who performed badly at the Battle of the Boyne but who were nonetheless penalized by confiscation and exile after the final victory of William had been achieved. Frost considered that the reputation of Clare's dragoons as brave fighting men was subsequently redeemed by their commendable performance in the wars on Continental Europe, and he suggested that their lot in poverty and exile was preferable to that of the small number of Catholics (including Frost's own family) who remained in possession of some estates in the county and suffered 'slavery and degradation at home under Penal laws' (567, 603).

This appraisal suggests that Frost seemed to think that it was Catholic landowners rather than priests or the more humble lay population who bore the principal brunt of the Penal Laws in Clare. However, while regretting the loss of power, influence, and land by Catholic proprietors in his county he seemed as ready, as was Wood-Martin in the case of Sligo, to accept what had occurred in the past as an accomplished fact. We have already noted his regret that the principal branches of the O'Brien family had sided with the government at critical moments in the past, but this did not dilute his respect for that dynasty as can be seen from his publishing in an appendix a 'pedigree of the family of O'Brien from Brian Boroimhe to 1717'. Similarly, while he recorded the slippage of land away from indigenous Catholic proprietors into the hands of Protestants, Frost showed nothing but respect for the descendants of these, mostly English adventurers, and illustrated his text with depictions of the nineteenth-century residences of some of their number. More particularly, when he instanced the questionable manner in which Thomas Spaight had first came into the possession of land in County Clare he mentioned in a footnote that 'this Thomas Spaight [was] the ancestor of the highly respectable families of that name in Clare, Limerick and Tipperary. . . [and was] also represented in Clare in the female line by Robert Carey Reeves, D.L. of Besborough, Killinena and by Francis Morice, Esq of Springfield, Sixmilebridge' (537). And while he had paused to celebrate the achievements of Clare's Dragoons in foreign service, Frost also occasionally saluted service by landed Protestant families from County Clare in British forces. Thus, when describing Coney Island on the Shannon he noted that there was a hill on the island 'on the summit of which stands a monument to the memory of one of the children of the late Field-Marshal Sir John Fitzgerald, KCB' (542). And in listing in his appendices the names of those who had served as Members of Parliament for Ennis in 1613–1880 and for County Clare in 1583–1886, and those from the County who, during the era of the Penal Laws, had converted 'from Popery to Protestant religion', he showed nothing but respect for the actions and decisions of these individuals.

By choosing to write county history rather than national history, Frost, like Wood-Martin, had found a vehicle through which he might encourage his readers to take pride in their county community by knowing something of its past. The social background of our two authors, as I have suggested, may explain why each remained attached to the existing social order. However, either one (or both) may also have been guided by the advice of John Mitchel, the Young Irelander of 1848, who when considering the injustices inflicted upon the indigenous population in Ulster at the time of the plantation in that province, exhorted his readers to welcome the descendants of the planters as potential members of a united nation since the land they occupied was held 'by far too old a title to be questioned'.[8] Our two authors may also have been inspired by Mitchel's further observation that

> when Irishmen consent to let the past become indeed History, not party politics, and begin to learn from it the lessons of mutual respect and tolerance, instead of endless bitterness and enmity; then, at last, this distracted land shall see the dawn of hope and peace, and begin to renew her youth and rear her head amongst the proudest of the nations.[9]

---

[8] John Mitchel, *The Life and Times of Aodh O'Neill, Prince of Ulster* (Dublin, 1845), viii.
[9] Mitchel, The Life and Times of Aodh O'Neill, xii.

Some historians in nineteenth-century Ireland may have been inspired by such sentiments but not so Canon Patrick White, who in 1893, the same year in which Frost's history appeared, published a book also entitled *The History of Clare and the Dalcassian Clans of Tipperary, Limerick and Galway*. This well-written work is far more engaging than that of Frost, but it differed sharply from what Wood-Martin and Frost had written because Canon White displayed scant respect for (and made little mention of) county or governmental institutions, and because his loyalties and admiration were fixed more on one segment of the population of the county, those 'at home and abroad' who were descended from what he described as 'the Dalcassian clans' resident in the lordship of Thomond, and also further afield, before Thomond was designated as County Clare in 1580.[10] Because his focus was different, Canon White had no reason to solicit respect for the existing social order as Wood-Martin and Frost had done, and his narrative, from the earliest times to his own day, seemed more concerned to use historical evidence to demonstrate that those who held the most prominent social positions in County Clare, and their ancestors, were but intruders upon property once held by the true leaders of the community. Thus, when exulting at the outset of the honours that accrued to Clare's Dragoons on the battlefields of Europe, he lamented that Carrigaholt Castle, once held by the Mc Mahons of the 'yellow dragoons', was in the hands of the Burton family, who, he implied, did not belong there (6). Members of the existing elite, as he saw it, were either strangers to or oppressors of the county community whose 'people [were] literally one family, bonded together by the well-defined ties of ancient blood and historic descent' (20). He might have added Catholicism as an even more potent bonding agent, since Canon White was using in a county context the same methods and assumptions that authors of Irish Catholic Nationalist history, such as Fr C. P. Meehan (whom he cited with approval), had previously employed in the writing of histories of the 'nation', the diocese, or the parish.

Catholic nationalist history, as opposed to the inclusive nationalist history advocated by John Mitchel, derived from church history which, in nineteenth-century Ireland, regardless of whether its authors were Protestant or Catholic, was invariably polemical and political because those who were trained in that craft knew how to use the historical record to demonstrate that the church of which the author was writing was the true

---

[10] P. White, *The History of Clare and the Dalcassian Clans of Tipperary, Limerick and Galway* (Dublin, 1893), title page and dedication. Further references are cited in the text.

church established by Christ and that all other churches were therefore deficient in one or several ways. Authors of such history conceded that the people with whom they were primarily concerned had suffered persecution as a test of their faith, but they also discerned occasional signs of divine (or providential) intervention in human affairs that encouraged those who experienced reverses to persist with their struggle in the certain knowledge that they would eventually be redeemed in a political as well as in a spiritual sense. Church history was therefore also prophetic history. Thus, while Canon White found himself having to end his *History of Clare* with 'the deplorable division caused in the national ranks by the unhappy fall of Mr. Parnell', he remained satisfied that the final political ambition of the people whose history he had recorded was within reach and that they would recover the 'right to self-government' of which the Dalcassian clans had been deprived in the sixteenth century (153, 375). Canon White's optimism stemmed first from the fact that Daniel O'Connell, backed by 'the priests and the people', and 'in tones of thunder', had commenced his campaign to secure the political and religious emancipation of the Catholic people of Ireland in County Clare. By electing O'Connell to Westminster, pronounced Canon White, 'Clare had killed with one blow Protestant Ascendancy and Catholic association', thus revealing his own antipathy to Catholics seeking negotiated concessions from a hostile government, as he was to Protestants enjoying a monopoly of power at the national or county levels (328). White was confident also because his people, or a reasonable percentage of them, had endured the vicissitude of the Great Famine, and he rejoiced particularly because, after the famine years, and with support from priests, preaching to them in 'their own Irish language', they had resisted 'the vigorous and persevering attempt' made to proselytize them. And he was encouraged also because 'the descendants of the Dalcassian clans' who had remained in the county had already recovered much of the land that had fallen into Protestant possession in past centuries, and he dedicated much of his history to showing how this land had come into Protestant possession in the first instance (6, 333, 365, 375).

This brief conspectus shows that Canon White's history of Clare bore many of the characteristics of a Church history that traced what had befallen a particular people from a lost golden age to the eve of a fresh dawn when those who had endured innumerable reversals and betrayals would recover their rightful inheritance. As he proceeded with his task, Canon White, as we noted in the case of O'Connell, isolated for praise particular individuals who, at various junctures, had defended those people whose cause he espoused. However, such heroes were few and he devoted greater attention to disparaging those who had betrayed their trust or oppressed the people and those to 'whom an evil fame popularly attaches' (295). In doing so he implied that misfortunate had always befallen such evildoers, almost as if by Divine decree.

Canon White began, as did most historians of Irish counties, with a moving description of the geography of Clare. This was clearly based on his own observations, even when he cited the publications of O'Donovan and O'Curry to authenticate what he had to say. Thereafter, he explained how 'for many centuries before the introduction of Christianity' to Clare, the Milesians and their descendants had fashioned 'a civilized government and a homogenous free people' that had no equivalent in the other countries of Northern and Central Europe in that the people there 'had learned to substitute law for mere force' (15). This civilization, he believed, was defective only in that the religion the Milesians had practiced had the 'one great blot' of encouraging human sacrifice, which defect was remedied when St Patrick, and in the case of Clare St Senan, brought Christianity to the country and the county (25–26). This success in Christianizing what was otherwise a perfect order was disturbed by the 'sacrilege' and 'unholy work' perpetrated by the Danish invaders whose 'desecration' of the religious settlement on Scattery Island was later avenged by Brian Boroimhe at the battle of Clontarf (1014) in which 'some will see the hand of Providence' (7, 43–47). Then came the arrival to Ireland (and to Thomond) of King Henry II and 'the English enemy' who extracted 'mock submissions', which lacked moral authority, from several Irish chieftains in Ireland including the O'Briens (130, 153). Worse was to follow in the sixteenth century when, in 1537, an Irish parliament 'consisting merely of the creatures of King Henry VIII' adopted that monarch's religious agenda for Ireland, and, when, in 1543, the ruling O'Brien surrendered his 'ancient dignity of Prince of Thomond' in favour of an English title. This, according to White, was part of a more general government 'policy' of extending crown authority in the country by 'bribing the chiefs with the plunder of the clans' (174–76).

What was happening in Ireland and in Clare was, according to White, but one dimension of 'a complete revolution in the religious and political life of Europe', which became more tangible in Clare in 1569 when the first Protestants settled in the county. This occasioned the papacy in 1571 to appoint Malachy O'Moloney as bishop of Killaloe to counter the activity of Protestants, but his work was diminished by 'the notorious Miler McGrath, a member of the Fermanagh family, [who] appeared in Thomond as Elizabeth's Archbishop of Cashel' (187–88). The ultimate tragedy, in the eyes of White, was that 'the degenerate O'Brien of that day' betrayed his clan, and after but 'a fitful opposition' to 'the English invaders' 'surrendered his strong places' in the county and 'sent his son Donogh to the English court as a hostage for his future good behaviour and to receive an English and Protestant education' (186–87, 191, 193). The defection of O'Brien, who was now earl of Thomond, and of his kin meant that when ships of the Spanish Armada were wrecked off the coast of County Clare in 1588 the survivors were tracked down and killed by a kinsman, Sir Turlough O'Brien of Ennistymon. This switch of allegiance meant also that when the lords of Ulster, with the aid of Spanish supporters, sought to reverse the conquest of Ireland, the earl of Thomond joined 'the English in the attack on the Northern Princes', leaving Tadhg Caoch Mac Mahon as 'the only one of note from Clare who took part . . . on the Irish side' at the 'disastrous defeat' at Kinsale (220–21).

The success of English arms and the refusal of King James VI and I to countenance a restoration of Catholicism to Ireland's towns left the country (and the county) open to exploitation by Protestant clergy and by adventurers 'taken from the lowest class in English and Scottish towns and cities' (243). White contended that the exploitation and injustices that followed were such that he considered that 'if ever a revolt was justified in any country it was that of 1641 in Ireland' (244). He was aware, as was James Frost, that the Catholic onslaught upon Protestant settlers associated with that insurrection had extended to County Clare and that the Protestant residents in County Clare who had survived the attack had given testimony of their experiences as part of the compilation known as the 1641 depositions. And Canon White knew, as did James Frost, that the most compelling Protestant testimony from Clare was that given by Maurice Cuffe concerning the siege of Ballyalla Castle. However, unlike Frost, but, like many Catholic authors who wrote before and after him, Canon White questioned the integrity of the Depositions as a historical source, claiming that 'a little careful enquiry' on his part had disclosed 'the fact that they were, for the most part, bold efforts of the imagination' (247). This rejection of the principal source on which the Protestant narrative of martyrology was based liberated White to exult in the participation by men from Clare in the Confederate War, to praise the involvement of Archbishop Rinuccini, the Papal Nuncio, in the siege of Bunratty Castle where 'he went into the trenches', to 'encourage on the men' by 'sharing their danger'. The result, he claimed, was that by the summer of 1646 'Clare had not so much as an openly hostile foot on her soil'. All, however, was to be reversed again by Ormond, Cromwell, and Ireton and most particularly by Morogh O'Brien, Baron, and later earl of, Inchiquin, a Clareman whose exploits on the English side 'secured him the unenviable title of Morrogh na Thothaine – Morogh of the burnings' (255). Having detailed the origins of Inchiquin, his association through marriage with the St Leger family in County Cork, and his switching of sides until Cromwell finally 'pushed him out of public life in Ireland', White condemned this most 'savage' and 'bitter' 'anti-Irishman' for his action as president of Munster in taking Cahir by treachery and then Cashel by force where he 'literally butchered without mercy by fire and sword in the sacred sanctuary . . . about three thousand men, women and children in and about the cathedral of Cashel' including twenty priests whose blood 'bespattered the altars upon which they had offered the Holy Sacrifice' (256). Canon White's indignation was such that he had so exhausted his vocabulary of denigration on Inchiquin that when it came to condemning Cromwell and his lieutenants, all he could say was that even the 'cruel, and savage and sanguinary . . . exploits' of Inchiquin paled by comparison with the 'ruthless deeds' of Cromwell, that 'psalm singing apostle of the Reformation' (258).

This brought Canon White to discuss the promotion in the county of a 'second great confiscation' that consisted of the assignment of some land to Catholic families who were to be 'transplanted' there from other counties in Ireland, the expulsion from the county of the priests who had persisted there, the effort to 'starve out Catholicism for want of pastors in Clare and Connacht', the formation of an Irish brigade on the continent which led to the 'first flight of the Wild Geese from Clare', and then 'the rush for plunder' that introduced to the county a great number of the Protestant landowning families whose descendants remained in possession of those lands even to the time of writing. He pointed out that among the few indigenous proprietors to survive were 'the chief families of the O'Briens – notably the earl of Thomond, the earl of Inchiquin and the Dromoland O'Briens', an achievement that Canon White found unsurprising given 'their well known temporizing policy' (293). And to give point to what would already have been apparent from his narrative, he recounted the success of Máire Rua Mc Mahon, the widow of Conor O'Brien of Lemenagh and Dromoland, in securing for her son the property that should have fallen into state hands because of the death of her husband when fighting in the service of the crown. She recovered the land, he claimed, by marrying Cornet Cooper, a Cromwellian officer, after she had ridden to Limerick in search of General Ludlow with the offer that she would become the wife of any officer of his choosing provided the O'Brien property was exempt from confiscation (262).

Canon White considered that the Cromwellian disruption marked the ultimate break with the past in County Clare, since, in his view, the reign of Charles II marked a continuing erosion of the wealth and influence of Catholics, the persistent persecution of priests – this time at the instigation of the earl of Orrery – and the build-up of 'all the elements for strife' that duly came to a head when the rule of King James II was challenged by William of Orange. It was then that Viscount Clare, who Canon White considered the only honourable man among the old aristocracy, formed his regiment of dragoons to support King James, with the result that after the Jacobite cause was beaten the government proceeded with what Canon White described as the third confiscation of Clare property. Defeat led also to the departure from the county of Clare's dragoons together with 'their wives, their children, their families'; the flouting by the government of the terms of surrender agreed upon at Limerick; and the enactment of the Penal Laws, which led to the 'ferocious, savage religious and civil persecution of the defeated Irish Catholics'. This enactment, in White's opinion, left England with 'a black record on the face of its history' such as was borne by 'no other country claiming to be regarded as civilised – Russia alone hardly excepted' (301).

Canon White's account may be considered an elaboration at the county level of the Catholic grand narrative that was being written by other priests at the diocesan or national levels. He further revealed how his approach to county history had been influenced by Catholic Church history when he detailed the misfortune that had befallen those individuals he considered most responsible for the degradation of Catholics. We have already noted his suggestion that the victory of Brian Boroimhe over the Danes was providentially decreed, and he similarly considered it 'curious' that the 'descendants' of the apostate Miler McGrath, 'like those of Martin Luther', had reverted to Catholicism and that 'some of them were by Cromwell transplanted into Clare' (188). Then when it came to the hated earl of Inchiquin, Canon White explained how he too had converted to Catholicism when serving as a soldier on the Continent during the years when the Cromwellians were dominant in Ireland. Then, after he had returned to Ireland following the Restoration of Charles II, Inchiquin persisted in that faith and 'died a Catholic' in 1673. It was obviously not appropriate for Canon White, as a priest, to speculate if his conversion had secured salvation for Inchiquin, but White seemed confident that it had done nothing to redeem his reputation in the mind of those he had offended in his earlier years. He sustained this by explaining how Inchiquin was, 'by his own request, buried in St Mary's Cathedral in Limerick', then a Protestant place of worship, but that not even this choice had saved Inchiquin from the revenge of the people given that a recent investigation of his tomb had revealed that there were no human remains in his coffin. This, for White, lent credibility to the popular belief that soon after Inchiquin had been buried 'his body was taken by night and flung into the river by some of the citizens who regarded it as desecrating the holy place' (257). Further humiliation awaited Inchiquin, according to Canon White, because his title failed in the male line in 1741 and reverted to the earl of Thomond in 1800. Even then it 'did not last long' because 'by the death without issue in 1846 of William, Marquis of Thomond, the house of 'Morogh the Burner was wiped off the face of the earth' (257). Canon White seemed satisfied that the same humiliation had befallen John Fitzgibbon, 'a man of obscure family', whom he considered guilty of 'treason to his country' for assisting in the passing of the Act of Union and was 'made earl of Clare for his treachery'. In this case Fitzgibbon died in 1802 leaving no male representative, which meant that his title also became extinct (328).

The death of the Marquis of Thomond in 1846 also brought an end to those that Canon White referred to as 'the absentee English O'Briens'. He further noted that financial difficulty had previously brought an end to their influence in County Clare because in 1712 a large part of the Thomond estate had been put up for sale. Catholics were debarred from purchasing any of the property because of the Penal Laws, which meant that the principal purchasers, who were Protestant families already in possession of estates in Clare, were able to consolidate their positions in the county from then forward to what Canon White referred to as the present day. In identifying the purchasers, Canon White thought it fair to mention that not all of them dealt harshly with those who had to accept tenancies from them. However, by the simple act of listing their names – Ivers, Burtons, Gores, Westbys, MacDonnells, Westrops, Stackpools, Henns, Scots, Gabbetts', and others – Canon White was making it evident that their time of dominance in Clare was at an end given that they clearly did not belong to what he had defined at the outset as the Thomond family 'bonded together by the well-defined ties of ancient blood and historic descent' (295, 20).

We have up to this point looked at three works published in Ireland in the late nineteenth century that represented themselves as county histories. In doing so it has emerged that each was distinctive but that Canon White's work proved to be different in concept and purpose from the other two.

Wood-Martin and Frost, like authors of county histories in Victorian England, each looked positively at the county as an institution from the moment of its creation, and wrote to encourage their readers to take pride in the achievements of their particular county up to that time and to work cooperatively into the future in the interest of the common good. Each recognized that the populations of their respective counties were diverse in composition and that different families had established roots at different times and under particular circumstances. They were both obviously conscious that diversity had given rise to communal conflict in the past and was likely to do so into the future, but they seemed to think that by disentangling county history from national history there was a better chance that communal harmony would prevail within their respective counties even in the event of politics at the national level, and at Westminster, being turbulent and divisive. Each, as we noted, came from a landowning background (one Catholic and the other Protestant), and this too, I have suggested, explains the conservatism of each and their seeming fear of what a turbulent future might bring.

Canon White came from a very different background in that he was the parish priest of Kilrush when he published his book, and some references in his text suggest that he had previously served as a priest in the parishes of Carrigaholt and Miltown Malbay. His opening chapter on the geography of County Clare shows that he was also had an intimate knowledge of East Clare, which is unsurprising given that he had been born and raised in Tulla. Given his social background and vocation, it is not at all surprising that the county community he defined was limited to the parishioners in the parishes in which he had served together with their counterparts in the other Catholic parishes of County Clare whether these belonged to the Killaloe diocese or that of Kilfenora. As a priest, he would have been keenly aware of what he would have regarded as the injustices that this community had suffered in past centuries, and he would also have been trained to emphasize the travails that priests and their parishioners had suffered under the Penal Laws with a view both to enhancing the respect of priests within their parishes and deepening the faith of the community. In this respect it is significant that where James Frost had contended it was Catholic landowners who had been most disadvantaged by the Penal Laws, Canon White insisted that it was the priests of County Clare who had suffered most gravely under the Penal Laws as they had done also under the rule of Cromwell.

In pointing to these occasional differences in interpretation between Frost and White I am not for a moment suggesting that Canon White was setting out to dispute what James Frost had written of the history of the same county, and there is no evidence that either had seen the work of the other in advance of their being published in the same year. However, each author would have been familiar with another volume relevant to their interests, which was Canon Philip Dwyer's *The Diocese of Killaloe*, which had been in circulation for fifteen years and touched upon many of the same topics that were of interest to Frost and White.[11] Dwyer's work was primarily an assembly of manuscript material on which he commented, and the evidence presented, and the commentary offered, was with the purpose of presenting a Protestant narrative of the past, since Philip Dwyer had been a canon of the Church of Ireland and the principal Church of Ireland minister in the town of Ennis in his capacity as vicar of Drumcliffe.

We know that James Frost was familiar with Canon Dwyer's history since he made frequent respectful reference to it and drew heavily upon the documentary evidence that Dwyer had assembled even when he differed with the arguments he was expounding. Canon White, on the other hand, refrained from making specific reference to his Protestant counterpart, although he too drew upon the sources that Canon Dwyer had assembled and even questioned their reliability as he formulated counters to some of the arguments that Dwyer had advanced. This would have surprised nobody at the time since one of the factors that sustained an interest in all Irish historical writing of the nineteenth century was what John Mitchel referred to as the 'historical dispute' conducted by the Irish Catholic Church with the Anglicans.[12] Such disputes, usually between clergymen, concerned such matters as the character of the early Christian church in Ireland and whether it was Protestant or Catholic, challenges over whether clergy in each of the two churches could trace an unbroken line of ordination back to the bishops of pre-Reformation times thus proving that they belonged to the church brought to Ireland by St Patrick, and charges and counter-charges concerning the sincerity of the Church of Ireland in its supposed evangelization mission. Canon Dwyer had taken a decidedly Protestant position on these and other contentious theological points. Moreover, he had asserted that Catholics were not the only ones who had suffered in past times in Clare, since the clergy of the Church of Ireland there had experienced three bouts of persecution in the space of some fifty years during the seventeenth century. The first onslaught, led by Catholics against Protestants at the instigation of Rome, commenced with

[11] Philip Dwyer, *The Diocese of Killaloe from the Reformation to the Close of the Eighteenth Century* (Dublin, 1878).

[12] John Mitchel, preface to *The Life and Times of Aodh O'Neill* (reprint of the 1845 edition; New York, 1874), xvi–xvii.

the insurrection of 1641, and according to Dwyer persisted during the years of the Confederate Wars when the Papal Nuncio encouraged it. This was followed by a second persecution, this time conducted by the militant Protestants who had accompanied Cromwell to Ireland and who had 'put down' the Church of Ireland 'with as effective an animosity as the Nuncio had expressed when our diocesan ministers were all dead or had fled away'.[13] And the third persecution in succession fell upon the Protestants in the county when during the reign of King James II their clergy again saw the need to flee for their safety lest they suffer the same fate as had befallen the Protestant clergy in 1641. Canon Dwyer believed that flight was the correct course given the 'intolerable pressure' that Lord Tyrconnell's government had subsequently placed on the lay Protestants who had remained in the county when, again at the instigation of Catholic clergy, the government used the 'yellow dragoons' of Lord Clare to enforce a 'reign of terror' upon Protestants by billeting soldiers in their houses and forcing them to bear the burden of supplying the horses of the dragoons (371, 372, 387).

As he catalogued the litany of woes that Protestants in Clare had endured, Canon Dwyer acknowledged that Catholic priests in the county had also suffered years of 'unparalleled misery' after Cromwell had usurped power and that the 'popery laws' enacted during the reign of King William were 'very arbitrary, oppressive and cruel' (409). While he regretted this 'policy of exasperating retaliation and repression of the Irish Roman Catholics' into which King William had been 'coerced' by his parliament (411), he also believed that there was no doubt that the 'three great confiscations' of the lands of Catholics in Country Clare, and throughout in Ireland, over the course of the seventeenth century 'were the direct consequence [and] the inevitable retaliation which the Roman Catholics of Ireland brought down upon themselves by making themselves the tools of the Roman, and chiefly Episcopal, agents of the Pope, and of the continental foes of England and liberty' (338).

Such an interpretation of events and such a rationalization of the Penal Laws would have proved unpalatable for any Catholic, so it is not surprising that both James Frost and Canon Patrick White saw the need for counter-narratives. Of the two, Canon White's *History of Clare*, which in the preface he described as a 'kind of elementary history for general readers', became the more comprehensive rejection of what Canon Dwyer had to say in that it persistently represented the Protestant landowners of

---

[13] Dwyer, The Diocese of Killaloe, 289. Further references are cited in the text.

Clare as a parasitic presence, whose inadequacy as defenders of their community had been most recently exposed during the years of the Great Famine. On this he provided some searing insight, based on what older parish priests of his acquaintance had told him of the way in which priests had put their own lives at risk when ministering to those most in need at the moment of their worst tribulation. Such description, as well as his account of several priests of Clare encouraging their people to support O'Connell, substantiated his case that priests were the natural and most trustworthy leaders of their community in the present as in the past. More tellingly, the only references he made to the institutions of the Victorian state were to workhouses, which he represented as places of degradation rather than of social amelioration.

It is not my intention in presenting Canon White as an author who was politically engaged to suggest that either Wood-Martin or James Frost was politically indifferent to what was happening about them. The likelihood is that they too were keenly aware of present politics and fearful of what the revolutionary changes that were proceeding concerning the ownership and management of land would involve for people of their social background and political allegiances. They were therefore, in a sense, seeking to escape from the harsh realities of their own time by writing histories of their respective counties which they hoped would, in turn, foster communal harmony at the local level by demonstrating how populations of diverse origins and allegiances had overcome their past differences to create a harmonious society in which all people might participate as equals regardless of ethnic or confessional background. Canon White differed from these authors (and also from Canon Dwyer) because those who belonged to the community he had defined had only partly overcome the hardships and injustices imposed upon their ancestors by a hostile government. For him, therefore, county history, by virtue of its immediacy, could be even more effective than either national history or church history to alert people to the need to mobilize themselves, under the guidance of their priests, to seek remedy from the injustices from which they still suffered. This perspective of Canon White, no less than that of Wood-Martin and James Frost, contributed to the efflorescence of the writing of county histories in Ireland from the era of Parnell forward to the present, and the contributions of Wood-Martin and Frost sustain my original proposition that some historical writing conducted in Parnell's Ireland was designed to calm rather than heighten the political and denominational animosities that we associate with that time.

Parnell's Grave, Glasnevin.

Photograph by Robert French, c. 1900. National Library of Ireland, Lawrence Photograph Collection

PART II

After Parnell
The Irish Literary and Historical Imagination

CHAPTER 9

Parnell and James Joyce's Dubliners
Strategies of Failure

Frank McGuinness

The city in James Joyce's collection of stories, *Dubliners*, is a haunted place, populated by multitudes of ghosts, clamouring to be seen and heard in ways that require special skills to decipher the power of their presence, their absences, bearing testimony to the contacts, the secrets that bind the living and the dead. Such strange geography requires sensitive mapping, as if Joyce sees his task as that of cartographer able to imagine the twists and turns, the inclines and the heights, even the abyss of the human minds and souls of all shaped by this city of ambiguities in this country of maddening riddles, for Dublin and Ireland take dominant roles in every page of Joyce's writing. His obsession is then with his nation's living and dead, and in no other work of Irish fiction does that conjunction, that 'and', cause more deliberate confusion than *Dubliners*. The aria that ends the final story of the book, as snow immobilizes the whole island, bestows an eerie benediction created by this prose, 'he [Gabriel Conroy] heard the snow falling faintly through the universe and faintly falling, like the descent of their last end, upon all the living and the dead'. An eerie benediction because it seeks to conjoin, to entangle, these opposites, living, dead, transforming both, until it seems like an act of theatrical defiance, indeed Shakespearian defiance as in the metaphysics of *Hamlet*, the dead are living, and the living dead, here, in this terrain, these shifting borders of the conscious and subconscious, where phantoms we can be trained to perceive bear witness to the intricate treacheries and hopes abandoned not only of times past, but also time present and time to come.

And one of the most potent, most troubling, most adored, and most tragic of these phantoms Joyce himself identifies as that strange spirit, called forth in his essay 'The Shade of Parnell', a 'spectral figure with the signs of death upon his brow'.[1] It is he is who visits the Christmas feast of

---

[1] James Joyce, 'The Shade of Parnell' (1912), in his *Occasional, Critical, and Political Writing*, ed. K. Barry, trans. C. Deane (Oxford, 2000), 196.

the Dedalus family, bringing violent disruption, unhinging the battle of church and state in *A Portrait of the Artist as a Young Man*. In a key story from *Dubliners*, 'Ivy Day in the Committee Room', Parnell's defeated followers gather, some wearing his emblem of the ivy leaf, in their bare roost on the October anniversary of his death, punctuating their humdrum existence, now purged of memories when Parnell offered more than hope of Home Rule, by scraping a few shillings canvassing for two self-serving candidates deaf to the pulse of debate, indifferent to radical change, all such ambition abandoned, waiting only for the comforting pop of stout bottles, listening to the bathetic recitation of a poem whose formulaic grief at the Chief's death conveys the scale of their utter abandonment and hopeless despair. The King has been killed, his people now are marked only by his passing. A price must be paid for what has been done, and that price leaves behind as legacy lethargy and petty bickering, backbiting and suspicions of spying, the only eloquence that can be summoned as evidence of any political will a serious dilution of that drama and those speeches of Parnell that 'caused his listeners' souls to tremble ... those strategic triumphs' as Joyce hailed them in 'The Shade of Parnell'. The whole story progresses through scenes of forlorn security, where the glory days of Parnell's career are rooted so far in the past that all who were once invigorated by the great man have settled themselves now nowhere near the borders of insurrection. Parnell's long march once threatened to lead his people forward in victory. Parnell is dead – these words, that terrible statement of fact, ring like a funeral knell to the hopes of liberation in the story, in the book, in the country.

If that truth aborts all prospect of decisive politics in the committee room, illuminated by a poor fire's flickering embers, the whole story diagnoses what afflicts the men gathered here – they are exclusively male. And it is as if there is a sexual wound disempowering those left after the chief whose very potency led to his downfall. The men of Ireland as a consequence now would appear to suffer from terror of their bodies as deep as their panic in the face of the betrayal of Parnell. It is not so much that they are indifferent to women and to men as that they are incapable of allowing such thoughts to create desire in any shape or form. The shadow cast by the catastrophe of Parnell's career darkens and indeed disables the males who once found their will to live, to act, to change, propelled by his enormous energy, now buried with him in the grave. 'Ivy Day in the Committee Room' illuminates dimly the scale and sorrow of this malfunction, but it is in the story that precedes it in *Dubliners*, 'A Painful Case', where the depth and breadth of this terrible timidity find the voice and the vision of what has cursed the Irish heterosexual since the fall of Charles Stewart Parnell through his liaison with Mrs Katherine O'Shea.

James Duffy, the tyrannical, timid male at the core of 'A Painful Case', works as a bank cashier, residing in his Chapelizod digs, chosen to be as far as possible from the other, in his words, mean, modern, pretentious suburbs of Dublin, where his quarters have the severity of a cell, prison or monastery. The trappings of his solitary days and nights are scrupulously stark. He rigs his living space following the dictates of an austere geometry, the furniture largely a severe contrast of iron bedstead and washstand and four cane chairs, all of his own choosing, nothing inherited, his history dating from these bleak objects, his pleasures rooting themselves in diversions of the mind, permitting himself access to books – a sturdy copy of Wordsworth a mainstay of his library – translating from the German Gerhart Hauptmann's instructive drama, *Michael Kramer*, allowing himself access to classical music concerts, especially Mozart, these being his sole redress to public entertainment. Throughout the narrative, even from its earliest paragraphs, a sense of struggle – a vigorous, conscious struggle to impose shape and discipline – emerges from Duffy, an individual, a Saturnine individual we are told, who 'abhorred anything that betokened physical or mental disorder'. His necessary routines, even his dietary habits – lunch of dry arrowroot biscuits and a beer in Dan Burke's, dinner in the same eating house in George's Street – thrives on the regulation and the rationing of resources Duffy fastidiously imposes on the regime with which he controls the desires and demands of his corporeal nature, following the dictates of the rule he has devised to curb fleshly anarchy and protect the purity of his celibate self. It is a life that is as dry and direct as the questions and answers encoded in the Maynooth Catechism Duffy keeps on his bookshelf, although it is stressed he has neither 'church nor creed'. He has instead faith, supreme, absolute faith in his sacred, superior powers of denial, exercised in his work, in his leisure, in his highly formal play. James Duffy is in essence a man without sin, scoured since baptism, certain to an almost angelic degree of salvation, barely aware of temptation about to fall.

She takes the shape of a married woman, Mrs Emily Sinico, who, out of the strange blue, talks to him before a concert begins in the Rotunda, lamenting the poor attendance, pitying the artists who will perform to so few admirers. This is the first sign of sympathy – he never gives alms to beggars and walks the streets protected by his stout hazel stick – to disturb Duffy's universe, physical and moral. The silence broken, Duffy speaks back to her, quickly gauging her age, her status, the changing shapes of her beauty, the precise attractions of her eyes. 'The eyes were very dark blue and steady. Their gaze began with a defiant note but was confused by what seemed a deliberate swoon of the pupil into the iris, revealing for an instant a temperament of great sensibility.' His face was of a harsh character and his mouth unamiable; we learn about this hard fellow, yet 'there was no harshness in the eyes' and so he seems to devour with relish what he sees in the woman, a few years younger than himself, when he observes, 'The pupil reasserted itself quickly, this half-disclosed nature fell again under the reign of prudence, and her astrakhan jacket, moulding a bosom of a certain fullness, struck the note of defiance more definitely.'

These rapid observations betray a hunger roaring to be satisfied, but for a man like Duffy, who has feasted only on sensual famine, other procedures come more naturally, and so most slowly but with increasing comfort more surely a tentative tenderness is allowed to develop between these strangers, man and woman.

They exchange cultural confidences. She admires his intellect, this he encourages. He shares with her some secrets, disclosing his contempt for Dublin's 'obtuse middle class which entrusted its morality to policemen and its fine arts to impressarios'. Her seafaring husband so ignores his wife's charms, he believes this friendship confines itself to their passion for music and that Duffy's visits to their abode – Duffy's dislike of 'underhand ways' forces Emily to invite him into their family home – these are ways of pursuing the daughter of the house. But if the man continues to place savage restraint on what stirs him, the woman does not follow such deprivation, possessing as she does an unruly heart whose need will out, no matter what consequence. She dares catch his hand passionately and 'pressed it to her cheek'. In that unfaithful instant he will banish her from him. He will not risk, not commit the crime of infidelity – not stain himself with the sin of adultery, and nowhere else in *Dubliners* does the shade of Parnell make its most dark, most troubling, and ironically perhaps most alluring presence felt. Duffy will not consider such an act of disobedience. He recoils from it as if it would defile him. He will not countenance such liberties between them. He is so attuned to the punishment, spiritual and secular, following on from this subversive act of illicit union that he eradicates such possibilities even from his consciousness. If in their chaste attachment and conversations male and female have been given separately glimpses of paradise together, the sensual, frantic touch of flesh ensures that on Duffy's part, at least, revulsion drives them from any possible Eden of their creation. If Duffy believes, as he asserts early in the story, that 'he lived at a little distance from his own body', then in the moment of revulsion that same body becomes only his own at more than a little distance, having faith in nothing but its fierce control of instincts warped in the service of a soul imagining itself ascending to 'angelic status' but in reality perverting its human needs, disguising them as commandments brought down from the mountain of Duffy's monstrous self-regard. 'We are our own', Duffy has sermonized to Emily Sinico, and in colossal error she has taken that 'our own' to mean 'together'. Because of this, she suffers the loss of a man she imagines could love her, a lesson learned as brutally as Nora does of her husband Torvald in Ibsen's *A Doll's House* when he violently rejects her redeeming efforts to save him from near-fatal illness.

No such attempt to save Duffy prolongs the plot of 'A Painful Case'. He next reads four years later in an evening paper details of the court report that tells Mrs Emily Sinico has been struck by the engine of a slow train at Sydney Parade coming from Kingstown at the crossing near her home. There is the strong implication she was drunk and that her death is suicide. As Duffy reads this to his appalled shock, he first castigates her for the weakness of her addiction that led her inexorably to this extremity and extinction. Bile spews from him in a series of almost rapturous accusations against her corpse. Then he stumbles into some sense of self-blame that he may have at least slightly contributed to her wretched state of unhappiness. He wanders through pubs and through the darkening city itself, watching strangers in huddles, of whatever sexual combination, making whatever love they devise or grab from each other, not wanting him observing their secret, strange, sheltering trysts. Finally, he knows he is utterly, absolutely isolated on this earth.

Each and every stage in the evolution of 'A Painful Case' centres on failure – failure of communication, failure of nerve, failure of will to do as desired. Purity, its preservation, its sterility, have protected James Duffy but at rigorous, ruinous cost. A juror asks, You saw the lady fall? And a witness answers, Yes. The court intricately, simultaneously condemns Duffy and Sinico as Parnell and Katherine O'Shea stood jointly condemned. That fall is how Duffy has let love be consummated, the woman fallen indeed, but also broken by the train, her face mangled, her body mutilated, yet these injuries have not immediately caused her death. Rather, it is her heart; in the words of the court, 'shock and sudden failure of the heart's action'. Duffy knows what has been lost. There was a way to escape from the barren landscape of his life, his way out, his revolt, which comes down to having courage to commit an act of adultery, and he aggressively, implacably rejects that liberation. He chooses instead to remain in servitude to the safety his virginity bestows upon himself. He is a man identified as a creature who dares not run the risk of copulation, especially with a woman who already has a husband, even if that husband is so indifferent to his wife she scarcely exists for him. As Duffy's panic at reading of the death mounts, it is as if Parnell stares Duffy in the eye, reducing him to pious rubble, fleeing from any point of contact with the saga of the disgraced leader whose story seems to implicate all who inherit the fall of that man. Parnell and Katherine O'Shea might as well have turned metaphorically into an Adam and Eve who pass on to all coming after them the quicklime of scandal, the negating impotence of the likes of James Duffy, living as one in thrall to his future like his past, like his present, a man untouched by any history but his own loss, damned by his solitariness, his cruelty, and his loneliness.

Is this why Duffy describes himself as 'outcast from life's feast'? Is there something more than this feast from which in the story's closing paragraphs he twice excludes himself? What in effect is Duffy seeking to remove from his psyche? Could it be time itself, its subtle workings, the capacity to change, to shatter all certainties? Has he been in the business of creating his own ice age wherein he can deny all signs of transition, of transformation, all entry to his deepest, darkest imagination, in absolute denial of the sexual act of mutual consent that will unlock the prison doors of his profound conformity, trapped as he is without friend or lover, eradicating the possibility that friend is lover, maintaining as he does that 'love between man and man is impossible because there must not be sexual intercourse and friendship between man and woman is impossible because there must be sexual intercourse'? This empty aphorism is his consolation. James Duffy, a man created in his own image, is resolutely determined in his perfect exile, untroubled by the fear of woman until that fear eats him alive, without the resources as he is to withstand the tumult of passion changing all before, beside, behind it, interior and exterior, that sex engenders in the marvellous mire of its unleashing, be it man with man, woman with woman, or man with woman.

Such panic seeps into the very syntax of Joyce's story. To take just two examples, at crucial junctures the pace of plotting contracts to deliver vital objective information. Is this habitual abruptness or something more stylistically revealing? After Duffy and Mrs Sinico end their acquaintance, we are told in a single sentence, 'Four years passed.' Then shorty after comes the spare information, 'His father died,' the only familial fact about Duffy offered. The concision with which these historical details are delivered charge them with reluctance to dwell too deeply on what such momentous news entails and ultimately demands, and that of course is knowledge of mortality, the notion and nature of mortality itself. If James Duffy is ultimately unmanned by the spell of his sexuality, his deeply vexing, deeply unsettling heterosexuality, he is equally petrified by death – death that comes to him in the strange, unearthly caress of Emily Sinico. 'She seemed to be near him in the darkness. At moments he seemed to feel her voice touch his ear, her hand touch his. He stood still to listen. Why had he withheld life from her? Why had he sentenced her to death? He felt his moral nature fall to pieces.' Now a being both alive and dead, this woman has in more ways than one crossed the line at Sydney Parade, her sentencing him to whatever destiny has in store for James Duffy, the inescapable meeting of life-in-death and death-in-life. She comes to him in various guises and for various reasons, perhaps not least in company with the lost leader, Parnell, as reprimand for Duffy's enormous error. In the catalogue of misreading and misadventures that goes to make up the personality and progress of this same James Duffy, one sentence screams out in error. Abandoning years earlier his attempts to impose his own particular slant at the meetings of an Irish Socialist Party because of his supposed intellectual superiority to the working men assembled there, Duffy informs Emily Sinico that 'No social revolution . . . would be likely to strike Dublin for some centuries.'

Within two years of the publication of *Dubliners*, events would prove Duffy radically wrong. Though Joyce in 'The Shade of Parnell' dreams the dead leader would not be vindictive towards the new Ireland, of course the same events would not entirely appease his troubled and troubling spirit. The Rising would leave the capital in ruins, its architecture as devastated as Duffy's lost serenity and security of mind, each possessed by completely unanticipated, unruly transgressions against authority, one colonially imposed, the other a private act of submission to the defiant, damning powers of the flesh, damnation taking shape as doubt.

> He began to doubt the reality of what memory told him. He halted under a tree and allowed the rhythm to die away. He could not feel her near him in the darkness nor her voice touch his ear. He waited for some minutes listening. He could hear nothing: the night was perfectly silent. He listened again: perfectly silent. He felt that he was alone.

So it is that the story's final sentence should most oddly, most appropriately read about Duffy, 'He felt he was alone.' A short step from singular to plural in national terms translates that lonely single self alone – *mé féin* – to *sinn féin*, ourselves alone. Sinn Féin's ensuing election victory would entail the triumph, the disruption, the division, the most terrible division of parliamentary politics and debate, the raising – but not the exorcizing, never the exorcizing – of the ghost of Parnell, whose sin was his treacherous country's damnation but the man's own salvation, an adventure, an ecstasy denied to the chaste and celibate, abandoned and broken James Duffy.

CHAPTER 10

'The Rhythm of Beauty'
Joyce, Yeats, and the 1890s

Edna Longley

Some critics polarize Joyce and Yeats by invoking the Irish Literary
Revival. I want to question this practice, of which the most extreme
instance is Len Platt's *Joyce and the Anglo-Irish* (1998): 'The Joyce
text ... is *devoted* to an undermining of revivalism's status as cultural
nationalism, and to a displacement of the Yeatsian Protestant tradition
from the round tower of Irish literary culture.... The social and cultural
gulf between Joyce and Yeats finds expression in two aesthetics so different
as to be radically incompatible.'[1] Such binary readings often had a context
in the Northern Irish Troubles, but their effect continues. In *The Strong
Spirit* (2012), Andrew Gibson again set Joyce against 'the revivalism of the
1890s', calling this 'very much the preserve of a privileged class and
thriving on its English connection'.[2] Yet, as Clare Hutton has shown,
the 'Scylla and Charybdis' chapter of *Ulysses* provides a far more nuanced
sociocultural snapshot of Dublin literati circa 1900: here Joyce 'acknowl-
edg[es] the complexity of literary traditions in Ireland'.[3] The catch-all
(or catch-some) category 'revivalism' is a retrospective imposition. In
Stephen Hero 'the compact body of national revivalists' does not mean
Yeats and co.[4]

'Revivalism', like the equally retrospective 'post-colonial' paradigm from
which it derives, can overdetermine narratives of Irish literary history
between 1890 and 1915. Thus, it tends to repress the aesthetic intercourse
(and mutual admiration) between Yeats and Joyce, while magnifying their
class or sectarian differences. This reprises the way in which the Easter

---

[1] Len Platt, *Joyce and the Anglo-Irish: A Study of Joyce and the Literary Revival* (Amsterdam, 1998), 232.
[2] Andrew Gibson, *The Strong Spirit: History, Politics, and Aesthetics in the Writings of James Joyce,
1898–1915* (Oxford, 2012), 150.
[3] Clare Hutton, 'Joyce and the Institutions of Revivalism', *Irish University Review* 33 1 (2003):
117–32 (127).
[4] James Joyce, *Stephen Hero*, rev. ed., ed. John J. Slocum and Herbert Cahoon (New York, 1944), 43.
Hereinafter cited as *SH*.

Rising itself changed the literary past. Yeats immediately feared that 'all the work of years has been overturned ... all the freeing of Irish literature and criticism from politics'.[5] In 1923 Ernest Boyd prefaced the revised edition of his book *Ireland's Literary Renaissance* by lamenting:

> Now that political preoccupations are supreme, literature in Ireland has been relegated to the second plane. There is no sign of the influence of James Joyce in his own country.... Irish criticism is too largely the monopoly of the patriotic, whose unimpeachable sentiments concerning Ireland are regarded as entitling them to pass judgment upon questions of aesthetics.[6]

The historical problematics of 'Irish criticism', which include reluctance to accept the Literary Revival (a literary-critical revival too) as foundational, affect the deployment of categories and paradigms.[7] Further, as Yeats studies and Joyce studies developed – sometimes in tandem, usually segregated, often segregated from Ireland – some formative literary and critical contexts receded. Fin-de-siècle Aestheticism, twinned with Symbolism, is one such context. But other problems arise when critics translate Aestheticism and Symbolism into proto-'modernism' instead of approaching that multifarious matrix on its own terms.[8] In 1941 a slightly closer witness, Louis MacNeice, combated an earlier tendency to polarize Yeats and Joyce (as symbolist versus realist) by returning them to the 1890s, to the religion of art, to their common ground as 'spoilt priests' with 'a fanatical devotion to style'.[9]

'Modernism', another retrospective paradigm, sometimes conjoins Joyce and Yeats, sometimes splits them, neither plausibly. Between the 1920s and the 1960s, even the adjective 'modernist' was not attached to Anglophone modern poetry in the sense that now centres on the disjunctive poetics of Pound and Eliot. Yeats invariably distances his own structures from theirs, as when he attacks Poundian form in the introduction to his *Oxford Book of Modern Verse* (1936): '[In *The Cantos*] I discover at present merely exquisite or grotesque fragments' (xxiv). Of course, Joyce's relation to 'modernism', as an imposed or imported paradigm, has also been thrown into question. Twenty years ago, Emer Nolan's *James Joyce and*

[5] Allan Wade, ed., *The Letters of W. B. Yeats* (London, 1954), 613.
[6] Ernest A. Boyd, *Ireland's Literary Renaissance* (London, 1923 [1916]), 7.
[7] See my *Yeats and Modern Poetry* (Cambridge, 2013), chapter 1.
[8] See Patrick McGuinness, ed., *Symbolism, Decadence and the Fin de Siècle* (Exeter, 2000).
[9] Louis MacNeice, *The Poetry of W. B. Yeats* (London, 1976 [1941]), 176.

Nationalism influentially repatriated him from its critical clutches. In *Yeats and Modern Poetry* (2013) I may have tried to do the same for Yeats; but in Joyce's case the repatriation emphasizes politics more than aesthetics: 'far from being dominated by what was later constructed as an ahistorical and abstract modernist agenda, *Ulysses* [is] centrally concerned with British-Irish historical, political, and cultural relations'.[10] That seems another binary proposition. It's true that some critics conflate a 'modernist agenda' with a nationalist or anticolonial agenda. That is, they construe Joycean form as his means of annihilating the British Empire, the Irish Literary Revival, English literature, and possibly Yeats, in one fell stylistic swoop. Yet perhaps Joyce's art is about more than this. Even careful formulations put the paradigmatic cart before Pegasus: 'postcolonial studies offers ways of articulating nationalism, both imperialist and anti-imperialist, and modernism as interdependent rather than opposed phenomena'.[11] George O'Brien brilliantly remarks of some Joyce criticism: 'The Ireland-of-the-Welcomes treatment deprives us of his exile.'[12] If there is also now an Irish critical climate more welcoming to Yeats, equally we should not deprive ourselves of Yeats's inner exile: of its effects on his poetry, on modern poetry – and on Joyce. From one angle, 'exile' is the symbolic locus of art: a realm populated by artist-heroes, like the wandering Oisin or Stephen Dedalus, who incarnate their creators' fin-de-siècle aesthetic self-consciousness.

Two 'isms' that belong more precisely to this literary period are Parnellism and Paterism. The former category is familiar, but its intersection with the latter may be less so, and may tighten the fin-de-siècle bond between Yeats and Joyce. Yeats both grasped and represents the fall and death (1891) of Charles Stewart Parnell as a window of cultural opportunity. Glossing his poem 'Parnell's Funeral' (1933), he says: 'This new dispute broke through all [party] walls . . . we began to value truth . . . free discussion appeared among us for the first time, bringing the passion for reality, the satiric genius that informs *Ulysses*, *The Playboy of the Western World* . . . .'[13] Some might see this as Yeatsian 'revivalism' engrossing Joyce. Others might take Kevin Barry's point that 'Joyce's international and cult status has concealed the ways in which his work is part of an articulate and

[10] Gibson, *The Strong Spirit*, 1.
[11] Derek Attridge and Marjorie Howes, eds., *Semicolonial Joyce* (Cambridge, 2000), 11.
[12] George O'Brien, 'The Joyce Problem', *Dublin Review* 15 (2004): 28–37 (33).
[13] W. B. Yeats, *Collected Works, vol. 1: The Poems*, ed. Richard J. Finneran (New York, 1985), 674.

broad debate within the Irish literary revival'.[14] 'Parnell's Funeral' revisits
1890s 'debate':

> Come, fix upon me that accusing eye.
> I thirst for accusation. All that was sung,
> All that was said in Ireland is a lie
> Bred out of the contagion of the throng,
> Saving the rhyme rats hear before they die.[15]

'Contagion of the throng' seems to remember 'The Day of the Rabblement' (1901), where Joyce (a supporter of the literary theatre) accuses
Yeats of betraying the avant-garde by seeking 'popularity': 'If an artist
courts the favour of the multitude he cannot escape the contagion of its
fetishism and deliberate self-deception, and if he joins in a popular
movement he does so at his own risk' (*OCPW*, 51). Yeats's seeming
quotation implies that Joyce helped to stiffen his avant-garde backbone.
In any case, 'rabblement' and 'contagion of the throng' give an Irish twist
to the fin-de-siècle stand-off between artist and bourgeoisie. 'Parnell's
Funeral', while scorning other nationalist worthies, transforms Parnell into
an artist-hero, artist-exile, artist-mask: 'Their school a crowd, his master
solitude.'[16] Perhaps 'that accusing eye' is Joyce's or involves a Joycean
'I told you so.'

Parnellism, in the shape of a clash between artist and mob, has been
attacked as antidemocratic, as patronizing the Irish people. Thus, Gibson
thinks that Stephen's Parnellite 'melancholia' subjugates his art to 'revivalism': 'his proud aloofness emerges as a form of dependence'.[17] Obviously, Yeats can never win if Irish literary dynamics, under the sign of
Parnell, is seen as a zero-sum political game rather than a matter of artistic
cross-currents. Parnell's 'solitude', which Gibson anachronistically attaches
to Stephen, is a latter-day mask for Yeats's disappointments. In 'Parnell's
Funeral', Parnell as artist-hero figures a complex literary moment and its
dissolution. It was integral to this moment that Ireland's window of
cultural opportunity opened when literature, partly under the influence
of Walter Pater, had become unusually occupied with its own workings. It
raised the stakes for literary values, possibilities, and forms that the
redemption of Irish culture from politics mapped onto the Symbolist

---

[14] James Joyce, *Occasional, Critical, and Political Writing*, ed. K. Barry, trans. C. Deane (Oxford, 2000), xxix. Hereinafter cited as *OCPW*.

[15] W. B. Yeats, *The Collected Works, I: The Poems*, ed. Richard J. Finneran (New York, 1985), 285. Hereinafter cited as *WBYP*.

[16] Yeats, *Collected Works*, 286.   [17] Gibson, *The Strong Spirit*, 153.

revolt against 'exteriority' and 'rhetoric'. Since politics had not really gone away, Ireland constituted a crucible that peculiarly tested the high claims being made for art.

Similarly, Joyce tested, rather than displaced, Yeats's own claims. In one aspect, *A Portrait of the Artist as a Young Man* replays Yeats's culture wars during the 1890s. Joyce puts psychological and social flesh on intellectual or political positions with which Yeats had to contend during his crusade for Irish literature and criticism. It is significant that the novel revisits the turbulent reception of Yeats's play *The Countess Cathleen*: 'A Libel on Ireland! . . . Blasphemy!'[18] Joyce introduced the play to students in Trieste, along with other plays by Yeats and plays by Synge. He translated it into Italian, and was obsessed by a song from the play: 'Who Goes with Fergus?' (perhaps construed as an artistic-heroic summons). He regretted missing Synge's *Playboy* and the anti-*Playboy* riots, for which the *Countess Cathleen* row may stand in. *Stephen Hero* more explicitly makes its pro-tagonist a test case for artistic principles, the principle of art. Here Joyce's chief laboratory is the mainly Catholic milieu of the university that Yeats indicts in 'On Hearing That the Students of Our New University Have Joined the Agitation against Immoral Literature' (1912). In *Stephen Hero* Stephen encounters a range of 'patriotic and religious enthusiasts' (*SH*, 164). These often represent the 'Irish Ireland' ideology, which favoured the language movement and damned the literary movement as alien. A fellow-student says that 'our peasant has nothing to gain from English literature' (*SH*, 58); a Gaelic teacher says that English 'is the language of commerce and Irish the speech of the soul' (*SH*, 64); and the university's president attacks 'writers who usurp the name of poet, who openly profess their atheistic doctrines and fill the minds of their readers with all the garbage of modern society' (*SH*, 96). He also tells Stephen that 'the cult of beauty is difficult' and that Aestheticism 'often begins well only to end in the vilest abominations' (*SH*, 101). The reference is to Oscar Wilde, no doubt. Yet Stephen's 'conversations with the patriots' (*SH*, 70) are con-versations, not mutual polemics, and he is himself comically dubbed a 'fiery-hearted revolutionary', a 'heaven-ascending essayist' (*SH*, 84–85). These terms suggest the artist who transmutes politics and religion into something else. In any case, the *Künstlerroman* can have a *mock*-heroic dimension, which need not invalidate its premises. In *Portrait* Lynch deflates Stephen by asking: 'What do you mean . . . by prating about

---

[18] James Joyce, *A Portrait of the Artist as a Young Man*, ed. H. W. Gabler and W. Hettche (New York, 1993), 5:1454–55. Hereinafter referred to as *Portrait*. References are by chapter and line number.

beauty and the imagination in this miserable Godforsaken island?' (*Portrait*, 5:1474).

Again, Stephen is not just the would-be poet as hero. He is also a literary critic and Pateresque aesthetic philosopher: an 'essayist'. A critic, even a Wildean 'critic as artist', seems an unlikely hero for any novel. Yet, in both fictions, criticism is Stephen's most prominent literary activity. Like Joyce's critical essays, his critic-hero belongs to the Revival's literary-critical dimension. Yeats especially had to counter the idea, which Boyd saw as resurgent in 1923, that nothing mattered but the Irish people's opinion of any work. Joyce graphically illustrates the problem of criticism in the 'malignant episode' (*Portrait*, 2:794) where, to the cry of 'Catch hold of this heretic', Stephen's classmates beat him with a cane and cabbage-stump for preferring Byron to Tennyson (767). It's one image of Irish 'debate' that Stephen should be grotesquely martyred for the religion of art. Yet Stephen as scathing critic can himself appear the 'tormentor' (796). Readers may sympathize with Davin when he induces the 'cold violence' of Stephen's comment about the 'old sow', after urging innocently: 'a man's country comes first. Ireland first, Stevie. You can be a poet or mystic after' (5:1052–55). Nonetheless this, like much else in *Portrait* and *Stephen Hero*, echoes resistance to Yeats's contention that literature is 'almost the most profound influence that ever comes into a nation'.[19]

In *The Strong Spirit*, Gibson demonstrates the vast extent to which *Portrait* is conscious of Yeats and other Revival writers. But he sees this as primarily evincing Stephen's/Joyce's struggle with the nets of 'revivalist discourse'.[20] Even such a struggle, based on Joyce's youthful immersion in Yeats, would testify to literary rather than political power. And is 'revivalist discourse' just 'revivalist discourse'? That discourse (or, rather, variegated literary effects) would have been less powerful if not entangled in other meshes – like the lure of being 'a poet or mystic' or both. The literary movement was not only about Ireland; hence, its appeal to Joyce. But Gibson stuffs all its sources, like all its effects, into 'revivalism', as when he says: 'Revivalism at the end of chapter 4 [of *Portrait*] figures chiefly ... as [George] Moore's aestheticism.'[21] Again, an old charge against Yeats's 'Celticism' is its 'English connection', to quote Gibson. But the 1890s were not only about England either. The 'Celtic element' contributed to

[19] W. B. Yeats, *Collected Letters, I: 1865–1895*, ed. John Kelly and Eric Domville (Oxford, 1986), 397–8.
[20] Gibson, *The Strong Spirit*, 149.   [21] Ibid., 181.

transnational revolt against exteriority. Joyce memorized Yeats's heretical religion-of-art testaments 'The Tables of the Law' and 'The Adoration of the Magi'. Similarly, his early career as a poet is indebted to the fin-de-siècle aesthetic elaborated in Yeats's introduction to his anthology *A Book of Irish Verse* (1895, 1899). For Yeats, the new Irish poets are 'distinguished . . . by their deliberate art, and . . . preoccupation with spiritual passions and memories'.[22] *Chamber Music* deploys Yeatsian tropes: twilight, faery, sighs, paleness, long hair, soul, 'dewy dreams', 'dappled grass'.[23] Such debts, woven into *Stephen Hero* and *Portrait*, are not cancelled by (varying degrees of) irony or by later satire: 'the twattering of bards in the twitterlitter between Druidia and the Deepsleep Sea'.[24] Joyce did a fair bit of poetic 'twattering' himself. *Chamber Music* comes under the Symbolist rubric of soul-music, even if Joyce's rhythms are less subtle and various than Yeats's, and draw on traditions of art-song rather than folksong.

Walter Pater (1839–1894) lurks somewhere 'in the twitterlitter'. In the late nineteenth century, Pater had a cultish impact on emergent writers: his stress on craft ('deliberate art'), his formulation of 'aesthetic poetry', his Anglicisation of *l'art pour l'art*. Pater's *Studies in the History of the Renaissance* (1873) became 'religion of art' gospel, especially its account of the Mona Lisa and its conclusion, which ends: 'Of such wisdom, the poetic passion, the desire of beauty, the love of art for its own sake, has most. For art comes to you proposing frankly to give nothing but the highest quality to your moments as they pass, and simply for those moments' sake.'[25] Yeats gives Pater star billing in the *Oxford Book of Modern Verse*. Besides starting the anthology with a free-verse lineation of Pater's Mona Lisa prose, he proclaims that this art criticism 'dominated a generation', and says of the 1890s: 'Poetry was a tradition like religion . . . and it seemed that [poets] could best restore it by writing lyrics technically perfect, their emotion pitched high, and as Pater offered instead of moral earnestness life lived as "a pure gem-like flame" all accepted him for master.'[26] Pater's signature ideal, 'to burn always with this hard, gemlike flame, to maintain . . . ecstasy',[27] had widespread heretical appeal. In Trieste, Joyce transcribed passages from Pater's *Marius the Epicurean*

[22] W. B. Yeats, *A Book of Irish Verse* (London, 2002 [1899]), xxvi.

[23] James Joyce, *Collected Poems* (New York, 1957), 23, 32.

[24] James Joyce, *Finnegans Wake* (New York, 1939), 37, 17. Hereinafter cited as *FW*.

[25] Walter Pater, *The Renaissance: Studies in Art and Poetry* (1893), ed. Donald L. Hill (Berkeley, 1980), 190.

[26] W. B. Yeats, ed., *The Oxford Book of Modern Verse* (London, 1936), viii–ix.

[27] Pater, *The Renaissance*, 189.

(1885) and *Imaginary Portraits* (1887). His essays on James Clarence Mangan imitate Pater's elaborate style, adopt/adapt Pater's ideas, and represent Mangan as a proto-aesthete who 'refused to prostitute himself to the rabble or become a mouthpiece for politicians ... one of those strange aberrant spirits who believe that the artistic life should be nothing other than the continuous and true revelation of the spiritual life' (*OCPW*, 134).

Since Joyce's Mangan essays are sometimes held to counter Revival biases by setting up an ideal type of the Irish Catholic writer, it is interesting that they should belong to Paterian common ground. Adrian Frazier virtually represents Pater as the driving ecumenical force behind the entire literary movement: 'George Moore, Edward Martyn, W. B. Yeats, and James Joyce all found themselves ... in reading Pater.'[28] If Moore's *Confessions of a Young Man* influenced *Portrait*, it was partly because Moore mediated Pater. Stephen's aesthetic philosophizing is ostensibly conducted in relation to Aquinas, Newman, and Catholic theology. But Pater-parody sits next to Newman-parody in 'The Oxen of the Sun', and it is hard to draw sectarian lines where the religion of art is concerned. Different streams of 'spilt religion' (T. E. Hulme's hostile term) merge in 'devotion to style'. For MacNeice, Joyce's early prose 'out-Pater[ed] Pater'.[29] Pater, a high Anglican before he lost his faith, like Newman before his conversion, was himself a devotee of Aquinas. Moreover, the ethos of 'aesthetic' literature was metaphorically, if not literally, Catholic. It might have been made for Joyce, and Joyce made some of it.

Perhaps it would highlight Pater's impact on Joyce if this were more often configured with his impact on Yeats. Although his presence in Joyce's works is well documented, Frank Moliterno noted in 1998 that 'comparative scrutiny of Pater and Joyce [had] remained peripheral for decades'. One reason may be that Joyce, who rarely names Pater, 'repressed' his centrality to 'the artist as a young man'.[30] Besides Pater's stylistic influence, and the influence of his 'devotion to style', *Marius* supplied a blueprint for the artist-hero and the Paterian 'moment' served as a model for the Joycean 'epiphany'. This is Alan D. Perlis's summary:

[28] Adrian Frazier, 'Queering the Irish Renaissance: The Masculinities of Moore, Martyn, and Yeats', in *Gender and Sexuality in Modern Ireland*, ed. Anthony Bradley and Maryann Giulanella Valiulis (Amherst, MA, 1997), 8–38 (8).
[29] MacNeice, *The Poetry of W. B. Yeats*, 176.
[30] Frank Moliterno, *The Dialectics of Sense and Spirit in Pater and Joyce* (Greensboro, 1998), 1, 3, 148.

[Pater's] Aesthetic Hero ... who makes his art his life ... is distinguished by his finely tuned senses that let the world of impressions bathe him completely and even, in washing through his mind, consolidate with consciousness into an epiphanal moment which is no longer the object's alone, but the object and the self welded by a 'hard, gem-like flame'.[31]

Moliterno rebukes a critical tendency to think that Joyce and other writers quickly 'outgrew' Pater (145). After all, he was still on Yeats's mind in the mid-1930s – or significantly recalled to mind by new versions of exteriority and rhetoric. Admittedly, Joyce was then parodying Pater's famous sentence about Mona Lisa: 'She is older than the rocks among which she sits.'[32] This becomes Anna Livia's '*I am Older northe Rogues among Whisht I Slips*' (*FW*, 105, 18). In 'Lestrygonians' Joyce has AE (George Russell) quoting from the same passage: 'What was he saying? The ends of the world ... Something occult: symbolism. Holding forth.'[33] Yet parody does not 'displace' its target. The Pater-inflected epiphany indeed belongs to 'Symbolism' (hardly just a brief literary phase): 'a sudden spiritual manifestation, whether in the vulgarity of speech or of gesture or in a memorable phase of the mind itself ... the most delicate and evanescent of moments' (*SH*, 216).

'Epiphany' also belongs to the interface between poetry and prose. It may define the 'prose-poem'. Since the fin de siècle was about quintessence, its quintessential genre was lyric, viewed by Pater as the most complete literary fusion of form and matter: Yeats's 'lyrics technically perfect, their emotion pitched high'. Joyce began as a lyric poet, and 'the eloquent and arrogant peroration' of Stephen's essay on 'Art and Life', replicated in Joyce's first essay on Mangan, affirms: 'The poet is the intense centre of the life of his age to which he stands in a relation to which none can be more vital. He alone is capable of absorbing in himself the life that surrounds him and of flinging it abroad again amid planetary music' (*SH*, 85; *OCPW*, 60).

Besides 'beauty', a keyword for Pater is 'ecstasy': a word that recurs in Stephen's reveries and which suggests a quasi-sexual consummation between the artist and beauty. In Joyce's first stab at self-portraiture, he writes: 'it was impossible that a temperament ever trembling towards its ecstasy should submit to acquiesce, that a soul should decree servitude for

---

[31] Alan D. Perlis, 'Beyond Epiphany: Pater's Aesthetic Hero in the Works of Joyce', *James Joyce Quarterly* 17.3 (Spring 1980): 272–79 (274).

[32] Pater, *The Renaissance*, 99.

[33] James Joyce, *Ulysses*, ed. Hans Walter Gabler (New York, 1984 [1986]), 158. Hereinafter cited as *U*.

its portion over which the image of beauty had fallen as a mantle'.[34] In *Portrait* itself, Stephen transfers 'beauty' to the artwork – ecstasy's fulfilment as 'aesthetic stasis':

> Beauty expressed by the artist cannot awaken in us an emotion which is kinetic or a sensation which is purely physical. It awakens, or ought to awaken ... an aesthetic stasis, an ideal pity or an ideal terror, a stasis called forth, prolonged and at last dissolved by what I call the rhythm of beauty.... Rhythm ... is the first formal aesthetic relation of part to part in any aesthetic whole or of an aesthetic whole to its part or parts or of any part to the aesthetic whole of which it is a part. (*Portrait*, 5:1147–57)

At the epiphanic interface, Stephen's definition of form as 'the rhythm of beauty' parallels what Yeats meant in 1900 by 'the symbolism of poetry': the entire poem as 'a musical relation': '[W]hen sound, and colour, and form are in a musical relation, a beautiful relation, to one another, they become as it were, one sound, one colour, one form, and evoke an emotion that is made out of their distinct evocations and yet is one emotion. The same relation exists between all portions of every work of art.'[35] Like Stephen, Yeats abjures kinesis as an impurity: 'The purpose of rhythm ... is to prolong the moment of contemplation'; poets should 'cast out ... those energetic rhythms as of a man running'.[36]

   To adapt another of Pater's influential propositions, Joyce's prose aspires to the condition of poetry: hence, perhaps, *Finnegans Wake*. His art, like Yeats's, originated in an aspiration to create highly crafted, ultimately symbolic, 'spiritual manifestations'. Shelley was another shared master. Yeats thought that Joyce had 'certainly surpassed in intensity' – that 1890s noun – all other contemporary novelists.[37] To this day, Irish novelists often keep one eye on poetry. So how should we rate Stephen as poet? Or Stephen's poem set amid Joyce's prose in *Portrait*: a villanelle that combines qualities of Yeats and Ernest Dowson? Dowson helps Stephen to eroticize Yeats's symbolic Rose. The poem is also 'supersaturated', as Stephen's mind is said to be, by spilt religion (*Portrait*, 5:2335). Like Yeats in the 1890s, Stephen replaces religious ritual with poetic incantation, the would-be rhythm of beauty: 'Are you not weary of ardent ways, / Lure of the fallen seraphim? / Tell no more of enchanted days' (1749–51).

---

[34] Quoted in James Joyce, *A Portrait of the Artist as a Young Man*, ed. Chester G. Anderson (New York, 1964), 260.

[35] W. B. Yeats, *Collected Works, IV: Early Essays*, ed. Richard J. Finneran and George Bornstein (New York, 2007), 116.

[36] Ibid., 117, 120.   [37] Wade, *The Letters of W. B. Yeats*, 651.

As he composes his villanelle, sexual and creative arousal beget a series of epiphanies, of which the poem is itself only one instance, or from which it emerges. Or, behind the scenes, the prose may have emerged from the poetry: some prose epiphanies are as verbally extravagant and more rhythmically interesting: 'The earth was like a swinging smoking swaying censer, a ball of incense, an ellipsoidal ball.' The passage continues ambiguously: 'The rhythm died out at once' (1571–73). Stephen's crystallizing of his emotions swings from desirous fantasy to precise memory, from Paterian ecstasy to dark projections:

> If he sent her the verses? They would be read out at breakfast amid the tapping of eggshells. Folly indeed! The brothers would laugh and try to wrest the page from each other with their strong hard fingers. (1717–21)

Another rhythm there. The whole sequence reflexively implicates Yeats, aesthetic and generic shifts, literary reception. The *Countess Cathleen* episode follows.

The jury appears to be out as to whether Joyce thinks the villanelle a good poem. Perhaps as elsewhere in *Portrait*, he is having his stylistic (or free-indirect-stylistic) cake and eating it: moving between the heroic and mock-heroic, the poetic and mock-poetic. Or perhaps he represents Pater's 'desire of beauty', where the erotic and aesthetic meet, as a necessary phase for the 'young' artist. Gibson questions 'the seriousness with which some critics have treated [the villanelle]', which 'surely represents a hiatus in or slackening of Stephen's modernity, a kind of recidivism . . . Here he is still remote from the adult Joyce: hence the resurgence of a Yeatsian vocabulary.'[38] For Gibson, Stephen must always mature in a predetermined 'modern' direction, or advance the work of national liberation, rather than undergo stages of literary apprenticeship which (as for Yeats) count in themselves. This parallels the idea that writers quickly outgrew Pater or Aestheticism or Symbolism and hurried on to 'modernism', without the 1890s leaving a more indelible imprint. Pound hoped to make Yeats an imagist poet, but admitted that he would always be 'romanticist, symbolist'.[39] Perhaps Joyce, shadowing Stephen, partly remained these things too. Further, Pater does not really advocate 'aesthetic stasis', even if his prose style inclines to that condition. Here Stephen, though not Joyce, misreads him. Pater's influence (as on Virginia Woolf) included his relativistic stress on shifting perception, consciousness-streams. He

---

[38] Gibson, *The Strong Spirit*, 199.
[39] Ezra Pound, review of Yeats's *Responsibilities*, *Poetry* 9 (December 1916): 150–51.

conceives the 'moment' in both art and life as belonging to the phenom-enal flux: 'impressions unstable, flickering, inconsistent, which burn and are extinguished with our consciousness of them ... that strange, perpet-ual, weaving and unweaving of ourselves'.[40] In 'Scylla and Charybdis' Stephen says, apparently with Joyce's sanction: 'As we, or mother Dana, weave and unweave our bodies ... so does the artist weave and unweave his image' (*U* 186). *Portrait* weaves and unweaves the Aesthetic Hero. In 'The Symbolism of Poetry' Yeats says that artists are 'continually making and un-making mankind'.[41]

Now for some 'what if' literary criticism. Had the Easter Rising not occurred, might we think rather differently about Yeats and Joyce around 1914 – the year when *Portrait* began to be serialized, when Yeats published *Responsibilities*? Pound praised both works for their 'hardness'. Taken together, they show how far the Irish literary 'movement' (Yeats's term, less loaded than 'revival' is now) has come in poetry and prose. They also involve retrospects on that movement, including its relation to Parnellism and Paterism. This is epitomized by the links between some poems in *Responsibilities* and Stephen's diary. Parnell is directly present in Yeats's 'To a Shade', indirectly present in Stephen's diary entry on Gladstone and 'A Race of Clodhoppers' (*Portrait*, 5:2669–71). Joyce detested Gladstone for 'effect[ing] the moral assassination of Parnell with the help of the Irish bishops' (*OCPW*, 142). Poems and diary share three keywords: 'away', 'conscience', 'father'.

As for Paterism, in 'The Grey Rock' Yeats invokes dead 'aesthetic' poets from the Rhymers' Club to counterpoint the poem's fable of a goddess betrayed by a mortal. Art too can be betrayed: once again by courting popularity, by making the correct ideological moves to secure 'a troop of friends'. Dowson and Lionel Johnson are praised for keeping 'the Muses' sterner laws' (*WBYP*, 103). Yeats's persona in *Responsibilities*, like Ste-phen's in *Portrait*, is often the embattled artist-hero. 'To a Shade' (*WBYP*, 109) tells Parnell's ghost: 'they are at their old tricks yet' – now with reference to art (Hugh Lane's proposed gallery), as formerly to politics. In the last stanza Parnell assumes the mantle of artist-exile: an 'unquiet wanderer' urged to leave Dublin: 'Away, away! You are safer in the tomb.' 'Away! Away!' with a not wholly different inflection begins Stephen's diary entry for 16 April (*Portrait*, 5:2777). In both 'To a Shade' and the diary, Dublin's coast figures freedom: 'that salt breath out of the sea / When grey

---

[40] Pater, *The Renaissance*, 187–88.   [41] Yeats, Collected Works, IV: Early Essays, 116.

gulls flit about instead of men'; 'the black arms of tall ships that stand against the moon, their tale of distant nations' (2779–80).

Responsibilities is haunted by dead artists (including Synge) who represent values ignored by the 'loud host', vilified by the 'old foul mouth' of the anti-Lane and formerly anti-Parnellite press (*WBYP*, 105, 109). In Yeats's epilogue-poem, Lady Gregory's Coole, the locus of inner exile, figures sanctuary for art's 'priceless things': 'A sterner conscience and a friendlier home' (127). As in 'The Grey Rock', 'stern' signifies inviolable literary and critical standards. In step with this sterner Aestheticism, Yeats's poetry has, of course, moved on since 1900: *Responsibilities* reflexively marks how the battle with Irish audiences has changed his poetry. Thus 'Paudeen' (108) revisits the clash between artist and bourgeoisie, with poetry now better fitted for that encounter. Initially, the poem's own rhythm is infected by the Paudeen voice (compare Stephen fearing his muse's brothers): 'Indignant at the fumbling wits, the obscure spite / Of our old Paudeen in his shop.' But a 'rhythm of beauty', implicitly toughened by culture war, extricates itself to suggest the ideal reciprocity between art and audience: 'a curlew cried and in the luminous wind / A curlew answered.' This is an epiphany about epiphanies (Yeats and Joyce share sea-birds as aesthetic icons). The poem finally symbolizes itself as 'a sweet crystalline cry': a harder aesthetic object.

If *Responsibilities* dramatizes an artistic mid-life crisis, *Portrait* dramatizes an earlier rite of passage. Both works involve the 'father' in this transition, in tensions between art and life. Yeats's prologue-poem apologizes to his 'old fathers' because his only progeny is 'a book' (*WBYP*, 101). *Portrait* ends with Stephen substituting Daedalus, his symbolic 'old father' in art, for his actual father. Stephen's rite of passage thus far is condensed into the diary. Here the potential artist-exile meets a range of people who reinforce or challenge his 'revolt': Davin, his father, John Alphonsus Mulrennan with his story of the old man who had 'red eyes and short pipe' (*Portrait*, 5:2748). The latter, whose speech evokes Synge, may combine patriarchal perils of the language movement and the literary movement. This is again a series of epiphanies: some based on everyday circumstance, others on 'phases of the mind', as when Stephen's future or future art is symbolized as the sound of hoofs that 'shine ... as gems' (2734) – a Pater echo? The epiphanies drafted earlier (interestingly, 'gems' replaced 'diamonds'), and closest to prose-poems, may be more ironically viewed than Stephen's 'new secondhand clothes' and so on. (2785). Stephen himself criticizes the horse-epiphany: 'Vague words for a vague emotion' (2737–38). Yet, as dreams or prophecies of the artist's life, the more visionary epiphanies seem partly ominous. Moreover, by sandwiching the visionary with the mundane, the new with the secondhand, and by making Stephen correct himself or backtrack, Joyce brings the multiple aspects of an emergent artistic personality closer together. He packs his pre-*Portrait* epiphanies (and poetry) into Stephen's luggage. Various roads and rhythms are left open as work in progress.

The diary's penultimate sentence concentrates the mutual challenge of life and art: 'experience'/'smithy'. Compare Yeats's 'The smithies break the flood' in 'Byzantium' (*WBYP*, 253). Stephen's 'uncreated conscience', like Yeats's 'sterner conscience', retains the 1890s idea that life should imitate art. And, like the invocations of 'The Grey Rock', his prospectus for exile, which fuses 'soul' with craft, is a religion-of-art prayer. So is his appeal to the 'old artificer' – who may subsume the not-yet-so-old artificer Yeats:

> Michael Robartes remembers forgotten beauty and, when his arms wrap her round, he presses in his arms the loveliness which has long faded from the world. Not this. Not at all. I desire to press in my arms the loveliness which has not yet come into the world. (*Portrait*, 5:2723–27)

Gibson comments: 'Stephen finally "overcomes" Yeats, the nineties, the backward look, and the tone and mood of the forlorn Anglo-Irish endgame.'[42] Once again, no literary game is zero-sum. Nor is the impulse behind Yeats's poetry ever reducible to forlorn Anglo-Irishness. Nor does this (Oedipal) epiphany seem so clear-cut. I would argue that the 1890s 'desire of beauty' remains alive in Stephen – and Joyce: that in *Portrait*, as in *Responsibilities*, Pater and Parnell combine to new effect. We might read the foundational aesthetic intercourse between Yeats and Joyce (the ground of more than modern 'Irish' literature) in less proleptic terms, whether those of proto-modernism or post-1916 Irish nationalism or both. Stephen's reflection on 'He Remembers Forgotten Beauty' might alternatively suggest that the 'beauty' pursued by Yeats's early poetry has impelled Joyce to discover his own 'rhythm of beauty'.

---

[42] Gibson, *The Strong Spirit*, 199.

CHAPTER 11

'Ingenious Lovely Things'
Yeats's Adjectives

Helen Vendler

Poets find arresting ways to employ all the parts of speech, down to 'a', 'an', and 'the'.[1] I have normally written about Yeats's poems as wholes, but recently I have been struck by his idiosyncratic use of various parts of speech. Although nouns or verbs might seem the first items to look into, I choose here – because Yeats's poetry is so often descriptive – to scan the notable and often odd adjectives in the later poetry that have both delighted and puzzled me. Their mutual relations, both to their nouns and to each other, provoke questions, pose difficulties. The classic instance of such cohabitation appears in the famous compound adjectives closing 'Byzantium': 'That **dolphin-torn**, that **gong-tormented**, sea' (the bold-face throughout this essay is mine). Can a sea of mire and blood be **torn**? Can a gong **torment** a sea? Such questions help us penetrate Yeats's imaginative moves; without understanding those we cannot comprehend the poem. Let me offer a more unobtrusive instance: How am I to imagine the field expressionistically sketched in the lines printed in bold below?

> Although the summer sunlight gild
> Cloudy leafage of the sky,
> **Or wintry moonlight sink the field**
> **In storm-scattered intricacy**,
> I cannot look thereon.
> ('Vacillation' V, *The Winding Stair*, 1933)[2]

---

[1] I discovered this truth about 'a' ('an') and 'the' when I was writing on the purposes assigned to each by Wallace Stevens: to my frustration, the early concordance then available did not list either word. Current digitized concordances make searches possible, but we still lack such concordances for many notable poets, for example, Hopkins. Sometimes the chaos of manuscripts (as in the case of Whitman) has so far precluded a complete concordance.

[2] Quotations from the published poetry are taken from *The Collected Works of W. B. Yeats, vol. 1: The Poems*, ed. Richard J. Finneran (New York, 1989), referenced in the text by title or page number. Boldface has been used to single out adjectival phrases. I do not include in my remarks passages much rewritten at a later date, and only in the case of 'Ancestral Houses' (below) do I make comparisons with manuscript materials.

What kind of intricacy can be storm-scattered? How does a storm scatter intricacy? What were the individual components, once unified but now scattered, of the previous intricacy? Why is the field made to *sink* by wintry moonlight? And why (more to the point) does Yeats resort to this perplexing terrestrial scene when the celestial summer scene preceding it is far more intelligible? (The Shakespearean 'gild' and the Keatsian 'cloudy' confer some traditional familiarity on the sunny sky, but no such echoes occur in the winter landscape.). Querying Yeats's adjectives in the later poetry brings us, with extraordinary intimacy, into his imagination – its idiosyncrasy, its leaps, its conjunction of dissimilar categories of thought, its assimilation of several categories into a single phrase.[3]

But before commenting on adjectives drawn from the later poetry, I must glance, for contrast, at Yeats's early adjectives, which are often almost empty of specific meaning: **pale**, **dim**, **old**, **young**, **great**, **woven**, **heavy**, **strong**, **mournful**, **proud**, and **sweet**. They serve either to veil the poems in a mist of dimness and pallor or to provide vague extensions of size, space, or time. When the younger Yeats resorts to semantically meaningful adjectives, he tends to ration them to one per noun, creating simple syntactic units:

> The **woods** of Arcady are **dead**,
> And over is their **antique joy**;
> Of old the world on dreaming fed;
> **Grey Truth** is now her **painted toy**;
> Yet still she turns her **restless head**:
> But O, **sick children** of the world,
> Of all the many **changing things**
> In **dreary dancing** past us **whirled**,
> To the **cracked tune** that Chronos sings,
> Words alone are **certain good**.
> ('The Song of the Happy Shepherd', 1889)

Yeats does in his late ballad-poems retain his early practice of pairing a single (and often linguistically uninteresting) adjective with a single noun,

---

[3] Still baffled by the imaginative infrastructure of these two lines, and certain that a poet would have better instincts than I in explaining them, I put the query to the poet Jorie Graham. She suggests that a formerly regular field of vegetation, say, a post-harvest wheat field, would lose its untroubled appearance and, as the vegetative detritus is scattered by a storm, would take on a new inscrutable patterning in which the previously solid field is made, under wintry moonlight, to sink into obscurity as the scattered stalks become the intricate figure upon that ground. She also comments that poets often, in condensing an image clear to them, retain its significant aesthetic components, sacrificing visual clarity to emotional accuracy.

restricting the speaker's range in import to preserve the appearance of 'folk-diction'. I quote from a ballad published in the 1930s:

> **All men** live in suffering,
> I know as few can know,
> Whether they take **the upper road**
> Or stay content on **the low,**
> **Rower bent** in his row-boat
> Or **weaver bent** at his loom,
> **Horseman erect** upon horseback
> Or **child hid** in the womb.
> ('The Wild Old Wicked Man')

Even when Yeats – as in the last four lines here – decides to reverse the normal English order of precedence (adjective followed by noun) to noun followed by adjective, the effect felt is still one of folk-archetypes, even of stereotype: if a rower, it will be one **bent** in his row-boat; if a weaver, one **bent** at his loom; if a rider on horseback, then **erect**; and if a child is **hid**, where but in the womb? Information lodged in such adjectives (including **upper** and **low**[er]) is minimal. We read such poems with already consti-tuted ballad expectations.

However, in Yeats's later meditative poems, successive adjectives offer complex intellectual moves compelled by simultaneous but differing men-tal perspectives. We are taken aback by the phenomenon in 'Nineteen Hundred and Nineteen' of strange (peculiar, unusual) adjectives closely cohabiting. To indicate my interest, I have borrowed the title of my essay from the provocative adjectival clusters in the opening stanza of 'Nineteen Hundred and Nineteen':

> **Many ingenious lovely** things are gone
> That seemed **sheer** miracle to the multitude,
> **Protected** from the circle **of the moon**
> That pitches **common** things about. There stood
> Amid the **ornamental** bronze and stone
> An **ancient** image **made of olive wood** –
> And **gone** are Phidias' **famous** ivories
> And all the **golden** grasshoppers and bees.

The three adjectives that introduce Yeats's lament – **many, ingenious, lovely** – set us a riddle. What is ingenious is rarely called lovely, what is called lovely is rarely called ingenious (and neither category is normally thought to be a 'miracle'). At the poem's opening declaration, we have no idea of the **many** ephemeral 'things' that might generate such anomalous joint adjectives. While **ingenious** is usually predicated of clever inventions, and **lovely** of natural beauty, the supernatural 'miracle' is rarely attached to either cunning ingenuity or beautiful 'things', no matter how lovely. To obscure the sense further, Yeats immediately withdraws the word 'miracle', linking it alliteratively to the naïve 'multitude' who would make such an uninformed judgement. Even when he places the **many ingenious lovely** 'things' in superlunary space, where they are **protected** from time in a way that **common** 'things' are not, he still refuses context. Where in time and space were those **many** vanished 'things?' In what fashion were they **ingenious** and in what ways **lovely**? Although Yeats then mentions **ornamental** bronze and stone, the artefacts glanced at are not specified – Are they bronze vessels or bronze statues? Are they marble statues or grave steles? Nor does 'an **ancient** image **made of olive wood**' appear either ingenious or lovely; it is merely an archaic ungendered sculpture (made of consumable wood, in apparent contrast to lasting bronze or stone). We understand only when the voice breaks off after 'olive wood' that the poet's imagination has been tempted to move beyond the conceptual and aesthetic realm of **ingenious** and **lovely** into a transcendent realm, in which images need not be lovely or ingenious to be venerated. Determined to remain on earth, the poet interrupts his swerve toward the sacred to resume his original categories. Only as the stanza ends do we discover that the basic referents for **ingenious lovely** things are intricate artefacts, though still undefined in theme – we do not know what was depicted by 'Phidias' **famous** ivories'. Finally, outlandishly, insects form the climax of the whole hyperbolic list: 'And all the **golden** grasshoppers and bees'.

We normally read to the end of a sentence before fixing the meanings of its words, but here we cannot proceed easily to the end, blocked as we are en route by the sheer number of perspectives imposed not only by the unresolved opening adjectives of 'Nineteen Hundred and Nineteen' but also elsewhere in the stanza. We are hindered in our advance through the stanza by the sudden interpolation of an unfinished sentence, itself retarded by the unresolved presence of a solid 'the' accompanied by a vague 'An': 'There stood / Amid **the** ornamental bronze and stone / **An** ancient image made of olive wood.' Only after the poet breaks off can the poem return, in its penultimate line, to its generating adjective, **gone**:

> Many ingenious lovely things are **gone**
> . . .
> And **gone** are Phidias' famous ivories.

Although Yeats's long periods frequently keep us in syntactic suspense, here it is the adjectives that by their incongruity compose a drawn-out and suspenseful problem of identity: 'Which vanished "things" were **inge-nious**, **lovely**, **protected**, **ornamental**, and **ancient**?' The riddle is sup-ported by the order – not an immediately lucid one – in which the unrelated adjectives appear. Before the poet's memory stand **many** things (an adjective arising from a visual perspective): How shall he differentiate the various items in his contemplated multipart assemblage? Following upon **many**, the adjectives completing the stanza imply a variety of perspectives in the poet's imagination as his list tentatively unfolds: the perspectives include the intellectual (**ingenious**), aesthetic (**lovely**), social (**protected**), architectural (**ornamental**), and historical (**ancient**). As the apparently 'spontaneous' first of the poet's reflections, the minute **inge-nious** is an odd choice, odder as soon as it is joined to **lovely**, and still odder as it is joined to **protected**. **Protected** demands clarification: 'By what power?' and 'From what danger?' In the striking ascription of a single shared distinguishing adjective – **ornamental** – to coupled bronze and stone, Yeats establishes not only a cultural and aesthetic homogeneity but also a common location and historical era in which the bronze and stone appeared together to a spectator's eye. Yet the poet has not yet defined – in any recognizable way – the space and time of these 'things'. The adjective **ancient** at last places the 'things' in a remote, not recent, past – but we are immediately troubled by the fact that the wooden 'image' as described seems neither **ingenious** nor **lovely**; and **famous** (where? among whom?) contributes to the social vagueness of the list while adding renown. Only the last two lines allow us to arrive at a secure knowledge of the ingenious and lovely Greek artefacts of ivory and gold, those 'things' that were in the mind's eye of the poet (along with that anomalous wooden image) before he even pronounced his first word. It is not self-evident, however, why golden insects would provide the stanza's climax.

Imagine the stanza paraphrased in syntactically natural prose, revealing itself immediately to the reader:

Those archaic lovely arts of ancient Greece are gone:
Phidias's ivories and the ingenious golden bees mentioned by Thucydides,
Things that seemed miraculous to the naïve multitude,
And to all of us seemed immortal, protected from that destruction inflicted by
    time on common things.
– Amid ornamental bronze vessels and marble columns
There stood on the Acropolis the ancient sacred olive-wood image of Athena –
That too is gone.

The obscure adjectival unspooling of the actual stanza is, by contrast to this prose paraphrase, a deliberate holding effort, enacting the musing mind of the poet as he contemplates the lost aggregate of Greek art – and, with a sharp break in tone, swerves briefly into a sacred image antecedent to, and beyond, the realm of art. The temptation to rise to the transcendent with Athena is firmly resisted by the poet, who returns to his original intellectual and aesthetic categories.

We might expect the poet to continue with explanatory causation: under what assault did the artworks vanish? Instead, we find, in the second stanza, a leap to the poet's own century as he counters his intellectual and aesthetic adjectives of nostalgia with a relatively empty set of contemporary modifiers: **pretty, indifferent, old, public, future, fine,** and **worst.**

> We too had many **pretty** toys when young;
> A law **indifferent** to blame or praise,
> To bribe or threat; habits that made **old** wrong
> Melt down, as it were wax in the **sun's** rays;
> **Public** opinion ripening for so long
> We thought it would outlive all **future** days.
> O what **fine** thought we had because we thought
> That the **worst** rogues and rascals had died out.

Like the adjectives of the previous stanza, those of the second, too, arise from several different mental perspectives: **pretty** from an ironic aesthetic of the trivial; **indifferent** from a legal stance; **public** from a political angle; **future** from the temporal perspective that has wrenched the poet's mind away from the ancient past. **Fine**, an adjective as scornful as **pretty**, arises from a sardonic judgement of value, while the hierarchical **worst** adds the perspective of vindictive social condemnation. It is worth enumerating the poet's points of view because his hostile scan of the present imitates his construction of the past: we see a rapid succession of incongruous adjectives uttered in a single stanza. We ask: Have we exhausted the jostling perspectives of the poet as he aggressively opposes the present to the past, erasing nostalgia by contempt?

No: the proliferation of perspectives continues, as Yeats imposes in the fourth stanza another immediate and swift conjunction of adjectives bizarrely unlike in diction and imagery: **dragon-ridden, drunken, murdered, scot-free, fighting.**

> Now days are **dragon-ridden**, the nightmare
> Rides upon sleep: a **drunken** soldiery
> Can leave the mother, **murdered** at her door,
> To crawl in her own blood, and go **scot-free**;
> The night can sweat with terror as before
> We pieced **our** thoughts into philosophy,

> And planned to bring the world under a rule,
> Who are but weasels **fighting** in a hole.

Even before we see the nouns to which these active adjectives are matched – before we learn that mythical dragons infest human days, that a young mother has been atrociously murdered, that the drunken soldiers who murdered her go (colloquially) 'scot-free', and that the fighting political opponents are men likened to feral ferrets – we live in a deliberately incoherent atmosphere in which young mothers and dragons and bestial savagery keep company. The early title for 'Nineteen Hundred and Nineteen' was 'Thoughts on the State of the Modern World': surveying modernity, Yeats's imagination rapidly pours forth another series of (apparently) disordered spectacles, just as it had when he advanced from the ingenious to the lovely to the ancient, showing us (in his immediately truncated glance at the ancient 'image') how quickly his imagination refuses a contemplation of the transcendent. Repudiating his youthful taste for **dim** and **pale**, Yeats in his powerfully metaphorical late adjectives draws from many distinct and taxing compartments of feeling, thought, and imagination. As we see him agitatedly displaying a mixing of metaphorical dragons and 'real' mothers and soldiers, we enter a realm of surreal description where thoughts converge unerringly from periphery to centre. We have come far from seeing a single adjective accompanying a single noun: we have become incorporated into a myriad-minded personality whose imagination, having taken on 'the state of the world', is beset by insistent clamouring adjectives, each claiming to represent a necessary perspective.

There are other notable adjectival behaviours populating the later poems, of which one, persisting from the early work, is the poet's frequent use of adjective phrases beginning with 'of':

> A sudden blast **of dusty wind** and after
> Thunder **of feet**, tumult **of images**.
> ('Nineteen Hundred and Nineteen')

The younger Yeats, fond of this adjectival possessive, wants it to be undisturbing, rural, immemorial:

> The cry **of a child** by the roadway, the creak **of a lumbering cart**,
> The heavy steps **of the ploughman**, splashing the wintry mould,
> Are wronging your image that blossoms a rose in the deeps **of my heart**.
> The wrong **of unshapely things** is a wrong too great to be told.
> ('The Lover Tells of the Rose in His Heart', 1899)

The information content of the early phrasing is conventional: a child's cry, a cart's creak, a ploughman's heavy steps, the heart's 'deeps'. As a catalogue of 'unshapely things' this conventional list will pass factual muster, and the creative use of the ears –rather than the eyes – to note 'unshapeliness' (in a cry, a creak, a heavy footfall) dramatically enlarges 'shape' from its primary visual reference to the aural. So far so good, but these youthful lines depend on clichés. In the passage from 'Nineteen Hundred and Nineteen', 'a sudden blast **of dusty wind**' far exceeds, in linguistic interest, 'the cry **of a child**', just as a 'tumult **of images**'[4] creates a surreal storm more imaginatively exciting than the 'realistic' creak **of a cart**. The later Yeats, in short, takes a rather placid adjectival template – a/the **X of Y** – and crams it with depth. So, for instance, in 'Chosen' (the sixth poem in the sequence *A Woman Young and Old*) the phrases in 'of' are eventful: the speaking woman struggles for 'an image on the track / **Of the whirling Zodiac**' and imagines her lover finding rest on 'the maternal midnight **of my breast**'. One cannot foresee as one reads what adjective will modify the Zodiac's 'track' or how the woman will characterize her 'breast'. Even a single genitive phrase in late Yeats can be pregnant with surprise: in 'Parnell's Funeral' we see first 'A bundle of' – of what? – **of tempestuous cloud** and later 'the contagion of' – of what? – **of the throng**. Yeats compels us to reflect on how and why his metaphorical tempest causes clouds to assume the shape of a household 'bundle', and on how and why a 'throng' can bring (like a disease) the threat of 'contagion' of semantic content.

Yet another adjectival behaviour common in Yeats is repetition of semantic content, which in both early and late work adds an aura of either incantation or insistence. He had loved linguistic linkages formed by incremental returnings of almost any part of speech, as in the conscious repetitions of several different ones – the pronoun, the verb, the preposition, the possessive adjective, the noun – in the experimental 'He Wishes for the Cloths of Heaven' (1899):

> I would **spread** the cloths **under your feet**:
> But **I**, being poor, **have** only **my dreams**;
> **I have spread my dreams under your feet**;
> **Tread** softly because you **tread** on **my dreams**.

Repetition, in such an instance, is the index of a magical incantation. It transforms words as it goes, by sleight of hand summoning **tread** to follow

---

[4] *OED*, *tumult*, s.v. 3: fig. Great disturbance or agitation of mind or feeling; confused and violent emotion.

spread, so that phonetic resemblance is not confined only to the line-endings in rime riche. And to compound the poem's ritual effect, Yeats is willing to repeat a word by its homonym, as another 'magic' transformation almost invisibly changes the grammatical function: **have** as 'possess' becomes **have** as an imperfect auxiliary. The 'magic' can also stealthily alter the mood of a single verb in a single line: **tread** as an imperative becomes, four words later, 'you **tread**' as an indicative.

In the late poetry we find highly worked repetitions of this sort, but in contrast to the medieval embroidery of 'He wishes for the cloths of heaven', the late imaginative texture – with an unexpected plainness proper to age – can repeat an unchangingly emphatic word as the frustrated poet's search reviews the recurrent features of its imaginative past:

> I **sought** a **theme** and **sought** for it in **vain**,
> I **sought** it daily for six weeks **or so**.
> Maybe at last, being but a broken man,
> I must be satisfied with my **heart** . . .
> . . .
> What can I but enumerate **old themes**?
> First that sea-rider Oisin led by the nose
> Through three enchanted islands, allegorical dreams,
> **Vain** gaiety, **vain** battle, **vain** repose,
> **Themes** of the embittered **heart**, **or so** it seems,
> That might adorn **old** songs **or** courtly shows.
> ('The Circus Animals' Desertion')

Although in the second stanza there are several polysyllabic adjectives (their syllables mounting and declining in pleasing symmetry – 2, 3, 5, 3, 2 – **broken, enchanted, allegorical, embittered, courtly**), and although each of these offers its own perspectival genesis (respectively, physical, magical, literary, emotional, historical), the adjective that most draws attention to itself is the conspicuously monosyllabic **vain** (because its triple anger is 'predicted' in the first two lines not only by the tripling of **sought** but also by the initial adverbial phrase 'in **vain**').

The fourfold repetition of **vain** performs a conventional demonstration of through-composed unity, but like other late reduplications contributes markedly to changes in tone. The three thrusts of **sought** enact the poet's increasingly hopeless determination; the triple adjectival **vain** prefaces – and therefore pre-emptively destroys – the subsequent emotional hopes for sexual gaiety, vigorous battle, and deserved repose; and the dismissive **old** of '**old** themes' – rejecting personal idealizations no longer valid – changes hue to become the nostalgic **old** of '**old** songs'. As usual, the later Yeats gets double value from almost any ordinary stratagem of rhetoric by expanding, deepening, and varying it in performance: against the putatively simple **vain** of 'in **vain**' he sets the complex tripled adjective, repudiating as **vain** (empty) the gaiety derived from sexual illusion, satirizing as **vain** (futilely undertaken) a battle lost, and lamenting as **vain** (useless) the reparatory work of rest. In this way, Yeats – with a single adjective which alters in meaning at each repetition – can take on the 'chameleon' quality Keats ascribed to the poet.

When I asked myself, as I was rereading 'Meditations in Time of Civil War' (1928), what aspect of its ottava rima overture – 'Ancestral Houses' – generated its dense resonance, it was, I saw, Yeats's use of adjectives. Many were already familiar: **old**, **our**, **great**, **rich**, **every**, **long**. But outvying those were successive polysyllabic adjectives relying on ostentation ('**escutcheoned** doors') or modifying unexpected nouns into personifications ('**slippered** Contemplation') or juxtaposing mutually cancelling antonyms ('**marvellous empty** sea-shell'). The texture of the verse is compressed even in the first stanza, where its central reduplication ('**Life** ... rains down **life**') emerges within an opulent adjectival texture – even while subverting its descriptive riches not only by its ominous beginning, 'Surely', but also by the curt dismissive comment, 'Mere dreams, mere dreams!'

> Surely among a **rich** man's **flowering** lawns,
> Amid the rustle of his **planted** hills,
> Life overflows without **ambitious** pains;
> And rains down life until the basin spills,
> And mounts more dizzy high the more it rains
> As though to choose **whatever** shape it wills
> And never stoop to a **mechanical**
> Or **servile** shape, at **others'** beck and call.
> **Mere** dreams, **mere** dreams!

As I said earlier with respect to the late ballads, Yeats never lost his liking for phrases combining a single adjective and a single noun. In the early 'Song of the Happy Shepherd', the chosen adjectives are occasionally imaginative – 'the **cracked** tune', '**clanging** space' – but the incessant reiteration of the syntactic template of adjective-plus-noun begins to seem an unconscious tic. In the later work, Yeats's riddling adjectives, even when matched with a single noun, tend to require some intellectual labour. As we first encounter 'Ancestral Houses', for instance, the adjectives, because of their oblique attachment to their nouns, demand attention. Is it the lawns themselves that flower? Who **planted** the hills, and what does the adjective **planted** mean in this context? (Its political meaning would be clear to an Irish reader, but the word **planted** remains magnetized toward vegetation by the nearby aura of **flowering**.) What specific pains are those created by ambition? What would a **mechanical** life-shape be, and how would life manifest a **servile** shape? And it is not simply the individual, free-standing phrases linking adjective to noun that ask effort; one wants to discover, in each poem, the conceptual organization linking such telling phrases to Yeats's expert overarching differentiation of aesthetic structure, tone, and form.

The first two drafts of the opening stanza of the poem ultimately called 'Ancestral Houses' (included in the manuscript materials of *The Tower*[5]) reveal how indispensable his adjectives are to Yeats's compositional invention. As he begins to write, his draft entirely lacks notable adjectives except for **supreme** (which he includes merely as an intrinsic part of the underlying Latin phrase *summum bonum*). I indicate by italics below the phrases Yeats will *strike out* in the subsequent draft:

> *What if that supreme good that all* our kin
> Thought *Thought*
> *Thinks most could magnify, diminishes*
> *And taking our greatness with* our bitterness,
> O what if all that most delights mankind
> And seems to magnify diminishes
> *Taking our greatness with our bitterness.*
> Because our greatness is our bitterness.

Reconsidering his intellectual conundrum of the relation of [achieved] greatness to [coincident] bitterness, Yeats sketches a second draft of these lines, correcting their bare vagueness by enriching them with a set of complex social contexts – a landowner, a landscape, history, will, and freedom of choice. The tentative inserted social adjectives of the second draft, in boldface below, transmute the first draft into something more recognizably human: (italics, as earlier, mark words later deleted):

> The **rich** men's houses rise in **flowery** lawns
> Then **wide** plantations [?rise] upon the hills:
> [?**Matured**] without **ambitious** aches or pains
> Life *can* pour out gains on gains till the cup spills
> And yet by spilling mounts & **greater** *gain* gains
>   [?*my*] mind

---

[5] W. B. Yeats, *The Tower (1928): Manuscript materials*, ed. Richard J. Finneran with Jared Curtis and Ann Saddlemyer. (Ithaca, 2007). The quoted excerpts can be found on p. 153.

> Where I *could* can choose **whatever** shape it wills
> And never grovel at **others** [*sic*] beck and call
> To **servile** shape or grow **mechanical**.

Yeats is still resorting in this second draft to pre-formulated phrases – 'rich men's houses', 'aches or pains', 'gains on gains' – but all are subsequently cancelled in favour of more studied diction. The poet briefly considers writing in the first person singular, referring to his mind both subjectively ('I') and objectively ('it') – '[?*my*] mind // Where I *could* can choose whatever shape it wills' – but decides to remain in the collective first-person plural, confirming the poem as a social lyric as well as a personal one. Although 'we' can serve as a universal collective (as it often does in Wordsworth or Auden), here Yeats implicitly inserts an Irish spectator contemplating a special subset of Irish society – the rich in their 'big houses'. The spectator is part of the national 'we', but he is not among the smaller group of **rich** men.

In his second stanza, Yeats exultantly places the **abounding glittering** jet of natural life in its man-made architectural basin. Yet for the spontaneous original fountain he immediately substitutes a desolate contemporary form:

> though now it seems
> As if some **marvelous empty** sea-shell flung
> Out of the **obscure** dark of the **rich** streams,
> And not a fountain, were the symbol which
> Shadows the **inherited** glory of the rich.

After his conflicting adjectives of aristocratic past and impoverished present – the **abounding** jet and the **empty** shell – Yeats flings into the imagination's foundry a third, enigmatic, component necessary to his myth of origin – 'the **obscure** dark of the **rich** streams' – obviating his original binary contrast of the rich inherited past and the futile present. Although the twice-repeated definite article '*the*' appears to give a locatable origin for the shell (it was flung out of *the* **obscure** dark of *the* **rich** streams') it denies shape – whether that of a fountain or of a shell – to that mysterious origin. There are affinities between this '**obscure** dark of the **rich** streams' and the equally obscure '**rich dark** nothing' of 'The Gyres' in that they both facilitate the burgeoning new. **Dark** matures into its adjectival form in '**dark** nothing' and its nominal form in '**dark** between the polecat and the owl' as the poet claims that in the future,

> Lovers of horses and of women, shall
> From marble of a broken sepulchre

Or **dark** betwixt the polecat and the owl,
Or any rich, **dark** nothing disinter
The workman, noble, and saint.

(293)

The passage might seem realistic in its restorative prophecy were it not for the weird and uninterpretable '**dark** betwixt the polecat and the owl'.[6]

In 'Ancestral Houses' (as elsewhere) Yeats multiplies an adjective's import by alteration of its context or syntactic function. When we first hear the word 'rich' it is a commercial adjective – 'the **rich** man' – but when it reappears as an adjective, it belongs to nature – 'the **rich** streams'. And on its next appearance Yeats uses it as a collective noun – 'the **rich**'. The malleable nature of the word **rich** allows Yeats to use it serially to describe an archetypal man, nature, and society. The **rich** – a noun – that ominously closes the stanza with the phrase 'the inherited glory of the **rich**' reveals that the glory 'shadowing' the '**Ancestral**' house is but a legend of past achievement, no more present to the contemporary eye than the obscure **dark** of the **rich** streams whence it issued.

The matrix of 'Ancestral Houses', as considered in Yeats's second stanza, is both socially and personally emotional: there were material and passionate motives behind the construction of these 'big houses', relegated now – by Yeats's adjectives **ancestral** and **inherited** – to a legacy of dead life. Yeats's adjectives stall in a shackling and shackled circle – **violent, bitter, powerful, bitter, violent** – having at its centre the material motive for the master's erecting of the graceful estate – to make its **violent** and **bitter** owner **powerful**. The personal motive is Yeats's dismayed suspicion of the intrinsic entwinement of Thanatos and Eros. The **powerful** man's fear of Thanatos drives him to summon architects and artists – themselves, like him, **bitter** and **violent** – to erect an antithetical shrine to Eros, honouring its permanent qualities of sweetness and gentleness, permanent because nominalized from the adjectives 'sweet' and 'gentle' into the platonic nouns 'sweetness' and 'gentleness'.

---

[6] The polecat (with brown fur and a vile skunk-like smell) is always figurally pejorative; the word is sometimes used as an appellation for a prostitute (*OED*). If the owl (standing, as usual, for wisdom) is at the opposite end of the allegorical spectrum from the polecat, the descriptive phrase may mean that both the owl-wisdom of intuition and the polecat-revulsion of the senses equally inhabit realms that are **dark** to rational knowledge. As Yeats ventures a location for the 'nothing', he first speculates that the immemorial human archetypes can be reactualized from the Christian legacy of 'marble of a broken sepulchre'; then – rejecting the Christian guess – he wonders whether perhaps the archetypes can be excavated from the mysterious 'dark' of both senses and intuition; then – as he gives up on the nothing's unknowable nature – he cries out his frustrated '**any rich, dark** nothing'.

Some **violent bitter** man, some **powerful** man
Called architect and artist in that they,
Bitter and **violent** men, might rear in stone
The sweetness that all longed for night and day,
The gentleness none there had ever known.

What would it be to live a placid life free from ambitious pains, the sort of life Yeats had never been able to arrange for himself? And can art arise afresh in the Irish post-war life of '**slippered** Contemplation?' In the Christian contrast between the active and the contemplative life, the ascetic contemplative choice is reckoned the more virtuous; but Yeats, as he imagines the leisurely and unworried meditations of the rich man's wealthy heirs, doubts that 'slippered Contemplation' free of hardship could ever produce worthy art:

O what if gardens where the peacock strays
With **delicate** feet upon **old** terraces,
Or else all Juno from an urn displays
Before the **indifferent garden** deities;
O what if **levelled** lawns and **gravelled** ways
Where **slippered** Contemplation finds his ease
And Childhood a delight for **every** sense,
But take our greatness with our violence?[7]

---

[7] Yeats attempts to rewrite this sceptical outcome in 'The Gift of Harun Al-Rashid' (1923) where man loses bitterness as he is rewarded by the 'honeycomb' of marriage. The courtier-speaker reports a colloquy between himself and the newly married caliph: 'And thereupon a colloquy took place / That I commend to all the chroniclers / To show how violent great hearts can lose / Their bitterness and find the honeycomb' (446). 'The gift of Harun Al-Rashid' is not always convincing as it allegorizes Yeats's own marriage in conventional pragmatic and romantic ways. The invented Arab context now seems fusty and fin-de-siècle, the mise-en-scène 'orientalist'. Still, there are occasional memorable passages, especially when Harun Al-Rashid describes his wife's speech in sleep as she announces new truths, especially ones abstracted from life contexts. Yeats resorts to a wonderful perspectival account of abstract truths: 'Self-born, high-born, and solitary truths, / Those terrible implacable straight lines / Drawn through the wandering vegetative dream' (449).

The six adjectives predicated of the truths – that they are self-born, high-born, solitary, terrible, implacable, and straight – require that the reader find a plausible perspective from which to arrive at each. The first is individual, the second social, the third monastic, the fourth Blakean, the fifth judgmental, and the sixth geometric, while the seventh adjective, a passive one, 'drawn', is the fulcrum between the implacable straight lines and the dream. Similarly, the reader must adopt – rapidly, in succession – the two perspectives creating the adjectives attached to dream: the first, 'wandering', belongs to the cognitive perspective of judgement, as it characterizes the erratic nature of the dream, while the second, 'vegetative', belongs to a philosophical perspective. The dream – neither a dead 'mineral' thing nor a free 'animal' thing – is alive, but detained in the middle passive realm of the vegetative.

The habitation of slippered ease may delight children, who require nothing more than sense pleasure, but it is not sufficiently invigorating – as Yeats reluctantly concedes – for epic manliness, the battle valour of the founder that begins in violence and ends in death. The powerful and bitter master departs to gain martial and commercial power, leaving behind his beautiful ancestral house and gardens, but while he is away his descendants, weakened by living in peace within that sumptuous house and its beautiful gardens, may dwindle to cowards:

> But when the master's buried mice can play,
> And maybe the great-grandson of that house,
> For all its bronze and marble, 's but a mouse.

Although Yeats recognized his own contemplative nature in naming this sequence 'Meditations', he was no reclusive monk; his personal and social battles, his stubbornness and aggression in constituting a modern literature in Ireland, lie within his scorn for – as well as his envy of – 'slippered Contemplation'.

Yeats's perspectival clusters of adjectives ('**Many ingenious lovely** things') and his single but repeated adjectives ('**Vain** gaiety, **vain** battle, **vain** repose') achieve their results by accumulation. But there is yet another adjectival property exploited by Yeats, one belonging not to the distinctions of a cluster but rather to single adjectives. Single adjectives standing alone have the excellent capacity – if they are inherently contrastive adjectives – to achieve a double exposure; behind their assertions lies a shadow environment populated by their implicit opposites, which are almost invisibly brought to mind. In 'Byzantium', 'The **unpurged** images **of day** recede' can hardly be imagined except in the shadow of its implied counter-truth: 'The **purged** images **of night** advance', just as 'The Emperor's **drunken** soldiery are **abed**' is intelligible only because behind it abides the normative contrast of 'The Emperor's **sober** soldiery **stand on watch**.' In such cases, negative specification – of the **unpurged drunken** daytime routine-at-present – becomes suggestion-by-contrast of the positive purged, sober, nocturnal purification-to-come.

While the ever-antithetical Shakespeare of the sonnets tends to be explicit in his contrastive lyric adjectives ('For I have sworn thee **fair**, and thought thee **bright**, / Who art as **black** as Hell, as **dark** as night'), Yeats allows an antithetical adjective to stand alone while it silently summons its logically implicit opposite. I rewrite (in italics, with apologies to Yeats) the lines of 'Byzantium', making clear the antithetical shadow lines behind its 'golden handiwork'. The enameled bird,

Planted on the star-lit golden bough,
Perching on the sunlit golden bough
Can like the cocks of Hades crow,
Can like the cocks of heaven crow,
Or, by the moon embittered, scorn aloud
Or, by the sun contented, praise aloud
In glory of changeless metal
In glory of changing life-flesh
Common bird or petal
Splendid bird or petal
And all complexities of mire or blood.
And all simplicities of sinlessness.

It is as though Yeats were playing with us a game of antonyms: behind the stationary **planted**, the transient *perching*; behind the nocturnal **star-lit**, the diurnal *'sun-lit'*, and so on. The contrasts are so conceptually linked that the phrase **of Hades** cannot fail to summon *of heaven*, nor **moon**, *sun*. The procession of implied antitheses continues: **embittered**/contented; **scorn**/praise; **changeless**/*changing*; **metal**/*flesh*; **common**/*splendid*; **complexities**/*simplicities*. And behind the deadly sins implied in **mire** [Luxuria], **fury** [Ira], and **blood** [Superbia – but also Luxuria and Ira], we glimpse, painfully, the unattainable figures of sinless love and peace. In short, within Yeats's exhausted but envious repudiation of the day's unpurged images, we perceive an adjectival 'shadow poem' – not one of Byzantine ghostly purgation but rather a sinless one of human joy. The technique of the silent, summoned, ghost word is frequent in Yeats's later work, as he in effect writes a double-exposure single line, the stated fact necessarily recalling its unstated antithesis. (I have spoken here of adjectival contrasts, but of course any substantive part of speech can be mined for its implicit contrastive value.)

'Byzantium' offers not only adjective clusters (**that dolphin-torn, that gong-tormented** sea) and single contrastives (**unpurged**) but also a new possibility: the unstable and unsettling shuffling of adjectival phrases. Though formed on the earlier 'simple' template 'X of Y' in which the pre-positioned and post-positioned stable nouns, – the *cry* of the *child*, the *creak* of the *cart* – have a 'natural' connection, the problematic 'attributions-in-*of*' that appear in 'Byzantium' present no such 'natural' links between the abstract and the concrete. Instead, they link, with their baffling 'of', abstract to abstract, uncontextualized:

complexities of mire or blood
complexities of fury
furies of complexity

As we attempt to arrive by logic at Yeats's import, we deduce that mire has its own complexities, analogous to, but distinct from, the complexities of blood; that fury has complexities similar to, but distinguishable from, those of mire or blood; and that complexity itself has furies. However, the rational unvexing of these phrases is not the point; rather, the point is that the complexities of one's own failures – those storms of lust, anger, and bloodshed – defeat any disentangling of their essences into simpler form. In the insoluble rage and self-condemnation of old age, adjectives boil in a fury of the inexpressible.[8]

In 'Ancestral Houses' the sudden change in tone from the coarse third stanza (**violent** and **bitter**, etc.) to the phonetic subtleties of the fourth garden stanza is created almost exclusively by a succession of first unexpected and then threadbare adjectives: the unexpected **delicate** of peacock's feet is succeeded by the conventional **old** of ancestral terraces; the surprising **indifferent** modifying the compound noun '**garden** deities' adds the marble busts of classical gods to the peacock's feet and the formal vista of old terraces; and, when **gravelled** and **levelled** almost rhyme both graphically and aurally, it is as if language had produced in '**-elled**' a universal garden suffix. Although the stanza of the outdoor garden scene generates the indoor house scene of stanza 5, the choice of adjectives distinguishes the twins: while stanza 4's adjectives are peculiar in their ascription of unexpected qualities to their nouns (**delicate** to peacocks' feet, **indifferent** to garden deities, and **slippered** to 'Contemplation'), stanza 5, with its adjectival anticipation of the decline of the ancestral house, offers the clichés of a tourist brochure: '**escutcheoned** doors', '**polished** floors', '**great** chambers', '**long** galleries', and '**famous** portraits'. Invention lapses into an inertia of public language, adjective by adjective, until we feel the beautiful mansion stiffening into rigor mortis.

Yeats often takes pains in the later poetry to impose, as in 'Ancestral Houses', implausible linkages of adjective and noun, and he feels free as well to abandon realistic notation in favour of a continual mismatching of

---

[8] In 'Byzantium' the adjectives mount into two of Yeats's most urgent adjectival compounds, 'dolphin-torn' and 'gong-tormented', both said of the sea, of the 'dolphin's mire and blood' (that kenning for the impure mortal tide beating at the breakwater of the Emperor's golden smithies). I once heard Oliver Edwards (a professor of German who had been one of Yeats's younger friends) recite 'Byzantium' after the fashion of Yeats's own reading, which Oliver had begged the poet to repeat so that he could fix and remember the Yeatsian sounds and phrasing. Two aural features resonated in the closing line as Oliver Edwards reproduced it: the first was the exaggerated and intensifying echo of 'tor-n' in 'tor-men-ted', and the second was the poet's pronunciation of those adjectives with both a rolled 'r' and a deliberate prolongation of both vowels and consonants in the parallel phrases: 'That dolllphinn-torrrrnn, that gonggg-torrrmmennnteddd sea'. (One can hear versions of that kind of prolongation in Yeats's recorded readings.)

what we could call figure and ground. In 'Blood and the Moon', upon the generalized ground 'the world', Yeats applies his most grotesque figure – '**this pragmatical, preposterous** pig'. His contempt derives theoretically from Berkeleian Idealism, but Yeats voices it in two farcical alliterating adjectives, each more abnormal in modifying its mutual alliterating noun, 'pig'. 'Pragmatical' – obsolete in contemporary usage (see *OED*, s.v. 'pragmatical', 3) – is unfailingly pejorative: 'officious, meddlesome, interfering; intrusive'; and, of a person, 'conceited, self-important, pompous; opinionated; dogmatic, unbending'. (There is scarcely a more entertaining set of derisive pages in the *OED* than those of 'pig' and its compounds.) Against a meddlesome and opinionated society, Yeats is willing to stretch his adjectives of caricature as far as **preposterous**. A caricature – whatever its exaggerations of feature – must nonetheless be modelled on a recognizable counterpart, and Yeats turns to the unkillable genre of animal fable as he inscribes 'the world' as an Orwellian preposterous, pragmatical pig.

Caricature, too, governs the opening of 'News for the Delphic Oracle', in which the **golden** codgers represent the geriatric body as one still sighing after sex, just as the **Holy** Innocents, reliving their death, represent infant masochistic pleasure as 'their wounds open again'. 'Man-picker Niamh' is another such caricature, like the globe-trotting 'Madam' in 'Under Ben Bulben' whose 'bowels are in heat' as she gazes upon 'half-awakened Adam'. Yeats's jeering adjectives of satirical portraiture measure the distance he has travelled – or has been forced to travel by age, experience, and aesthetic taste – from the paler adjectives of his Celtic twilight. Yet portrait caricatures of **golden** codgers or **Holy** infants are not Yeats's strongest adjectival suit in old age. He is better at monstrous sights and apocalyptic events: we recall, in 'The Second Coming', the **blank** and **pitiless** gaze, the **rough** beast and the **slow** thighs, as well as Yeats's breath-taking coupling (in 'The Gyres') of the adjective **irrational** with 'streams **of blood**' or the glossing of **nightmare** as **numb**. Such unanticipated but eerie moves disturb the mind striving to follow the poet, as he first joins an abstract adjective (**irrational**) to an unbearable sensual phenomenon (streams of blood), and then, giddily reversing syntactic direction, attaches a sensual adjective (**numb**) to an abstract concept (nightmare). He intends that we should flinch as **sensitive** arrives unexpectedly among the felt horrors:

> **Irrational** streams **of blood** are staining earth;
> . . .
> What matter though **numb** nightmare ride on top
> And blood and mire the **sensitive** body stain?
>
> (293)

Yeats's later meditative poems, even the more apparently sedate ones, have to manage the accumulated perspectives, jostling for precedence, of the aged poet's mind. Among the later works, the poem that set him the most difficult adjectival task, I believe, was the ceremonious 'The Municipal Gallery Revisited' (319–21), in which he must characterize, as he walks through the Gallery, not only the paintings that he sees but also the persons represented by the art. He has to supply blank factual accounts ('a **revolutionary** soldier kneeling to be blessed') while providing his own estimate of the inner life of the persons portrayed ('A soul **incapable** of remorse or rest') and judging the success of the art itself ('A **great ebullient** portrait certainly'). He must mimic the vertiginous passage of time, measured by years hardly distinguishable from minutes ('I met her all but **fifty** years ago / For **twenty** minutes in some studio') and must represent the cruel brevity of human life by compressing a whole existence into a diptych: 'Hazel Lavery **living** and **dying**'.[9] He must – in spite of all his reverence for Coole – despair as he admits the failure of his prophecy of its future:

> **Childless** I thought 'my children may find here
> **Deep-rooted** things', but never foresaw its end.

As Yeats walks through the Gallery, approaching portraits of friends and intimates, he must keep his own elegy in touch with literary tradition high and low, alluding – in a single phrase – to 'An image **out of Spenser** and the **common** tongue'. He must render not only both the particular ('John Synge himself') but also the collective ('John Synge, I and Augusta Gregory ... / We three alone in modern times had brought / Everything down to that **sole** test again'). Yet as soon as he has identified their cultural work with a 'scientific' methodology – bringing everything down to 'a single test' – he has to concede, as he had in 'The Circus Animals' Desertion', that 'It was the dream itself enchanted me.' The '**sole** test' had been the writers' old fantasy – impossible in modernity – of a felt continuity between high and low social classes: 'Dream of the noble and the beggarman'.

These are only some of the far-ranging obligations of description for 'The Municipal Gallery', which alludes to Irish public history, the art of painting, the meaning of friendship, and the poet's age, with personal pain

---

[9] This phrase represents two separate paintings: Hazel Lavery in blooming youth and Hazel Lavery ghostlike on her deathbed. By twinning the brief participial adjectives living and dying, Yeats makes the life speed to the death.

and pride overarching all. There are hidden implications: when Yeats presents his triumvirate, it is not the expected 'John Synge, Augusta Gregory, and I' or perhaps (with respect to age and gender) 'Augusta Gregory, John Synge, and I'. No: Yeats has just seen the Mancini portrait of Gregory and is coming to the portrait of Synge (painted by Yeats's father). Flanked by the dead, Synge to the right of him, Gregory to the left, Yeats puts himself between them – offering the poem as his proffered self-portrait. He moves as a living witness among ghosts, performing his memorial mourning and adjuring the future spectator to 'think where man's glory both begins and ends, / And say my glory was I had such friends.' We see here Yeats's mastery of the unassertive adjectival effect: '**Man's** glory' slips without effort into the contrastive '**my** glory', and the inconspicuous gesture in **such** deftly implies the whole preceding inventory of Yeats's associates.

I offer this brief and incomplete sketch of Yeats's powerful inventiveness within the potential of a single part of speech to suggest that when we wish to account for the heady density of a given late poem – or even a given late line – there is scarcely an adjective that does not repay scrutiny. Nor can there be any reflection on the total 'meaning' of these complicated poems without a scrutiny of Yeats's inventions in all the parts of speech. Our rapid required head-turning from perspective to perspective as we read the later Yeats replicates within ourselves Yeats's instant, searching, successive, and simultaneous responses – intellectual, psychological, sensual, and emotional. It is an effect dizzying to us but characteristic of Yeats's original, ambitious, and wide-ranging poetic practice at the height of his imaginative power.

CHAPTER 12

Modernism in the Streets
Pearse and Joyce

Declan Kiberd

In his essay 'Ghosts', Patrick Pearse summoned the spirit of Charles Stewart Parnell to stand beside those of Tone, Davis, Lalor, and Mitchel in the canon of Irish separatism.[1] His speech at the grave of O'Donovan Rossa in 1915 was delivered in close proximity to the Parnell monument at Glasnevin Cemetery. It rejected the sort of 'Ivy Day' platitudes denounced by James Joyce in a short story in *Dubliners*; and it called for action. Prior to the delivery of that speech, the city of Dublin had been put into lockdown by Thomas MacDonagh, in what was effectively a rehearsal for the Easter Rising.

For Pearse, Parnell was 'a flame that seared, a sword that stabbed'.[2] He epitomized the 'triumph of failure' idea which would underlie the insurrection. Parnell was a type of the misunderstood artist, an unrecognized redeemer. Herbert Howarth wrote of his influence on subsequent Irish writers and speechifiers: 'The Irish committed the crucial act of killing their prophet, and the guilt, the desire to purify the guilt, the belief that this guilt sanctified, the belief that sacrifice assures rebirth, gave them irresistible vigour in the next generation.'[3] Joyce endorsed the linked critique of parliamentarianism, mocking not just the ward-heelers of Dublin city council but also the 'bankrupt' nationalist party at Westminster, who 'have given proof of their altruism only in 1891, when they sold their leader, Parnell, to the pharisaical conscience of the English Dissenters without extracting the thirty pieces of silver'.[4] For true-blue republicans, Parnell remained 'unfallen' among parliamentarians,[5] one who had never used violence but never repudiated those who resorted to it.

---

[1] Pauric Travers, 'The Political Speeches of Charles Stewart Parnell', *Studia Hibernica* 31 (2001–2): 243
[2] Ibid., 243.
[3] Herbert Howarth, *The Irish Writers 1880–1940: Literature under Parnell's Star* (London, 1955), 45.
[4] James Joyce, *Critical Writings*, ed. Ellsworth Mason and Richard Ellmann (Ithaca, NY, 1959), 196.
[5] Sean Farrell Moran, *Patrick Pearse and the Politics of Redemption* (Washington, 1994), 94.

The funerals of Parnell and O'Donovan Rossa were staged events which reduced the sense of felt distance between street and stage. Throughout most of the nineteenth century, Dublin had worn the mask of an occupied capital. George Moore, in *A Drama in Muslin*, had described it as a sick city, its plaster falling like scabs from a diseased body, its labourers battered. The poverty-stricken citizens stared, often at no more than a few feet of distance, at aristocratic revellers borne on carriages into Dublin Castle. 'One would think they were a lot of hungry children looking into a sweetmeat shop', complains one party-goer; 'The police really ought to prevent it.'[6] Over forty years later, sweet shops would be a major target of looters, according to James Stephens in *The Insurrection in Dublin*: 'there is something comical in this looting of sweetshops – something almost innocent and childlike. Possibly most of the looters are children who are having the sole gorge of their lives.'[7]

The notion of reclaiming the streets as zones of autonomous selfhood recurs through the Irish revival, coming to a climax when Pearse sees insurrectionary Dublin as once again worthy to take its place beside the Paris of the Commune. Helena Molony described how in the early years of the century, no respectable person would walk after twilight on the side of O'Connell Street frequented by British soldiers; and so she and Maud Gonne began distributing handbills against recruiting and advising young women not to consort with the Tommies. Both women sometimes lured soldiers into alleyways, where these soldiers were then beaten up by nationalist males, a stratagem denounced as obnoxious by Arthur Griffith. The streets were already a heavily contested space. Joyce sets an altercation between Stephen Dedalus and some soldiers in the Nighttown episode of *Ulysses*, enacted in 1904.

Joyce's project was to reclaim the streets for art, in keeping with the wider democratic programme which impelled his previous books. They are all celebrations of walkers in the city; and they register movement through the streets in terms of a freedom of the mind, each building, statue, or shop functioning as an aide-memoire. In his work the streets of Dublin are raised from being zones of disease and danger to places of amenity and civic pride. Street people, far from constituting a problem, become one of the main subjects of an art which describes how they circulate and achieve a sense of their own massed power.

---

[6] George Moore, *A Drama in Muslin* (Gerrards Cross, 1986), 171.

[7] Quoted in *Handbook of the Irish Revival 1891–1922*, ed. Declan Kiberd and P. J. Mathews (Dublin, 2015), 425.

The Easter Rising, like *Ulysses*, was an answer to a question which had never exactly been asked. It was a gesture out of an uncertain future, an act whose meaning would become clear only in retrospect when people learned how to decode it. When James Connolly told Patrick Pearse that their comrades were going out to be slaughtered, the latter responded by saying that, although most of their fellow-citizens would not understand its meaning at the time, eventually they would. This seems close enough to the trajectory of modernist experiment: first incomprehension or opposition; then belated, if still somewhat baffled adoption; ultimately some kind of celebration. The 'triumph of failure' is the subtitle of the most influential biography of Pearse;[8] as an idea it has a clear lineage in the early history of modernism.

One of its sources, strangely enough, is an essay on Shakespeare's English kings, written by Walter Pater in 1889. He challenged the tendency of efficiency-worshipping imperialists to heroicize Henry the Fifth and belittle Richard the Second: in Pater's reading, the one who loses his life may save it. Doomed complexity is preferable to, as well as more poetic than, a merely administrative guile. Oscar Wilde was one of many critics who followed Pater in pointing out that Richard the Second spoke most of his play's turbo-charged poetry. Imperial England's worship of success had led only to the wearing of hollow crowns. If Henry represented the failure of triumph, Richard epitomized the triumph of failure. W. B. Yeats detected this underlying structure within most of Shakespeare's great plays: a clash between a base usurper and a sensitive poet.

Yeats rewrote that contrast as the clash between Cuchulain and Conchobar: 'a wise man who was wise from very wisdom and an empty man that thrust him from his place'.[9] It was, in effect, the story of what England had done in Ireland. Joyce, in due course, also Celticized Shakespeare. In the 'Scylla and Charybdis' episode of *Ulysses*, Stephen Dedalus reads his own fate in that of the playwright: 'the theme of the false or the usurping or the adulterous brother is to Shakespeare what the poor are not, always with him. The note of banishment, banishment from the heart, banishment from home, sounds uninterruptedly from *The Two Gentlemen of Verona* onward, till Prospero breaks his staff.'[10]

---

[8] Ruth Dudley Edwards, *Patrick Pearse: The Triumph of Failure* (London, 1977).

[9] W. B. Yeats, *Essays and Introductions* (New York, 1955), 108.

[10] James Joyce, *Ulysses*, annotated and ed. Declan Kiberd (Penguin Modern Classics, 1992), 271–72. Hereinafter cited in the text by page number.

That Shakespearean theme of doomed complexity is taken up in the 'Aeolus' episode of *Ulysses*, where Professor McHugh depicts the Celts as those who went forth to battle but always fell: 'we were always lovers of lost causes' (169). 'Aeolus' is set mainly in the premises of the *Freeman's Journal* and is a study of the windy rhetoric practised by ineffectual nationalists in 1904; but Joyce also adds the structural irony that the site was but a stone's throw from the epicentre of the Easter Rising of 1916 in Dublin's General Post Office. Professor McHugh is himself something of a Paterian, and so was Joyce. 'Material victory is the death of spiritual predominance', he told Georges Borach: 'Successful states only become colonisers and merchants.'[11] 'But the Greek . . .', intones McHugh (169), as if speaking for the author of *Ulysses*. This triumph-of-failure motif outlasts all such moments in revivalist texts, to be taken up even more comprehensively by Samuel Beckett in later decades. For Beckett 'to be an artist is to fail, but as no other dare fail'.[12] Success meant nothing to him, but he often spoke of the vivifying climate of failure.

A central intuition behind all such cases (and many other non-Irish instances) was summed up by Irving Howe in a brilliant aphorism: 'Modernism must always struggle but never quite triumph – and in the end it must struggle in order not to triumph.'[13] Howe and sociologist Daniel Bell wrote an analysis of this ambiguity as they watched radical activists and hippies take their agendas out of bohemia and onto the high streets of New York and San Francisco in the 1960s. The New York Intellectuals (so self-named) were unsure whether notions of a multiple self or of an ever-innovating style should become so generally current; they feared that in such a transformation modernism might become a mere fashion system, commodified and coarsened, thereby losing its cutting edge. They had no doubt, either, that the break-out of these codes from bohemia into the mainstream was a phenomenon signalling 'the decline of the new'. Within a few months during the Summer of Love, Howe and Bell had coined a name for this development: 'modernism in the streets'.[14]

But all of this had happened before – long before, in the streets of Dublin of 1916, which also were invaded by artists, poets, intellectuals, and bohemians. The year 1916 was a case of 1967–68 *avant la lettre*. In a novel published in 1965, *The Red and the Green*, Iris Murdoch depicted

[11] Cited in Willard Potts, ed., *James Joyce: Portraits of an Artist in Exile* (Dublin, 1979), 68.

[12] Samuel Beckett, *Disjecta: Miscellaneous Writings*, ed. Ruby Cohn (New York, 1984), 145.

[13] Irving Howe, 'The Idea of the Modern', in Howe, ed., *Literary Modernism* (New York, 1968), 13.

[14] The phrase is fully elaborated by Daniel Bell in later sections of his *The Cultural Contradictions of Capitalism* (New York, 1973).

the Easter rebels as existentialists before their time, who chose to become authentic to themselves and who knew as actors how to commit themselves to the quality of an action. In 1967, in months when Haight-Ashbury was at its noisiest, William Irwin Thompson published *The Imagination of an Insurrection: Dublin Easter 1916*, in which the values of the flower children – mysticism crossed with political radicalism, anti-imperialism fused with raised consciousness – are mapped onto the Easter rebellion. That book was, sadly, a year late for the fiftieth anniversary commemoration, but spot on for the Summer of Love. The most belated race in Europe once again?

Or the most premature? In Zurich of 1916 James Joyce walked through streets which played host to many other European radicals, V. I. Lenin, and Tristan Tzara. He was also hard at work on the most futuristic narrative to come out of World War I. Lenin had yet to take the sealed train that would bring him in the following year to the Finland Station, but he said in an essay published in the summer of 1916 that the misfortune of the Irish was that they had risen somewhat too soon, before the revolt of the European proletariat had fully matured.[15] Had they waited until 1917, when mass defections threatened to take many nations out of the war and when colonial revolts erupted across the world, they might have chosen their time more fittingly and helped detonate a world-wide revolution. As it was, Lenin's essay remains one of the rare occasions on which the Irish have been accused of getting up too early in the morning.

That Zurich of revolutionaries has been immortalized by Tom Stoppard in *Travesties*. One exchange in it goes as follows:

> – What did you do in the Great War, Mr Joyce?
> – I wrote *Ulysses*. What did you do?[16]

Ulysses was, among other things, a protest against the Great War and against the imperial misuse of a classic pedagogy which had helped to give rise to it. In the second episode, Stephen Dedalus contemplates the links between a violent history, physical-contact sports, and the class in Roman history which he has just given, but his processing of these links seems to arise from Joyce's own proximity to scenes of aerial bombardment in Locarno, 1917: 'I hear the ruin of all space, shattered glass and toppling masonry, and time one livid final flame' (28). The pacifist politics

[15] V. I. Lenin, 'Lessons from the Easter Rebellion', quoted in *Handbook of the Irish Revival*, 450.
[16] Tom Stoppard, *Travesties* (London, 1974), 50.

espoused by Leopold Bloom in subsequent episodes was doubtless conditioned by news Joyce was receiving from Dublin. For instance, Bloom's suggestion that it is madness to arm young soldiers in the face of a large civilian demonstration was probably added by Joyce following the murder of civilians at Bachelors' Walk in the aftermath of the Howth gun running.[17] Indeed, Bloom's combination of anti-imperialism and pacificism might more generally be traced to the influence of Joyce's class-mate and fellow-pamphleteer, Francis Sheehy Skeffington.

The object of Patrick Pearse and his followers in 1916 was to take Ireland clean out of the European conflict, for they feared that a distinctive Irish identity, refashioned in the years of the Revival after 1891, was in danger of disappearing in the trenches.[18] This was the main burden of a discussion between Pearse, Desmond FitzGerald, and Joseph Plunkett inside the General Post Office, as they sought moral justification for their action. Joyce was at that very time creating *Ulysses* for a somewhat similar reason: out of a fear that the Dublin of his youth might disappear, just as Dante projected a Florence which he thought in peril of evaporation. As early as 1907, in an essay in *Il Piccolo della Serra* of Trieste, Joyce drily observed of Ireland: 'If she is truly capable of reviving, let her awake, or let her cover up her head and lie down decently in her grave forever.'[19] In fact, Dante had made eerily similar complaints about Florence: 'you are like a sick woman who cannot find any rest on her soft bed, but turns continually to ease her pain'.[20]

This imaging of beloved, endangered landscape in terms of a beleaguered female is yet another link between Pearse and Joyce; and their writings are linked also, of course, by the theme of betrayal. Pearse wrote in what many read as his signature poem:

> Mise Éire
> Sinne mé ná an Cailleach Béarra
>
> Mór mo ghlóire
> Is mé do rug Cuchulain cróga
>
> Mór mo náire
> Mo chlann féin do dhíol a máthair
>
> Mise Éire
> Uaigní mé ná an Cailleach Béarra

---

[17] See F. X. Martin, *The Howth Gun Running* (Dublin, 1964).
[18] Desmond FitzGerald, *Memoirs 1915–16* (London, 1968), 142–43.
[19] James Joyce, *Critical Writings*, ed. E. Mason and R. Ellmann (Ithaca, NY, 1959), 174.
[20] Charles Williams, *The Figure of Beatrice: A Study in Dante* (New York, 1961), 154.

> I am Ireland
> I am older than the Old Woman of Beare
>
> Great my glory
> I that bore Cuchulain the valiant
>
> Great my shame
> My own children that sold their mother
>
> I am Ireland
> I am lonelier than the Old Woman of Beare.[21]

That poem feeds into the opening phrasing of the 1916 Proclamation of the Republic: 'Irishmen and Irishwomen ... Ireland through us summons her children to her flag.' That this is no sexist attempt to project onto Mother Ireland a femininity which the (mostly male) rebels are denying in themselves is manifest in the Proclamation's equal address of women as of men (and that at a time when women were yet to be entitled to vote).

Pearse's lyric connects in its text and imagery to one published in 1900 in a volume of his favourite poet of classical Irish, Seathrún Céitinn (Geoffrey Keating). In a poem titled 'Óm Sceol ar Árd-Mhagh Fáil', Céitinn complained of an outraged Irish womanhood

> Deor níor fágadh I gcár do bhrollaigh mhínghil
> Nár dheolsad ál gach cránach coigríche
>
> A drop was not left in the plain of your smooth bosom
> Which is not sucked up by the brood of every foreign sow.[22]

J. C. McErlean's edition of Cétinn's poems, songs, and laments was a volume used by Pearse in those same Irish-language classes attended by the young Joyce. He went as a lover of languages but also because he was attracted by Kathleen Sheehy (who would feature as Gaelic Leaguer Miss Ivors in 'The Dead'); but he was soon repelled because Pearse (himself still young and callow) could not praise the expressive powers of Irish without disparaging those of English – something Joyce could not abide. Those famous lines of Céitinn must have echoed in Joyce's head when he inverted them, while holding to their central meaning, in his own 1916 Proclamation, *A Portrait of the Artist as a Young Man*:

---

[21] Patrick Pearse, *Plays, Stories, Poems* (Dublin, 1924), 323–24. Hereinafter cited as *PSP*.
[22] J. C. McErlean, ed., *Dánta, Amhráin is Caointe Sheathrúin Chéitinn* (Dublin, 1900), 15. Translation by J. M. Synge in TCD Synge Ms 4387, f.54,v.

– Do you know what Ireland is? asked Stephen with cold violence. Ireland is the old sow that eats her farrow.[23]

'Mo chlann féin do dhíol a máthair' indeed.

The fate of Parnell, a leader betrayed by his own followers, gave added force to such lines in the period of Revival, impinging as heavily on Pearse as on Joyce. A central theme of Joyce's Exiles in 1912 is – appropriately, given the foundation of the Ulster Volunteers in that year – that of a covenant betrayed. But it is also of 'the faith of the master in the disciple who will betray him'.[24] Four years later, the example of the Ulster covenanters had turned Pearse from moderate Home Ruler to militant republican separatist; but he acted upon the principles espoused by Richard Rowan in his play: of a Christ-like (or Parnell-like) martyr to truth who will willingly incur incomprehension and betrayal on the path to freedom.

* * *

Joyce and Pearse were not mere rebels, who knew what they were against. Rather, they were revolutionaries, who attempted to sketch what they were for. Being still both young men in 1900, they saw themselves as shock-troops of the modern. Each had a heightened sense of belonging to a cutting-edge generation. Pearse refers repeatedly in his essays to his generation's particular 'task' and to the unsatisfactory, treasonous peace made by its fathers. Joyce's characters, like the writer, shared in this need to self-invent: to become 'himself his own father'. Part of this impulse was the abolition of lineage: like others of their generation, both men sought affiliation rather than filiation (to borrow the useful distinction made by Edward Said).[25] They were fascinated by how newness comes into the world and in the contours of an invisible republic which may yet become discernible:

> O wise men, riddle me this: what if the dream come true?
> What if the dream come true? – if millions unborn shall dwell
> In the house that I shaped in my heart, the noble house of my thought.
>
> (*PSP*, 336)

---

[23] James Joyce, *A Portrait of the Artist as a Young Man* (London, 1960), 203. Hereinafter cited as *Portrait*.

[24] James Joyce, *Exiles* (London 1973), 52.

[25] See especially the title essay in Said's *The World, the Text and the Critic* (Cambridge, MA, 1984); and also Robert Wohl, *The Generation of 1914* (Cambridge, MA, 1979).

There is no fundamental difference between these lines and the closing determination of Stephen Daedalus in Joyce's 1916 book 'to forge in the smithy of my soul the uncreated conscience of my race' (*Portrait*, 253).

If the future is what artists already are, both men were futurologists. They dreamed of what was to come and hoped that the contours of such a society lay folded in the dreamscapes of their writings. They could be intolerant of even the most gifted members of the previous generation: the youthful Pearse derided Yeats as a 'harmless' English poet of inferior rank, and the equally intolerant Joyce told the poet that he had come 'too late to help him'. This is another sense in which both men carried the agenda of a new generation with a defiant, conscious pride. In *A Portrait of the Artist as a Young Man*, Joyce could not help labouring the point all those years after his strange meeting with Yeats: 'Michael Robartes remembers forgotten beauty and, when his arms wrap her round, he presses in his arms the loveliness which has long faded from the world.... Not this. Not at all. I desire to press in my arms the loveliness which has not yet come into the world' (Portrait, 251). Pearse, for his part, also renounces the old-fashioned beauty of the ailing female and turns away from her to a more uncertain but futuristic image:

> Dhallas mo shúil
> is mo chluas do dhúnas;
> chruas mo chroí
> is mo mhian do mhúchas.
>
> Thugas mo chúl
> ar an aisling a chumas,
> is ar an ród sco romham
> m'aghaidh a thugas.
>
> I blinded my eye
> and I closed my ear;
> I hardened my heart
> and I stilled my desire.
>
> I turned my head
> on the vision I had shaped,
> and to this road before me
> I turned my face.
>
> (*PSP*, 324)

Each writer sought a dream of which he could not directly speak. He could speak only of having sought it.

The technical problem which they faced was similar. How can one express the unknown, when all that is available comes in the language of the known? For Joyce that problem was summed up in the dilemma of Moses, bearing down from Mount Sinai the tablets of the law in the language of the outlaw. For Pearse and his co-insurrectionaries, the inner vision animating them could not be fully expressed in any available language: the vague, fizzy, recycled lettering of the Proclamation text seems to signal that problem. (Some of the font had to be broken to improvise necessary letters; other parts dismantled so that it could be used in making later paragraphs.) The young Joyce, in his years as member of the Theosophical Society in Dublin, was keenly aware of the challenges posed for any mystic by art. As Thomas MacDonagh was to write in *The Irish Review* of 1914: the mystic 'has to express in terms of sense and wit the things of God that are made known to him in no language'.[26]

If the problems confronted by Joyce and Pearse were somewhat similar, so were the technical solutions arrived at. Each presented his radical new vision as a revival of something very old, and each purported to discover the future in the past. Each knew that the best way in which to be original was to go back to origins. So Joyce employed Homer's *Odyssey* to gift-wrap Europe's most experimental modernist narrative (and to make his Irish subject matter more palpably European). He thus secured a hearing even among some conservatives by presenting the revolutionary as a return to deepest tradition. That had been the technique of the French revolutionaries of the 1790s, as they wore Roman togas to disguise the fact that they were revolutionary businessmen, a new meritocracy crusading against inherited wealth and calling for an energized society in which careers were open to talent.[27] Pearse was well aware of these tactics and deployed them himself. Arguing for a child-centred education, he said it would merely be a return to the tradition of Clonmacnoise monasticism. And James Connolly, in *Labour in Irish History*, argued that socialism would signal a restoration of a lost world in which land was held for the people, the only difference being that now it would be retained for them by the state rather than a chieftain.[28] All of these examples are part of a French revolutionary technique.

They are also an element of what might be called a corrected pedagogy as practised by Joyce and Pearse. Joyce was hugely critical of the imperial system of education, much imitated by his own Jesuit teachers in

[26] Thomas MacDonagh, 'Language and Literature in Ireland', *The Irish Review* 4 (March–April 1914): 176–82.
[27] On this phenomenon, see Harold Rosenberg, *The Tradition of the New* (Chicago, 1982), 155ff.
[28] James Connolly, *Labour in Irish History* (Dublin, 1966), 1–15.

Clongowes and Belvedere Colleges. *Ulysses* has its own Hellenizing alternative, based on a truer classicism: an older man, wise in the ways of the world, counsels a youth. Pearse ran his school at St Enda's on a similar basis, owing as much to Ruskin and Morris as to Celtic tradition. Contrary to some recent televisual depictions of it as some sort of madrasa, St Enda's was thoroughly modernizing, according to science a profile it had yet to achieve in other school's programmes, and allowing boys to vote in a democratic manner on whether the sport of the summer term would be hurling or cricket. But this did not prevent Pearse from exploring and heightening also the monastic connection: he said that at Clonard a carpenter's son named Kevin sat alongside the son of a king Colmcille, under the gaze of a charismatic teacher; 'and thus it was that men learned not only the humanities but all gracious and useful arts'.[29]

* * *

Pearse's theology was radical and even his harshest critics admit a religious dimension to his thought. Joyce is less often depicted as a religious analyst and even his warmest supporters depict him as an errant secularist. But both men seem really to be extraterritorial Catholics, somewhat in the manner of today's liberation theologians. Their frustrations were not with what the priests taught them so much as with the fact that the priests did not seem to believe or practice it themselves. Readers of the Christmas dinner scene in Joyce's *Portrait* will recall how the men at table lament the ways in which the ecclesiocracy denounced and excommunicated Fenian rebels. This tradition of extraterritorial Catholicism helps to explain the overt use of rosary beads in prayers at the post office in 1916: the leaders, having like FitzGerald, Pearse, and Plunkett established the ethics of their deed, were keen by such symbolic demonstration to show that they rejected those bishops and priests who saw their oath-bound secret societies as sinful.

The climax of *Ulysses* is itself a kind of corrected Catholic pedagogy, taking the form of a radical eucharist. Bloom, who had earlier distributed bread to hungry seagulls, gives Stephen coffee and a bun. Stephen in an earlier book had told his mother that he would not receive his Easter communion: he would not go for it, so let it come to him. Now it has come borne in a most unlikely fashion by an ad-canvasser of partially

---

[29] Séamas Ó Buachalla, ed., *A Significant Irish Educationalist: Educational Writings of Patrick Pearse* (Cork, 1980), 377.

Jewish background. This is a throwback to a scene in the *Odyssey*: when Odysseus meets a one-eyed monster, he bribes the monster with drink, which anticipates the words of Jesus consecrating bread and wine: 'Take, Cyclops, and drink. Wine goes well with human flesh.'[30]

Pearse's own fusion of pagan energy and Christian sensitivity came to a focus on the figure of Cuchulain (who died, of course, strapped to a post, anticipating Jesus on the cross). That fusion had been part of an ethic of English public schools, which wished to produce 'muscular Christians' combining a smiter's robustness with the exquisite delicacy of a man of feeling – a sign that, for all the ideas of a corrected pedagogy informing some Revivalist depictions, the Cuchulain rendered by, say, Augusta Gregory might at times seem to be an English public schoolboy in the drag of a Celtic hero. But there was something more extreme about Pearse's own blending of pagan and Christian rhetoric, which managed to be offensive not just to many pious Christians but also to some early twentieth-century pagans. In his essays, Pearse did for Cuchulain what Joyce did for Odysseus, managing to x-ray many of the outlines beneath the surface of the tale: 'The story of Cuchulain symbolizes the redemption of man by a sinless God.'[31] The Táin he reinterpreted as an unconscious retelling (and foretelling) of the story of Calvary. Pearse was aware that later Christian monks might have been tempted to reconfigure scenes of the old tales along more Christian lines, but he preferred to believe that the ancient tellers really had foreseen a Christian element in their narrative.

This is rather like Ernst Bloch's notion that every text contains an 'ideological surplus', answering less to the needs of its time than to those requirements which will emerge only in the future.[32] What unnerved contemporary Catholics and Celticists was the extent to which Pearse mingled references to Colmcille and Cuchulain, as if they were part of a promiscuously formed continuum. No wonder that J. J. Horgan was sufficiently upset to call the Rising a sin and Pearse a heretic. The 'excess of love' which worries Yeats in his treatment of the event is itself a phrase taken from Pearse's concelebration of his two exemplars, that excess of love

---

[30] On this, see Theodor Adorno and Max Horkheimer, *Dialectic of Enlightenment*, trans. John Cummins (London, 1979), 67.

[31] Patrick Pearse, 'Some Aspects of Irish Literature', in Pearse, *Songs of the Irish Rebellion* (Dublin, 1924), 156.

[32] Ernst Bloch, *The Principle of Hope*, 3 vols. (Oxford, 1986), 3:932.

which was 'the inspiration alike of Cuchulain and Colmcille, the inspiration that made the one a hero and the other a saint'.[33]

The corrected pedagogy supplied by Joyce at the climax of *Ulysses* has, of course, been found by some commentators to have a homoerotic dimension – Mulligan in the book says no less to Stephen when he suggests that Bloom 'looked upon you to lust after you' (279). In much the same way, Pearse's idealization of boys at St Enda's has come under critique. Yet both cases seem instances of what the French might call *croyant, pas pratiquant*. Joyce, after all, had immense reservations about the *Blutbruderschaft* of World War I, which is one of many reasons why he chose a draft-dodger such as Odysseus rather than a warrior like Cuchulain as role model; but he also deeply understood the male bonding which was such an intensified backdrop to, and product of, life in the trenches in the war. Pearse was himself far more of a European in thought than he sometimes pretended: his ideas of men beautifully jeopardizing their lives for one another accord all too easily with the 'dulce et decorum' rhetoric of Charles Péguy and Rupert Brooke. Even the troubling speech at O'Donovan Rossa's graveside about the need for bloodshed to redeem Irish manhood has analogies in Sigmund Freud's 1915 statement that, whereas before the war life was shallow as an American flirtation, now in the era of mass graves it has recovered its full content and meaning.[34]

Functioning as public intellectuals, and able to assume a definite audience for their ideas, both Joyce and Pearse wrote important essays about Ireland – Pearse mainly for a national audience, Joyce (as time and circumstance allowed) either for a native or international readership. Each was aware that the self of an author is something of a pose, an affectation – a realization all the stronger for Irish thinkers in the decade after the death of Wilde, who has said that the first duty in life was to adopt a pose. Each presented, as did so many public figures in those days, an idealized bodily self-image to photographers. Each man in many essays casts himself as an inheritor of the Enlightenment, of that public sphere which emerged in the eighteenth century. Joyce was severely critical of the compromises made with Westminster by the Irish Parliamentary Party – and his first statements along these lines come well before Pearse's. The ultimate default setting for each man in politics was Theobald Wolfe Tone. Each felt acutely the failure of Wolfe Tone's ideal of a republic to be realized. Joyce in *Ulysses* writes about 'the slab where Wolfe Tone's statue was not'

---

[33] Patrick Pearse, *Political Writings and Speeches* (Dublin 1924), 25.
[34] See Wohl, *The Generation of 1914*.

(293), recognizing that a republic still has to be made (like the uncreated conscience). Both responded richly to the west of Ireland as a symbolic space, while retaining the role of a metropolitan intellectual. Gabriel Conroy, at the climactic moments of Joyce's *Dubliners*, is drawn into a silent west of Ireland; and in the diary passages towards the close of *Portrait* Stephen recognizes that he will be forever haunted by images of the western peasantry, summed up by his meeting with Mulrennan. Yet both men felt a certain ambiguity about the 'west'; Angela Bourke has astutely noted Pearse's bourgeois refusal to have any Yeatsian truck with fairies, even in his stories of redemptive children.[35]

In the end, of course, there are major distinctions to be made between Joyce and Pearse. The former was first and last an artist, for whom Bohemia (if even it) was the native country; the latter an occasional artist and eventual nationalist for whom Ireland was be-all and end-all. Like other writer-leaders of the insurrection, Pearse might be seen as someone who turned from art to the fatal lure of action. Joyce, by contrast, always saw writing as the ultimate means of taking power – and he took his own revenge by pulverizing that very English whose expressive powers Pearse had once disparaged. Thompson, in *The Imagination of an Insurrection*, sees Pearse and the other 1916 poets as examples of an *artiste manqué* – a diagnosis which Pearse himself half-anticipated when he said that the Rising would relieve Ireland of 'three bad poets'. He was in fact a rather good writer, who maintained a high standard of work in both Irish and English; and, despite his allergy to fairies, he was capable in some of the poems quoted (and in others) of a profound mysticism.

But there is an intermediate stage, between surface realism and mystic intuition, which Joyce made his own – including the subconscious or semi-conscious, the free association of thought and feelings. Pearse, though he was in most other respects an early modernist, could never go there. Did something in him fear the depths of his own mind, that darker, ruminative, English side? He seems to have feared those zones, or perhaps his lived experience, being less rich and unconstrained than Joyce's, left him with less such material to draw upon.

Some of the insurgents of 1916 escaped from the General Post Office through tunnelled passages – Dublin's warrens of the unconscious. It's hard to think of Pearse as knowing of these places, but some among his followers clearly did.

---

[35] Angela Bourke, 'The Imagined Community of Pearse's Short Stories', in *The Life and After-Life of P. H. Pearse*, ed. Róisín Higgins and Regina Uí Chollatáin (Dublin, 2009), 141–55.

In 'Wandering Rocks', the central episode of *Ulysses*, the narrative as a whole is a rehearsal of the frustrations which impelled the 1916 rebels to action. A sense of resentment, with the vice-regal cavalcade but also with church power, bubbles not far below the surface. From one underground sewer Tom Rochford has rescued a choking man, and for this bringing-to-light of repressed humanity he is named 'a hero'. All allegiance to earthly power is highly ambiguous in report: as the vice-regal cavalcade passes, 'from its sluice in wood quay wall under Tom Devane's office Poddle river hung out in fealty a tongue of liquid sewage' (325).

The Rising is the future, unmentionable action which hovers behind Joyce's 1904 Dublin. But even its ideas of a Christ-like redemption are fully centralized in the text. When Bloom sees a poster advertising 'blood of the . . .' he wonders, 'who me?' Georges Borach observed, 'I can well imagine that his head was full of this mystery when he wrote *Ulysses* and therein lies the allegorical point of this story of new martyrdom.'[36] The links with Bloom as crucified 'jewman' are manifest in a text which has its own links with such poems as Plunkett's 'I See His Blood upon the Rose' or 'The Little Black Rose Shall Be Red At Last'. Joyce had long been interested, like Yeats, in the symbolism of roses and had caused Stephen to hope that somewhere you might eventually develop a green rose.

Pearse's own attempt to create a conscientious space saw him summon Cuchulain and walk into the post office. That was one way of reclaiming the streets. Another was Joyce's celebration of circulation and of the new forms of knowledge which a true democratic circulation might bring. Were their revolutions as doomed to commodification as Irving Howe and Daniel Bell proclaimed the insurrections of the 1960s to be? In the new state, the 1916 tradition lost its openness, as Pearse was reduced to a military uniform and his theological radicalism retrofitted to a conservative Catholicism. Likewise with *Ulysses*. It would eventually be reduced to an excuse for an annual Dublin drinking festival and Joyce to a literary cove with straw boater and glasses. The danger which attends all revolutionary acts had been warned against by Karl Marx – the tactic of invoking a past narrative in order to open a future one is forgotten, as two steps backward are taken but no jump into a future as exciting as it is unpredictable. The tactical use of old clothing is forgotten, as it becomes costume and even uniform.[37]

---

[36] Cited in Potts, ed., *James Joyce*, 35.

[37] See Karl Marx, 'The Eighteenth Brumaire of Louis Bonaparte', in *Surveys from Exile*, ed. David Fernbach (London, 1974), 94.

Yet the openness of both Pearse's and Joyce's thoughts remains available. Joyce thought the Rising a futile gesture, yet cheered when the threat of conscription was lifted in 1918 (a consistent opposition to militarism being another quality that quite distinguishes him from Pearse). The 'Circe' episode of *Ulysses* is filled with the sufferings of the city's poor; it develops through Stephen's altercation with British soldiers and ends with Dublin in flames: 'Brimstone fires spring up. Dense clouds roll past. Henry Gatling guns boom. Pandemonium. Troops deploy. Gallop of hoofs' (694). Taken in all probability from the pages of James Stephens, in his book *The Insurrection in Dublin*, this is indeed 1916 as a nightmare of history.

CHAPTER 13

Modernism, Belfast, and Early Twentieth-Century Ireland

Terence Brown

In 1996 in his Parnell lecture (published as Magdalene College Occasional Paper no. 15) Professor Paul Bew reminded us that among Parnell's achievements as a nationalist politician was an ability to keep in clear sight the concerns of Irish individuals who did not share a nationalist vision. Bew in this lecture drew attention to a speech by Parnell delivered in 1891 (appropriately in Belfast) in which he recognized the principle of conciliation as key to an Irish nationalist approach to the problem of Ulster Unionism. Arguably, it is a measure of the degree to which Parnell's insight was largely forgotten in early twentieth-century Ireland that the city of Belfast is a great unspoken in the large body of literature to which the term 'Irish modernism' has been applied. I am not suggesting, however, that Belfast was felt to be the elephant in the room, in the period when the great Irish modernist texts were being composed (among which I would include obviously the works of Joyce and Beckett but also *The Tower* by Yeats), from the beginning of the twentieth century until after the Second World War, but rather that it was not part of the mental universe of these or other writers in any developed way. Inasmuch as it was for Yeats, for example, it was simply as a local manifestation of that 'filthy modern tide' he excoriated. Joyce makes the briefest of references to Belfast in *Dubliners* in 'Eveline' where a man from Belfast is the builder of what seem brashly obtrusive 'bright brick houses with shining roofs' among 'little brown houses'.[1] The ostentatiously encyclopaedic *Ulysses*, the book of the city, makes no reference to Belfast; the Orangeman Mr Deasy in 'Nestor' is sometimes assumed to be a Belfastman, but there are no clear grounds for this since membership of the order was not limited to Ulster in 1904 and its headquarters were in what is now Parnell Square. Beckett, who was of course educated north of the Irish border and spent a term teaching in Campbell College in East Belfast, makes no reference to the

[1] James Joyce, *Dubliners* (Penguin ed.; London, 1992), 29.

235

city in his work (the most northerly element in his Wicklow- and County Dublin–haunted imagination is the Fingal of *More Pricks than Kicks*).

The decades we associate with the emergence of Irish modernism in literature and with the successes of Irish nationalism for which Parnell had laid the foundations were strikingly among the most remarkable in the history of the northern capital, decades when in the context of British imperialism and international war it was fully incorporated into one of the largest conglomerates of industrial, engineering, and organizational activity the world had seen to that date. I am thinking of what the historian Christopher Harvie has termed the 'steam-boat internet'[2] of north British capitalism, with key cities of Belfast, Glasgow, Liverpool, and Manchester creating a hub for a globalized world. Belfast was of course along with Glasgow the shipbuilder in this titanic enterprise. As Jonathan Bardon in his *History of Ulster* records, by 1914, the year in which *Dubliners* was published, with its pushy Belfast builder, the firm of Harland and Wolff 'was responsible for almost 8 per cent of the world's output'. Belfast indeed had been the 'fastest-growing shipbuilding region ever since 1879, with an average growth rate of 7.8, twice the rate of Clydeside'.[3]

The *Titanic* represented the yard's apotheosis and dark night of the soul, an event that stirred the world's imagination but not that of the Irish modernists. Yeats's only connection to the event, as we learn from Ben Reid's biography of the much-travelling New Yorker John Quinn, who might well have been a victim of the catastrophe, was the fact that on board were a seal ring and a rosary owned by Lady Gregory. John Wilson Foster has given us a compelling impression of what kind of city Belfast was that produced such a ship (and other huge liners were to slip into Belfast Lough even after the *Titanic* tragedy) when he writes in his essay 'A Mechanical Age' (in his book *Recoveries*) of the ship as 'a giant product of an immense manufacturing network ... with Belfast at the centre of the web'. And he analyzes how the response to the sinking of the *Titanic* by H. G. Wells, Joseph Conrad, and Rudyard Kipling involved them in admiration for 'the figure of the engineer' as 'a socially neglected yet necessary and saving presence in modern society'.[4]

The Great War brought renewed business to the yard, to the linen industry (all those uniforms, tents, knapsacks and need for fabric meant business was brisk), and to the famed ropeworks. The end of the war

---

[2] Harvie used this term in a lecture at the John Hewitt Summer School in County Antrim.
[3] Jonathan Bardon, *A History of Ulster* (Belfast, 1992), 456.
[4] John Wilson Foster, *Recoveries: Neglected Episodes in Irish Cultural History* (Dublin, 2003), 52.

brought new opportunities to rebuild a depleted stock of shipping. By 1919, Bardon tells us, Harland and Wolff had 'orders of seventy-two vessels totalling nearly half a million tons and contracts for twenty-three sets of marine machinery'.[5] There were 30,000 employees, who when they streamed from work in the evening were, as a poet of the period evoked it, 'Terrible as an army with banners / Through the dusk of a winter's eve'.[6]

The poet in question was Richard Rowley, the pen name of Richard Valentine Williams, a 1877-born son of a cotton-handkerchief maker who joined the family business when he left school in Holywood, County Down, and wrote poetry and drama outside business hours. His family was very much the product of Belfast bourgeois society, the world of Forrest Reid's fiction and to some extent that of George Reavey (another Ulsterman with a walk-on part in the history of Irish modernism, with the obvious religious difference – the Reaveys were Catholic, the Williamses Protestant). One of Rowley's brothers became a professor of German at Cambridge, the other a professor of history at St Andrews. He himself was cultivated and travelled (his business took him to Europe and the United States) and his interests extended to the fine arts, in which he favoured the contemporary and modern. Although he was always uncomfortable with Yeats, he moved easily enough in the Dublin literary world. In 1917 the Dublin house Maunsel and Co. Ltd (most famously the publisher of Synge and the non-publisher of *Dubliners*) published his collection of poems *The City of Refuge and Other Poems* and followed that in 1918 with a further collection entitled *City Songs and Others*.[7]

These two volumes, as the titles suggest, were deliberate efforts by the Northerner to evoke and pay tribute to the Belfast that had built the *Titanic* and other great ships as it sought to allow urban existence its beauty as well as its epic achievements, even as the modernist T. S. Eliot was registering London as the site of enervated alienation (*Prufrock and Other Observations* was published in 1917). Where in Eliot's late romanticism city life expressed itself in terms of an almost decadent ennui, Rowley's romantic take on Belfast, as on London in one or two poems, was emotionally overblown. The city is deemed to be beautiful, as in a Shelleyan rapture:

[5] Bardon, *A History of Ulster*, 464.
[6] Richard Rowley, 'The Islandmen', in *City Songs and Others* (Dublin, 1918), 7.
[7] These biographical details are derived from Victor Price's 'Introduction', in *Apollo in Mourne: Poems, Plays & Stories by Richard Rowley* (Belfast, 1978), 1–15.

> Of Beauty have I made a dream
> To feed my spirit. Not the high
> And evident glory shed on wood and stream
> By summer dawnings, but the shy
> And unsung beauties of the street,
> Where all day long, the folk
> In hurrying thousands meet,
> And factories jet into the sky
> Their spiral clouds of smoke.[8]

This poem is entitled 'The City Beautiful'. One can also compare, once one acknowledges the obvious differences in poetic power, Rowley's poem 'A Beethoven Sonata' with Eliot's 'Rhapsody on a Windy Night'. Rowley makes a city echo with music and romantic nostalgia where Eliot makes his city a surreal extension of a disordered consciousness. Rowley's poem begins:

> As I tramped the streets of the City,
> On a night of windy rain,
> From the touch of hidden musician,
> Floated a sudden strain;
> It kindled a remembrance in my heart
> With a flash like a lightning's gleam,
> I wakened a long-dead vision,
> It stirred an old-time dream.[9]

In 'The Islandmen', Belfast's shipyard workers are rendered as the 'legions of labour'.[10] Where Eliot in *The Waste Land* has a crowd flow over London Bridge in a Dantean phantasmagoria ('I had not thought death had undone so many') Rowley honours those who 'March endless o'er the Bridge', the many individuals young and old who have taken on the heroic proportions of the ships their work brings into existence:

> Only strong hands
> Can give strength visible form;
> Only proud hearts can fashion shapes of pride.
> Iron and steel are dead
> Till man's creative will
> Shall weld them to the image he desires,
> Shall make a living symbol
> Of the strength and pride of his soul.[11]

---

[8] Richard Rowley, *The City of Refuge and Other Poems* (Dublin, 1917), 7.
[9] Rowley, *City of Refuge*, 18.   [10] Rowley, *City Songs*, 7.   [11] Ibid., 8.

Rowley's poetry of the city must appear to us now romantically elevated to the the point of vacuity, so conscious are we of the city as a zone of ineluctable ambiguity. Yet it is intriguing to read such attempts to paint Belfast in almost utopian terms since in the first half of the twentieth century it was usually registered, when it was registered at all, in dystopic terms – famously of course in MacNeice's poem 'Belfast', where the sectarianism that had one of its vicious cockpits in the shipyard that Rowley eulogized in 'The Islandmen' is manifestly related to MacNeice's disdainful repugnance for his natal city. An earlier example of such feeling is to be found in Forrest Reid's novel *Following Darkness* (1917), published as *Peter Waring* in 1937. This novel set in opposition a rural Ulster idyll with the social degradation of industrial Belfast. But it is hard to top for dystopic disgust Sean O'Faolain's gothic city of dreadful night as evoked in 1941 in his *An Irish Journey*. Two Royal Ulster Constabulary men are lit by flashes of light on the Falls Road in the wartime blackout:

> Those glimpses of light, the steadily tramping figures, two by two, looming unexpectedly, the towering warehouses, hardly seen, felt magnetically, the cavernous yards, the shrouded churches, more and more factory hulks, a sooty spire, all along that artery to the west, coalesced into a black-out of not only light but sweetness. One felt that nothing could indeed, have possibly come of that nineteenth century Sunday sleep and the red factories and the grey buildings, and the ruthlessness with which the whole general rash of this stinking city was permitted to spread along the waters of the lough and the screams of opposing hates. Glasgow has its gangs – razor-boys, safety blades stuck adeptly in their nails to slash the face across: but Glasgow is twice the size of Belfast. Double Belfast, I felt, and the whole foul place must go up in smoke.
>
> To think that this city rules the Six Counties – the lovely Bann valley, the Glens of Antrim, the lake country of Fermanagh, the Lagan valley, the plains of Armagh. It is horrible. All the hates that blot the name of Ulster are germinated here. And what else could be germinated here but the revenges of the heart against its own brutalization.[12]

One notes here, in the bottled venom, that Belfast is reckoned a Victorian city, its industrialism, whatever about its sectarianism, set against the Arnoldian categories of sweetness and light that could scarcely impact upon such a benighted manifestation of early capitalism. In this regard the passage (only two paragraphs in an extended execration) compares with MacNeice's poem, which, to be sure, evokes Belfast's grim sectarianism with its titanic cityscapes, but also hints at the proto-typical consumer

---

[12] Sean O'Faolain, *An Irish Journey* (London, 1941), 243.

society, developing in the 1930s. For MacNeice notes the city shops only to be repelled by their contents:

> And in the marble stores rubber gloves like polyps
> Cluster; celluloid, painted ware, glaring
> Metal patents, parchment lampshades, harsh
> Attempts at buyable beauty.[13]

In this stanza MacNeice's Belfast is entered as metonymy of what would become the post-industrial city. Neither of the representations of the city, neither that of MacNeice nor that of O'Faolain, has any regard for how the city, in the early twentieth century, despite the ugliness of its politics and of much of its civic life, possessed the capacity to participate in the extraordinary outpouring of technological, entrepreneurial, and organizational energy that was the north British capitalism I summoned to mind earlier. Which is to say that they do not appreciate in the least how Belfast was involved in the creation of twentieth-century modernity in its almost monumental phase. Joyce understood this new phase in human experience, as Joep Leerssen has reminded us in his thoughtful concluding chapter in his book *Remembrance and Imagination*. He notes there how in *Ulysses* in the 'Ithaca' episode 'the entire universe and the engineering skills of the empire concur in providing water for [Bloom] to make cocoa' and he observes: 'Thus, *Ulysses*, as well as being so many other things, becomes an immense effort at normalizing and calibrating the position of Dublin in space and time, at showing how much a part of the world it is, how synchronized with, and in proximity to, the rest of the world.'[14] That world is one in which industrialization has provided Dublin not only with clean water from the Roundwood Reservoir through a complex pattern of pipes and holding tanks but with an advanced electric tram system which dispatches its carriages at set times to the suburbs from the heart of the Hibernian metropolis. Accordingly, for Leerssen, Joyce's Dublin in *Ulysses* is with its 'dynamism and movement, and the insistent use of physical clock time ... rendered a metropolis ... the quintessential twentieth-century city'.[15] But if Joyce understood the dynamic energies of industrialized modernity and considered Dublin temporally in synchrony and spatially in proximity with it, he seems to have ignored the city to the north of Dublin on the island of Ireland, in the same time zone and very

---

[13] Louis MacNeice, *Collected Poems* (London, 2007), 25.
[14] Joep Leerssen, *Remembrance and Imagination: Patterns in the Historical and Literary Representation of Ireland in the Nineteenth Century* (Cork, 1996), 230.
[15] Ibid., 228.

approximate, that was an obvious, major manifestation of that very modernity.

It is very likely the case, as C. J. Ackerley has argued in his book *Demented Particulars*, that Samuel Beckett thought that his novel *Murphy*, published in 1938 through the good offices of Belfastman George Reavey (who acted as his literary agent), 'should do for his London ... what *Ulysses* had done for Dublin'. Ackerley notes how Beckett provides the city with 'an air of grubby plausibility' with 'much of the incidental detail [arising] directly from Whitaker's *Almanac* (1935), Beckett using it to plot the time-space coordinates of his novel in much the same way that Joyce had used Thom's *Directory* (1904) for *Ulysses*'.[16] Ackerley indeed argues that Beckett took a deliberate decision to 'Londonize' his text, making it a palimpsest of literary layering, evoking by way of recurrent allusion the world of Elizabethan and Jacobean drama and of eighteenth-century fiction. So the city in the novel is a place of sordid rooms, streets, parks, buildings, grim institutions, peregrinations (like those of Lenehan and Corley in Joyce's 'Two Gallants'), rides by bus, tube, and taxi. It does not give much sense that the city is the heart of an Empire with commerce and trade among its principal activities (if we except Celia's involvement with 'the trades') and we do hear almost comically of the Perseverance and Temperance Yards, the Vis Vitae Bread Co., the Marx Cork Bath Mat Manufactory. One of its most compelling scenes is when Murphy falls asleep among a flock of sheep in Hyde Park, giving the book a strange pastoral, almost bucolic interlude. Only at moments, as when Celia thinks she might return to her old beat as a sex worker in West Brompton, do we get a glimpse of the city as a commercial entrepot. She surmises that she might enjoy seeing once again 'the barges of waste paper on the river and the funnels vailing to the bridges'.[17] So if Beckett imagined himself, as Ackerley suggests, doing for London what Joyce had done for Dublin, it was scarcely to set the city in the centre of industrialized modernity or in modernity's temporal zone, even in a novel plotted with almost manic attention to chronology.

Yet even a work that seems almost deliberately to mock industrial society's powers (*Murphy*'s deadly garret heater with its Heath Robinson gas delivery system is an absurdist piece of engineering) cannot completely ignore the kinds of things North British capitalism, with Belfast as a key participant, was giving to the world. I am thinking of that black comic

[16] C. J. Ackerley, *Demented Particulars: The Annotated Murphy* (Tallahassee, FL, 1998), xx.
[17] Samuel Beckett, *Murphy* (Picador ed.; London, 1973), 87.

scene in the morgue at the Magdalene Mercy Seat, with its Scottish, North British doctor (the Hebridean Dr Angus Killiecrankie) and its golf-obsessed coroner.[18] The company assembled to identify the remains of Murphy, we are told, 'proceeded directly along a short passage flanked on either hand with immense double-decker refrigerators, six in all, to the post-mortem room, a sudden lancination of white and silver, to the north an unbroken bay of glass frosted to height of five feet from the floor and reaching to the ceiling' (146). So dehumanized does this engineered environment seem that Beckett immediately has us note that 'Outside the horns of yew had the hopeless harbour-mouth look, the arms of two that can reach no further, or of one in supplication, the patient impotence of charity or prayer' (146). In a moment of silence during identification 'the faint hum of the refrigerators could be heard' (148). And when it has been completed, 'They covered the tray and carried it out to the refrigerators' (150). Confronted with this bleak modern occasion, with is humming refrigerators and industrial-scale preservation and disposal processes (Murphy is bound for the crematorium), Neary cast his mind to other things as if to banish from consciousness what is taking place before his very eyes: 'Neary saw Clonmachnois on the slab, the castle of the O'Melaghlins, meadow, eskers, thatch on white, something red, the wide bright water, Connaught' (150). Neary's mind at a quintessential modern moment is with ancient Ireland, its heroes, and their burying places and is journeying westward like Gabriel Conroy at the end of 'The Dead', far from London, Dublin, or, indeed, Belfast.

[18] Ibid., 146–50.

CHAPTER 14

Too Rough for Verse?
Sea Crossings in Irish Culture

Claire Connolly

Turbulent Waters

Memories of Oliver Cromwell's bloody Irish campaigns were long-lived. In the late 1930s, as part of a national project run by the Irish Folklore Commission, a schoolgirl named Annie Morgan of Coaghill, Williamstown, County Galway, heard this account from John Gaffey, a forty-one-year-old farmer: 'When Cromwell died the earth refused to take him. Three times and each time the corpse was found near the grave. At last the people decided to throw him into the Irish Sea between England and Ireland. They did so and the part of the sea that Cromwell was thrown into, is rough the hottest day in Summer.'[1] Some of these details are repeated in another story that tells 'how Cromwell died in Ireland and was buried there, but the Irish soil rejected his body and the coffin was found on top of the grave each morning. Finally, it was thrown into the sea and sank down between Dublin and Holyhead, thereby causing that part of the Irish sea to be very turbulent ever since.'[2]

These stories understand the waters between Ireland and Britain as fomented by violent conflicts. They are a reminder of how the Irish Sea shapes a connection with an expansionist Britain, from the early modern period onwards. But even as conditions at sea are given a political explanation, we see the makings of a more intimate history of rough weather. To consider sea crossings in Irish culture is to encounter both certainty – enduring environmental realities experienced over centuries – and unpredictability, as weather events made haphazard work of history. Across the centuries, a great mass of people (soldiers and adventurers, landlords

[1] 'In the Penal Times', The Schools' Collection, vol. 13, p. 98, Dúchas.ie, www.duchas.ie/en/cbes/4591091/4589775/4615416. For help and advice given during research for this essay, I am grateful to Angela Bourke, Patricia Coughlan, Alex Davis, R. F. Foster, Breandán MacSuibhne, Diarmuid Ó Giolláin, Finola O'Kane, William Laffan, and Tony Lewis.
[2] Sean Ó Súilleabháin, ed., *Folktales of Ireland* (London, 1966), 283–84.

and migrant workers, businessmen, students, members of parliament) and goods (letters, books, wine, weapons, live cattle) moved between the islands. Individual experiences, sometimes colourful, sometimes mundane, can be found in disparate sources – state documents, inventories of goods, memoirs, diaries, and correspondence. Composed of stories that can be retrieved, at least in part, culture offers a special kind of archive of Irish Sea crossings: richly textured, patterned, often voicing the views of elites but sometimes able to give us the trace of ordinary lives. To track such perspectives is to move with history itself, as crossing the Irish Sea became a necessary, even routine, aspect of colonial modernity – so indelibly present in Irish and British history as to be almost invisible to us, barely marked, difficult to locate as a distinct cultural phenomenon – though that is just what I attempt here.

The Irish Sea has a singular and resonant place in a shared British and Irish imagination, and the simple question of its power both to connect and to divide has commanded political and cultural attention for centuries. A ninth-century Irish poem reminds us of the realities of life on an island surrounded by water, battered by waves that can carry invaders to its shores or keep them at bay:

> Is acher in gáith innocht
> Fu fuasna fairrgae findfholt
> Ní agor réimm mora minn
> Dond láechraid lainn ua Lothlind.

Frank O'Connor translated this as 'The Viking Terror':

> Since tonight the wind is high,
> The sea's mane a white fury
> I need not fear the hordes of Hell
> Coursing the Irish Channel.[3]

The voice is that of a monk safe indoors, enjoying a brief respite from seaborne Viking attacks. A powerful evocation of violent weather on the Irish Sea, the poem expresses enduring environmental realities that include the prevailing south-westerly winds that blow across open water; persistent strong tidal currents that are whipped up by the winds, meaning that unusually steep waves break in deep water; and numerous sandbanks along

---

[3] Frank O'Connor, 'The Viking Terror', in *Kings, Lords and Commons: An Anthology from the Irish* (London, 1962), 45. In a note to the poem, O'Connor compares ninth-century Ireland to London during the blitz: 'we waited for a moonlit night to sleep safe in our beds'. Lothlind/Lochlainn (in the genitive) means Scandinavia.

the east coast between Dublin and Wexford and on the Welsh coast around Anglesey, leading to the wreck of many ships. These conditions are currently worsening, as climate change brings more frequent storms.

As Unquiet as the Irish Sea

Jane Ohlmeyer describes the century that followed the Cromwellian plantation in terms of 'making Ireland English'. Turbulent seas ensued, and so did a new politics. But the process was hardly a smooth one: Ohlmeyer describes seventeenth-century state formation as 'haphazard, messy and clumsy'. Among the 'random accidents' that she lists are accidents of fertility, birth, and death alongside 'human attributes like ambition, determination, greed and snobbery'.[4] 'Political geography' also features on her list, and we could consider the impact of the weather on the Irish Sea as another kind of accident affecting the wider 'anglicizing agenda' (ibid.). Yet given that the rough waves of the Irish Sea are tossed up by currents whose actions have endured across millennia, perhaps their role is better understood as decisive, even determined?

One way of writing about the Irish Sea was to deny its roughness, as if to refute the suggestion that Ireland was not ready for incorporation into empire, a 'strange country' resistant to improvement and exploitation. Such a defensive formulation began to emerge in the seventeenth century, even as Cromwell's body started to churn up the sea. The earliest natural history of Ireland (authored by Gerard Boate, in 1652), has a chapter entitled 'The Irish Sea Not so Tempestuous as It Is Bruited to Be'.[5] Boate was a Dutch physician who went over to Ireland with Cromwell and died shortly after. From about 1644, he had been gathering information about the topography and environment of Ireland with his brother Arnold, resident in Ireland; Samuel Hartlib gathered these notes and published them in 1652.

Discussing 'the Nature of the Irish Sea, and of the Tides which go in it', Boate explains:

> That part of the Irish sea which divideth Ireland from Great Britain, is very much defamed both by ancient and modern writers, in regard of its boysterousness and tempestuousness, as if it were more subject to storms and raging weather than any other, and consequently not to be passed without very great danger. (ibid., 28–29)

---

[4] Jane Ohlmeyer, *Making Ireland English* (New Haven, CT, 2012), 476.
[5] *A Natural History of Ireland in Three Parts, by Several Hands* (London, 1652), 28.

So strong is this association, reports Boate, that it is a 'common proverb' to say 'as unquiet as the Irish Sea'. Yet that proverb is immediately met with a rejoinder from Boate, who goes via some of the earliest sources (Richard Stanyhurst and his annotations of Giraldus Cambrensis) to show us that 'The Irish sea is quiet enough, except when by high winds it is stirred, so as not only in the summer, but even in the midst of winter people do pass it to and fro.' 'True it is that some ships do perish upon this, but the same happeneth also upon other seas, who are all subject to the disaster of tempests and shipwracks' (29). Working through a kind of proto–Irish Sea archive while also calling up 'daily experience' for evidence of the sea's quietness, Boate insists that the Irish Sea is scarcely rough at all, and that if it is rough, well, then it is no rougher than other seas.

Boate's *Natural History* is representative of the new scholarship about Ireland that took shape after the Cromwellian revolution. As Toby Barnard has suggested, improving projects such as Boate's *Natural History* can be connected to later organizations including the Dublin Philosophical Society, the Royal Dublin Society, the Physico-Historical Society, and the Royal Irish Academy, on to the Ordnance Survey itself.[6] All represent the ways in which knowledge about Irish environments was shaped by colonialism and revolution. Boate's *Natural History* of Ireland constituted 'a detailed brochure for would-be planters and investors. Its observations were inseparable from a wider colonial project of conquest and colonization that saw 'about 40 per cent of Ireland' become the property of 'fresh Protestant owners' (ibid.). The scientific language of improvement underpinned a process whereby Catholic proprietors were assigned to history, part of 'the largest single shift in land ownership anywhere in Europe'.[7]

Where such language meets the sea, it is instrumental – in the mode of survey or inventory, listing possibilities for resource exploitation or extraction. Margaret Cohen notes in her study *The Novel and the Sea* that, in the early modern period, the sea is associated with the plain style characteristic of the mariner's craft, hostile to metaphors and literary grace notes, more concerned with present dangers than 'aesthetic grandeur'.[8] For her, the wider cultural change towards the 'sublimization of the sea' begins with *Paradise Lost*, where Milton used the threats and dangers that faced

---

[6] T. C. Barnard, 'The Hartlib Circle and the Cult and Culture of Improvement in Ireland', in *Samuel Hartlib and Universal Reformation: Studies in Intellectual Communication*, ed. Mark Greengrass, Michael Leslie, and Timothy Raylor (Cambridge, 1994), 281–97 (281–82).

[7] Mícheál Ó Siochrú, *God's Executioner: Oliver Cromwell and the Conquest of Ireland* (London, 2008), 248.

[8] Margaret Cohen, *The Novel and the Sea* (Princeton, NJ, 2013), 42–45.

mariners 'to model the kind of empowered agency that strives to go beyond the limits, to the point of overthrowing God' (ibid., 108). Cohen's observations about changing cultural patterns of representation serve to point us towards perhaps the best-known literary inscription of the rough waters of the Irish seas, albeit to a poem that is hardly Irish: Milton's 'Lycidas', in which 'the Author bewails a learned Friend, unfortunatly drown'd in his Passage from *Chester* on the *Irish* Seas, 1637'.

A young student at Cambridge, Edward King was drowned when the ship on which he was travelling from Chester to Dublin was wrecked off the North Wales coast. The route taken by King – along the Dee estuary, west around Anglesey, and into the Irish Sea – was one often chosen by travellers between Britain and Ireland in the seventeenth century. The silting up of the Dee estuary in the seventeenth century meant that the route gradually fell out of favour. Another possibility was to go further overland through North Wales and Snowdonia and across the island of Anglesea to Holyhead. But in the days before Thomas Telford's early nineteenth-century modernization of the route, the going was rough and dangerous, dependent on quick-moving tides and the shifting sands at Conwy and Menai (Fig. 5).

We now benefit, as John Kerrigan has remarked, from scholarship that returns Milton's 'Lycidas' 'to North Wales and the Irish sea'.[9] In the late 1990s, a scholarly map attempted to pinpoint the exact location of the sinking of King's ship, based on research into stage times, tide tables, and weather history (Fig. 6).

But we need not reduce Milton's poem to the limits of such detailed empirical research in order to appreciate that when Edward King boarded a ship in Chester, he placed himself at the mercy of the 'the remorseless deep', imagined in 'Lycidas' as closing over King's body. Milton conjures a negative geography of the Dee estuary, which opens out to the rough coastline of North Wales and Anglesea. In the poem, Milton reimagines the dead young man as a kind of watery spirit:

> Henceforth thou art the Genius of the shore,
> In thy large recompense, and shalt be good
> To all that wander in that perilous flood.[10]

---

[9] John Kerrigan, *Archipelagic English: Literature, History and Politics, 1603–1707* (Oxford, 2008), 227.
[10] Milton, 'Lycidas', ll. 183–85, in Robert Cummings, ed., *Seventeenth-Century Poetry: An Annotated Anthology* (Oxford, 2000), 310.

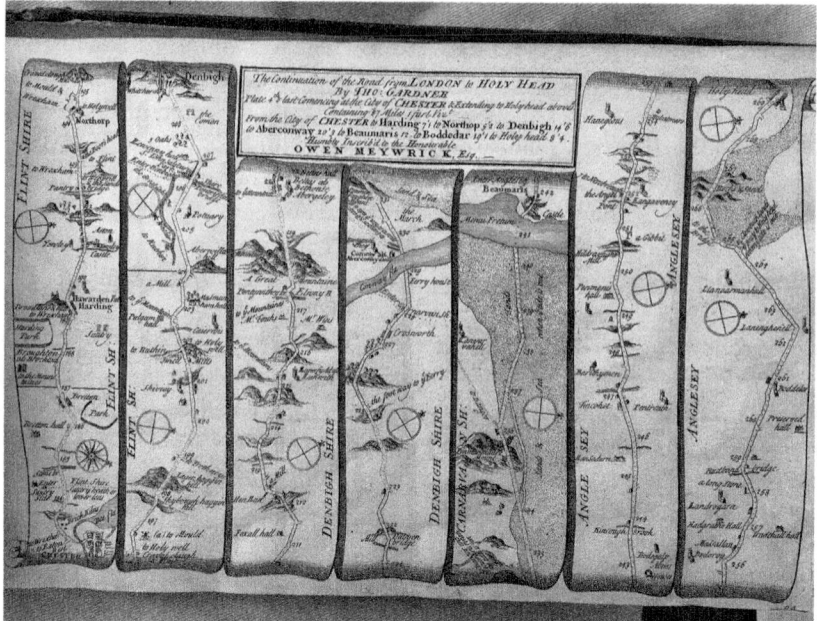

Fig. 5   The continuation of the road from London to Holyhead.
From *Paterson's British Itinerary: Being a New and Accurate Delineation and Description of the Direct and Principal Cross Roads of Great Britain* (London, 1785)

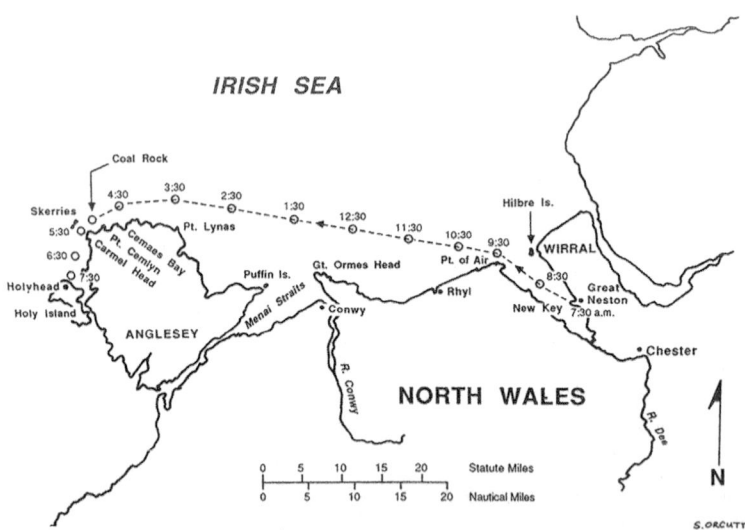

Fig. 6   S. Orcutt, sketch map in J. Karl Franson, 'The Fatal Voyage of Edward King, Milton's Lycidas', *Milton Studies* 25 (1989), 43–67

In analyzing the poem's geopolitics, Lawence Lipking has read 'Lycidas' as a poem that 'blends personal grief with a sense of how much the country has lost': 'Milton puts himself on the map by mourning for Britain'.[11] Lipking interprets the poem in terms of an assertion of English dominance over the seas and goes so far as to read Milton's spirit who guides the shore as a kind of border guard, in charge of 'keeping out and keeping in', policing 'all that wander in that perilous flood' (ibid., 213).

Among the volume of memorial poems on King's death (with 'Lycidas' as the final item) is one from which I have taken the title of this chapter. John Cleveland's 'Upon the Death of Mr King' (1638) snipes at the rigid quantitative metre of the Latin poems in the memorial volume: 'The sea's too rough for verse; who rhymes upon't, / With Xerxes strives to fetter th' Hellespont' (ll. 10–11). The reference is to Herodotus: when a bridge built by the Persian ruler Xeres over the Hellespont (the modern Dardanelles) was destroyed by a storm, the emperor ordered his men to give the sea 300 lashes and sank a pair of shackles in the sea.

The legendary idiocy of any effort to limit the sea's power allows Cleveland to make of King's drowning a modishly elaborate set of metaphors for writing, water, and 'grief's hydrography' (l. 8). Treating the sea in a style of strained conceit, the poem ends with the suggestion that the sea makes islands of all the university men, who must discard their books and allow their eyes to fill with water:

> We'll issue 't forth, and vent such elegies
> As that our tears shall seem the Irish Seas,
> We, floating islands, living Hebrides.[12]

The rocking-horse rhythm of the poem stands in contrast to Milton's broken lines, and Cleveland all too neatly rounds off his effort with the treble rhyming of elegies, seas, and Hebrides.

Waiting in Holyhead

A royalist propagandist who found in the Irish Sea the material and the rhythms of poetic loss and gain, Cleveland never himself made the journey from which he conjured so many literary arabesques. With Jonathan Swift, though, we come to a writer who knew this crossing well. In September of

---

[11] Lawrence Lipking, 'The Genius of the Shore: Lycidas, Adamastor, and the Poetics of Nationalism', *PMLA* 111.2 (1996): 205–21 (205).

[12] John Cleveland, 'Upon the Death of Mr. King', ll. 52–54, in Cummings, *Seventeenth-Century Poetry*, 345–57.

1727, he embarked on a return trip to Ireland, still riding high on the success of *Gulliver's Travels* (1726) but anxious for news of Stella (Esther Johnson), who lay dangerously ill in Dublin. It is probably a measure of Swift's worry for her fate that he turned away from Chester, where he encountered a delayed boat, and pursued instead the risky mountainous overland route in hope of boarding a packet at Holyhead. There he encountered bad weather, costly inns, and a long wait, only arriving in Dublin in early October. Stella died four months later. The two poems that Swift wrote in Holyhead, along with the journal he composed there over his seven-day stay, express memorable and eloquent rage at being trapped 'in the worst spot in Wales under the very worst circumstances', as he put it in the 'Holyhead Journal'.[13]

Swift was stuck in Holyhead because of the weather, but he was also trapped inside a densely bound knot of contingent circumstances. Anglo-Irish elites were at once reliant upon the sea and regularly subject to bad weather. Prevailing south-westerly winds mean ships are to this day more commonly stuck in Welsh rather than Irish ports, and readers may well have composed their own Holyhead journals, text messages, or tweets. An enraged and frustrated Swift tried to write his way out of his circumstances, and his poem 'Holyhead. Sept. 25. 1727' uses images of wind and tide to convey not so much restless movement of the sea but rather the confinement imposed upon an impatient passenger:

> Lo here I sit at Holy Head
> With muddy ale and mouldy bread
> All Christian vittals stink of fish,
> I'm where my enemies would wish.
> Convict of lies is every Sign,
> The inn has not a drop of wine
> I'm fastened both by wind and tide,
> I see the ship at anchor ride.
> The Captain swears the sea's too rough,
> He has not passengers enough.
> And thus the Dean is forc'd to stay
> Till others come to help the pay.[14]

In Holyhead, Swift also wrote a poem with the title 'Ireland', which begins: 'Remove me from this land of slaves, / Where all are fools, and all are knaves' (ibid., 330–332). The loathed Welsh port would become an

---

[13] Jonathan Swift, 'Holyhead Journal, 1727', in *The Prose Works of Jonathan Swift*, ed. Herbert Davis, 14 vols. (Oxford, 1939–68), 5:207.

[14] Swift, *Complete Poems*, ed. Pat Rogers (New Haven, CT, 1983), 329–30 (ll. 1–12).

ironic last recourse from bondage in his imagination: on 21 October 1735, he wrote to Alexander Pope 'as one going very fast out of the world', saying that 'my flesh and bones are to be carried to Holy-head, for I will not lie in a country of slaves'.[15]

Swift's seemingly accidental focus on Holyhead (he had meant to travel via Chester, just as Edward King did) now seems propitious, given the later history of the Welsh sea port as a key node in the nineteenth-century infrastructure of travel.[16] With the Union, improvements to the harbour and approach roads became a matter of some importance. The South Stack lighthouse was built in 1808, to guide packets in and out of the harbour, and a connection between Holyhead and Howth meant that ships could avoid the stretch of rocky Welsh coast encountered on a journey from Liverpool or Parkgate. In 1815, the Scottish engineer Thomas Telford was commissioned to survey and improve the Holyhead Road, setting in motion one of the first great infrastructure projects of nineteenth-century Britain. Telford built his suspension bridge over the Menai Straits (the first such iron suspension bridge in the world, completed in 1826) and greatly improved the road. From the 1830s, competing railway companies started to run from Holyhead to London. There were also a number of attempts to create a railway connection from London to Dublin and to the west of Ireland, which would link up with the trans-Atlantic steamship business. We can trace the significance of Holyhead in this new infrastructure in some famous twentieth-century Irish remarks about the Welsh port: these include Stephen Dedalus's opinion that 'the shortest way to Tara is *via* Holyhead' and Frank O'Connor's suggestion that 'an Irishman's private life begins at Holyhead'.

The introduction of steam on the Irish Sea was a key development. From May 1821, the steamships *Lightning* and *Meteor* began to carry the mail between Holyhead and Kingstown (previously, until the departure of George IV from the port in 1821, known as Dunleary, and renamed Dun Laoghaire by the Free State in 1920). The journey became a somewhat more straightforward matter, part of what Margaret Cohen calls the 'routinization' of the sea in the transition from sail to steam.[17] A journey from London to Dublin that could take up to four days before Thomas Telford's road improvements became a matter of some forty or so hours,

---

[15] Swift, *Correspondence, vol. 4: 1732–1736*, ed. Harold Williams (Oxford, 1965), 408. Swift died in 1745.

[16] On accident and circumstance, see Michael Rosenblum, 'Swift's "Holyhead Journal" and Circumstantial Talk in Early Modern England', *Eighteenth-Century Studies* 30.2 (1996): 159–72.

[17] Cohen, *The Novel and the Sea*, 179.

though experiences could still vary widely. Later, improvements in steam technology and new rail lines reduced the journey still further so that ten or twelve hours, with a four-hour sea crossing, came to seem normal. More broadly, these technological changes were part of the post-Union opening up of Ireland, which is also the fortification of Ireland: steamships berthed in new extended and recently fortified harbours to connect with a more extensive stagecoach network, military roads, and later rail links.

The visit of George IV to Ireland in 1821, the second year of his reign, can be seen as a pivotal moment in the story I am telling, and its traces are preserved on both sides of the sea. At Holyhead, a George IV arch (also known as the Triumphal Arch or Admiralty Arch) was erected in 1822–23, marking the northern terminus of Telford's road as well as the recent visit of the King. George IV's arrival in Howth and departure from Kingstown were also recorded in both places: his tiny footsteps were chiselled in granite at Howth harbour, while a memorial to his departure from Dun Laoghaire was erected in 1823 (as depicted in an engraving by George Petrie from 1828, Fig. 7). In William Thackeray's notorious description, the monument consisted of 'A hideous obelisk, stuck upon four fat balls, and surmounted with a crown on a cushion – the latter were no bad emblems perhaps of the monarch in whose honour they were raised'.[18]

Meanwhile, a painting, 'George IV on board the "Lightning", the first Post Office Steam Packet to Dublin, 12 August 1821' (Fig. 8), was commissioned to mark the king's departure from Holyhead. The king had intended to travel across the sea on the royal yacht, the *Royal George*, only to meet bad weather and rough winds on the Welsh coast. Instead, he and his party transferred to the steam packet *Lightning* and set sail on 7 August 1821. Just right of the centre of the painting, the mail boat can be seen with Holyhead harbour and the height of Caer Gybi visible in the distance, to the left of the image. The *Lightning* is shown in starboard broadside with smoke issuing from the funnel, illuminated by bright light, with the King and his group just visible on deck. We can see the *Royal George* with its fluttering royal standard to the left, flanked on the far left by the other steam packet, the *Meteor*. Both the *Lightning* and the *Meteor* lie flat on the water, firmly quelling the sea's action, while the older ships are tossed up by the waves. The transition from sail and steam is strongly marked: the painting is framed by the image of a frigate in bow view, receding into darkness as it fires a farewell salute, signalling the end of an era.[19]

---

[18] William Thackeray, *The Irish Sketchbook* (Gloucester, 1990), 3.
[19] Cf. also https://collections.rmg.co.uk/collections/objects/12111.html.

Fig. 7 George Petrie, 'Memorial of the King's Visit to Ireland, Kingstown'.
Engraving, Crawford Art Gallery, Cork

Seasickness

If the painting makes purposeful history of windy weather, its story rides roughly over the continuing realities of slow crossings in bad weather, which remained the experience of sea passengers throughout the age of steam. Daniel Maclise's evocative sketch of passengers aboard the ship *Severn* as it makes its way from Cork to Bristol tells a different story

Fig. 8   William John Huggins, 'George IV on board the "Lightning", the first Post Office
Steam Packet to Dublin, 12 August 1821'.
Oil on canvas, National Maritime Museum, London, Caird Collection

(Fig. 9). A familiar genre scene is transformed by Maclise's unusual choice
of a shipboard location, while his attention to slumped bodies and
hunched shoulders vividly captures the passengers' plight.

Such a predicament was often described in travel writing. John Gamble,
a retired Army surgeon with literary interests, offers a vivid account of the
bodily realities of travel in his *Sketches of History, Politics and Manners,
Taken in Dublin and the North of Ireland, in the Autumn of 1810*. In 1810,
Gamble crossed from Liverpool to Dublin (a distance of about forty
leagues, he tells us, on a crossing that lasted 'something more than twenty
six hours'). The weather was 'for once' kind and the passage 'favourable'.
But as he crossed the waters caressed by 'breezes, soft as the breath of
Love', 'wafted . . . gently to the Emerald Isle', Gamble could not resist the
chance to share with readers the more normal experience of travel along
this 'rough and lofty coast along which our vessel glided'.[20]

This is the same rocky coast on which the ship bearing Edward King to
Dublin foundered, its reputation as 'one of the worst hazards of the
Atlantic crossing' secured by its 'baffling combination of havens and

[20] Quoted in Breandán MacSuibhne, ed., *John Gamble, Society and Manners in Early Nineteenth-
Century Ireland* (Dublin, 2011), 16–17.

Fig. 9   Daniel Maclise, 'On Board the "Severn" from Cork to Bristol'.
Drawing, Victoria and Albert Museum (F.88:244)

hazards'.[21] The combination of strong tides and a shallow coastal seabed made navigation tricky. Here is Gamble: 'The whole of this coast is dangerous, even to a proverb; and many sea captains have declared they felt more anxiety in going from Holyhead to Liverpool, than in their passage from the West Indies to England.'[22]

Gamble is quick to move from the proverbial dangers of the coastline to the bodily realities of life on board: 'I would recommend every person who goes to sea for the first time to keep upon deck as much as possible, it is the most effectual method of avoiding sickness, and if at length he is obliged to yield to it, the tone and refreshment which the pure and cold air has given him shortens in duration, and weakens in violence.' Failing that (surely familiar) protection, Gamble recommends that '[w]hen a person is compelled by sea-sickness to quit the deck and betake himself to his berth, he should stretch himself as much at length as possible, with his head low and firmly pressed to the pillow, endeavouring to lose all motion of his own, and to accommodate himself to the ship's. Wine or spirits is bad; though, of the two, the latter diluted with water is preferable. The drink I would

[21] Ivor Wynne Jones, *Shipwrecks of North Wales* (Newton Abbot, 1978), 20, 92; cited in J. Karl Franson, 'The Fatal Voyage of Edward King, Milton's Lycidas', *Milton Studies* 25 (1989): 43–67 (50).
[22] Gamble in MacSuibhne, *John Gamble*, 17.

recommend is a highly-taken bottled porter, soda or seltzer water.' Lest there be any doubt of suffering from 'this nauseous disease', Gamble's list continues, finally ending with the suggestion of 'a small opiate plaister, applied to the pit of the stomach', the precursor perhaps to modern motion sickness tablets (ibid., 17–18).

Gamble's frankness sounds an unfamiliar note, however. More common is the kind of brisk advice offered by Mrs Delany, to her friend Mrs Dewes in April 1753, in advance of a crossing to Dublin:

> Don't apprehend anything from the sea. It is a disagreeable element to deal with, but it never hurts me any longer than whilst I am on board, and though I must confess, and I fear you will find whenever you make me happy by coming here, that a *ship is a most unpleasant thing*, yet the happiness it is to convey me to is a full amends for a few hours distress, and the passage is *seldom more* than *forty hours*, and often not much more than half that time.[23]

Even as she puts the unpleasantness of the ship to one side, Mrs Delaney's comments open up an improving vision of the Irish Sea with roots in Boate's natural history. The writings of Maria Edgeworth continue these contradictions of connection and disconnection, most particularly in her novels, where time and tide so often neatly align to serve the needs of her plot. But Edgeworth herself was all too familiar with rough sea crossings. A letter in 1791, addressed from an inn in Holyhead, reports that 'a thirty-three hours' passage' has left the family sick and sorry: 'all the sick pale figures around me with faint voices send their love to you and my uncle'.[24] Yet, in other letters, the family seem to make a kind of improving fiction of the crossing, discussing the motion of light on the water and making observations: 'When the sea was calm, I never was more entertained than with watching the various curiosities of sea manners, sea views & the ship; which by the by was as clean as any room at Edgeworthstown.'[25]

Sea Views

A striking example of the literary efforts to tame rough water in the name of 'sea manners' and 'sea views' comes from Gerald Griffin's tale, 'The

---

[23] *The Autobiography and Correspondence of Mary Granville, Mrs. Delany: With Interesting Reminiscences of King George the Third and Queen Charlotte. Edited by the Right Honourable Lady Llanover*, 3 vols. (London, 1861), 3:225.

[24] Maria Edgeworth to Mrs Ruxton, 1791, in *Life and Letters of Maria Edgeworth*, ed. Augustus Hare, 2 vols. (London, 1893), 1:17.

[25] Charlotte Edgeworth to Mary Sneyd, 25 Sept. 1802, National Library of Ireland MSS 10166-7.

Half-Sir', one of the *Tales of the Munster Festivals* (1827). Griffin grew up on the banks of the Shannon, the son of middle-class Catholic parents with an older brother who served in Canada with the army. Griffin went from journalism in Limerick to a rickety life as a jobbing journalist in London. In his Munster tales, Griffin writes powerfully about the dramatic effects of the Atlantic waves on the west coast of his birth, but in relation to the Irish Sea he is curiously keen to minimize its effects. In the following passage, a very slight agitation at sea is placed in relation to the confusion on shore as a varied group gather to embark from Dublin for London.

> The morning was a still and beautiful one – and the face of the bay, agitated only by the bulk of its own waters into that leaping undulation which we cannot describe otherwise than by referring the reader (in defiance of the imputation of a common-place affectation) to Claude Lorrain's embarkation pictures, looked clear and glassy green. The pier was crowded with passengers who were waiting to see their effects safely stowed before they took their own places in the vessel, with clamorous jingle-men and ragged, half-starved porters; members of the exiled parliament made up for the winter campaign; and adventurers of every description, who devoutly believed that gold and fame grew like blackberries upon hedges every where but in poor Ireland – and who, if they did not actually suppose that the houses in London were tiled with pancakes, and the streets paved with wedges of gold – yet would have staked their existence that something very good must be had there or so many people would not be constantly going and *never* returning; and lulled their hearts with the delicious promise of a delusion quite as vain, if not so palpably absurd, as that above alluded to of poor Whittington.[26]

Griffin's effort to find a visual correlative for the 'leaping undulation' of Dublin Bay leads him into a strange point of comparison. The imagined connection between Claude's Mediterranean blues and the dull waters of Dublin Bay seems highly improbable. Claude's settings are Italianate and explore the play of light and sun on water and buildings; his strict linear perspectives and subdued symmetries impose a kind of willed neoclassical order on the chaos that Griffin describes. The narrative charts the confusion of the passengers destined for likely disappointment in London (just what Griffin himself had experienced), even as the 'clear and glassy green' of the ekphrastic image smooths over such uncertainty.

The visual record yields further evidence of taming of the sea and the creation of perspective. John Laporte's view of Dublin Bay from Clontarf, from the topographical collection of George III (Fig. 10), is typical of the

---

[26] Gerald Griffin, *Tales of the Munster Festivals*, 3 vols. (London, 1827), 1:347–68.

Fig. 10   John Laporte, 'View of Dublin Bay from Clontarf' (1796).
Hand-coloured etching, © British Library Board (K.Top.53.21.c B20100-12)

effort of eighteenth-century views of Dublin to present a 'wholly positive' image of the sea.[27] The power of the tide and the surge of water in the bay is reflected in the building of fortifications designed to secure newly reclaimed land from the effects of the sea. Finola O'Kane has shown how the bay to the east of the city played a crucial role in securing Dublin's maritime identity in the eighteenth century, with extensive land reclamation enabling the city's 'swivel to the east'. O'Kane reads Laporte's image as part of a wider effort 'to place the city in a wide maritime and economic context', suggestive of its incorporation into empire and readiness for trade.[28]

But even as rough waves were kept at bay, these images tell their story. We can locate evidence of the bay's notorious storms in the depiction of the long ramparts in William Ashford's 'The Royal Charter School from Clontarf' (Fig. 11), built to save the shoreline from being washed away. James Arthur O'Connor's atmospheric 'A View of Irishtown from

[27] Finola O'Kane, *William Ashford's Mount Merrion: The Absent Point of View* (Tralee, 2012), 22.
[28] Finola O'Kane, 'The City of Dublin', www.bl.uk/picturing-places/articles/the-city-of-dublin.

Fig. 11   William Ashford, 'The Royal Charter School from Clontarf' (1794).
Oil on canvas, National Gallery of Ireland

Sandymount' (c. 1823, Fig. 12) maintains a delicate visual balance between the developing city and the distant bay. The ships, visible only by their topmost sails, are held at a distance by harbour walls, while a prominent church spire announces the onward march of urban development in Irishtown and Ringsend, urban villages belonging to the Fitzwilliam estate. The central group are arranged on sandy soil, near a makeshift structure for boats, at rest (or at play) under looming clouds, while lapping waves reclaim the land for the sea. Central to the painting, the ramparts not only divide land from sea but remind viewers of the wider history of land reclamation central to the success of the Fitzwilliam estate.[29]

An accomplished draughtsman as well as a talented painter, O'Connor left Ireland for London in 1822, sketching and seeking out new commissions but always displaying his remarkable talent for 'intimate, local scenes' such as this Dublin one.[30] O'Connor's Romantic style of painting has

[29] Ashford, a leading Irish landscape painter at the start of the nineteenth century, had received a commission from Viscount Fitzwilliam for a series of views that depicted the Mount Merrion estate and managed 'the absent point of view' (as per O'Kane, *William Ashford's Mount Merrion* and her 'Dublin's Fitzwilliam Estate: A Hidden Landscape of Discovery, Catholic Agency and Egalitarian Suburban Space', *Eighteenth-Century Ireland* 31 (2016): 92–116).

[30] Nesta Butler, 'James Arthur O'Connor', in *Art and Architecture of Ireland 2: Painting 1600–1900*, ed. Andrew Carpenter et al. (New Haven, CT, 2015), 395–98 (396).

Fig. 12   James Arthur O'Connor, 'A View of Irishtown from Sandymount' (c. 1823).
Oil on canvas, private collection

been connected to his 'enforced emigration' from Ireland and his 'View of Irishtown from Sandymount' might be seen to use the relationship between sea and land to express wider uncertainties, reminders of crossings that are shadowed by death and loss, haunted by psychological uncertainty (ibid., 397).

These are ideas that gather into a distinctive body of writing towards the end of the nineteenth century, from which point we can clearly discern something like the psychologization of the sea crossing and the beginning of an exploration of the affective power of rough waves. Such a possibility is darkly shadowed forth in Griffin's predictions of poverty in London and given a more concrete expression in Anthony Trollope's *Phineas Redux*. At the start of that novel, Phineas's potentially 'perilous' return to London and the challenges of parliamentary life are presented in terms of the responsibility of a man for his own self: a cumbersome 'possession', a man's self might however might be shed, half way across the Irish Sea:

> Doubtless there is a way of riddance. There is the bare bodkin. Or a man may fall overboard between Holyhead and Kingsto[w]n in the dark, and

may do it in such a cunning fashion that his friends shall think that it was an accident. But against these modes of riddance there is a canon set, which some men still fear to disobey.[31]

In Trollope's account of Phineas's 'revolvings', the young man 'walked up and down the long pier of Kingsto[w]n harbour', wondering 'what might not London do for him?' The question resonates with a longer history of Irish writers and artists for whom emigration was experienced as a necessity at once financial, professional, and emotional. Trollope's account of Phineas's plight recalls such tragic stories as the death of W. B. Yeats's uncle, the stockbroker Robert Corbet. An agent for the Royal Exchange Assurance Company, who sold off bankrupt estates after the Famine on behalf of Encumbered Estates Court, Corbet ran into money problems and committed suicide by jumping off the Holyhead mailboat in 1870. His death, as R. F. Foster remarks, 'brings together all the emblems signifying the decline of an Ascendancy elite'.[32]

Charles Stewart Parnell and Sea Storms

The history of travel continued to develop in this period. With the intensification of the railway system, the increased frequency of sea crossings, and a new infrastructural density came a kind of writing that itself works to build connections from sea crossings to discourses of identity. The life story of Charles Stewart Parnell provides particularly fruitful material through which to think about the many different aspects of my narrative, connecting up as it does routine journeys back and forth across the sea, infrastructural innovations, and affective connections over water.

Even in death, Parnell was fated to make a final passage across the Irish Sea. In 1891, his coffin was conveyed from Brighton to Willesden, before being carried on the Euston to Holyhead train and on to Dublin by steamer from Holyhead, accompanied by Parnellite members of parliament. In *King of the Great Clock Tower*, Yeats wrote of how on that 'stormy October morning' he had 'gone to Kingsto[w]n Pier to meet the Mail Boat that arrived about 6 a.m. ... expecting a friend, but met what I thought much less of at the time, the body of Parnell'.[33] The friend was Maud Gonne, who, as R. F. Foster explains, was returning from Paris to Dublin via Holyhead, devastated following the death of her child.

[31] Anthony Trollope, *Phineas Redux* (Penguin ed., London, 2003), 8.
[32] R. F. Foster, *W. B. Yeats: A Life*, 2 vols. (Oxford, 1997), 2:9.
[33] Quoted in A. N. Jeffares, *A New Commentary on the Poems of W. B. Yeats* (London, 1984), 333–35.

Onlookers, seeing her dressed in deep mourning, assumed Gonne was one of the Parnell funeral party.[34]

Parnell's body travelled a route with a family as well as a political history. His great uncle, Sir Henry Parnell, had chaired the Holyhead Road commission that backed Telford's plans and enabled his remarkable works. There is also a personal history, as told by Katherine O'Shea, who recounts Parnell's 'great love for sea storms' in *Charles Stewart Parnell: His Love Story and Political Life*. In that book, she tells a dramatic story concerning rough waves, though the body of water in this case is the English Channel. In 1887, while the *Times* forgeries were being investigated and just after the election of Captain O'Shea in Galway in 1886, Parnell and Katherine O'Shea took an end terrace house in Brighton – number 10 Walsingham Terrace. In her account of those months, they spent their time walking and riding on the Downs while he also continued to travel over and back to Ireland for shooting. In Brighton, Parnell occupied himself with mineralogy and amateur engineering, including a plan 'to invent a vessel which would so cut through the water as to obviate any sensation of the motion of the waves'. [35] (Before he met O'Shea, Parnell been known to seek relaxation from the stresses of parliament by playing with a boy's train set.)[36]

Katharine O'Shea describes the 'thing' he invented as like 'a treble torpedo-boat' and reports: 'He had no training in mechanics, nor did he know anything of shipbuilding or engineering, except such information as he obtained from the various books he read for amusement at rare intervals – but these models he made, and tried off the under-deck of the Chain Pier at Brighton, were extraordinarily ingenious.' Built in 1823, the Chain Pier at Brighton was designed to facilitate packet boats destined for Dieppe, part of the same modernizing moment as the works over which Henry Parnell had presided.

Concerning Parnell's model 'treble torpedo-boat', O'Shea offers a striking story concerning 'one rough, stormy day' at the Chain Bridge, looking out at the English Channel. Together, the couple 'tried the "float," though it was useless to do so, as the waves shattered the slight thing against the pier before Parnell could sink it to the required depth'. As the pair 'stood looking out at the great waves – so near, and shaking the whole pier-head

[34] Foster, *W. B. Yeats*, 2:115–16.
[35] Katharine O'Shea, *Charles Stewart Parnell: His Love Story and Political Life*, 2 vols. (London, 1914), 2:210.
[36] Paul Bew, 'Charles Stewart Parnell', in *The Oxford Dictionary of National Biography*, www.odnb .com, accessed 24 April 2019.

in their surge', Parnell picked up his lover, held her 'clear over the sea' and threatened to jump: 'Had I shown any fear I think he would have done it, but I only held him tight and said: "As you will, my only love, but the children?" He turned then, and carried me to the upper deck, hiding my eyes from the horrible roll and sucking of the sea beneath our feet.'[37] A 'near *Liebestod* as Foster suggests, Katharine O'Shea's story brings not only a personal story but a political one to a ringing climax, invoking as it does the political necessity of sea journeys, the emotional content carried on the waves, and the recurrent undertow of the material history of travel crossings.[38]

The meaning of such crossings formed part of the political discourse of political independence. Making the case of a form of self-government for Ireland, Gladstone drew on Henry Grattan, who had opposed the Union in 1800 on the grounds that the Irish Sea made for inevitable separation even as threats from overseas demanded a secure connection: Ireland, he wrote, 'hears the Ocean protesting against Separation, but she hears the sea likewise protesting against Union; she follows, therefore, her physical destination, and obeys the dispensations of Providence when she protests, like the sea, against the two situations'.[39] Gladstone's speech introducing the Government of Ireland Bill (the First Home Rule Bill) in 1886 echoed Grattan's invocation of the waves' dual message of division and interdependence: in his version, Ireland 'hears the ocean protesting against separation, but she hears the sea protesting against union'.[40] Independence in 1922 brought one kind of answer to these political questions, but the sea continued to speak of entangled relationships and difficult crossings.

Crossed Lives

Where political history teaches us to think about the sea as a source of either opportunities (discovery, commerce, empire) or threats (invasion scares that continued into the nineteenth and twentieth centuries), this chapter has sought to trace more intricate cultural patterns. Katharine O'Shea's story about her lover's model ship afloat under the Chain Bridge shows how a dramatic account of the affective energies of the sea could

---

[37] O'Shea, *Charles Stewart Parnell*, 152, 154.

[38] R. F. Foster, 'Mrs O'Shea's *Parnell*', in *Paddy and Mr Punch: Connections in Irish and English History* (London, 1995), 123–28 (135).

[39] *Speech (at Length) of the Rt Hon Henry Grattan in the Irish House of Commons, against the Union with Great Britain* (London, 1800), 16.

[40] H. C. G. Matthews, ed., *The Gladstone Diaries, January 1881 to June 1883* (Oxford, 1990), 10:cxxx.

resonate within and disturb a political narrative. In the century that
followed the death of Charles Stewart Parnell, cultural representations of
the sea's waves continued to express intimate, troubled histories. And even
in the period after political independence in 1922, the Irish Sea remained a
resource for writers who wished to explore experiences of identity, belonging, and gender.

In this final section of this chapter, I move to a poem that seems to
explore, inhabit, and amplify Grattan and Gladstone's image of double-
tongued waters. Belfast-born poet Louis MacNeice has been described by
Terence Brown as a poet who 'interiorised the machine age' in his writing
of travel by road, rail, and sea.[41] MacNeice was intimately familiar with
'the bloody boat home',[42] and section sixteen of his *Autumn Journal*
(1939) develops that poem's drama of the divided self via a powerful
image of rough waves. A certain knowledge as to the roughness of the
sea seems to enable a politically curious and open exploration of the
crossing of possibilities and positions:

> Why do we like being Irish? Partly because
>   It gives us a hold on the sentimental English
> As members of a world that never was,
>   Baptised with fairy water;
> And partly because Ireland is small enough
>   To be still thought of with a family feeling,
> And because the waves are rough
>   That split her from a more commercial culture;
> And because one feels that here at least one can
>   Do local work which is not at the world's mercy
> And that on this tiny stage with luck a man
>   Might see the end of one particular action.
> It is self-deception of course;
>   There is no immunity in this island either;
> A cart that is drawn by somebody else's horse
>   And carrying goods to somebody else's market.
> The bombs in the turnip sack, the sniper from the roof,
>   Griffith, Connolly, Collins, where have they brought us?
> Ourselves alone! Let the round tower stand aloof
>   In a world of bursting mortar!

---

[41] Terence Brown, '"What am I doing here?": Travel and MacNeice', in *Incorrigibly Plural*, ed. Edna
   Longley and Fran Brearton (Manchester, 2012), 72–84 (73).
[42] Louis MacNeice to Anthony Blunt, 13 July 1929. The letter is written from on board the SS
   Patriotic (Belfast Steamship Company Limited). Jonathan Allison, *Letters of Louis MacNeice*
   (London, 2010), 208.

Let the school-children fumble their sums
    In a half-dead language;
Let the censor be busy on the books; pull down the
    Georgian slums;
Let the games be played in Gaelic.[43]

Expressed in rough quatrains and employing varying line lengths, Mac-Neice's question, 'Why do we like being Irish?,' initiates a sequence of questions that seem to feel their way over and back across the sea, exploring the turbulent boundary between 'Irish valedictions and maledictions', as Edna Longley puts it.[44]

The question of the roughness of the waves lends formal shape to 'the restless currents and eddies of MacNeice's thought', while the proverbial roughness of the water gives material substance to the forms of division enacted within this poem.[45] Where the first question occupies an orderly twelve lines, the second question covers thirteen, thus breaking equilibrium. To be drawn into the vibrating questions of this section of *Autumn Journal* is to experience the daily flow of thought characteristic of this long poem as a surging and receding of possibilities. The movement of the poem itself imitates the action of the waves: not an easy movement back and forth between opinions but, rather, expression of contradictory possibilities as wavelike disturbances, an organized disturbance brought to bear on a state of rest. The division expressed by the poem's two questions enacts a split but also keeps faith with the wider aims of *Autumn Journal* as a poem that 'synthesises the loose ends of the 1930s into a personal and communal psychodrama', creating 'the effect of salvaging some prospects for the future from the wreck of the past'.[46]

Autumn Journal may well mark the end of one particular kind of poem about rough waves, with literature increasingly shaped by the possibility of air travel. Written in 1968, Welsh poet Harri Webb's 'Return Visit' opens with the view of Dublin from the airport bus and offers the mordant reminder that 'One damp green country / Is much like another.'[47] There are also poems that reframe the crossing via the view from overhead, including Austin Clarke's enigmatic meditations on a personal absence (a separation from a lost lover) from a short 1960 lyric with the telling title

[43] Louis MacNeice, *Autumn Journal* (London, 2012), 52–53.
[44] Edna Longley, *Louis MacNeice: A Critical Study* (London, 1988), 57.
[45] Glyn Maxwell, 'Turn and Turn Against: *Autumn Journal*', in Longley and Brearton, eds., *Incorrigibly Plural*, 171–89 (172).
[46] Longley, *Louis MacNeice*, 59.
[47] Harri Webb, 'Return Visit', in Webb, *Collected Poems* (Llandysul, 1995), 94.

'Menai Strait'. Rather than confine itself to the well-worn route via Holyhead, the poem offers an aerial perspective on a remembered lover, who returns via a vivid memory of sail and steam: 'But now that absence comes back / Over cloud-gap, Wales under wing-tip, / Tunnel, funnel, forgotten, / Fire-shovelled knots of slack'.[48] In Clarke's poem, the relationship between the past and the present situation is remade in that between the mailboat and air travel, with a lost world of sea crossings making an insistent return. His trio of words ('Tunnel, funnel, forgotten') echo in Thomas Kinsella's 'Handclasp at Euston' from 1960: 'Wales, / Wave and home; I close my eyes.'[49]

But rough crossings refuse to remain in the past. They live on in cultural memory even as developments in transport have reframed them as history. Austin Clarke once more captures this process in oblique lines from a long autobiographical poem entitled 'The Hippophagi': 'Weather reports / Lay bare our soul in ancient ports.'[50] That laying bare of the soul was to play a key part in the social history of twentieth-century Ireland, where emigration via the mailboat remained a reality both routine and inevitable: what Clair Wills refers to as 'the fated and determined nature of the emigrant's story'.[51] Edna O'Brien captures the impress of the journey over these rough waves when Cait and Baba set sail from Dublin to Liverpool at the end of her novel, *The Lonely Girl* (the second in *The Country Girls* trilogy, later filmed as *Girl with Green Eyes*). A pregnant friend asks Cait to send abortion pills from England, a reminder of the many women in twentieth- and early twenty-first-century Ireland whose terminations were 'pushed out of sight on the Liverpool boat'.[52] As the two young women leave Ireland on board the *Hibernia*, the ship itself seems to share and embody their lonely plight:

> Baba waved a clean hanky, and we leaned on the rails and felt the ship move and saw the dirty water underneath being churned up.
> 'Like a hundred lavatories flushing', Baba said to the foamy water as the seagulls rose up from their various perches along the rails and flew, slowly, with us. [53]

---

[48] Austin Clarke, 'Menai Strait', in Clarke, *Collected Poems* (Manchester, 2008), 227.

[49] Thomas Kinsella, 'Handclasp at Euston', in Kinsella, *Moralities* (Dublin, 1960), 14.

[50] Austin Clarke, 'The Hippophagi', in *Collected Poems*, 233–39.

[51] Clair Wills, *The Best Are Leaving: Emigration and Post-War Irish Culture* (Cambridge, 2015), 173.

[52] Mary Holland, 'An Issue the Liverpool Boat Can't Carry Away', *Irish Times*, 25 June 1986; quoted in Lindsey Earner-Byrne and Diane Urquhart, *The Irish Abortion Journey* (Basingstoke, 2018), 80. See also Lindsey Earner-Byrne, 'The Boat to England: An Analysis of the Official Reactions to the Emigration of Single Expectant Irishwomen to Britain, 1922–1972', *Irish Economic and Social History Journal* 30 (2003): 52–70.

[53] Edna O'Brien, *The Country Girls Trilogy and Epilogue* (London, 1988), 374.

Further out to sea, Baba prepares for life in London by doling out seasickness tablets 'in case we puke all over the damn ship': '"If I'm sick, 'twill spoil everything," Baba said as she burped, and then put a hand towel over her new dress, for safety's sake' (ibid.).

I have been describing a phenomenon that is possessed of both highly public and quietly intimate meanings – crossing centuries, countries, and lives in diffuse, extensive, and varied patterns. Yet it is also true that the crash of the rough waves of the Irish Sea has been condensed and crystallized within compelling metaphors. In Elizabeth Bowen's *The Last September* (1929), Lois draws on the remembered miseries of the sea crossing to feed an 'inner blankness': 'She was lonely, and saw there was no future. She shut her eyes and tried – as sometimes when she was seasick, locked in misery between Holyhead and Kingstown – to be enclosed in a nonentity, in some ideal no-place, locked and clear as a bubble.'[54] *The Last September* reimagines seasickness as a kind of negative freedom, allowing the past to invade the present via the intense image of a 'no-place' on board ship. As with Swift's suggestion of burial in Holyhead, Bowen finds in the sea's roughness a form of miserable release from both isolation and connection: sickness as strange resource, turbulent waters remade in painful memory.

[54] Elizabeth Bowen, *The Last September* (London, 2015), 89.

CHAPTER 15

'Myth, Fact and Mystery'
F. X. Martin, Medievalist and Historian of the 1916 Rising

Thomas Bartlett

The publication in the 1960s of a series of books and articles on the 1916 Rising by Professor F. X. Martin (hereafter FX), professor of medieval history at University College Dublin, constituted collectively a landmark in the serious professional study of the Rising.[1] In 1961 he published in *Irish Historical Studies* (*IHS*) two lengthy memoranda by Eoin MacNeill, titular head of the Irish Volunteers in 1916 and author of the countermanding order to them not to mobilize on Easter Sunday (Fig. 13).[2] One of MacNeill's memoranda was written just before the Rising and the other eighteen months later, and both appeared in print, heavily annotated by FX. The significance of these statements by MacNeill was quickly realized by an Irish public that had not ceased to be fascinated by the Rising and the circumstances surrounding it. Remarkably, *IHS* had to depart from its stated editorial policy of publishing nothing on events in Ireland post-1900 in order to bring out these documents, and such was the public interest that for the first time, and the last, this issue of *IHS* went into a second printing in order to meet the demand for copies. This publication was succeeded by collections of documents on the Irish Volunteers and the Howth gun-running, and a further collection of essays – *Leaders and Men of 1916* – followed in 1967: a substantial body of work by any standards.[3] It may be noted that FX was always at pains to

---

[1] In an appreciation of FX's work on 1916, Michael Laffan writes that his publications 'dominated the decade in terms of "1916 studies"'. See M. Laffan, 'The Decade of the Rising: FX Martin on 1916', in *Ireland, England and the Continent in the Middle Ages and Beyond: Essays in Memory of 'a Turbulent Friar', F.X. Martin OSA*, ed. H. B. Clarke and J. R. S. Phillips (Dublin, 2006), 327. My thanks to Professor Laffan for discussing F. X. Martin's writings with me.

[2] Rev. F. X. Martin, 'Select Documents: XX, Eoin MacNeill on the 1916 Rising', *Irish Historical Studies* 12.47 (March 1961): 226–72. The length of this select document was unprecedented in *IHS*.

[3] F. X. Martin, ed., *The Irish Volunteers, 1913–1915: Recollections and Documents* (Dublin, 1963); Martin, ed., *The Howth Gunrunning and Kilcoole Gunrunning, 1914* (Dublin, 1964); Martin, ed., *Leaders and Men of the Easter Rising: Dublin 1916* (Dublin, 1964). See also F. X. Martin, ed., 'Extracts from the Papers of Dr Patrick McCartan', *Clogher Record* 5 (1963), part two in *Clogher Record* 5 (1964), and a final part based on the McCartan papers, 'Easter 1916: An Inside Report on

(a)

(b)

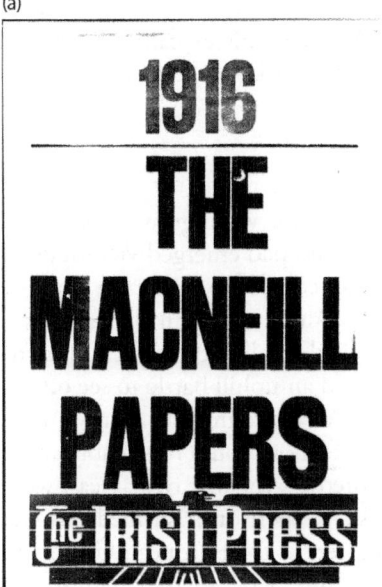

Fig. 13   Sensationalist news posters announcing F. X. Martin's publication of the
MacNeill Memoranda, April 1961.
FX Martin Papers, UCD Archives Department

point out that 'my 1913–23 Irish historical work is a side-line to my
medieval researches, but a delightfully distracting one'.[4] However, notwithstanding his numerous publications relating to the 'revolutionary
decade', it is, I think, unarguable that it was the publication of the
MacNeill memoranda in 1961 together with two lengthy review essays
in 1967–68 – in essence a single essay – published over two issues in *Studia
Hibernica*, that put the professional study of the Rising on an altogether
new footing. These review essays, entitled '1916 Myth, Fact and Mystery'
and '1916: Coup d'État or a "Bloody Protest"' (for convenience I will treat
them as a single piece), came in at some 150 printed pages – possibly the
longest review essay ever in any historiography – and addressed the

Ulster', *Clogher Record* 12 (1986). He also edited a volume entitled *The Easter Rising 1916 and
University College Dublin* (Dublin, 1966).

[4] FX Martin to Professor Denis Gwynn, 21 Dec. 1963: UCD archives, FX Martin papers, P189/239.
The 'side-line' continued: FX (with F. J. Byrne) later edited a volume of essays on *Eoin MacNeill:
The Scholar Revolutionary, 1867–1945* (Shannon, 1973) and, later still, edited Michael Tierney's
posthumously published biography of MacNeill, *Eoin MacNeill: Scholar and Man of Action* (Oxford,
1980).

arguments and opinions, the merits and demerits of some twenty-eight books and articles, some of them by FX himself.[5] FX explained its scope: 'I shall ... touch on most of the significant works on the Easter Rising published since 1916.'[6]

***

One of the more extraordinary aspects of these writings was that their author was a professor of *medieval* history, who had emerged victorious in 1962 from an epic and protracted four-way contest to claim the chair of medieval history at UCD in succession to Aubrey Gwynn SJ. FX was a member of the Augustinians and his principal published research hitherto had been on early modern Ireland.[7] He faced an uphill battle to see off his rivals for the chair, Drs Geoffrey Hand, J. A. Watt, and Rev. Dr Maurice Sheehy, all of whom applied for it, and all of whom could reasonably argue that FX was 'not really a medievalist'.[8] Moreover, the first two at least were outstanding medieval scholars: Hand was an expert on Irish medieval law and would later go on to a distinguished career at the European University Institute, and Watt, an authority on relations between the English and Irish in medieval Ireland, would subsequently become professor at the University of Newcastle. Sheehy was much the least qualified for the chair; Robin Dudley Edwards, professor of modern Irish history at UCD, reviewed Sheehy's application and dismissed it as insubstantial. Contrary to Sheehy's claim to have studied medieval history in the History Faculty at the Gregorian University in Rome, Edwards's investigations revealed that not only was there no medieval history department in that institution, there was no faculty of history there either. Moreover, Sheehy had not studied history as an undergraduate, had no experience of teaching history, and his soon-to-be published doctorate on papal letters and Ireland was wholly unimpressive: having read it, Edwards concluded that Sheehy was 'not equipped ... either to teach or to expound or perhaps even edit such

---

[5] The historian Hugh Kearney, a former colleague of FX, teased him that his review 'breaks two records. It is the first review to be longer than the books it is reviewing and, secondly, you are the first author actually to review yourself.' Kearney to FX, 23 June 1968: UCD Archives, FX Martin papers P189/273.

[6] F. X. Martin, '1916 – Myth, Fact and Mystery', *Studia Hibernica* 7 (1967): 7–126; Martin, 'The 1916 Rising – A Coup d'État or a "Bloody Protest"?', *Studia Hibernica* 8 (1968): 106–37.

[7] F. X. Martin, *Giles of Viterbo, 1469–1532* (Rome, 1960); Martin, *Friar Nugent: A Study of F. L. Nugent, 1569–1632, Agent of the Counter-Reformation* (London, 1962).

[8] Cited in the entry by Art Cosgrove on F. X. Martin in *Dictionary of Irish Biography*.

material'.[9] Edwards's colleague, T. Desmond Williams, professor of modern history at UCD, concurred. He too was resolutely opposed to Sheehy's candidacy but for other, mostly non-scholarly, reasons. Sheehy in his view was 'a miserable, disgruntled and totally unqualified priest'. Sheehy was indeed, like FX, a priest, but he was not just any priest. His brother, Monsignor Gerard Sheehy, was chancellor to the redoubtable John Charles McQuaid, Archbishop of Dublin, and Maurice Sheehy was a frequent visitor to the archbishop's palace in Drumcondra, assisting his brother in ordering and arranging the diocesan archives (a pet project of McQuaid's).[10] Not surprisingly, given McQuaid's intense interest in UCD appointments, Williams was not at all confident of a favourable outcome, for while Michael Tierney, then president of UCD appeared neutral, his 'advisors favour Dr Sheehy'. To counteract this powerful backing from the archbishop and his allies, it helped, to put it no stronger, that FX himself was friendly with President Tierney and had become acquainted with Mrs Éibhlín Tierney, a daughter of Eoin MacNeill, through his work in sorting out her father's papers with a view to publication. Nonetheless, as Williams again noted, 'It is all an appalling situation which requires considerable technique and diplomacy if we are to disentangle it successfully.'[11]

Until recently, there were a number of bodies in UCD that had a voice in the appointment of professors; the relevant faculty, the academic council, and the governing body were normally consulted concerning the suitability of the candidates, ranked in order of merit by the interview panel. Accordingly, Edwards and Williams submitted a resolution to the Faculty of Arts describing Drs Hand, Martin, and Watt as 'qualified' for the post; indeed, Martin and Watt were 'highly qualified'. As for Dr Sheehy, while his 'energy and ability' were acknowledged, and while he 'gives promise of good quality in future editorial work', he was not deemed suitable by Professors Williams and Edwards. The votes for the respective candidates varied from forum to forum, but the only concrete outcome was that Dr Hand, perhaps realizing that his academic future lay in a law department, dropped out of the race. Three candidates – Martin, Sheehy, and Watt – thus went forward to the decisive vote in the Senate of the National University of Ireland. Votes in favour in the Arts Faculty or the

[9] Material on Dr Maurice Sheehy's application in UCD archives, Robin Dudley Edwards papers, LA22/188.

[10] David Sheehy, 'Dublin Diocesan Archives: An Introduction', *Archivium Hibernicum* 42 (1987): 45.

[11] T. Desmond Williams to Herbert Butterfield, 29 May 1962, in Cambridge University Library, Butterfield papers, MSS 531/W328. My thanks to Professor Laffan for this reference.

Academic Council for individual applicants were no doubt welcome, but they carried little weight, and equally, adverse votes could be entirely ignored. All candidates were aware that the only vote that counted was in the senate, the ultimate appointing body. The NUI Senate consisted of the presidents of the NUI colleges, some senior academics, a handful of national politicians, and four county councillors, almost none of whom would have had any idea of the respective qualities of the candidates who sought their votes. Canvassing for votes was expected, indeed was more or less mandatory.[12] FX proved an enthusiastic and energetic canvasser.[13] He described the outcome of the contest in a letter to his former rival Geoffrey Hand.

> The week before the Senate election was pretty hectic. The last straw was when I found out, three days before the Senate [meeting], that Sean McEntee [at this time tánaiste in Sean Lemass's Fianna Fáil government] was phoning electors on behalf of Sheehy. I was dubbed (perhaps not by McEntee) as a Fine Gael candidate. The story *now* is that I won by a last minute blitz on, and capture of, the Fianna Fáil votes. Neither story is true. The scales were tipped at the Senate, I understand, by James Hogan [brother of a prominent Fine Gael politician and history professor] of UCC: he spoke on all three candidates, explained their qualities and left it to the electors.

Hogan's views may well have been coloured by interventions from Tierney, for the two men were on the right wing of the Fine Gael party, but it is unlikely that Williams or Edwards had any influence with him. At any rate, Hogan had reportedly described the exclusion of Hand in favour of Sheehy as 'a disgrace'. FX gave the following figures: first

---

[12] In his memoir *Vive Moi: An Autobiography* (London, 1965) the writer Seán Ó Faoláin described his epic struggle over the Chair of English at University College Cork against Daniel Corkery, according to Ó Faoláin, 'a man whose only previous teaching experience had been with small boys in a primary school'. Ó Faoláin recalled 'interviewing, or being interviewed by, one stout farmer [and member of the NUI senate] who was so hard at work saving his crop of hay on a day of high wind that to talk to him at all I had to walk alongside him shouting into the wind while he vigorously plied his hay fork'. Ó Faoláin lost out to Corkery, though in the event, he reckoned he was lucky: 'I would have been out of the place [UCC] within three years, or else stayed on and gone to seed' (258–61).

[13] In later years FX would relish relating how on one occasion while canvassing in Kerry, he needed to track down a county councillor who had a vote in the contest but who was out saving turf in the bog when FX called to his home. FX in full canonicals duly took himself off to the bog where he solicited the councillor's vote only to be told that he had given a solemn promise to Mrs Sheehy on her deathbed that he would vote for her son, Fr Maurice, when the Chair became vacant. Undeterred, FX identified himself as an Augustinian friar and proceeded to absolve the fellow from his solemn promise. Given that FX won the contest by just one vote, and after the elimination of Sheehy, it is tempting to speculate that this may have been the crucial vote.

scrutiny: Martin 14, Watt 11, Sheehy 5; second scrutiny, Sheehy having been eliminated: Martin 15, Watt 14. FX had won by the narrowest of margins.[14]

***

FX had gathered up essays, statements, private correspondence, and books on the 1916 Rising during his work in editing MacNeill's memoranda and in compiling his volume on the Irish Volunteers. In response to a request from Fr Dónall Cregan – president of St Patrick's college, Drumcondra, and a member of the editorial board of *Studia Hibernica*, which he had helped found in 1961 – he began to prepare a lengthy review article on this material. FX worked steadily on the review throughout 1967, and its core was based on books and articles published in the immediate decades after 1916. However, FX's determination to include comments and criticisms of the most recent publications – many of which had been published in 1966–67 to take advantage of the fiftieth anniversary of the Rising – undoubtedly gave the review 'a wayward and self-indulgent structure', as very often they were add-ons to the main text or simply inserted where relevant.[15] Finally, having toiled ceaselessly on this project, just before Christmas 1967, FX announced to the editor of *Studia Hibernica*, Stiofáin Ó hAnnracháin, that the piece was done: 'The "article" is finished', he wrote, adding, 'and I feel finished.'[16]

Publication, however, was by no means straightforward. Fr Cregan had already expressed alarm at the reported length of FX's forthcoming review, complaining that the 1967 issue of *Studia Hibernica* had had to be held back for it and claiming that several other articles had been 'bumped' to make way for it. In addition to the delay, the length of the article meant that the journal would have to seek a subvention of £150 from UCD to publish it.[17] A much more serious problem, however, was the many emendations to FX's text that appeared between preliminary 'galleys' and final proofs and that threatened to put an end to the whole project. FX expressed outrage at the 'tampering' with his text and threatened to take his review article elsewhere. Did Cregan not know that the *Irish Times* was

---

[14] FX to Hand, 25 Oct. 1962, 5 Dec. 1962, UCD FX Martin papers P189/352: P189/004. Watt may have suffered a disadvantage because he was English. As for Dr Maurice Sheehy, he later left the priesthood and married Frank O'Connor's widow, Harriet.

[15] Laffan, 'The Decade of the Rising', 329.

[16] FX to Ó hAnnracháin, 23 Dec. 1967, UCD archives, FX Martin papers, P198/273.

[17] Fr Cregan to FX, 20 March 1968, UCD archives, Martin papers 189/273.

interested in publishing the review in a series of articles and that a book
deal might follow?[18] Contrary to what was claimed, the alterations to his
text were not merely, FX wrote, 'changes of emphasis' here and there;
rather, they constituted a deliberate 'misrepresentation of my views' and
were a deliberate attempt at *suppressio veri, suggestio falsi* at the hands of the
editor and the editorial board. Ó hAnnracháin, the editor, had already
blotted his copybook by ringing the Bursar's Office in UCD seeking
information on the requested £150 subvention – his intervention on this
sensitive issue had caused FX much embarrassment – and FX was not
prepared to spare him his wrath. Ó hAnnracháin's explanation for the
textual changes was entirely 'ingenuous' (i.e., disingenuous?), and FX
threatened to go public: "It is time that somebody made a stand on this
issue against those who are falsifying Irish history, a small pressure group
who are imposing their viewpoint on the majority of the Irish people.' In
the end, following an apology by Ó hAnnracháin – 'no conscious attempt
was made to misrepresent you' – FX calmed down.[19] Provided his text was
entirely restored, he wrote, he was prepared to go along with publication in
Studia Hibernica. He did this out of esteem for Fr Cregan and also because
he well knew that to withdraw the review article publicly 'would probably
wreck the reputation of *Studia Hibernica* among scholars'.[20] Accordingly,
the suggested changes were abandoned, and FX's lengthy review article
duly appeared in the summer of 1968.

***

What made FX's review article and his earlier publication of the memo-
randa so valuable was, first, that he was prepared to challenge the hitherto
accepted, and indeed revered, narrative of 1916, one that placed Patrick
Pearse right at its centre, thus marginalizing Sean MacDermott, Eoin
MacNeill, Bulmer Hobson, and the others. It had until then been a
narrative that made all criticism impertinent, all questioning redundant.
That narrative could only be embroidered, but not challenged. Second,
FX's comments were measured on, and sympathetic to, the authors of the
works he reviewed. His harshest criticisms had usually to do with a lack of
footnotes and an absence of indexes. He could deal fairly with Desmond

---

[18] FX was in discussions with Methuen about a book from his review articles, claiming, 'I would prefer
an English to an Irish publisher': FX to Janice Price, Methuen, 17 Feb. 1968, UCD archives Martin
papers, P189/273. Methuen had published FX's earlier book on Friar Nugent.
[19] Ó hAnnracháin to FX, 15 March 1968, UCD archives, Martin papers 189/273.
[20] FX to Fr Cregan, 18 March 1968, UCD archives, Martin papers 189/273.

Ryan's near-hagiography of Pearse[21] as well as he could with A. T. Q. Stewart's stout defence of Ulster Unionism's gun-running and threatening civil war. And he was spot on in terms of undiscovered or ignored sources: he referenced the Bureau of Military History's witness statements and other documents held by them, and lamented their inaccessibility, cast as they were into what he styled 'The Limbo of Untouchable Things', that is, government archives (107); he accurately described the report of the Royal Commission on the Rebellion in Ireland as not just 'valuable but invaluable' in terms of its contents and appendices (26–27); and while he rebuked Max Caulfield for the lack of footnotes in his history of the Rising, he commended his energy in seeking out and interviewing members of the British army who had helped in its suppression (36). On a wider plane, he was ahead of his time in examining or at least touching on the wider significance of the Rising: he perceptively noted that the Rising could be seen as setting in train the dissolution of the British Empire, and while he did not mention Indian nationalists (or Jewish for that matter) he did note that 'Pearse was to be the model as much for the Breton separatists as for the Irish republicans' (37, 71). He could be witty too: he remarked that reading Seán Ó Faoláin's biography of Countess Markievcz led him to believe that Ó Faoláin had embarked on the work as an admirer of the Countess but had ended it 'in sympathy with her husband' (81). And he was frankly delighted at the way those who had denounced the rising in 1916 – the various churches, Trinity College Dublin, the print media, even that organ of the Ascendancy, *The Irish Tatler and Sketch*, had fallen over one another to commemorate and indeed celebrate its fiftieth anniversary. Third, his judgements were very often astute and challenging. He posed the question – still not satisfactorily resolved – 'Was the Ulster Volunteer Force the first fascist army in modern times? (56); and his remarks about the 'Great Oblivion' into which the Irish ex-servicemen fell after the Great War ultimately began the process of recovery and remembrance which fifty years on has become such a key feature of the historiography of the revolutionary era (68).

Insofar as FX addressed the question of the military planning and execution for the Rising, his verdict was unequivocal. 'The Rising was imaginatively planned with artistic vision and with exceptional military

---

[21] Mrs Desmond Ryan, however, was not too happy about the treatment of her late husband. Mrs Ryan to FX, 28 June 1968, UCD archives, Martin papers, P189/273. On the other hand, Bulmer Hobson – near invisible since 1916 – had been frankly delighted at how FX had restored his place in history in his earlier publications. 'I cannot tell you how much I appreciate what you have done': Bulmer Hobson to FX, 29 Nov. 1963, UCD archives, FX Martin papers P189/239.

incompetence' (9). The rebel headquarters – the General Post Office (GPO) – was a 'disastrous choice' (26); 'military bungling' (106) distinguished the Rising from the start; and the 'insurgents had no intelligible or, militarily speaking, intelligent blue print for an all-Ireland rising' (110). He noted that the Military Council of the Irish Republican Brotherhood had 'little competence in military affairs' and that those who had military experience – J. J. 'Ginger' O'Connell and Eimar O Duffy, for example – were kept completely in the dark in the planning for the Rising (111). Finally, he concluded that 'the Rising as it took place, *or even as it was to have taken place in its fuller form*, was ill-conceived and unrealistic as a military affair' (110, my emphasis). In his view, the military aspects of the Rising were secondary to its central purpose, which was the proclamation and declaration of the republic.

Later commentators have not significantly dissented from this judgement.[22] True, Barton and Foy described the insurgents' plan as 'imaginative, aggressive and optimistic', but this verdict was based almost entirely on the authors' reading, in my view flawed, of the so-called Ireland report, compiled by Casement and Plunkett for the German High Command in 1915.[23] Military men, such as Colonel P. J. Nally writing in the *Irish Sword* in 1966–67, did regard the rebels' choice of defensive localities as 'excellent' but noted the smallness of their forces, the absence of a supply chain, their lack of artillery and armoured cars, and their skeletal medical service. In addition, communications were poor between the rebel outposts, while those of the enemy were first-rate. Nally's main rebuke was directed at the British commanders for authorizing a madcap cavalry charge up Sackville Street, for persisting with a suicidal assault up Mount Street, and, especially, for executing the rebel leaders. On the whole, though, he concluded the British forces performed creditably in suppressing the Rising, given that they were taken by surprise and had poorly trained recruits to throw into the fray.[24] For the first time in an Irish insurrection, the rebels were better trained than the enemy – and it showed.

***

[22] The best recent work on the Rising, Charles Townshend's *Easter 1916: The Easter Rising* (London, 2005), praises FX's review articles as 'a unique cocktail of information, assessment and research agenda' (xvi–xviii).

[23] M. T. Foy and B. Barton, *The Easter Rising* (Dublin, 2011 [1999]), 22, 36–37.

[24] Col. P. J. Nally, 'The Easter 1916 Rising in Dublin: The Military Aspects', *Irish Sword* 8.29 (Winter 1966): 313–25 and 8.30 (summer 1967): 48–57.

I wish to conclude this brief examination of FX's review article, and other publications on 1916, with a fuller discussion of two of the points raised by him: one was a conclusion, the other was in the nature of a throwaway jocular remark. First, at the conclusion of his *Studia Hibernica* piece, FX comments:

> The rising caused many deaths and casualties, most of them were of innocent people. But one person to whom it dealt a mortal blow, who died unwept, unhallowed and unsung was the stage Irishman. The Hero supplanted the Fool .... The servile and feckless peasant threw off his rags to reveal himself as a disciplined, courageous soldier. In English eyes, the Irish were never the same again.

What FX was signalling here was that the Rising had finally scotched one of the most serious and persistent jibes against Irish rebels or Irish soldiers fighting at home: that they were always militarily incompetent. This was a charge that had a long history. It might be found in the writings of the twelfth-century apologist for English rule, Gerald of Wales, and it was brought forward again in commentaries by Edmund Spenser and Sir John Davies in the sixteenth and seventeenth centuries. Even foreign authors subscribed to the notion of innate Irish military inferiority: it is difficult nowadays to understand the anger caused among Irish nationalists by Voltaire's claim in the 1750s that while the Irish made good soldiers for other countries they were militarily useless in Ireland. It was in vain that nationalist writers such as Mathew O'Conor, Thomas Davis, and especially J. C. O'Callaghan sought to refute this 'calumny'. And yet, despite these persistent efforts at rebuttal, the vicious taunt showed no signs of going away. The perceived, apparently historically accurate, proven ineptitude of Irish rebels at home was both a powerful psychological weapon in the hands of the British government and an effective deterrent to Irish insurrection, though not of course to Irish conspiracy. Surely only a madman would dare brave the ridicule, the derision, the ignominy, and the scorn that were the inevitable outcomes of any attempt at armed rebellion. Bulmer Hobson later conceded that Irish people 'had been really brought to believe that armed resistance to the English occupation of Ireland was both insane and immoral', while Pearse noted grimly that we had been brought to accept that 'rebellion in all its forms is silly'. Riddled with spies and informers, paralyzed with indecision, poorly trained, poorly equipped, and poorly led, Irish rebels had always made a poor showing in the field, and as a result Irish rebellions were always futile, tragic, or farcical; 'insane or immoral' (Hobson); or, as Pearse put it, either 'a bloody debacle like '98 or a dreary fizzling out like '48 or '67'.

Hence the decision to press ahead with Rising on Easter Monday. With the capture of Roger Casement, the sinking of the arms-laden ship the *Aud*, and especially with the countermanding order issued by Eoin MacNeill, Easter Sunday, the planned date for the Rising, passed without incident. But the rebel leadership was undeterred and determined unanimously to strike the following day, Easter Monday. We can only guess at their motives, for none left a detailed statement of the thinking behind that decision. Undoubtedly a factor, perhaps a major factor in their fateful decision, was not to be subject to the catcalls and derision attendant on calling off or postponing action: that humiliating hallmark of Irish rebels had to be scotched once and for all. But would the rebels make a good fight? Their success, and its impact on British opinion, and indeed wider afield, were what FX was highlighting when he concluded his review article, and in this he was echoing the understandably bemused remarks by Mathew Nathan, Under-Secretary at Dublin Castle at the time of the Rising, in his evidence to the Royal Commission inquiring into the 'Rebellion': 'Apart from its ultimate futility', noted Nathan gravely, 'the conduct of the insurrection showed greater organisation, ability and military skill than had [previously] been attributed to the [Irish] Volunteers.' Or indeed to Irish rebels ever. And, as FX concluded, for the first time Irish rebels looked and acted like professional soldiers, while British regulars were made to look like amateurs in the 'six days that shook an Empire'.[25]

The second remark that FX made in his *Studia Hibernica* article, and that I propose to discuss briefly, was by no means as thoughtful as the earlier one. But it was suggestive. Here it is: in discussing what could be gleaned of the insurgents' plans – holding the line of the Shannon, marching the northern volunteers to Connacht via Tyrone and Fermanagh (without firing a shot!), even the expectation of a German landing in the west of Ireland, FX made this casual aside: 'It was a Napoleonic plan, but there was no Napoleon to supervise it and no Grande Armée to execute it' (117). Perhaps inadvertently, FX was highlighting, first, the key input into the planning of the Rising: the lessons drawn from the revolutionary and Napoleonic period in Irish history, a period that saw several French descents on Ireland. And second, the example of Napoleon himself, the

---

[25] This point about the impact of the Rising on English perceptions of Irish fighting men is further developed in my 'The Irish at War', in *Culture and Society in Ireland since 1750*, ed. J. Cunningham and N. Ó Ciosáin (Dublin, 2015), 347–58.

humble soldier who conquered half the world and whose story was an inspiration for many of the leaders of the Rising, notably, Patrick Pearse.

Insofar as an overall plan of the Rising can be discerned, it would appear that it owed almost all to that put together by Theobald Wolfe Tone and the French general Lazare Hoche in the 1790s. Very many of the Rising's leaders were steeped in the history of the ill-fated French incursions into Ireland in the 1790s, the course and outcome of the 1798 Rebellion, and the saga of Robert Emmet's failed rising in 1803. Tone's *Memoirs*,[26] with their numerous plans and projects for a French-led Irish invasion with a supporting Irish rebellion, were staple reading among the revolutionaries. The Germans would, it was hoped, take on the mantle of the French, or so Joseph Mary Plunkett and Roger Casement expected from their negotiations with the German High Command. In this they were to be cruelly mistaken, for the Germans had no intention of risking an army on a perilous sea voyage to Ireland – the disastrous British expedition to Gallipoli offering conclusive proof of the near-criminal recklessness of such amphibious landings far from home. Nonetheless, the point remains a fair one: FX had identified the military thinking of the rebel leadership as almost entirely derived from the lessons they had drawn from the period 1793–1815.

With regard to Napoleon, FX was also on sure ground in hinting at his posthumous influence on the rebel leaders. P. H. Pearse, in particular, it may be said, was besotted with Napoleon. At St Enda's, his school at Rathfarnham, he had what amounted to a museum to Napoleon, and the classrooms were decorated with busts and pictures of the great man. Padraic Colum recalled that Pearse's prize possession was a lock of Bonaparte's hair. '[Pearse] used to say', recalled Colum, 'hold your breath now while I'm showing you this.'[27] Not surprisingly, Desmond Ryan, Pearse's first biographer, accepted that Pearse had a Napoleonic complex that 'expressed itself in a fanatical glorification of war for its own sake'.[28] And while in the GPO during Easter Week, an observer noted Pearse as striking 'a Napoleonic attitude with his right hand on his breast'.

In other ways, too, Pearse's admiration for Napoleon was evident. He added lines in Irish to several poems so as to praise the man, and he was

---

[26] Published as long ago as 1826 in Washington, DC, and then reprinted in 1898 in an abridgement edited by Augustine Birrell (who in bizarre coincidence was to be Chief Secretary in 1916).

[27] Padraic Colum, *The Road around Ireland* (New York, 1926), 128.

[28] Ruth Dudley Edwards, *Patrick Pearse: The Triumph of Failure* (London, 1977), 342.

devoted to R. M. Johnston's book *The Corsican*.[29] This was a compilation of a 'diary' by Bonaparte 'derived entirely from Napoleon's own words, written and spoken', and while Johnston candidly admitted that 'it avowedly contravenes ... those rules for the treatment of historical documents', he was nonetheless certain that the book offered 'psychological illumination of a great career'. Pearse took the book with him everywhere. Colum remembered 'being with [Pearse] in the Abbey Theatre and seeing him read during the intervals a book called *The Corsican* that was made up from diaries, proclamations and despatches of Napoleon'. Pronouncements by the great general such as 'the art of warfare does not require complicated manoeuvres; the simplest are the best, and common sense is fundamental' would have been reassuring to Pearse, for though he was Director of Military Operations in the Irish Volunteers, he completely lacked military experience.

***

Rather like FX's lengthy review article, this assessment has, like Topsy, just 'grow'd and grow'd', and in doing so, much apparently extraneous material has been brought in. Yet such tangential digressions can be justified, for FX's essay as well as offering critical takes on most of the prominent publications on the Rising (up to 1966) also, as Charles Townshend notes, laid down 'a research agenda' for further studies. Moreover, in seeking to take the study of the Rising out of politics and into history, he set in train what later would be called (and condemned) as the 'revisionist project'. Indeed, more than twenty years after the publication of his *Studia Hibernica* articles, Pádraig Ó Snodaigh, a constant critic of FX, bracketed him along with Fr Shaw SJ (whose trenchant strictures on the Rising had appeared in 1972) as the 'two godfathers of revisionism'. In reality, FX's writings had little in common with Shaw's 'splenetic debunking' of the Rising, for Shaw was a Celtic scholar and a Jesuit, and his approach was that of a moral theologian, not a historian.[30] FX, by contrast, sought to forensically separate myths from facts and to reveal what had hitherto appeared mysterious about the 1916 Rising.

---

[29] First published in New York in 1910. The French writer Louis Le Roux claimed that Desmond Ryan gave Pearse the book. Le Roux, *Patrick H. Pearse*, trans. Desmond Ryan (Dublin 1932), 47.
[30] Felix Larkin, 'From Mythology to History: FX Martin and the historiography of the 1916 Rising', in *Rebellion and Revolution in Dublin: Voices from a Suburb, Rathfarnham, 1913–23*, ed. M. Hay and D. Keogh (Dublin, 2016), 213–14. My thanks to Mr Larkin for letting me read his article in advance of publication. F. Shaw, 'The Canon of Irish History: A Challenge', *Studies* 66 (1972): 113–57; and see C. Brady, ed., *Interpreting Irish History: The Debate on Historical Revisionism* (Dublin, 1994), 8.

CHAPTER 16

The 'Easter Rising'
Four Fallacies and Some Reflections

David Fitzpatrick

For most Irish people, 1916 signifies the 'Easter Rising' (otherwise rebellion), which caused more than 450 deaths, destroyed much of central Dublin, and radicalized Irish politics. For diverse reasons, this bizarre outbreak is celebrated as the foundation of modern Ireland. Militant republicans revere the rebels as role models, martyrs who vindicated violence without democratic sanction as a political instrument. Conventional politicians, while denying that the rebellion legitimized more recent terrorist campaigns, applaud the rebels for the egalitarian sentiments of the so-called proclamation of the Irish Republic. Most commentators accept that the rebellion, though lacking prior popular support, drew upon deep feelings of resentment against British oppression, latent desire for full independence rather than partial autonomy within the United Kingdom, and romantic attachment to grand gestures rather than plodding compromises. Some maintain that radical nationalism had gained support since the outbreak of European war in August 1914, as Irish casualties and wartime privations multiplied. What else could explain the rapid post-rebellion shift in popular support from John Redmond's Home Rule movement to the republican demands of what became known as Sinn Féin? If nationalists were not unreconciled separatists at heart, why were they so outraged by sixteen executions and the incarceration of a few thousand political dissidents?

Yet this portrayal of wartime Ireland, framed by hindsight, would have been unrecognizable to contemporaries. When Redmond's support for the imperial war effort split the nationalist Irish Volunteers in autumn 1914, only about 10,000 (6 per cent) repudiated Redmond's leadership. Apart from modest recruitment for the Irish Republican Brotherhood, there was little evidence before 1916 of declining nationalist endorsement of the 'constitutionalist' strategy. Most believed that Home Rule, having been enacted in September 1914 but suspended during the war, would indeed be implemented thereafter with some special provision for unionist Ulster.

Both Redmond and the Irish unionist leader Sir Edward Carson had ostentatiously supported the war against Germany, in the hope of strengthening their contending political claims once peace returned. They also sincerely hoped that pushing nationalists and unionists alike into the field of battle would erode domestic animosities and reconcile potential rebels (unionist as well as nationalist) to future coexistence within the Empire. Asquith's Liberal government, even after unionists including Carson were admitted into coalition in May 1915, had done its utmost to avoid alienating nationalists, exempting Ireland from conscription in February 1916.

Prior to the rebellion, this entente seemed to be working quite well. Though military enlistment was sluggish by British standards, about 210,000 men were recruited or mobilized in wartime Ireland. Of these, about 35,000 died (the oft-cited figure of 49,400 includes Irish servicemen raised in Britain or overseas and Britons in Irish regiments). This represented the greatest military deployment in Irish history (about 1,600 rebels 'rose' in 1916 of whom fewer than 100 died). Most nationalist newspapers supported the 'war effort', if less whole-heartedly than their unionist and British counterparts, and numerous Catholic nationalists as well as Protestants backed the boys at the front by knitting socks, working as volunteer nurses, or buying war bonds. Instead of being engulfed in the civil war that had threatened to erupt over Home Rule in 1914, wartime Ireland seemed unexpectedly united.

Far from sowing general disillusionment and stifling enlistment, reports of horrific Irish casualties initially gave extra moral force to Irish pro-war propaganda. Of the three Irish divisions raised for the 'New Armies' in 1914, the first to reach the front line was the Tenth, which played a conspicuous part in the Suvla landings at Gallipoli in August 1915. Its exploits and losses, like those of three Irish regular battalions deployed at the first landings at Helles in April 1915, were promptly mythologized by Redmond's publicists as proof of the irrepressible Irish martial spirit. Yet the Irish sacrifice at Gallipoli never became the focus of national pride as in Australia or New Zealand, partly because the first Gallipoli (Anzac) Day was also Easter Tuesday 1916.[1] Nor did later nationalist generations extol the gallantry of the Sixteenth (Irish) division at Guillemont or Ginchy in September 1916.

---

[1] David Fitzpatrick, 'Imperial Loyalties: Irishmen, Anzacs, and the Conflict of Empires at Gallipoli', *The Irish Sword* 30.121 (2016): 305–31.

The nearest Irish counterpart to the Anzac cult was instead centred on 1 July 1916, the first day of battle at the Somme, in which the Thirty-sixth (Ulster) division fought with undeniable if reckless courage at Thiepval. The division suffered almost 2,000 fatalities in July 1916, just exceeding the Tenth division's losses at Gallipoli. The fact that most of these Ulster soldiers were recruited from Carson's Ulster Volunteer Force, many being Orangemen, made it simple to link their cause with William of Orange's triumph at the Boyne (on 1 July 1690) and the pursuit of 'civil and religious liberty'. For unionist Ulster, the charge of the Ulster Division was a potent proof of Ulster's commitment to King and Constitution. Commemoration of the battles of the Boyne and the Somme was quickly fused, being as fundamental for the new state of Northern Ireland founded in 1921 as the 'Easter Rising' was for the Irish Free State.

In portraying Ireland's 1916, we must therefore incorporate several narratives apart from the 'terrible beauty' of Yeats's Easter rebels. For unionists, the rebellion confirmed deep-seated suspicions, highlighting Ulster's deeper patriotism as exhibited a few weeks later at the Somme. For Home Rulers, still predominant among Irish Catholics, the rebellion was an external shock with profound consequences but shallow historical roots, whereby a few dissidents skilfully exploited popular emotions to discredit rational nationalism. Though many Redmondites were eventually 'converted' to Sinn Féin's doctrine of 'self-determination', their pragmatic outlook prevailed in 1921–22 when most self-determinators accepted an Irish Free State of twenty-six counties within the British Empire. All of these narratives have resurfaced in events and debates prompted by the centennium, demonstrating that the bequest of 1916 remains as ambiguous and contested as ever.

***

Yet it would be naïve to suppose that the recent orgy of centennial commemoration has transformed public perceptions of 1916 from narrowly nationalist celebration to modishly pluralist self-questioning. Instead, the predominant outcome of both official and private commemoration in the Republic of Ireland has been to reinforce the belief that the rebellion was a noble, patriotic, and justified act of collective sacrifice, tainted only by the failure of subsequent generations to act on the prescriptions of the 'proclamation' issued on Easter Monday. Social critics extolled its aspirations for 'cherishing all the children of the nation equally', abolishing distinctions according to sex or religion, and pursuing the creation of a republic representing all citizens of a pre-existing Irish nation, suppressed by centuries of occupation and oppression.

The proclamation was cited as a stark reminder of the nation's failure to complete a social revolution by eliminating internal divisions 'carefully fostered by an alien government'. Child-abuse lobbyists repeatedly misrepresented the 'children' of the proclamation as juveniles rather than citizens, until quashed by Emeritus Professor John A. Murphy's painstaking corrective manifestos. Critics of Brexit exulted in the reference to 'gallant allies in Europe', and proponents of votes for emigrants rejoiced that Pearse's nation embraced Ireland's 'exiled children in America'. Radicals, socialists, and feminists all used the foundation text to berate politicians for their conservatism and timidity, a line disingenuously taken up by almost all politicians to discredit each other. Irish public debate thus resembled a conclave of fundamentalist Christians, squabbling about the true meaning of the Gospel, excoriating rival sects as traitors and sinners, yet all affirming an unshakeable devotion to the sacred text.

One of the oddest aspects of this collective obsession with belatedly implementing the revolutionary urtext was the widespread belief that the debate itself was a triumphant proof of Ireland's new-found maturity and pluralism. Previous governments and parties, it was implied, would never have had the courage to point out the radical and feminist strands in early republicanism. In fact, the involvement of socialists and women in the rebellion had been recognized and celebrated throughout the preceding century. The 'Connolly tradition' of 1916 had long been invoked by socialist and Labour advocates and historians in their aspiration to transform a Free State or pseudo-republic into a 'workers' republic'. Ever since R. M. Fox's *Rebel Irishwomen* (1935), historical accounts of the rebellion had given perhaps exaggerated attention to the 'neglected' involvement of women. This tendency had been accelerated, not ignored or retarded, by the jubilee celebrations in 1966.[2] Cumann na mBan veterans were represented on local jubilee committees; post-primary scholarships were sponsored for ten girls in recognition of 'the part played by women in Ireland's historic fight for freedom', including 'women fighters'; 100 girls from the Dublin Camogie Association appeared in a commemorative pageant at

[2] Roisín Higgins, *Transforming 1916: Meaning, Memory and the Fiftieth Anniversary of the Easter Rising* (Cork, 2012). Higgins, while supplying evidence of the involvement of women in the official commemoration, deplores the fact that 'the historical position of women during the Easter Rising was not used as a way of forcing debate on the position of women in the 1960s' (82). The issues of gender and class are virtually ignored in Mary E. Daly and Margaret O'Callaghan, eds., *1916 in 1966: Commemorating the Easter Rising* (Dublin, 2007).

Croke Park; and 200 women were among the 1,800 Dublin veterans assembled opposite the General Post Office (GPO) on Easter Sunday.[3] Though limited in scope, the prominence given to women in the jubilee undermines the smug belief that only the globalized Ireland of 2016 was sufficiently grown-up to cherish all the metaphorical children of the imagined nation equally.

Essential to the official programme, and allocation of its €48 million budget, was the need to avoid triumphalism through various balancing acts. One should celebrate not merely actors but victims, civilians as well as fighters, police and military as well as rebels. The adoption of multiple historical perspectives and sites for re-enactment was undoubtedly an advance. Likewise, the attempt to counterbalance celebration of the rebellion with respectful interest in the Thirty-sixth (Ulster) Division's destruction at the Somme was preferable to rigid partisan demarcation between the commemoration of these episodes (as practised in Northern Ireland). The pursuit of balance further required inclusion of the exploits of the Sixteenth (Irish) division at Guillemont and Ginchy. Here again there was nothing new, such parallels having been drawn by the late F. X. Martin in 1968, Edna Longley in 1992, the late Keith Jeffery in 2000, and many others.[4]

Yet a deep moral imbalance remained between celebration of the rebellion as a noble if flawed assertion of sovereignty, and denigration of Irish involvement in the Great War as a catastrophic error resultant from deception and manipulation of the masses by unscrupulous politicians. In retrospect, most agreed that the Great War was an avoidable tragedy in which all the major powers were complicit and in which all those who served were their victims. By contrast, the rebellion was depicted as a triumphant demonstration of the capacity of a nation accustomed to victimhood to seize control of its destiny through acts of personal heroism and calculated violence. The effect of this polar analysis was to rob those who served in the Great War of the dignity attached to moral actors making rational choices and to exaggerate the agency and rationality of rebels who were, in many cases, duped and manipulated by their secretive and deceitful leaders, the signatories of the 'proclamation'.

---

[3] *Irish Times*, 4 and 19 Feb., 18 March 1966; *Irish Press*, 11 April 1966; see also Higgins, *Transforming 1916*, 45, 53, 118.

[4] F. X. Martin, '1916 – Myth, Fact, and Mystery', *Studia Hibernica* 7 (1967 [1968]): 7–126 (esp. 62–65); Edna Longley, 'The Rising, the Somme, and Irish Memory', in *Revising the Rising*, ed. Máirín Ní Dhonnchadha and Theo Dorgan (Derry, 1991), 29–49; Keith Jeffery, *Ireland and the Great War* (Cambridge, 2000), chapters 2 and 4.

Even though the prevailing commemorative narrative owes much to tradition, in substance if less in language, it has been accompanied by a truly impressive explosion of public engagement with matters once the preserve of teachers and historians. Encouraged by the digital release of sources such as testimony for the Bureau of Military History and military pension files, thousands of lay researchers have developed expertise on personal experiences of the rebellion and the Great War, often linking historical records with their own family or local background. Scores of exhibitions in museums and libraries throughout the country, even north of the border, have made photographs, letters, and artefacts accessible to the public. 'Roadshows' and public appeals have unearthed many more valuable documents in private hands for copying and return.

Tens of thousands of Irish people and tourists have participated in public re-enactments, masquerading as the contending forces of 1916. Tourists were shepherded around Dublin on '1916 tours' featuring barricades and military sites. Tacky 1916 souvenirs, republican kitsch, and glossy pseudo-histories abounded, soon to be consigned to bargain basements. Art installations, some votive, some parodic, have colonized parks and public spaces as well as galleries. The artistic parodists included Rita Duffy, whose 'emporium of objects for sale, from Countess Markievicz dress-up dolls (ball gown or military uniform?) to Lady Lavatory and Imperial Palaver soaps and Black and Tan boot polish' so delighted Fintan O'Toole. Architects of the official programme such as Maurice Manning, chairman of the 'expert advisory group', have rightly celebrated the resultant 'democratization of access to our historical sources' and, one might add, democratization of history-making.[5]

Yet democratization has come at a price. Giddy with the discovery of documents and personal stories, private commemorators have understandably fallen back on familiar narratives to provide a framework for understanding them. In this they have been enthusiastically assisted by curators, re-enactors, and academics, feeding the insatiable public demand for reassuring platitudes dressed up as postmodern insights. As public interest fades, conscientious scholars may revert to their proper function as cautiously revisionist critics and blushing subverters of accepted wisdom, for which their reward will be academic acclaim, public indifference, and a sense of selfless virtue. Meanwhile, let them enjoy their place in the setting sun!

***

[5] *Centenary Conversations*, supplement to *Irish Times* (29 Sept. 2016).

In order to highlight what went wrong in the centennial commemoration of what is generally remembered as the 'proclamation of the Irish Republic' and the 'Easter Rising', let me address four fairly obvious yet widely held fallacies concerning these events.

1. The term 'rising', according to the *Concise Oxford Dictionary*, has multiple meanings: 'resurrection; insurrection, revolt; boil, pimple'. With its dual connotations of Pearse's 'risen people' and Christ's ascent from the dead, 'rising' has become the favoured word for describing what erupted in Dublin on 24 April 1916. Yet contemporaries almost universally called it a 'rebellion' or an 'insurrection' (signifying 'an incipient rebellion'). The terms 'rebellion' and 'rebel' were used proudly by participants, while the phrase 'Ireland ... strikes for her freedom' was preferred in the first declaration of the provisional government. The word 'rising' appears only in its second declaration: 'The country is rising in answer to Dublin's call, and the final achievement of Ireland's freedom is now, with God's help, only a matter of days.' Yet God failed to help and the country did not rise.

2. Strictly speaking, no rebellion occurred in Dublin at Easter 1916, Christ's resurrection having been celebrated on the previous day (Easter Monday has no religious significance). The rebels had indeed planned to strike on Easter Sunday, despite the inevitable disruption of church services, with the intention of dramatizing Pearse's linkage of the national and Christian resurrection narratives. Eoin MacNeill's countermand of mobilization may have postponed the outbreak beyond Easter, yet later generations have found the liturgical association irresistible.

3. No 'proclamation of the Irish Republic' was read out by Pearse from the non-existent steps of the GPO or posted around Dublin on 24 April 1916. Not could it have been, because the signatories had already sworn 'allegiance to the Supreme Council of the Irish Republican Brotherhood and Government of the Irish Republic'.[6] What was actually proclaimed was 'the Irish Republic as a Sovereign Independent State', the second stage in an interminable process.[7]

---

[6] This passage appeared in the oath administered to initiates of the Irish Republican Brotherhood after 17 March 1873, slightly varying the formula in the Supreme Council's message of 24 April 1868: T. W. Moody and Leon Ó Broin, 'The I.R.B. Supreme Council, 1868–78', *Irish Historical Studies* 19.75 (1975): 286–332 (esp. 299, 304, 314).

[7] Though the word 'proclamation' does *not* appear in the Easter Monday address, a second address was issued to 'the Citizens of Dublin on the momentous occasion of the proclamation of a Sovereign Independent Irish State now in course of being established by Irishmen in Arms'. This was loosely recapitulated in the final paragraph: 'We have lived to see an Irish Republic proclaimed. May we live

4. It therefore seems reasonable to conclude that there was no 'Easter Rising' and no 'proclamation of the Irish Republic' in 1916. Surely, though, as W. B. Yeats put it, 'all' had been 'changed, changed utterly' by whatever did occur? Alas, no. As the syntax of 'Easter 1916' makes clear, what Yeats believed to have been 'changed utterly' was not Ireland but the reputation of those who had organized the rebellion, the people 'with vivid faces' whom he used to mock at the club (shrill-voiced Constance Markievicz, that 'drunken, vainglorious lout' John MacBride). Just in case readers had been intoxicated by his rhetoric into imagining that Ireland too had been changed, Yeats painstakingly wrote 'it out in a verse' all over again, naming four signatories as individuals who were 'changed utterly: a terrible beauty is born'. That beauty, as the colon proclaims, resided not in post-rebellion Ireland but in the personal transfiguration of the rebels.

***

It may be objected that these points are merely pedantic, having no bearing on the deeper significance of the rebellion. On closer inspection, they illuminate some of the most tendentious aspects of 1916 commemoration over the intervening century up to the present day.

1. By adopting the term 'rising', celebrants claimed the legacy of previous 'risings' in 1798, 1848, and 1867, confirming the nation's supposedly unsatiated desire to overthrow British rule by force. The official commemoration concentrated on the connection with 1848. Every school in the Republic was presented with a national flag (based on Meagher's tricolour raised in 1848), secondary schools being supplied by the American-sponsored Thomas Francis Meagher Foundation.[8] Associated epithets such as 'the risen people' also elided the actual conflict of April 1916 with the subsequent revolution, a prolonged process of realignment shaped by many other factors only loosely connected with the rebellion. These included the exercise of arbitrary coercion, Lloyd George's subsequent attempt to implement partition, the botched threat of conscription in 1918, and the novel possibility (however remote) of winning independence through a

to establish it firmly'; facsimiles in *Sinn Féin Rebellion Handbook* (Dublin, *Weekly Irish Times*, 1916), 1, 4a.

[8] For antecedents of the tricolour, see Brian Hand, 'The Fabric of a Deathless Dream: A Short Introduction to the Origins and Meanings of the 1916 Tricolour Flag', in *Making 1916: Material and Visual Culture of the Easter Rising*, ed. Lisa Godson and Joanna Brück (Liverpool, 2015), 16–24.

post-war peace conference rather than Westminster. Though the rebellion had a significant part in generating these threats and opportunities, most would eventually have applied even in its absence. It follows that the very word 'rising', ubiquitous in commemoration, seriously exaggerates its influence on Ireland's future, as well as its continuity with Ireland's past.

2. The spurious association with Easter encouraged devout celebrants to accept unquestioningly the rebellion narrative of self-sacrifice, resurrection, and national redemption. This narrative is deeply misleading, because it suppresses several inconvenient facts. Most of those 'sacrificed' in 1916 were neither rebels nor their opponents, but civilians. Though Pearse protested that his belated surrender was designed to avoid 'the further slaughter of Dublin citizens',[9] the rebels had knowingly initiated the conflict in a crowded residential and business district, which was bound to cause civilian carnage. By adopting the Easter motif, celebrants made it easier for Catholics to accept the morality of the rebellion despite its glaring disregard of Catholic doctrine. This precluded the use of force without a popular mandate, an intolerably oppressive government, the exhaustion of non-violent alternatives, and a reasonable prospect of success. None of these conditions applied in April 1916: even Birrell's wartime government had proved to be surprisingly mild despite much goading from the Irish Volunteers. The association with Easter was asserted so strongly in 2016 that the main official ceremonies and the associated Dublin parade were held, as in 1966,[10] on Easter Sunday (27 March). Contrary to the ecumenical ethos of the proclamation, however, this schedule resulted in forced abandonment of the most solemn religious services of the year in the two Church of Ireland cathedrals, yet not in the Catholic pro-cathedral.

3. The supposed 'proclamation of the Irish Republic' has caused untold mischief by inviting every republican faction to claim the Easter inheritance and by linking republican ideals to those of 'her secret revolutionary organization, the Irish Republican Brotherhood', the very antithesis of democratic thinking. As a secretive self-perpetuating elite, actually preferring the use of force to any inclusive political

---

[9] Pearse's order of 27 April 1916 did *not* accept responsibility for civilian deaths, offering unconditional surrender 'in order to prevent the further slaughter of Dublin citizens, and in the hope of saving the lives of our followers now surrounded and hopelessly outnumbered': facsimile in *Rebellion Handbook*, 4.

[10] *Irish Times*, 11 April 1966; Higgins, *Transforming 1916*, 37.

process, the Irish Republican Brotherhood and its 1916 advocates provided a grimly appropriate example for future devotees of 'physical force', as confirmed by the murder of a Northern Ireland prison officer by the 'New IRA' shortly before Easter 2016. The misleading phrase 'proclamation of the Irish Republic' was repeated ad nauseam. All schools were supplied with versions in Irish as well as English, and Trinity College published dozens of centennial translations into Russian, Chinese, Arabic, Turkish, and thirteen other languages on its votive website. The anachronistic treatment of the proclamation as a document for our own times was central to school commemoration, pupils being invited to enter a competition to invent a 'proclamation for a new generation' in English, Irish, or any other language. In primary schools, it was directed that 'a member of the Defence Forces will present the national flag in a short ceremony that will involve a reading and explanation of the Proclamation, an outline of the history of the national flag and its correct protocols'. The flag was again to be 'prominently' displayed in all schools on 'Proclamation Day' (15 March). The militaristic theme was even more prominent than in 1966, when flags and proclamations were likewise distributed throughout the school network but without army involvement.[11]

4. The incantation 'all changed, changed utterly', apart from being a blatant misrepresentation of Yeats's words, also conveys a grossly simplified vision of Ireland's subsequent history. Scholars have spent decades showing how little changed after the rebellion and subsequent revolution, which so conspicuously failed to eliminate clientelism, 'Anglicization', economic stagnation, social inequality, and religious intolerance. Here, at last, I find common ground with those who have written of a proclamation (and a revolution) betrayed. Historians have continued to collude in the fantasy that all was 'changed utterly' by the rebellion and that by coining this phrase Yeats had offered a deep historical insight. The tag gave its name to a History Ireland 'hedge school' in the National Library, an autumn schools conference arranged for the National Museum, and an exhibition in Trinity College. The Irish ambassador to Hungary, when likening the significance of the 'Easter Rising' to that of Hungary's 1848 revolution, felt that 'Yeats summed it up perfectly in his famous words'.[12] Even Roy

---

[11] *Irish Times*, 22 April 1916; Higgins, *Transforming 1916*, 48–49.
[12] Events scheduled for 8 and 16 Nov. (postponed because of industrial action to Jan. 2017), 26 Feb., and 2 Sept. 2016.

Foster endorsed this interpretation of 'changed utterly' in his *Vivid Faces*.[13] Furthermore, Foster's sympathetic and affectionate depiction of the 'revolutionary generation', most of whom had no part in the rebellion, gave credence to the rebels by treating them as products of a great cultural and imaginative upsurge of independent minds escaping the torpid intellectual atmosphere of Redmondite nationalism. Foster recognized, however, that the imaginative sweep of the 1916 'generation' left little imprint on the practical conduct of revolution in 1919–21: 'The mature revolution was far more monocultural, and more ethnically defined, than the pre-revolution.'[14] For historians, as for the public, 1916 nostalgia remains a powerful unifying sentiment.

***

One of the most striking oddities of the popular and official commemorative consensus was its sentimental militarism, echoing that of the rebels and thus tending to vindicate the use of violence for political ends. This was evident in the prominent part taken by the Irish army in the Easter Sunday parade and other events. A military band played 'Danny Boy' and 'Mise Éire', an army officer read the proclamation, and the president and the taoiseach reviewed a procession including the Defence Force, police, fire brigade, prison service, and ambulance officers.[15] The military trappings of the official programme mollified Sinn Féin, which in the Republic (but not always in Northern Ireland) was happy to concentrate on the egalitarian aspirations of the rebels, rather than on their iconic status as military exemplars for later generations of IRA 'volunteers'. Sinn Féin abandoned its provocative plan to beam tricolour lights on to the GPO and belatedly absolved itself of responsibility for a mawkishly sinister exhibition at the Ambassador Theatre, 'Revolution 1916'. For €15, customers were invited to:

> Follow in the footsteps of the 1916 leaders as you travel back in time. Relive the Rising in a series of special sets from the GPO, to Moore St and then take the final walk from the condemned cell in Kilmainham to the stonebreakers yard. View the largest private collection of 1916 artefacts and

---

[13] 'When Yeats completed "Easter 1916" in the September of that year, the next phase of the revolution still hung in the balance; but ... [by 1921] those quiet Dublin streets conjured up at the beginning of Yeats's poem would be "utterly changed" in their way': R. F. Foster, *Vivid Faces: The Revolutionary Generation in Ireland, 1890–1923* (London, 2014), 25.
[14] Ibid., xxiii. [15] *Irish Times*, 28 March 2016.

weapons from the Irish Volunteers organization including original proclamation, Howth Mausers and Michael Collins's gun.[16]

The marriage of convenience between Sinn Féin and its political rivals was
only slightly spoiled by dissident republicans, who clear-headedly lauded
the men of 1916 as pioneers of urban terrorism rather than self-sacrificing
idealists with 'vivid faces'. A montage of the rebel leaders briefly displayed
as a poster in Newry starkly made the point that they should be revered as
killers, not sacrificial victims.[17] Very few historians or public figures
questioned the militaristic tone of the commemorative programme. An
exception was John Bruton, so often at odds with public opinion even
when taoiseach, yet implacably rational:

> I question whether we should treat the 1916 Rising and Proclamation as the
> foundation event of our democracy – as we did this year.... Instead of using
> the official ritual of 1916 commemoration to rekindle our national ideology
> around something that was inherently unrealisable, we should instead
> commemorate the entire process that led to our present statehood, with
> special emphasis on the landmarks that did not involve the use of force.[18]

This certainly was not the message of the taoiseach who was in office
during the commemorations. In his address when opening a Witness
History interpretative centre at the GPO, Enda Kenny resorted to a string
of republican clichés in 'phoenix flame' mode:

> It was on this site, 100 years ago, that Padraig Pearse read aloud the
> Proclamation of the Irish Republic in an act of brave defiance that lit the
> touchpaper leading to the culmination of centuries of struggle for Irish
> freedom. From the ashes of the Rising, the subsequent War of Independ-
> ence, and Civil War arose a free and democratic Irish state.... We owe
> much credit to the early nation builders who built up our public institu-
> tions as unassailable pillars of democracy.[19]

His interpretation was guided by eminent historians. In March 2015, the
late Professor Ronan Fanning had called provocatively for 'shameless
celebration' of this 'seminal moment in the birth of the Irish republic',

---

[16] Flyer, promising 'live reading of the proclamation every day at Monday outside the theatre', and
offering tickets on www.revolution1916.ie (punctuation and apostrophe *sic*; website now defunct).

[17] Poster observed by the author from a bus to Dublin airport on 21 April 2016, but removed before
his return journey, camera at the ready, three days later. The poster juxtaposed an image of the
signatories with one of modern 'volunteers' in Balaclavas. An election for the Northern Ireland
Assembly was held on 5 May.

[18] *Centenary Conversations.*   [19] *Irish Times*, 26 March 2016.

asserting (as if it were self-evident) that no 'British government would have ceded power to a native Irish government without the use of violence'.[20]

In the wake of the 1916 centenary, let us be wary of the seductive deceptions that continue to disguise the less savoury aspects of this momentous event. With six years to come of the 'decade of centenaries', there will be many further opportunities to revisit, reinterpret, and twist past events in pursuit of a better future. As the focus of commemoration moves from mass mobilization to terror and counter-terror, and on to partition and civil war, it will be increasingly difficult to establish any consensual narrative of events, even one so problematic as the heroic version of Easter 1916. Will the effort prove to be worthwhile?

[20] Address to Fine Gael national conference, Castlebar, 21 Feb. 2015: *Irish Times*, 2 March 2015.

CHAPTER 17

Late Style Irish Style
Contemporary Irish Poetry and the Problem of Belatedness
Clair Wills

Was Parnellism the end of something or a beginning? As with most either/ or questions the safest way to respond is probably with 'both', or perhaps 'neither'. So Roy Foster argues in Chapter 3 in this volume that Yeats's well-known claim that 'the modern literature of Ireland, and indeed all that stir of thought which prepared for the Anglo-Irish war, began when Parnell fell from power'[1] has blinded us to the persistence of political activity in the years after 1891, and particularly that associated with women. Joep Leerssen locates the idea of new beginnings – revival, rising, renaissance – in the context of broader European developments; by emphasizing the comparative aspects of European national-reformist movements, he shows how Irish beginnings and endings should themselves be understood as part of a larger cultural geography. Nonetheless, with the benefit of a bit less hindsight than we can muster today, the sense that Parnell's fall caused a decisive break in Ireland's political history seemed clear to his contemporaries, the Irish writers and politicians who outlived him. And it was not merely that parliamentary politics could no longer be thought of as on the side of Ireland's future, but that past and future were divided on generational lines. Joyce's *A Portrait of the Artist as a Young Man* neatly dramatizes the argument Yeats made in his Nobel Prize-winning speech (indeed, perhaps the example was in his mind) as the young Dedalus turns from the melancholy politics of his Parnellite father ('Poor Parnell! he cried loudly. My dead king!') to devote himself to an art fitted for 'the uncreated conscience' of his race. Across Europe young male writers (Rilke, Conrad, Mann) were engaged in the same rejection of past authority, figured in the new genre of the *Künstlerroman* and its

---

[1] 'The Irish Dramatic Movement' (1923), reprinted in W. B. Yeats, *Autobiographies* (London, 1955), 559.

refusal of social 'Bildung'.[2] But in Ireland that refusal was couched in post-Parnellite terms.

If Irish youth was on the side of revolution (political revolution and the revolution of the word), this was not because Irish age was wedded to reformist and ameliorist versions of social progress, but because progress in itself appeared to have stalled. Joyce's representation of Irish political and cultural life as in a state of paralysis was a critique of the older generation for *not* having given way to the present, for continuing its ghostly existence beyond its time. It may be indicative that both the fathers of Yeats and Joyce chose to live the last decades of their lives in what Colm Tóibín has called 'a sort of aftermath',[3] accepting they were part of a generation that had been surpassed. John B. Yeats died in New York in 1922, having spent the last fifteen years of his life separated from his family and living in a boarding house. W. B. Yeats diagnosed in him a 'lack of will'. John Stanislaus Joyce died in 1931 in a Dublin boarding house, and did not see either of his eldest sons for the last nineteen years of his life. His son James identified in him a lack of 'courage'. It is surely no accident that the ghostly aftermath in which these men spent their old age coincided with Ireland's youthful beginnings as an independent country. Their own youth had run in parallel with Ireland's struggle to construct its history as one of self-making rather than serial defeat and acquiescence. As the past generation they were placed in an impossible bind, both preparers and makers of emancipation, and by default those who had failed to secure freedom. They were both too early for the national movement and too late.[4] They were at the beginning of something, but they outlasted its end.

Parnell himself has figured as a symbol of the anachronistic and untimely in Irish literary history. For Yeats the proud, heroic figure of Parnell stood for all that was antithetical to what he regarded as the corruptions of the hypocrisy-ridden, democratic Christian age. Parnell was a 'self-creating' individual, in the mould of Synge, Swift, and a gallery of other Protestant heroes, able to master his wayward Celtic temperament through silence and reserve. Yeats particularly liked recounting one story of

---

[2] See, for example, Joseph Conrad, *Youth* (1898), Thomas Mann, *Tonio Kröger* (1903), Rainer Maria Rilke, *The Notebooks of Malte Laurids Brigge* (1910). See also Franco Moretti on the crisis of the European *Bildungsroman*, in the appendix to *The Way of the World: The Bildungsroman in European Culture* (London, 1987).

[3] Colm Tóibín, *Mad, Bad, Dangerous to Know: The Fathers of Wilde, Yeats and Joyce* (New York, 2018).

[4] For a discussion of the life of John B. Yeats in the context of his contemporary Henry James's preoccupation with the idea of being 'too late', see my review of Tóibín's book: Clair Wills, 'Prodigal Fathers', *New York Review of Books*, 20 Dec. 2018.

Parnell's habits of self-conquest, namely, that when giving a speech at the Rotunda in Dublin in 1890 he clenched his hands so tightly that his palms bled. The garrulous and undisciplined Irish public, he argued, were drawn to 'the solitary and proud Parnell as to her anti-self'.[5] Parnell symbolized everything that the Irish people were not, and for that very reason they needed to destroy him. Yeats puts it pithily in his 1934 poem 'Parnell's Funeral', where he represents the popular crowd as a pack of hounds, dragging down a noble stag.

> An age is the reversal of an age:
> When strangers murdered Emmet, Fitzgerald, Tone,
> We lived like men that watch a painted stage.
> What matter for the scene, the scene once gone:
> It had not touched our lives. But popular rage,
> *Hysterica passio* dragged this quarry down.
> None shared our guilt; nor did we play a part
> Upon a painted stage when we devoured his heart.

An age is the reversal of an age. The concept of lateness is not easily squared with the theory of history as a series of cycles, reversing and superseding one another, which was central to Yeats's view of civilization. Lateness presumes a continuum, if not necessarily a teleology, a point in time when it is possible to be 'late' or even 'too late'. If time proceeds as a series of cycles, how do we tell whether, when we appear to be late, we may not in fact be too early?

Elsewhere in this volume Joep Leerssen has discussed the general sense, at the turn of the twentieth century, of European literature's 'historical belatedness'. Yeats's rejection of any alliance with decadence (the 'old age and coming decline' of English literature) was based on his belief that Irish literature was still in its formative stages ('we are a young nation with unexhausted material lying within us'). His argument is not so different from the claim in the 1916 Proclamation that precisely because they have come late to history, and have understood its unexhausted material, the revolutionaries could form the vanguard of the future, repurposing the past in the present. 'In every generation the Irish people have asserted their right to national freedom and sovereignty; six times during the past three hundred years they have asserted it in arms.' The Rising is therefore timely – it has to happen in the current generation. But it is also untimely,

---

[5] See W. B. Yeats, *Autobiographies* (London, 1955), 195. For a discussion of this passage, see David Dwan, *The Great Community: Culture and Nationalism in Ireland* (Dublin, 2008), 189–99.

in that through the rebels' actions speak 'the dead generations through which [Ireland] achieves her old tradition of nationhood'.

In what follows I want to address this idea of productive anachronism by considering literary belatedness, and my focus will be primarily on contemporary writing. My title alludes to the Palestinian critic Edward Said's last book *Late Style* and to his interpretation of Theodor Adorno's essay on late Beethoven.[6] Said begins his reflections on lateness with some thoughts on the idea of timeliness in general, and particularly our sense that certain behaviours, certain ideas, certain events, are appropriate to particular stages in life. So the death of a child seems more tragic than the death of an elderly person; or the lusty behaviour of an old man more embarrassing than that of a young one. It is precisely this form of anachronism that Said favoured in his account of late style. Rather than privileging reconciliation and serenity, harmony and resolution as the mellow fruits of a ripe old age, he prizes the knobbly, spiky, inedible products of maturity, art that insists on its own contradictory and alienated relationship with the social order of which it is a part. Adorno's example was the disorderly, fragmented, nature of Beethoven's late masterpieces, which still remember, but with extraordinary distortions, the usual musical forms; for Said it was Lampedusa's 1958 novel *The Leopard*, with its emphasis on social disintegration, the failure of revolution, irredeemable stasis, and the end of a whole way of life, or the dislocated, studiedly anachronistic poems of Constantine Cavafy.

It is in this sense that Parnell, Yeats's intransigent hero, might be said to be an example of wilful and productive anachronism. In the 1913 poem 'To a Shade' Yeats addresses Parnell as an 'unquiet wanderer' who is both too late and too early for the Ireland of his time: Yeats tells him to go back to the grave since 'the time for you to taste of that salt breath / and listen at the corners has not come'. The unseasonable figure of Parnell chimes with the sudden experiences of understanding and enlightenment which, as so often in Yeats's poetry, are untimely moments, moments which, as he puts it in 'The Cold Heaven', are both 'out of season' and 'out of all sense and reason.'

The emphasis on untimeliness rather than tardiness is helpful in expanding and moving beyond the biographical sense of late style. As Said was at pains to point out, the concept of lateness brings with it all the dangers of addressing works of art as though they were merely expressions

---

[6] Edward W. Said, *On Late Style* (London, 2006). See also Theodor W. Adorno, *Essays on Music*, ed. Richard Leppert (Berkeley, 2002).

of personality, the result of a maturing sensibility. Yes, he holds on to the belief that being near the end, close to death, almost exiled from the experience of life as continuum, is what precipitates the new idiom characteristic of late style. But what is important about late style is its uncompromising, disillusioned commentary on the present. The detachment of the late stylist is not simply a matter of existential fatigue. It reflects a culture which itself is disintegrating. In the face of that decay, late style sets aside consolation, accepts irredeemable loss, denies us the comforts of an optimistic humanism; Said says it is 'without synthesis, transcendence or hope'. It renders disenchantment, yet also pleasure, without resolving the conflict between them.

***

The question of resolution lies at the heart of Derek Mahon's poem 'Dreams of a Summer Night' – a poem that explicitly references Said's concept of late style. Mahon's recent work pits the writer's biographical sense of lateness (lateness as personal, as age) against a broader cultural consciousness of belatedness – the sense that we are all late modern individuals, inhabiting a late planet, all too soon to be overcome by the corruptions we have visited upon it. It is 'late' poetry, preoccupied with the current ecological crisis, and dealing surprisingly directly with issues such as climate change. In the face of our complicity with the industrialization and commodification of life and landscape, our fondness for air travel and 'third world' tourism, for example, which is both a means of escape and a heightened form of consumerism, Mahon weighs up the rival claims of science and art as responses to global catastrophe.

'Dreams of a Summer Night' is positioned as the last poem in the 2011 volume, *New Collected Poems*. Mahon finds himself up late on a June night, in Kinsale, a small town on the coast of West Cork, when the light never really fails. As the girls sleep upstairs in the house, he puts on Mozart's oboe concerto, KV 134.

> It's far from what Said meant by late style
> Since it was written by a twenty year old;
> But I'm late listening, taking it all in
> Like a dreamt 'gentle concord' in the world.[7]

---

[7] Derek Mahon, *New Collected Poems* (Oldcastle, 2011); further quotations are from this edition. See also Mahon, *Against the Clock* (Oldcastle, 2018).

For a composer dead at thirty-five, perhaps the work produced in his twenties could be characterized as late, but this, as Mahon points out, is hardly the point. Mozart is now, by default, late-listened-to, interpreted in the context of a decadent late capitalist culture, in which it is impossible to separate mobility from consumerism, from the destruction of the planet, and from what has recently been termed the globalization of indifference. Mahon is making the same point as Said here – that lateness has less to do with individual biography than we might think. It is a consequence of an artist's ability to recognize a culture's belatedness.

The question of whether art can offer redress or resolution is central to the poem. That gentle concord echoes Theseus's question to Lysander at the end of *A Midsummer Night's Dream*:

> I know you two are rival enemies.
> How comes this gentle concord in the world . . .?

How come you and Demetrius aren't still trying to murder each other, as you were yesterday? It is an image of the way that magical artifice, the work of poetry or music or dream, may reconcile irreconcilables. In fact, the idea of reconciliation is mostly figured in the poem through the work of Ingmar Bergman, not only *Smiles on a Summer Night* (Bergman's own version of *Midsummer's Night's Dream*), but also *Wild Strawberries*. Bergman's 1957 film is the story of an old man coming to terms through memory (and something more than memory: the re-realization of the past in waking dreams) with the crises and mistakes of his youth. The lonely and irascible Isak Borg journeys from Stockholm to his home university of Lund to receive an honorary degree, and on the way encounters his past (his childhood, youth, and unhappy marriage) as though it was still present and unchanged. *Wild Strawberries* offers the viewer a famously disturbing and much-copied series of images of being out of season or out of time – in particular the clock face without hands, which punctuates the nightmares in which Isak questions the boundary between the living and the dead. Yet the film as a whole works its way towards wholeness, at the very least completion. As Isak says towards the end of the film, after the day's real and dream events have unfolded: 'I caught myself in the middle of the ceremony turning the events of the day over in my mind. It was then that I decided I would recollect and record everything that had transpired. In this chain of events, randomly scrambled together, I thought I could make out a most remarkable causality.' A chain of events, randomly scrambled together – it is this kind of anti-chronological, ahistorical causality which interests Mahon, who charts his own series of waking nightmares through the poem. We may be out of season geographically, ecologically, and morally, but he holds to his faith in the critical function of art.

This is lateness in the sense of completeness, or at the very least acceptance of the broken whole – the gentle concord born of the long night of the summer solstice when late is never too late, when darkness never really comes. Mahon's poem sets up a relatively simple distinction between the world seared with trade and bleared, smeared with toil (echoing Gerard Manley Hopkins), a world of war and oil, on the one hand, and the soul's imaginings, on the other. The poem asks whether, after the Irish gold rush and slump, after 'the global hurricane, the rule of money', it is down to dream, and to poetry, to take on the task of being 'instrumental in the soul's increase'. If all this sounds a bit wet, Mahon is all too aware of that fact. He tries to undercut our scepticism by accusing himself of being soppy in the course of the poem – yet he ends by holding to the efficacy of what he calls his 'seasonable dreams', 'to keep me right and ward of disbelief'. In fact, in what looks like a direct challenge to Yeats's analogy in 'The Cold Heaven' between being out of season and being out of all sense and reason, Mahon rhymes reasonable with seasonable in the poem, and not just once.

I do not offer this reading of 'Dreams of a Summer Night' as an example of late style so much as an explicit reflection on the concept. What Mahon is confronted by in these recent elegiac poems, obsessed with the effects of climate change and the devastation of the planet, is the way that irony and disbelief collude with the forces of corruption. The straightforwardly positive invocation of *Wild Strawberries* conjures ideas of forgiveness between generations, the lost possibilities of youth, and an almost Christian insistence on the possibility of reconciliation and redemption. Most of all it offers Mahon a way of affirming the value of the aesthetic as a site of resistance. In fact, in the poem he explicitly refers to the mystery of the autonomous artwork, 'those strange impulses circuiting the brain'.

A chain of events randomly scrambled together is a fragile enough image for the critical function of art and particularly so in an Irish context, weighing as it necessarily does against Yeats's search for 'befitting emblems of adversity', from *The Tower*, or Seamus Heaney's corresponding search for what he called 'symbols adequate to our predicament' around the time he was writing his 1975 volume *North*. Heaney's preoccupation with adequacy developed into a sustained attempt to conceptualize the forms of redress, balance, and reconciliation that it was poetry's right and duty to perform. Mahon's affirmation of his faith in dream comes from the same source, though he formulates it very differently – not redress and balance but critique – the necessary resistance that art performs in standing up for itself as art. Yet, remarkably, Heaney also turned to the image of a chain in his final volume of poems, published in 2010. It is a volume that explicitly reflects on what it means to be late, or even too late.

In the first part of an early sequence in *Human Chain*, the sound of a boiler starting up propels Heaney back to a childhood moment with his parents, in a place which 'could have been Grove Hill':

> Where I'd often stand with them on airy Sundays
> Shin-deep in hilltop bluebells, looking out
> At Magherafelt's four spires in the distance.
> Too late, alas, now, for the apt quotation
> About a love that's proved by steady gazing
> Not at each other but in the same direction.[8]

The lines pick up familiar strands in Heaney's work: the recall of an intensely private, familial world which holds its own against broader definitions of the public; the ease with which colloquial speech and the language of the everyday become one with the rhythms of the poem (that seemingly natural string of compound words – 'shin-deep in hilltop bluebells'). Perhaps above all the poem reminds us of the importance to Heaney of recall in and of itself, of remembering as an act of piety towards the past and the dead, and one intimately associated with place. Perhaps no other poet in recent years has shown such sustained engagement with the belief in memory as a means of recovering community and human solidarity in solitude.

This poem begins in medias res, and proceeds by means of verb-less stanzas, offering a series of unfolding snapshots of personal experience. By contrast, many of the poems in *Human Chain* do the work of building the bond between then and now through an involved and sometimes awkward syntax. Like plumbing laid bare, there is something pleasing and honest about this skeletal architecture, caught in phrases such as 'It was evening before I came to / To what I was hearing'; 'And now the man who drove them here will drive / Them back, and by evening we'll be home'; 'Me at the time not thinking'. Even as the syntax draws together past and present these poems insist on the difference between what the poet can see now and what he could see in the past, but also on the difference between what he thought he saw in the past and what he now understands that he saw then. This difference is crucial, as in that gap lie lost moments of

---

[8] Seamus Heaney, *Human Chain* (London, 2010). Further quotations are taken from this volume.

connection which cannot be retrieved. Terms such as 'uncoupled', 'apart', 'nothing but chaff', 'it didn't happen' seem to seed each other throughout the book. Despite the human and humane chain which is forged through the volume there are wound the poems cannot salve. There are some things for which poetry is too late.

So many of Heaney's poems have come down on the side of possibility that we may miss the significance of the voice which says it is 'too late, alas, now'. Belatedness is a mark of lyric poetry of course, and of the elegy in particular, where it is the poet's task to turn coming-too-late, showing up after the end of life to record it, into durable monuments of remembrance. There are certainly poems in *Human Chain* which make the turn towards fulfilment, or at the very least offer a balance between what has been lost and what remains to come. So, for example, 'Route 110' is an autobiography structured around Aeneas's descent into Hades, a poem in which the bus ride to 'Cookstown via Toome and Magherafelt' becomes a journey of survival through a neighbourly underworld. The passage through deaths mourned, and 'bodies / Unglorified', ends with the birth of one 'Whose long wait on the shaded bank has ended', a return to the light. Yet in general the shadow of lateness in *Human Chain* has darkened – reminding us that links break, connections fail, that we make the return from the underworld, if we make it at all, scrubbed clean of memory and experience.

As this volume reminds us, as much as thoughts of death, late stylists are haunted by their own previous work. In a volume preoccupied with ghosts the poems themselves read like afterlives of previous selves, as Heaney returns to ideas of childhood and physical memory, to what he called in an earlier sequence 'Squarings' – a kind of formal balancing out and equalizing of the rival claims of past, present, and future. But what I am suggesting is that these images are being recycled, returned to in a manner that reveals their redundancy, even futility, as the poems chart a form of exile from the richness of the material world. 'The Baler', for instance, ends with a dying man who can no longer bear to watch a sunset, but it is a sunset that has already been evoked as a 'dusk Eldorado'.

If it is curious that both Heaney, in 2010, and Mahon, in 2011, reflect on what it means for poet or a poem to be 'too late', it surely becomes worthy of remark when we notice that a third poet, Paul Muldoon, considers the same question in his 2012 volume, *Maggot*. The long central sequence in the volume, 'The Humors of Hakone', is broadly set in the area near Mount Fuji in Japan. At its heart it features a decomposing Japanese corpse cum corpus, which becomes the inspiration for an exhaustive list of all the of things for which we, poet and readers, will always be too late:

> A corduroy road over a quag had kept me on the straight and narrow.
> Now something was raising a stink.
> A poem decomposing around what looked like an arrow.
> Her stomach contents ink.
>
> Too late to cast about for clues
> either at the purikura, or 'sticker-photo booth', or back at the Pagoda.
> Too late to establish by autolysis, not to speak of heat loss,
> the precise time of death on the road to Edo.[9]

The exhaustive and exhausting detail with which Muldoon insists on all the things we cannot know prompts the question, What are we not too late for? Is there any knowledge or understanding to be gleaned from the body of the poem? The volume is stuffed full of attempts to find meaning, either through divination, the interpretation of portents and omens, or through forensics, the interpretation of remains – what he calls the poem cadaver. Muldoon has long been preoccupied with the status of the poem itself as an aesthetic remnant, the residue of violence and terror, and the questionable pleasure that we take in it. In one of his earliest poems, 'Dancers at the Moy', the unusual spring of the dance floor is one by-product of the massacre of hundreds of horses, their buried bones giving a lightness to the step. But in *Maggot* the clear before and after of event and aesthetic product has broken down, so that we are in a world of endless creation and destruction, of composition through decomposition.

The manifold cancers, maggots, and worms in these poems are agents of death but also figures of renewal – so, for example, maggots are introduced to wounds to clean and disinfect them, to stop rot as much as to further it. Perhaps the most disturbing treatment of this antithesis comes in 'Moryson's Fancy', a poem which rings the changes on a passage from Fynes Moryson's *An History of Ireland*, dated 1599 to 1603. Moryson provides the epigraph to the poem 'A most horrible spectacle of three children (whereof the eldest was not above ten years old), all eating and gnawing with their teeth the entrails of their mother'. It is the ability to become accustomed to what another poem calls 'common torment' (and yet another suggests is common torture, to which we have all become accustomed) that enables survival.

---

[9] Paul Muldoon, *Maggot* (London, 2012). Subsequent quotations are from this volume.

The poem is interested in Moryson's spectacle and what it tells us, or what can and cannot be read from it. It begins with a portent, signalled by a hare:

These three children for whom their mother at first seemed asleep
may have known a hare running to the right from a fold
of her skirt would have them leap
into an inauspicious stretch of Fermanagh bog

where generation after generation would learn to mitch and cog
rather than follow their callings as scholars.
Check out the cuffs. Check out the collars.
Check out the flesh farthingales
through which they so resolutely ate.
Maybe they'll yet look into their mother's entrails
and somehow haruspicate

that the Muldoons will lose their hold on the ancient barony or Lurg
and be reduced to ferrying pilgrims to Lough Derg.
Maybe they'll be forewarned also of how to tackle
this most horrible spectacle
of themselves as a synonym
for savagery, a stain
on the integrity of the nation, for while they acted on a whim
their whim will nonetheless sustain

the will of generation after generation through the hard slog . . .

The children become their own prophesy, a synonym for their own actions, read as savage when, as Muldoon puts it, they acted on a whim. In other words, they are misread. Muldoon has always been interested in repetition, in the closed circle, the serpent with its tail in its mouth. Here the circle completely ties up past and future. We watch the spectacle of the children in the past foretelling their own future, through generation after generation. The past anticipates the future as a never-ending cycle of state and counter-state violence, passed on through generation after generation.

We will return to the question of the preordained, and the divination of what Muldoon calls the 'iffy inevitability' of this pattern. But let us do so via the idea of 'spectacle', introduced by 'Moryson's Fancy', for Muldoon suggests that spectacle in itself has a role in forming the closed circle through which, he implies, we accustom ourselves to comment torment.

The first sequence in the book is 'Plan B', a typically weird sequence in which a number of interrelated narratives both do and do not connect – narratively and grammatically – including the visit of Edward VII to the Cork Exhibition of 1903, the KGB, and the execution of an elephant by

Thomas Edison while demonstrating the dangers of alternating current. There is clearly an ironic reflection here on Victorian ideas of progress, culminating in the 1903 exhibition, but this is married to a display of Edwardian manners, deportment, elocution, the learned performance of being in the world, and of worldliness. The use of polite, exact, and studied diction seems to be caricatured by the precise syntactical structures, for example, in the first poem in the sequence:

> On my own head be it if, after the years of elocution and pianoforte,
> the idea that I may have veered
>
> away from the straight
> and narrow of Brooklyn or Baltimore for a Baltic state
>
> is one at which, all things being equal, I would demur.
> A bit like Edward VII cocking his ear
>
> at the mention of Cork. Yet it seems I've managed nothing more
> than to have fetched up here.

We could call this elocution as circumlocution. If I read the grammar here correctly, that first sentence translates as 'It's my responsibility if I don't like the idea of being in the Baltic.' But in Muldoon's poem – and in the volume as a whole – the syntactical architecture becomes its own edifice of artifice. Grammar here is far from being merely functional. It is a capricious actor or agent in its own right; we repeatedly find orphaned concepts and grammatical dependencies which seem to but do not add up.

This issue of causality is, I believe, vital to an understanding of the problem of lateness as it is addressed in this volume. The 'Plan B' sequence traces the causal relationship between a seemingly arbitrary chain of events and state terror. This is most easily expressed in the vignettes about Thomas Edison, who, keen to gather an ever-larger audience for himself and his experiments, in 1903 turned the execution of an elephant into a vehicle for showmanship, trying to prove that the rival technology of alternating current was a bad thing. He gathered a large crowd for his demonstration and had it filmed. (The footage is online on YouTube.) New technologies are not just implicated in but are the vehicle for the development of mechanisms of brutality and state terror, moving from entertainments such as the film of the electrocution of Topsy to the electric chair to the mechanization and technologization of state control. The volume as a whole keeps shifting between images of non-mechanized torture – pitchforks and iced water – to images of contemporary Western state terror, the violence of which, Muldoon suggests, is hidden behind a smokescreen of technology (smart bombs, for example) and linguistic circumlocution (terms such as extra-ordinary rendition, for example). The story of Edison's staging of violent death as entertainment reminds us not only that such circuses are used as trials for new forms of violence but that they are also a screen or camouflage for that violence.

Although there are clearly narrative threads running through the sequence (Edison, Edward VII, the KGB) the poem is really powered by linguistic associations. So, elocution becomes circumlocution, but also electrocution, and inexorably, the unspoken execution. The poem does not just set up the relationship between state power and entertainment as a problem to be identified. It is also about the ways the poet's linguistic deportment, his ability to balance out these images, and keep them all in play inside his lightly built and oh-so-ingenious structure, is itself complicit in the cover-up. Who knew, Muldoon asks, that 'forensics' derives from 'forum', that it originates in public performance, rhetoric, and political persuasion?

We seem to have strayed a good distance from the idea of lateness, untimeliness, and anachronism. To bring us back it may be helpful to reconsider the relationship between lateness and decadence. In Derek Mahon's poems – knowing, urbane, ironic – the artworks of a late, decadent culture still offer a site of resistance to the world of war and oil, precisely by insisting on their own aesthetic integrity. We might think something similar is going on in Muldoon's poetry, which seems to willingly invite the charge of literary exhaustion. He offers up his confections so knowingly, exquisitely performing his perfect elocution and his flawless etiquette, revelling in artifice, insisting that this is work that is refined, exact, and – arguably – living off itself.

The cover of the Faber edition of *Maggot* shows a photograph by the artist Chris Jordan of a dead albatross chick, its opened gullet filled with plastic that it has picked up from the ocean. The bird has fed on the waste of late capitalism, and the photograph, its tone both elegiac and admonitory, clearly says, 'late planet'. It inhabits the same world as Mahon's seabirds grounded by oil. But the cover photograph also directs us to Muldoon's translation of Baudelaire's 'The Albatross' and to Bauldelaire's poem 'Carrion', from *Les Fleurs du Mal*, another poem about a corpse, and one to which Muldoon explicitly alludes in 'The Humors of Hakone', mentioned earlier. Here is the beginning of Baudelaire's poem in a translation by William Aggeler:

My love, do you recall the object which we saw,
That fair, sweet, summer morn!
At a turn in the path a foul carcass
On a gravel strewn bed,
Its legs raised in the air, like a lustful woman,
Burning and dripping with poisons,
Displayed in a shameless, nonchalant way
Its belly, swollen with gases.[10]

Baudelaire ends his poem with a classic flourish, the immortality trope claiming the poet's right and ability to stop the rot and arrest the processes of putrefaction. In *Maggot* Muldoon puts that claim in question, while also upholding it, in his own habitual have-and-eat-cake balancing act. He explores the body as waste matter, deadly flesh wounds, leprosy, the body as 'a footnote to the loss of its own heat', the poem its own 'protruding tongue'. And at the same time he constructs an elaborately patterned verbal cage, a kind of kaleidoscope for the display of this violence and decay.

If the modern world, and all its torments, has grounded Baudelaire's albatross for good, can the poet survive any better as scavenger or maggot, by feeding off the body of experience, disinfecting it, and preserving it in aesthetic patterns? The balance of hope and doubt is reflected in the engineered divergence of pattern and patterned, which often seem to go their separate ways in these poems, betraying the strains on poetry itself in contemporary culture – not least the obscurity and uncertainty of the relation between the poet and his audience. The artful automatism of Muldoon's verse confronts us with the anxious possibility that poetry itself has started to feel belated, 'too late to divine the mess we've made', as he puts it in 'The Humors of Hakone' or, as in the final lines of 'A Hummingbird': 'Like an engine rolling on after a crash, / long after whatever it was made a splash.'

***

Lateness is relative. Late style cannot be categorized according to an identifiable list of characteristics – it is something we attribute to artists. Nonetheless the extent to which late practitioners turn their attention to interpreting late style – Said on Lampedusa, Mahon on Bergman, or

---

[10] Charles Baudelaire, *The Flowers of Evil/Les Fleurs de Mal*, trans. William Aggeler (Fresno, CA, 1954).

perhaps Leonard Cohen on Cavafy – suggests an attempt to test the limits
of silence before it is 'too late'.

In Said's formulation, following Adorno, late style comes about when
artists become exiled from their addressees and from their communities. In
Heaney's case, we might say that the disjunction was the result of too
much success rather than too little of it. He found a vast international
audience, but his dialogue was with his readers, not the consumers of a
Heaney brand or the collectors of signed editions. And it is for his readers,
not his audience, that his late poems of personal exile have significance. As
we have seen, Muldoon has taken to self-mockingly parading his creden-
tials as far as poetic elocution is concerned – performing his own exile from
his readers. Hence, perhaps, Muldoon's other persona – as rock musician
and lyric writer – trying to comment on contemporary culture through a
medium that actually has some resonance and purchase within that
culture. It is an uneasy compromise but might be regarded as an attempt
to get beyond what Adorno himself, towards the end of his life, saw as the
looming dead-end of an uncompromisingly rejectionist late modernism.

It will not have escaped readers' attention that, while promising a
discussion of Irish late style, I appear to have given something much more
like reflections on the crisis of global modernity: Mahon's war over oil;
Muldoon's concern with US imperialism, and complicity with state terror.
That is obviously partly because global concerns are Irish concerns, even if
Irish concerns are not always global ones. Nonetheless, I want to hold on
to the Irishness of these explorations of late style. I have already touched on
the heightened sense in Irish poetry of the problem of irreconcilability –
the search for 'befitting' emblems and 'adequate' symbols, in the face of
lack of fit, and the failure of language to be adequate to the violence and
corruptions of the twentieth century. But I am also suggesting that
anachronism, exile from time, and untimely causality have a particular
purchase in Irish letters. In contrast to the idea of time as chronology,
certainly in contrast to the revolutionary sense of the forward march of
history (the Republican faith that 'our day will come'), Irish literature in
the twentieth century has tended to emphasize stasis, entrapment, circu-
larity, and repetition – the failure to move on to a modern future: Yeats's
gyres, the stories of stasis and paralysis in Joyce's *Dubliners*, the cyclical
narrative of Kavanagh's 'The Great Hunger', Flann O'Brien's peculiarly
Irish hell which goes 'round and round' in *The Third Policeman*, the
repetitions and rewindings of time in *Waiting for Godot* and *Endgame*.
To follow just one of these threads: many critics have pointed out that the
tragedy of Patrick Maguire in 'The Great Hunger' foreshadows Irish realist

fiction and drama of the 1960s, and particularly the late naturalism of John McGahern, Brian Moore, Edna O'Brien, and Tom Murphy. All of these writers work with plots which drag their protagonists back into a cycle of familial violence, which seems to prove the failure of generation. When Kavanagh writes of Paddy Maguire that 'he would have changed the circle if he could' or that 'There is no tomorrow, but only time stretched for the saving of the hay', we are not so far from the clock face without hands, a kind of constitutive anachronism to the Irish twentieth century, which may be one source of the forms of Irish late style.

Index

Note: *page numbers in bold refer to illustrations*